Weaponized Words

Strengthen your understanding of the persuasive mechanisms used by terrorist groups and how they are effective in order to defeat them. *Weaponized Words* applies existing theories of persuasion to domains unique to this digital era, such as social media, YouTube, websites, and message boards to name but a few. Terrorists deploy a range of communication methods and harness reliable communication theories to create strategic messages that persuade peaceful individuals to join their groups and engage in violence. While explaining how they accomplish this, the book lays out a blueprint for developing counter-messages perfectly designed to conquer such violent extremism and terrorism. Using this basis in persuasion theory, a socio-scientific approach is generated to fight terrorist propaganda and the damage it causes.

KURT BRADDOCK is Assistant Teaching Professor in the Department of Communication Arts and Sciences at the Pennsylvania State University, USA. He researches the persuasive effects of terrorist propaganda and how that propaganda can be challenged. He has also advised multiple governments, non-governmental organizations, and practitioners on effective counter-messaging strategies.

Weaponized Words

The Strategic Role of Persuasion in Violent
Radicalization and Counter-Radicalization

Kurt Braddock

Pennsylvania State University

CAMBRIDGE
UNIVERSITY PRESS

CAMBRIDGE
UNIVERSITY PRESS

University Printing House, Cambridge CB2 8BS, United Kingdom

One Liberty Plaza, 20th Floor, New York, NY 10006, USA

477 Williamstown Road, Port Melbourne, VIC 3207, Australia

314–321, 3rd Floor, Plot 3, Splendor Forum, Jasola District Centre, New Delhi – 110025, India

79 Anson Road, #06–04/06, Singapore 079906

Cambridge University Press is part of the University of Cambridge.

It furthers the University's mission by disseminating knowledge in the pursuit of education, learning, and research at the highest international levels of excellence.

www.cambridge.org
Information on this title: www.cambridge.org/9781108474528
DOI: 10.1017/9781108584517

© Kurt Braddock 2020

First published 2020

A catalogue record for this publication is available from the British Library.

ISBN 978-1-108-47452-8 Hardback
ISBN 978-1-108-46487-1 Paperback

For Mom,
who taught me that to beat the monsters that scare us,
we have to hold fast and look them in the eye.
It's the only way to learn their weaknesses.

Contents

Figures

Tables

x

Acknowledgments

I have read my fair share of books about communication theory, terrorism, radicalization, and all manner of other topics. At the beginning of all of them, there has been some form of thanks to individuals who had been personally or professionally important to the author and had supported the work that went into the development of the manuscript. Too often, I have skimmed past those acknowledgments, eager to find the information I sought and apply it to my own research. I suppose it's impossible to understand the value of colleagues and loved ones for writing a book unless one goes through the experience themselves. I will no longer make that mistake.

The process of writing this book has shown me, with sharp clarity, that taking on a project of this scale is impossible without leaning on others for support. Here, I would like to thank several people who served as my support system, and without whom this book would not exist.

Foremost, I would like to thank Cambridge University Press for believing in this project and supporting it at every step. In particular, I owe an immense debt of gratitude to Commissioning Editor Janka Romero. Her enthusiasm and advice have guided the development of this book from the initial submission of its prospectus up through its final publication. As a first-time author, I am incredibly grateful to Janka for all her help, and can only hope to work with such wonderful editors in the future. Also from Cambridge University Press, I would like to thank Editorial Assistant Emily Watton for all her help in resolving practical issues associated with book publication. Without Emily, I would have been entirely unable to navigate the logistics of publishing *Weaponized Words*.

Though a publishing house and its team are fundamental to a book's completion, emotional support from loved ones is of no less importance. In this vein, I thank Brooke Cairns for her patience as I worked on *Weaponized Words*. Enduring long nights in which I was locked away in my office, mood swings resulting from impending deadlines, and incessant statements of self-doubt about the quality of my writing, Brooke never wavered. She insisted that not only would I complete the book, but that it would be great. While I leave judgments of the book's quality to you, Brooke's continuous love and support was vital to its completion. For that, I will never be able to repay her, though I will remain eternally grateful.

I would also be remiss if I didn't acknowledge the decades of support I have received from my family and how that support has contributed to the writing of this book. My mother (Gail), who passed away in 2013, was always a source of enthusiastic support for every endeavor I have attempted. I miss her every day and hope that she would have been proud to see that her son has contributed to the safety of the world in some small way. My father (Earl) has been a steadfast supporter of mine as well, continuously pushing me to succeed on whatever path I took.

Growing up, my siblings and I took different routes to adulthood – routes that we still walk today. Eric is an artist. Kelly is a singer and a photographer. I am an academic. Despite our divergent interests, we have always supported each other in what we do. My brother remains one of my closest confidants and has never failed to state his pride in my work. My sister shares my work with her friends, eager to express the influence it has in some circles. Though my family has regularly over-stated my skills and influence as a researcher – a tendency that I don't correct out of my own pleasure in making my family proud – I am ever-grateful to them for serving as enthusiastic pillars of support.

I am also lucky to have some of the best friends within the discipline that a person could ask for. Throughout the production of this book, John Horgan, Paul Gill, and John Morrison have provided me with constant encouragement, insight, and perhaps most importantly, reprieve from my own work schedule. From offering to review early drafts of the chapters to discussing the book's progress over pints, these gentlemen helped to keep me grounded. At a time when I was often lost in work, they were quick to ensure that I made time for fun and camaraderie.

In the same vein, I would be remiss if I did not express my gratitude to James Price Dillard, my one-time PhD advisor and life-long mentor. While writing *Weaponized Words*, Jim was quick to offer welcome advice and excitement in equal measure. Even more valuable has been Jim's philosophy and approach to empirical research. He has instilled in me the notion that to be part of the academy is a privilege earned and enjoyed by few, and with that privilege comes the responsibility to reveal and explain objective truths for the betterment of one's fellow man. I hope that this book meets a level of empirical rigor that would make Jim proud and makes the world better in some small way.

I also owe thanks to Denise Solomon, Chair of the Department of Communication Arts and Sciences at Penn State and source of moral, academic, and social support. As Chair, Denise is responsible for all the goings-on in the Department, and (by the nature of the job) must ensure that its members meet their institutional obligations. Still, she allowed me the freedom to pursue this project, which at times required a significant amount of my attention. Denise appreciates the role that research plays in the development of knowledge, an appreciation she has cultivated in the Department as its leader. Without this appreciation and her patience, I never would have been able to finish this book.

Also central to the development of this book are researchers whose work has directly impacted my own, many of whom I count as friends. These include (but are not limited to) Dan Köhler, Alastair Reed, Haroro Ingram, Amarnath Amarasingam, Emily Moyer-Gusé, Mick Williams, Aaron Zelin, Graham Macklin, Robin Nabi, Andrew Glazzard, Michael Pfau, Bobi Ivanov, and Josh Compton.

I have similarly had the benefit of receiving experience and feedback from practitioners in the fields of counterterrorism and countering violent extremism. Some of those who have been particularly supportive include Adela Levis at the US Department of State, Ross Frenett and Vidhya Ramalingam of Moonshot CVE, and Mattias Sundholm and E. J. Flynn of the United Nations Counterterrorism Executive Directorate (UN-CTED).

Of course, the accomplishment of any professional goal requires help from personal friends. I have been lucky to have some of the best. I want to give special mention to two of my oldest friends, Dustin Dellinger and Jim Haas, for their continuous enthusiasm about my work. Never has a scotch tasted so good as when we had our celebratory toast following the completion of *Weaponized Words*. Other friends who have been equally supportive are Zoe Marchment, Emily Corner, Devi Margolin, Bart Schuurman, Lindsay Stanek, Kira Harris, Sarah Carthy, Lauren Camacci, Jennifer Malloy, Andy High, Sarah Beth Hopton, Al Palait, Ally Gross, Samantha Kutner, and Marissa Cosgrove.

I am also appreciative of the various establishments that suffered my presence while I wrote this book. I spent countless hours hunkered down in the back of Evermore Coffee Roasters, tapping away at my laptop over endless Caffé Americanos. Its owners, Ryan and Lauren Vaxmonsky, were ever-gracious hosts. They allowed me to arrive early and leave late – all the while expressing enthusiasm and curiosity about the book in equal measure. The amazing drinks they provided and the excitement they expressed were no small part of this book's coming into existence. I similarly spent dozens of working lunches at Dooney's Pub, where

Max Bigelow was always quick to alleviate the stresses of writing the book with a kind word. Max was there when I wrote the first paragraph of *Weaponized Words*, and he was there when I typed the very last period at its end. He is an inseparable element of its creation.

I would also like to paradoxically thank the arrogant pundits, charlatans, fake academics, and false prophets who have claimed that social science has no place in the debate about effective counterterrorism or counter-radicalization policy. Your claims have, in part, motivated me to write this book. You have asked what empiricism and science can offer that your obsolete perspectives and simplistic solutions can't. Here is one researcher's answer.

And finally, I want to thank my dog Sulley. The writing of this book was no small endeavor, and at times, caused me a significant amount of stress. I owe Sulley thanks for showing me that no matter how urgent work is, no matter how imminent deadlines are, no matter how much writing there is left to do, there is always time to take a deep breath, relax, and maybe doze off for a few minutes. Thanks, buddy.

Introduction

We can't kill our way out of this war.
                            US Air Force Lieutenant General Robert Otto[1]

Hence to fight and conquer in all your battles is not supreme excellence;
supreme excellence consists in breaking the enemy's resistance without
fighting.   Sun-Tzu, *The Art of War*, Chapter 3-2[2]

I know what you're thinking. I can practically sense your confusion
through the page. You've seen the damage that can be done when radical
white nationalists, Islamic extremists, and violent political dissidents
spread their messages unchallenged. You've watched as terrorist groups
have lured unsuspecting recruits with promises of vengeance and glory.
You've witnessed the bloody ends of terrorist propaganda, and you
opened this book eager to strike back against it.

Then you saw the Table of Contents and were greeted by words you'd
sooner expect to encounter on a college course syllabus than in a book on
fighting violent radicalization and terrorism. Narrative theory. Communicative inoculation. Reasoned action. Discrete emotions.

This, you might be thinking, *is not what I signed up for.*

Don't panic. It's perfectly understandable if you feel caught off-guard.
After all, discussions about terrorism rarely include any mention of
communication or psychology theories. Although you might not yet be
familiar with these theories and the principles that underpin them,
they're central to the processes that sustain terrorist groups and their
activities. They explain why terrorist propaganda resonates with some
audiences, and most importantly, they can help guide our efforts in
fighting that propaganda with strategic messages of our own.

That's why you're here. You're here to learn about how we can fight
violent extremism at its ideological source and ultimately save the victims
of terrorism – both those killed in potential attacks, and those that
become sufficiently misguided to perform them.

1

Pursuit of these goals through strategic persuasive communication is what led me to write this book. For years, the theories and perspectives you'll encounter here have explained how and why certain messages are persuasive. Research on healthcare, politics, education, business, sex, friendship, and scores of other topics has demonstrated the value of persuasion theory for predicting and influencing beliefs, attitudes, and behaviors of target audiences. Somehow, these theories and perspectives have slipped through the cracks in efforts to fight terrorist propaganda. This has been a missed opportunity.

These decades-old communication and psychology theories are loaded weapons on a shelf – weapons that we have yet to really deploy on the communicative front of the battle against violent extremism. It's time we use them. To do so, this book will show how each of these theories can be used to analyze the psychologies of our target audiences, inform which content should appear in our messages, and guide the distribution of our messages to those we mean to turn away from terrorism.

Before we get to that, it's important to understand what we are up against. After all, terrorist groups can (and do) develop persuasive messages that help them achieve strategic goals. The effectiveness of these messages can also be explained by the theories we'll discuss.

So, before we begin to talk about how to use our own "weapons," I want to tell you a story that shows how terrorist groups use communicative weapons of their own, and how those weapons can cause significant damage. Originally reported by the *New York Times*[3] in 2015, this is a story about a vulnerable young woman named "Alex."

∴

It all started so innocently. She was only curious.

After seeing an ISIS video showing the execution of James Foley in August of 2014, "Alex" wanted to understand how anyone could justify it. "I was looking for people who agreed with what they were doing, so that I could understand why they were doing it." As a lonely 23-year-old living with her grandmother in an isolated part of Washington state, Alex spent much of her time online. Rather than go on dates or attend parties, Alex would watch movies on Netflix or update her social media accounts. So naturally, when she looked for ISIS supporters to talk to, she turned to Twitter.

Her search didn't take long. She had no problem finding individuals who claimed to be part of ISIS – individuals that were willing, even eager, to talk to her. In virtually no time, she was part of a social community that the seclusion of rural Washington failed to provide. Within a few weeks,

Alex had built online relationships with several ISIS supporters. They politely responded to any questions she asked, all the while teaching her about Islam and its rituals. Gradually, these conversations led Alex to question whether the media's portrayal of ISIS was accurate. Despite widespread proof of the group's brutal actions, she became skeptical, even defiant.

"I knew that what people were saying about them wasn't true. I don't think that the Islamic State is as bad as everyone says; I think that their atrocities are exaggerated. I think that they brought stability to the land. I think that it might be one of the safest places to live in the Middle East."

Over time, Alex's engagement with her new "friends" on Skype and Twitter led her to question her own Presbyterian upbringing and the lessons of the church that she valued for years. One of these new friends, Hamad, assured her that she didn't need to abandon her religion – but also described Christianity as flawed in a way that could only be corrected by Islam. After some consideration (and a conversation with a dismissive pastor at her church), Alex agreed to one of the central tenets of Islam – that Jesus was a prophet of God, but not *part* of God as described in the Bible. After Alex affirmed her new belief to Hamad over Skype, he pressed her:

"So, what are you waiting for to become a Muslim?"

∴

Shortly after these exchanges, Hamad vanished from Skype. This was no great threat to Alex's continued interest in Islam and ISIS. By the time Hamad disappeared, Alex had made more than a dozen online friends who were sympathetic to ISIS and more than happy to tell her all about the group. Other supporters quickly filled the social void left by Hamad's absence, including a 51-year-old married man living in the UK.

"Faisal," Alex recalled. "He's my friend."

Alex spoke with Faisal almost daily, sometimes for hours. Most of the time, the two of them would talk innocently – discussing tea, gardening, and other things. Sometimes, though, Faisal would talk to Alex about more substantive topics, like Islam. He taught her the proper methods of Islamic worship, including the need for Muslims to place their foreheads on the ground during prayer, just as Jesus had done. Alex was a good student to Faisal; she complied with his instructions.

After a few weeks of Skyping with Faisal, Alex turned a corner. She asked him how one would go about converting to Islam. Faisal made the process easy for her, saying that she could convert by testifying that "There is no God but Allah, and Muhammad is his messenger" on Twitter. A few days after Christmas, just four months after seeing the James Foley video, Alex logged on to make her declaration. For her conversion to be official, she needed two Muslims to acknowledge it. Just after 9:00 in the evening, Alex made her online testimony with Faisal serving as one of her witnesses. Within hours, Alex's Twitter followers had doubled in number.

Alex made one last post before going to bed that night.

"I actually have brothers and sisters. I'm crying."

∴

The gifts started arriving in January.

Cash. A prayer rug. Hijabs. Books that pushed a stricter version of Islam. Pamphlets that laid out the duties of subservient women. And of course, chocolate – always chocolate.

Some Twitter users grew concerned for Alex after hearing about her conversion and the gifts she was receiving. Some suggested that she should stop associating with the people who have changed her in such a short period of time. She protested, "… cutting off ties is hard, and they gave me stuff." Despite claims that she told Faisal to stop sending gifts, packages continued to arrive. It was shortly after Valentine's Day when Alex found that the gifts and companionship came with some conditions.

Her online "friends" told her to stop following *kuffar* (Islamic non-believers) on social media. The fact that Alex still followed some of her Christian friends led an online ISIS supporter to accuse her of being a spy. Faisal vouched for Alex; but introduced her to another Twitter user who spent hours interrogating her. After being questioned about her online activities, she was cleared of being a spy. Faisal praised Alex's "beautiful character" afterward. He then told her that getting someone to marry her wouldn't pose much of a problem.

Alex giggled nervously as she recalled talking about the possibility.

"Faisal found a guy that would marry me. The information he gave me was he's 45 [years old] and bald. But he's a very good Muslim."

∴

Faisal began to pressure Alex, telling her that it was a sin for a Muslim to live among non-believers. Gradually, their conversations turned to her traveling to "a Muslim land," which Alex understood to be Syria – the home of the ISIS capital. In early 2015, Faisal offered to buy her tickets to Austria to meet her future husband. Although Alex's 11-year-old brother would need to accompany her (as ISIS women are required to travel with a male relative), she was sure it wouldn't be a problem.

At this time, Alex started to wonder if Faisal had been speaking with other women about the possibility of traveling to Syria. After making light of the fact that he was, in fact, speaking with other women on social media, Alex Googled her "friend." She found a catalogue of terrorist incidents that Faisal was connected to.

In 1995, Faisal was arrested and imprisoned for possession of firearms, bullets, shotgun cartridges, timers, and explosives. In 2000, he was arrested again for suspicion of plotting a large-scale explosion. Police found a garbage bag outside a building where Faisal had met a Bangladeshi immigrant; the bag contained plastic gloves, a scale, and HMTD – a highly explosive compound. At that time, investigators found a file called the "Mujahedin Explosives Handbook" on Faisal's computer. Nine years later, Faisal was arrested by Bangladeshi security forces for running a bomb-making factory out of an orphanage that was operated by a charity he led. Court proceedings associated with this incident said that Faisal "had chalked out a blueprint for grooming each child as a militant." Although Alex asked Faisal about these accusations, he dismissed them as unfair persecution due to his being Muslim. Their conversations continued.

By this point, Alex's grandmother had noticed that Alex wasn't sleeping much. Often awake and on her tablet chatting at all hours, Alex's constant engagement with shadowy online figures led to several fights with her grandmother, who eventually barred her from accessing the Internet at night. After multiple conversations with Alex about what she was doing online, her grandmother confronted Faisal on Skype. She asked him about the proposed trip to Austria, the promise of marriage to a bald stranger, and her abandonment of her Christian faith. Faisal downplayed everything. He promised never to contact Alex again.

Rukmini Callimachi, a reporter with the *New York Times* and expert on issues related to radicalization and terrorism, attempted to contact Faisal on multiple occasions to comment on Alex's story. Callimachi tried to reach him through Skype; she sent him multiple e-mails; she even sent letters to the address from which he shipped Alex gifts. He never answered.

Having been exposed as a likely ISIS recruiter, Faisal seemed to vanish into the ether.

∴

Alex's story is all too common. ISIS has seduced countless people with its propaganda, thousands of whom have gone on to engage in violent activity on behalf of the group.[4] As quickly as counterterrorist forces have eliminated these violent radicals, others have emerged in their place. ISIS may have lost its grasp on its physical territory in late 2017,[5] but the group's propaganda continues to inspire others to attack civilians at all corners of the globe.

Of course, peace and security sometimes require the targeted killing of active terrorist fighters. This is a natural result of confronting violent adversaries. But the continued effectiveness of terrorist propaganda shows that we can't kill our way out of our struggles against violent extremism. We need to understand the persuasive nature of terrorist propaganda. We need to challenge the ideologies that drive terrorist activity. Most of all, though, we need to fight back against terrorist messaging to turn would-be radicals away from violence.

In recent years, policymakers, government officials, and researchers have tried to accomplish these very things. Several large-scale initiatives have been implemented under the umbrella of "countering violent extremism."[6] Many of these efforts have focused on countering terrorist messaging to challenge terrorist groups' ideologies, and hopefully, convince potential recruits that supporting terrorism is not a viable form of political action. Though these efforts have been well-intentioned, their execution has left much to be desired.

For example, in late 2013, the now-defunct Center for Strategic Counterterrorism Communications (CSCC) at the US Department of State launched a counter-radicalization messaging campaign called "Think Again, Turn Away."[7] This program was designed to challenge ISIS online propaganda by sharing stories, images, and arguments that contradict the ISIS ideology. The messages shared by the CSCC on Twitter were typically taken from the media, and showed the threats posed by ISIS, as well as the hypocrisies of the group's actions. It did not go over well.

CSCC posts quickly deteriorated into "embarrassing" flamewars between CSCC personnel and ISIS supporters. Tweets were ridiculed by ISIS sympathizers. Even CSCC officials became "supremely uncomfortable" about the organization's efforts, given that the US Department of State's seal was attached to the distributed messages. The State Department has since improved its approaches to online counter-messaging, but as the "Think Again, Turn Away" initiative shows, its first efforts were largely a failure.

This begs the question: What did we miss? Where have we gone wrong in our strategic counter-messaging efforts? The answers to these questions depend on the context in which we attempt to fight terrorist propaganda. In the case of "Think Again, Turn Away," it seems that the CSCC failed to recognize that when a message's targets (ISIS sympathizers, potential ISIS recruits) do not trust the message's source (the US Department of State), the message will simply be dismissed or ridiculed. This issue – called source credibility – has been a subject of persuasion research for decades.

Although this is only one example, it reveals a recurrent shortcoming of many counter-messaging efforts intended to challenge terrorist propaganda – they are not founded on proven communication theory and practices. That's where this book comes in.

Specifically, this book will provide readers with two fundamental kinds of knowledge related to violent radicalization and communication. First, it's important that we understand why terrorist propaganda can be so persuasive in some cases. So, this book will use long-standing persuasion theory to show how certain kinds of terrorist propaganda have effectively drawn individuals to support (or engage in) terrorism.

Second, we must use our extensive knowledge of communication and psychology to inform our counter-messaging strategies. Stated plainly, we must base our counterterror and counter-radicalization efforts on theories and practices that have been proven effective. We can no longer overlook how much the psychological effects of communication affect the adoption (or abandonment) of terrorist ideologies. So, this book will discuss these communicative phenomena and show how they can be harnessed, mastered, and ultimately leveraged to dissuade support for terrorism.

Without understanding (1) why some terrorist propaganda is persuasive to certain people or (2) how we can maximize the effectiveness of our own counter-messages, we are essentially shooting at targets in a dark room, blindly hoping that one of our shots hits its mark. We can't afford to engage in trial-and-error when the development and implementation of counter-messaging programs takes time, money, and resources. More importantly, terrorist propaganda has real consequences – both for those exposed to it, and those that are victimized by terrorists who have been seduced by it. Preventing these consequences requires us to be painstaking in how we challenge terrorist messages.

We need to be thorough. We need to be systematic. We need to be scientific. And most of all, we need to be right.

∴

Before delving into how communication theory and practice can inform efforts at counter-radicalization, it is important to understand the phenomena that we mean to fight. So, the first chapter in this book explains the process of violent radicalization, how it occurs, and how it relates to engagement in terrorism. Specifically, Chapter 1 will describe how violent radicalization has been defined in the past, as well as how it can be thought of as a specific type of persuasion. When we consider violent radicalization to be a persuasive process (that is, a process of belief and attitude change), we can begin to think about how persuasion theories and practices can be used to address the problem.

After defining violent radicalization (and discussing how certain persuasive strategies can promote or discourage it), Chapter 2 turns to past efforts at counter-radicalization. As indicated above, these efforts have not been guided by tried-and-true communication or psychology theory. Nevertheless, it's important to review them to understand what has worked, what hasn't, and why.

Once we've covered the foundations of persuasion and violent radicalization, we can begin to think about specific theories and perspectives that (1) explain how terrorist groups try to gain support for their actions and ideologies, and (2) inform the development of future efforts to challenge terrorist propaganda. The first of these perspectives concerns the use of narratives. For decades, communication researchers have recognized the persuasive effectiveness of narratives, showing them to affect people's beliefs, attitudes, intentions, and behaviors in several domains. Health behaviors, political decisions, sexual activity, acceptance of others, environmental awareness, technology adoption, and even belief in conspiracy theories have been shown to be affected by exposure to narrative messages. Despite overwhelming evidence showing the potential for narratives to affect audience beliefs and attitudes, they have rarely been explored as tools for preventing violent radicalization. Chapter 3 addresses this gap in our knowledge – showing not only how terrorists have used narratives to achieve their strategic goals, but also how we can use narratives to thwart those goals.

In Chapter 4, we turn to one of the most reliable, time-tested theories of persuasion – inoculation theory. Most people are familiar with the concept of inoculation as a form of protection from illness; however, in the same way that a yearly shot can guard against the flu, communicative inoculation has been shown to protect against the adoption of problematic beliefs and attitudes. Much like narratives, communicative inoculation has been shown to be effective for decades across a wide range of domains. Unfortunately, inoculation has not been used to prevent the adoption of beliefs and attitudes that promote the use of terrorism. This chapter builds on new counter-radicalization research to show how analysts and policymakers can harness the persuasive power of inoculation to protect against the spread of extremist ideologies and behaviors.

Chapter 5 describes how the theory of reasoned action (TRA) – a classic model of persuasion and behavior – explains terrorist groups' attempts to radicalize potential supporters. In its simplest form, the TRA predicts that someone will intend to engage in a behavior because of their beliefs and attitudes about (1) the behavior itself, (2) what others think about the behavior, and (3) whether they can perform the behavior. Terrorist groups go to great lengths to influence audiences' beliefs and attitudes about their activities, meaning the TRA can help us investigate their persuasive efforts and how they might influence their targets. More importantly, however, we can also use the TRA to carefully design messages intended to dissuade support of a terrorist group. This chapter shows how this might be done.

When we get to Chapter 6, we shift our focus. Whereas Chapters 3–5 feature perspectives and approaches with strong emphases on cognitive processes, Chapter 6 will cover some of the most critical targets of terrorist messaging – audience emotions. Specifically, this chapter will discuss how terrorist groups' messages play on audiences' emotions to foster support for their ideologies and activities. Of course, analysts and practitioners have also tried to fight terrorist propaganda by influencing audience emotions. However, researchers have yet to scientifically examine the psychological implications of arousing different emotions in counter-radicalization messaging. Chapter 6 will fill this gap in our understanding by describing how empirical research on different emotions – happiness, sadness, guilt, shame, anger, and jealousy – can be used to construct messages that will effectively turn people away from supporting terrorist groups.

At this point in the book, we'll have covered four critical persuasion theories and perspectives. It's unlikely that terrorist groups think about applying these theories and perspectives to hone their propaganda, but the persuasive principles that underpin their messages have nevertheless driven their effectiveness in the past, and will continue to do so in the future. In addition, advances in communication technology and shifting strategic objectives in the twenty-first century have the potential to fundamentally change how terrorists try to engage with audiences. With this in mind, Chapter 7 uses information from the previous chapters to consider some impending challenges related to the persuasiveness of extremist propaganda.

Ultimately, the goal of this book is to offer ideas for challenging terrorist groups' persuasive messages to reduce audiences' risk of violent radicalization and involvement in terrorism. Although each chapter will offer specific guidelines on using the aforementioned theories and perspectives to develop specific counter-messages, the final chapter features specific suggestions on how we can pull together insights from the earlier chapters and emerging communication technologies to fight back against terrorist groups and their propaganda.

∴

Despite Alex's close calls with the Islamic State, her grandmother's intervention seemed to have brought her back from the verge of joining the group.

Alex gave her grandmother access to her Twitter account and e-mail, and her grandmother immediately changed the passwords to these accounts. She took Alex on a vacation to help her to reconnect with her family and forget her time talking with Hamad and Faisal. The family returned to something resembling normalcy. Unfortunately, it was short-lived.

One day, while on vacation, Alex waited for her grandparents to go to the beach. Once she was alone, she logged into Skype – an account that her grandmother had forgotten to restrict. As soon as she logged on, Faisal sent her a message. Alex responded. The two talked.

Months later, Alex and Faisal were still communicating online.

∴

It doesn't need to be like this. We can persuade the Alexes of the world to reject the Hamads and Faisals – to ignore the violent ideologies they peddle. We can convince individuals who are at risk for perpetrating violence to think for themselves and pursue peaceful means of political or ideological change. We can give potential terrorist recruits the communicative and psychological tools they need to avoid being seduced by groups that would use them as expendable pawns. We have the knowledge of persuasion to fight back against terrorist propaganda – we just need to use it.

It's time we load our weapons by transforming our knowledge of persuasion and psychology into actionable strategies for fighting extremist propaganda.

Let's begin.

Notes

1 James Bruce, "Inside the West's Secret War against ISIS," *The Arab Weekly* (July 3, 2016). Available at https://thearabweekly.com/sites/default/files/pdf/2016/07/03-07/p1000.pdf.
2 Sun Tzu, *The Art of War* (translated by P. Harris) (London and New York: Everyman's Library, 2018).

3 For the complete account on which this story is based, see Rukmini Calli-machi, "ISIS and the Lonely Young American," *New York Times* (June 27, 2015). Available at www.nytimes.com/2015/06/28/world/americas/isis-online-recruiting-american.html, and Poh Si Teng and Ben Laffin, "Flirting with the Islamic State," *New York Times* (June 27, 2015). Available at www.nytimes.com/video/world/100000003749550/flirting-with-the-islamic-state.html.

4 James P. Farwell, "The Media Strategy of ISIS," *Survival: Global Politics and Strategy* 56, no. 6 (2014): 49–55; Ashley Kirk, "Iraq and Syria: How many Foreign Fighters are Fighting for ISIL?" *The Telegraph* (March 29, 2016). Available at www.telegraph.co.uk/news/2016/03/29/iraq-and-syria-how-many-foreign-fighters-are-fighting-for-isil/.

5 Anne Barnard and Hwaida Saad, "Raqqa, ISIS 'Capital,' is Captured, U.S.-Backed Forces Say," *New York Times* (October 17, 2017). Available at www.nytimes.com/2017/10/17/world/middleeast/isis-syria-raqqa.html.

6 See Laurie Fenstermacher and Todd Leventhal, eds., *Countering Violent Extremism: Scientific Methods & Strategies* (Wright-Patterson Air Force Base, OH: Air Force Research Laboratory, 2011).

7 Rita Katz, "The State Department's Twitter War with ISIS is Embarrassing," *Time* (September 16, 2014). Available at http://time.com/3387065/isis-twitter-war-state-department/. Greg Miller and Scott Higham, "In a Propaganda War against ISIS, the U.S. Tried to Play by the Enemy's Rules," *The Washington Post* (May 8, 2015). Available at www.washingtonpost.com/world/national-security/in-a-propaganda-war-us-tried-to-play-by-the-enemys-rules/2015/05/08/6eb6b732-e52f-11e4-81ea-0649268f729e_story.html.

Part I

The Battlefield

Foundations of Persuasion, Radicalization, Violent Radicalization, and Counter-Radicalization

1   Words are Loaded Pistols: Radicalization and Persuasion

In the introductory chapter, I talked quite a bit about persuasion, radicalization, and how the two might connect. To better understand (1) where these concepts meet, and (2) how our understanding of the former informs our methods for dealing with the latter, I'm afraid we need to do a few academic chores. Most importantly, we need to conceptualize the topics that serve as the foundation of the book.

To do this, I'll first outline various perspectives on the nature of radicalization to identify common thematic elements across the different ways that radicalization has been understood. In doing so, it becomes possible to properly explain how radicalization and related concepts pertain to persuasion. By connecting persuasion to radicalization, I can present the central theses that underpin the rest of the book, and most importantly show you the potential value of persuasion theory in efforts to counter radicalization processes. I'll also provide three case examples to illustrate how persuasion relates to radicalization.

In short, this chapter will review past research on the process of radicalization, use this research to develop a workable definition for radicalization, and show how it is inherently related to persuasive communication.

First things first – let's review how the experts have understood radicalization.

Models of Radicalization

To grasp the nature of radicalization, we first have to develop an informed definition for it. Specifically, we must contend with problematic issues surrounding the term, especially with respect to the myriad ways that it has been conceptualized. By engaging with the literature on radicalization, we can draw lessons from how the process has been understood in the past.

This raises one problem, though. Researchers in multiple disciplines have studied radicalization, and as a result, no two conceptualizations

15

of the process are alike. Scholars from education,[1] history,[2] psychology,[3] business,[4] rhetorical analysis,[5] political science,[6] and several other fields have engaged in research on what they call "radicalization" or "radicalism," leading to countless context-specific conceptualizations.

For starters, consider the intense upsurge in research on radicalization in terrorism studies in recent years. In March of 2019, a Google Scholar search for all publications mentioning "terrorism" and "radicalization" between 1990 and 2005 yielded 3,110 results. The same search for years between 2006 and 2019 yielded 17,200 results. Radicalization, it seems, is a hot topic of interest.

The vast increase in the number of researchers exploring radicalization has an upside. As a multidisciplinary domain within social science, the study of terrorism (and all related concepts) benefits from input from different kinds of researchers, practitioners, and analysts.

That said, one downside to the size of the literature on radicalization is that there is little consensus about what radicalization actually is. So, to highlight key elements of radicalization as identified by past work, I performed a systematic review of papers on the topic. Specifically, I evaluated papers that met at least one of multiple criteria. The paper must have:

- attempted to formally explicate radicalization as the central focus of the writing,
- stated an explicit definition for radicalization as part of a larger study on political violence (or other related phenomena), or
- provided a framework for radicalization as part of a larger study on political violence (or other related phenomena) but only provided an implicit definition for the term.

To identify work that meets at least one of these criteria, I tracked down seminal research within terrorism studies to identify the means by which the authors built their conceptualizations for radicalization.[7] I also used these papers as launching pads from which I could identify other studies by way of the research these papers cited. As a final step in my hunt for research on radicalization, I searched multiple academic databases (e.g., PsycInfo, Google Scholar) for papers mentioning radicalization that had not been identified in the previous two steps. This produced several new papers for me to evaluate.[8]

As expected, this process produced many definitions for radicalization, all of which differed in subtle ways. Luckily, there are commonalities across some of the definitions that allow us to get an idea about some of the central elements of the radicalization process. Grouping these elements into categories shows that radicalization has been conceptualized in four principal ways.[9]

Some experts have thought of radicalization as a form of *identity negotiation*, whereby individuals assimilate beliefs and attitudes consistent with those of an extremist group at the cost of their own unique psychological characteristics. Others have treated radicalization as the *acquisition of "motivational knowledge"* from ideological leaders. Still others emphasize *social networks* as foundational in radicalization, arguing that the process occurs as a function of interactions with trusted others who have extremist beliefs and attitudes. Finally, some have thought of radicalization as a form of *incremental commitment* to an extremist group facilitated by specific social and psychological changes.

It is important to note that these categories are not mutually exclusive. Radicalization can be simultaneously characterized by any combination of these descriptors. However, different experts have emphasized some characteristics over others when conceptualizing the process of radicalization. The four categories of conceptualizations reflect these points of emphasis.

Let's consider these categories one by one to see if we can't develop a comprehensive understanding of the process.

Radicalization as Identity Negotiation

Several experts have emphasized the importance of personal identity in the radicalization process. For instance, Dr. Anthony Stahelski of Central Washington University has performed extensive research on social and psychological conditioning in cults, which he has used to inform research about radicalization with respect to terrorist organizations. Stahelski has claimed that individuals become greater threats for engaging in ideologically motivated violence when they experience changes in their perceptions of their own identities.[10] This process of identity negotiation is comprised of several steps, many of which have been investigated by other researchers in the context of terrorism and political violence.

Depluralization

For most people, meaningful and personally relevant group memberships are critical for healthy psychological development.[11] Generally, individuals address their needs for belonging, association, and membership by affiliating with several kinds of groups. These groups can be based on familial relations, tribes, friendships, interests, recreation, education, or any number of other shared characteristics. Being in multiple kinds of groups facilitates an individual's sense of belonging and affiliation, but no one group (except maybe family) is completely essential to an individual's self-concept.[12] As such, individuals can move in and out of social groups with little psychological discomfort. By being affiliated with multiple groups in this way, individuals avoid depending on any one group as the only basis for their identity.

To get people to adopt their ideologies, extremist groups must minimize the importance of their other social groups and become their most critical group affiliation.[13] This can be accomplished by physically isolating individuals from the other social groups they are part of. When this is impossible, some extremist groups pressure target recruits to voluntarily avoid their other affiliations while they strengthen their social links to the extremist group itself.[14] This allows for the creation of a new reality for the individual – one that is defined entirely by the extremist group.

Self-deindividuation and Other-deindividuation

Once individuals have abandoned their outside affiliations, they become more vulnerable to losing the personal identity they cultivated as a function of those affiliations.[15] They replace their personal beliefs, attitudes, values, and behavioral patterns with those expected by members of their new group. In doing so, they lose their perceptions about right and wrong outside the context of the extremist group and develop an alternative set of goals and norms consistent with the group's ideology.[16] Perceptions of reality – particularly with respect to how different social forces affect one's life – become aligned with those offered by the group's leadership. Akhtar described this step as a surrendering of personal values on "the altar of group approval."[17] As this happens, the person may cease to think of himself as an individual with unique psychological characteristics, but will instead consider himself to be a cog in a larger machine – a deindividuated component of a larger system dedicated to the achievement of the extremist group's goals.[18]

While individuals undergo self-deindividuation, they can also experience a parallel process where they deindividuate people who do not belong to their group.[19] As an individual comes to believe that their social conditions are affected by external groups (a common tenet of extremist ideologies), they may also come to perceive those groups as a uniform collection of enemies.[20] When this occurs, the individual develops beliefs that treat all members of enemy groups as homogeneous. This is a critical step in the context of political violence, as people tend to demonstrate greater aggression against those they do not see as distinct entities.[21]

As someone (1) replaces their personal identity with an identity based on their affiliation with an extremist group and (2) comes to perceive group outsiders to be part of a single homogeneous mass, the individual's worldview has been simplified such that it contains only two groups: "us" and "them."

Dehumanization

After categorizing people such that they are part of the individual's in-group (i.e., us) or out-group (i.e., them) and stripping those who fall into the latter category of any individuating characteristics, new adherents to extremist ideologies may ascribe positive attributes to the in-group and negative attributes to the out-group.[22] In this stage of the radicalization process, individuals begin to consider out-group enemies as subhuman, referring to them as animals, pests, vermin, demons, or monsters.[23] By perpetuating the idea that the members of enemy groups are part of a deindividuated, subhuman collective, extremist groups rationalize violence against those perceived enemies.[24]

Stahelski adds that once violence against out-group enemies has been justified and performed, radicalized individuals may also engage in "demonization" whereby they become convinced that their enemies are the manifestation of a "cosmic evil."[25] This serves as a psychological coping mechanism to help perpetrators avoid feeling remorse for their violent actions.

∴

Taken together, the phenomena described above characterize radicalization as a process whereby an individual replaces their personal identity with a collective identity based on the beliefs, attitudes, and proposed behaviors of an extremist group. These beliefs, attitudes, and proposed behaviors are communicated to the individual in the form of messages that advocate for the abandonment of social ties to any groups outside the extremist group.

Although this definition describes how perceptions of self- and other-identity affect the radicalization process, it fails to address several issues related to *how* individuals radicalize. For instance, how do individuals *learn* the beliefs and attitudes that they are expected to adopt? What sources provide vulnerable individuals with the information that serves as the basis for their radicalization?

Although it suffers from shortcomings of its own, another perspective on radicalization provides some insight into the mechanisms that allow extremist ideologies to be conveyed from established members to developing radicals. This perspective argues that radicalization is a function of knowledge transfer.

Radicalization as the Assimilation of Motivational Knowledge

It is widely understood that terrorist groups cannot survive without senior members transferring their knowledge to new recruits. Most research in this area has focused on the importance of technical knowledge transfer for achieving the group's objectives. Information on constructing explosives,[26] circumventing security systems,[27] exploiting the media,[28] and collecting intelligence on potential targets[29] is regularly taught and learned in terrorist organizations. To effectively plan their attacks, it is essential for members to obtain and implement this kind of knowledge.

That said, these groups cannot survive only by knowing how to build a bomb and turn off alarms. The performance of terrorism sometimes requires adherence to extremist ideologies that promote and justify the use of violence; the tenets of those ideologies need to be taught as well.

In this vein, *motivational knowledge* relates to information designed to inspire potential recruits by instilling the group's ideology.[30] Whereas technical knowledge assists in the physical execution of a violent act, motivational knowledge helps in the development of a mindset capable of performing one.

∴

In discussing al-Qaeda, terrorism expert Bruce Hoffman once argued that the group's ability to survive "[was] not predicated on the total number of jihadists that it may have or have not trained in the past, but on its continued ability to recruit, to mobilize, and to animate both actual and would-be fighters, supporters, and sympathizers."[31] Although Hoffman's claim was specifically about al-Qaeda in the wake of its 2001 attacks, it rings true for extremist organizations of all ideologies. It contends that the radicalization of new recruits through the dissemination and assimilation of motivational knowledge is the lifeblood of such organizations. Before potential recruits can be taught how to elude security forces, organize operations, or use weaponry, they are taught about the ideology of the group for which they will support the use of violence.[32]

The Analysis Unit of the Royal Canadian Mounted Police (RCMP) has highlighted the importance of teaching and learning extremist ideologies as a fundamental component of radicalization. Specifically, in the late 2000s, the RCMP defined radicalization as "the process by which individuals are introduced to an overly ideological message and belief system and taught or encouraged to follow thought or behavior patterns that could eventually (but not always) lead to extremist activity or direct action."[33]

This emphasis on learning as a key mechanism in the radicalization process has some basis in research on ideological assimilation. James Forest, former Director of Terrorism Studies at the US Military Academy, argued that knowledge of an extremist movement's history, objectives, and motivations plays a central role in inspiring potential recruits to engage in violence on behalf of its ideology.[34]

Some cases of violent extremism have highlighted the importance of motivational knowledge in the radicalization process. For instance, both the alleged "shoe-bomber" Richard Reid and the "20th hijacker" Zacarias Moussaoui had connections to the Finsbury Park mosque in north London.[35] While attending the mosque, it is likely that the two would-be terrorists were exposed to the extremist teachings of Sheikh Abu Hamza, who was arrested in 2004 for terrorism-related offenses.[36] A similar situation emerged out of the Quds mosque in Hamburg, Germany. Several al-Qaeda recruits, including the leader of the 9/11 hijackers, Mohammed Atta, attended the mosque and were inspired there.[37]

Even decades ago, the transfer of motivational knowledge was thought to be central to the radicalization process. In the 1970s and 1980s, the Provisional Irish Army (PIRA) required recruits to attend training sessions where they were taught about Irish Republicanism, what the PIRA's ideology means to the recruit, as well as the movement's policies.[38] These lessons did not provide the recruits with any military knowledge that would help them carry out attacks for the Provos, but they built group cohesion and solidarity among new PIRA fighters, thereby strengthening their dedication to the group.[39]

∴

Arguments for the motivational knowledge model define radicalization as a process whereby beliefs, attitudes, behaviors, and values consistent with extremist ideologies are taught by established members of extremist organizations to potential members.

Like any system of beliefs, extremist ideologies must be learned before they can be adhered to. That said, a conceptualization of radicalization that focuses on the introduction to, teaching of, and encouragement for an extremist ideology does not explain why some individuals come to accept the tenets of the ideology while others do not. As such, it seems that the acquisition of motivational knowledge is, by itself, insufficient for explaining how someone commits to an extremist ideology.

There is another perspective on radicalization that seeks to explicitly address some of the issues that contribute to one's acceptance of extremist ideologies and, sometimes, terrorist behavior. This perspective focuses on social affiliations as the fundamental driver of radicalization.

Radicalization as the Function of Social Network Affiliation

Based on research related to the origins and evolution of global terror networks, Marc Sageman argues that radicalization results from an individual's interactions with others in their social circle.[40] Sageman contends that through immersion in a social echo chamber in which similarly minded others reinforce each other's claims, individuals' beliefs and attitudes regarding an extremist ideology crystallize and intensify. Rather than focus on specific psychological mechanisms for belief and attitude change, the social-network perspective of radicalization highlights only that these mechanisms largely occur in the context of interpersonal relationships with others who are psychologically engaged with an extremist ideology.

Many researchers have adopted this perspective as an accurate representation of the nature of radicalization. For instance, Carlyle Thayer explained that the radicalization trajectories of the 7/7 London bombers were facilitated by regular meetings in study circles and at their mosque. Through these repeated meetings, the three attackers grew more socially conservative, insulating them from many of their peers. Thayer argued that when applied to cases like the 7/7 bombers, the social-network perspective shows that the "social bonds among groups of friends that predate formal recruitment into the global jihad" are critical to the radicalization process.[41]

Terrorism experts Thomas Hegghammer and Edwin Bakker similarly analyzed cases of radicalization among groups of individuals involved with the al-Qaeda network. In evaluating the motivations of new recruits to al-Qaeda in the Arabian Peninsula, Hegghammer showed that "group dynamics such as peer pressure and intra-group affection seem to have been crucial" to the radicalization process.[42] Bakker examined the cases of 242 al-Qaeda members, finding that their movement towards terrorism did not occur because of formal recruitment efforts by the group, but because of social networks of friends or relatives.[43]

Classic analyses of political extremists have produced similar results. Researchers have shown that in the 1970s and 1980s, an individual's involvement with European extremist groups was largely a function of personal connections with others who were already involved. Donatella Della Porta found that among members of Italian left-wing groups, more than 75 percent had at least one friend who had already been participating in the movement when they became initially involved.[44] In analyses of another left-wing terrorist group – the German Red Army Faction (i.e., the Baader-Meinhof Group) – Friedhelm Neidhardt[45] and Klaus Wasmund[46] discovered that most new recruits into the RAF were socially connected before their involvement.

As these examples illustrate, an individual's social connections can play a central role in their movement towards violence.

Though social-network approaches to understanding extremism and terrorism are varied, they generally highlight three phases that characterize the process:[47]

(1) The development of social affiliations with an extremist movement through friendship, kinship, discipleship, or religious connections,
(2) The intensification of beliefs and attitudes consistent with the movement's ideology through interactions with like-minded others, and
(3) Formal acceptance into the movement through the social connection that introduced them to the movement and/or its ideology.

So, although this perspective is primarily concerned with the context in which radicalization occurs (i.e., social networks), we can nevertheless deduce how it would inform the conceptualization of radicalization. The social-network radicalization perspective would define radicalization as an intensification of beliefs and attitudes consistent with an extremist movement's ideology resulting from affiliations and interactions with others who have a common interest in the tenets of that ideology.

Radicalization as Incremental Social and Psychological Change

As suggested by the three types of models described above, the term "process" is invoked to describe radicalization in different ways. Despite this tendency, there are relatively few definitions for radicalization that *emphasize the incremental nature* of the process. For instance, Stahelski[48] conceptualizes radicalization as a series of steps, but those steps are couched in a greater emphasis on identity change rather than radicalization's phasic nature.

In contrast to Stahelski, Sageman, Bakker, Hegghammer, or any of the other scholars cited in the previous sections, there are some researchers who have conceptualized radicalization by giving primary emphasis to its progression-based character. Of the definitions that emphasize the process-based nature of radicalization, there is a critical distinction to be made. Some researchers have described radicalization as fundamentally sequential, occurring in successive steps of increased ideological commitment. Others have defined the radicalization process as unstructured, occurring over a series of phases that can be nonlinear in terms of psychological or behavioral devotion to an extremist ideology.

Let's have a look at both categories.

Radicalization as Linear Change in Beliefs, Attitudes, Intentions, and Behaviors

In an early model of radicalization, Clark McCauley and Sophia Moskalenko described the process in largely linear terms.[49] They defined radicalization as "a change in beliefs, feelings, and behaviors in directions that increasingly justify intergroup violence and demand sacrifice in defense of the ingroup."[50] As part of this model, they argued that radicalization of behavior (like taking more risks for an extremist group, engaging in violence for a political cause) is directly related to an individual's beliefs and attitudes, such that those who engage in more radical behavior likely have more radical mindsets. In short, they argued that "those who do more" tend to have stronger feelings about the extremist group and its ideology than "those who do less."[51] Several social movement researchers share this perspective.[52]

Based on the assumption that greater ideological commitment is related to more extreme behaviors, McCauley produced a model characterizing radicalization as a process in which individuals progress up through various levels of a pyramid as their beliefs, feelings, and behaviors reflect stronger justifications of violence against some enemy.[53] Figure 1.1 depicts this first iteration of the pyramid model.

Figure 1.1 McCauley's first Pyramid Model of Radicalization
Source: Adapted from McCauley, "Jujitsu Politics." Copyright © 2006 by Paul R. Kimmel and Chris E. Stout. All rights reserved. Reproduced with permission of ABC-CLIO, LLC, Santa Barbara, CA.

In this model, individuals who sympathize with or support the goals of violent extremist groups – even if they disagree with the violent means by which they pursue those goals – represent the base of the pyramid. Using Irish republicans during the Troubles as an example, McCauley explained that the base of the pyramid would be comprised of individuals who believe that the British should be entirely uninvolved with Ireland. These individuals may not throw stones at British soldiers or detonate bombs at military checkpoints, but they agree with the Irish Republican Army's motivations for doing so. At the top of the pyramid are individuals who are "hardcore" Irish republicans that engage British soldiers in combat for the sake of the republican cause.

By structuring actors in terms of their support for terrorism in this way, McCauley's original pyramid model conceptualizes radicalization as a linear path towards violent activity, characterized by increased levels of ideological commitment that justify that activity. This would suggest that for an individual to engage in increasingly violent behavior (i.e., progress toward terrorism), they must undergo a parallel process of belief and attitude change consistent with the extremist group's ideology.

In a model similar to the first McCauley pyramid model, Fathali Moghaddam described the progression towards terrorism to be like climbing a staircase.[54] In the staircase model, Moghaddam argued that people begin on a "ground floor" where they consider why they experience injustice or live in unsatisfying social conditions. If an individual is frustrated by their situation, he will progress to the "first floor" where he will consider options for resolving his frustrations. If his frustrations are projected onto an entity that is believed to be the cause of his misery, he moves to the "second floor," where he grows aggressive towards that entity and regards it as an enemy. As anger towards the perceived enemy grows, some individuals will become sympathetic to violent tactics that terrorist groups use and come to morally align with the group's objectives. This represents movement to the third floor. From here, some sympathizers will go on to engage in "us-versus-them" thinking like the depluralization and deindividuation processes described by Stahelski. At this point, on the "fourth floor," the individual is likely ideologically and socially committed to a terrorist cause, with little likelihood of abandoning the ideology or, if they were already recruited, little chance to leave the group. The final step in the progression is movement to the "fifth floor," where the individual engages in a terrorist action.

Figure 1.2 provides a visual depiction of Moghaddam's staircase model. The doors on each floor represent behavioral options for the individual being radicalized. Moghaddam argues that individuals have

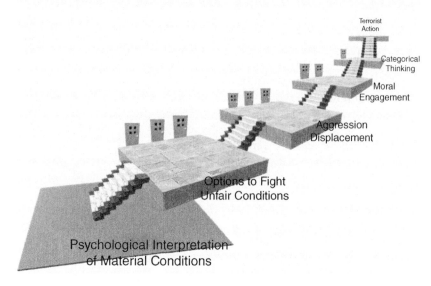

Figure 1.2 Moghaddam's Staircase to Terrorism model
Source: Adapted from Moghaddam, "The Staircase to Terrorism."

fewer and fewer options as the individual's beliefs and attitudes about the group and its enemies come into closer alignment with an extremist group's ideology. In this way, the staircase model of radicalization and terrorism is much like McCauley's pyramid model – in both models, those who "do more" tend to have stronger ideological affiliation to the group than those that "do less."

Both McCauley's pyramid model and Moghaddam's staircase model have a commonsensical appeal to them. It seems logical that as someone develops more radical beliefs and attitudes, they are more likely to engage in radical behavior. However, there is some evidence to suggest that the linear process suggested by these models does not capture several details associated with radicalization and its relationship with engagement in violent action.

For example, there are several cases of individuals who participated in violent behavior on behalf of a terrorist group without having adopted the group's ideology before having done so. Andrew Silke described forced conscription practices employed by the Ulster Defence Association (UDA) as they tried to bring new members into the group during the Troubles of Northern Ireland.[55] To ensure that their ranks were always filled with new fighters, the UDA would forcibly recruit young people who had yet to adhere to loyalist values to fight for the group.

The activities undertaken by these forced conscripts would place them at the apex of the pyramid in McCauley's model and on the "fifth floor" in Moghaddam's model. After all, they made significant personal sacrifices and took substantial risks in support of the UDA. However, their political views at the time of their conscription were not consistent with the behaviors they were forced to perform. If they had been, the threat of physical harm would not have been needed to motivate their engagement in violence. This phenomenon is not uncommon; child soldiers in Africa[56] and tribal supporters in Afghanistan[57] have also been found to engage in violence on behalf of extremist groups without showing any affinity for their ideologies.

As these cases demonstrate, radical behaviors can occur without the corresponding beliefs or attitudes. Alternatively, individuals can adhere to radical beliefs or attitudes without engaging in the corresponding radical behaviors. More simply, the "non-radicalized" often engage in violence, and the "radicalized" often do not.

To illustrate, consider the exceedingly small numbers of individuals who engage in terrorism despite holding what most would call radical beliefs and/or attitudes. In 2008, for example, the Palestinian Center for Policy and Survey Research questioned hundreds of adult Palestinians about attacks against Israel. Of the 1,270 individuals surveyed, more than 800 reported supporting the launch of rockets from the Gaza strip against Israeli civilians.[58]

According to the pyramid or staircase model, these individuals would be considered "radicalized," as most would argue that supporting armed attacks against non-military targets represents a radical position. Despite that almost 75 percent of respondents reported holding this position, only a small proportion of Palestinians have ever taken up arms against Israeli civilians or military targets.

Again, the direct relationship assumed by the abovementioned models does not hold. Radicalization of beliefs and attitudes does not perfectly correlate with engagement in violent activity.

∴

In contrast to the linear process-based models described thus far, there are other conceptualizations of radicalization that challenge the notion that the process is marked by direct relationships between beliefs, attitudes, and behaviors. These conceptualizations also emphasize that radicalization is incrementally phasic in nature, but not necessarily causally antecedent to violent activity. I call these models "nonlinear," and we'll turn to them next.

Radicalization as Nonlinear Change in Beliefs, Attitudes, Intentions, and Behaviors

Whereas the pyramid and staircase models for radicalization seemed to indicate a direct relationship between radicalization of beliefs and attitudes and increasingly violent behavior, some models have rejected the view that radicalization and terrorism are necessarily connected. Through his work on radicalization and its behavioral manifestations, John Horgan showed that individual trajectories into (and out of) terrorism are not always connected to beliefs and attitudes. Like McCauley, Moghaddam, and other process-focused researchers, Horgan described radicalization as a "social and psychological process of incrementally experienced commitment to an extremist or political ideology."[59] Unlike McCauley and Moghaddam's early conceptualizations of radicalization, however, Horgan also argued that "the way in which individuals make choices about their involvement ... in terrorism is complex and not reducible to a single behavioural dimensions."[60] Horgan's argument, in short, is that the process of radicalization is incremental and phasic, but is by no means a straight line from passive indifference to zealous engagement in terrorism.

Later iterations of the McCauley pyramid model were adapted to stress the nonlinear nature of radicalization. Again working with Sophia Moskalenko, McCauley developed the "double pyramid model" to distinguish psychological radicalization from violent behavior.[61] In contrast to the single pyramid model developed in 2006, the double pyramid model disaggregated beliefs and attitudes and behaviors such that they were no longer perfectly correlated. More specifically, this model proposes that individuals can "reside" at incongruent positions in what the authors called the "opinion pyramid" and the "action pyramid."

At the base of the opinion pyramid are individuals who have no opinion about an ideological cause (neutral individuals). Just above neutral individuals are those who may agree with a terrorist group's cause and/or goals, but perhaps not the violent means they use to pursue them (sympathizers). Above sympathizers is another group of individuals who agree with the terrorist group's cause and/or goals, as well as the violence used by the group (justifiers). Finally, at the apex of the opinion pyramid are those who feel they have a responsibility to engage in violence on behalf of the cause (personal moral obligation).

In the action pyramid, the base is comprised of individuals who do nothing to support a political group or cause (inert individuals). Above

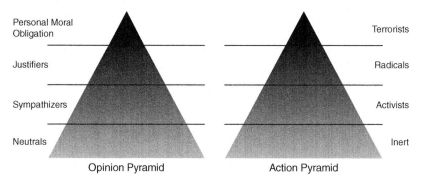

Figure 1.3 McCauley and Moskalenko's Double Pyramid Model of
Radicalization
Source: Adapted from McCauley and Moskalenko, "Understanding Political
Radicalization."

the inert are those who have partaken in legal political action for the sake of
the cause being advocated (activists). A small group of individuals may
emerge from activists who engage in illegal activity on behalf of the cause
(radicals). Finally, at the apex of the action pyramid, some individuals will
go on to engage in illegal violent action that targets civilians (terrorists).

McCauley and Moskalenko emphasize that the levels in both pyramids
are not "connected" by a stairway, as in Moghaddam's model. Individuals can jump from one level to another, skip levels, or move down the
pyramids as their situation dictates. Moreover, individuals can "exist" at
any point on either pyramid and not be in the equivalent level on the
other pyramid. For example, some individuals may feel a personal moral
obligation to defend a cause and/or ideology, but only engage in legal
activity to do so. This individual would reside at the apex of the opinion
pyramid (personal moral obligation), but only the second level of the
action pyramid (activists). Figure 1.3 offers an illustration of McCauley
and Moskalenko's double pyramid model.

The double pyramid model indicates that there are a wide number of
factors that may contribute to an individual's engagement in terrorism.
Although radicalization of beliefs and attitudes (resulting in feelings of
personal moral obligation to defend an ideology with violence) may put
someone at increased risk for engaging in violent activity, there are other
issues to consider.

Horgan's conceptualization of radicalization explicitly highlights these
factors. Based on cognitive behavioral therapy (CBT),[62] Horgan argues
that radicalization trajectories can culminate in any number of behavioral
outcomes, all of which are contingent on three situational factors: personal factors, setting events, and social/political/organizational factors.[63]

For Horgan, personal factors are any psychological experiences an individual undergoes during any stage of the radicalization process. These factors vary from person to person, and can include emotional states, personal experiences, feelings of dissatisfaction, identification with those they perceive as victims, and other things.[64]

Setting events are related to the influence of variables that are "part of the individual's socialization into family, work, religion, society, and culture."[65] These institutional factors are considered effectively unchangeable and are commonly understood as so-called "root causes of terrorism."[66] Some examples include poverty, lack of access to education, unemployment, and relative deprivation.

Finally, social/political/organizational factors relate to the social context in which an individual becomes concerned with political expression and ideology.[67] Here, Max Taylor and Horgan recognize the role of the extremist group in the radicalization process, arguing that how the group expresses the ideology can affect the radicalization trajectory of individuals exposed to it.

For Horgan and Taylor, radicalization is a complex process that is impossible to reduce to a linear progression from a starting point (political apathy) to a defined ending point (engagement in terrorism). Instead, radicalization is a function of the interplay between personal factors, setting events, and the social, political, or organizational context in which someone lives and operates. Those undergoing radicalization can shift roles as they grow more (or less) ideologically committed, indicating that there is no "end point" of radicalization. Instead, it is a constant negotiation of one's values, situational factors that facilitate or hinder certain behaviors, expectations related to outcomes of those behaviors, and one's role within an extremist movement.

In this model, radicalization occurs over time, but rarely follows the same pattern for any two individuals. In essence, this model argues that radicalization trajectories are as different as the people that experience them.

∴

Having now covered the four points of emphasis that have framed how radicalization has been understood, we can begin to see which characteristics are fundamental to the process. In doing so, it becomes possible to conceptualize radicalization in a way that accounts for the importance of persuasion.

In the next section, I will highlight elements of the radicalization process that are common to all the perspectives outlined in this chapter.

I will then offer a definition for radicalization based on these elements. As you may have already guessed, one of these elements is inherently related to communication and how it can influence the beliefs, attitudes, intentions, and behaviors of those who are exposed to it.

Radicalization as Persuasion

Despite conceptual disagreements about the nature of radicalization, there are themes that cut across the different ways it has been conceptualized that allow us to boil it down to its fundamental defining characteristics.

In comparing the different perspectives, we see three things that are consistently mentioned in expert descriptions of the radicalization process.

(1) Radicalization is phasic in nature. Although there is disagreement about what constitutes a "phase," radicalization is largely understood to be a cumulative process that occurs over time and across multiple personal, political, and social events.
(2) Radicalization is characterized by increased commitment to beliefs and attitudes consistent with an extremist ideology, but not necessarily a parallel commitment to engage in violence on behalf of that ideology.
(3) Radicalization is driven – at least in part – by exposure to content that advocates beliefs and attitudes consistent with an extremist ideology.
    (a) Identity negotiation model: Movement through the different stages of identity negotiation involves exposure to messages that frame the importance of different groups relative to the extremist group.
    (b) Motivational knowledge model: Acquisition of motivational knowledge requires communication between a teacher (i.e., an ideologically committed individual) and a student (i.e., a budding extremist).
    (c) Social network model: The pull of social networks is contingent on communicative relationships between the potential extremist and valued others within his or her social circles.
    (d) Incremental commitment model: Part of the social/organizational factors that incrementally influence beliefs and attitudes towards an extremist ideology involve the appeal of messages to which budding extremists are exposed.

If the language used in number (3) seems familiar, it should. There is a term for the transmission and reception of messages that are designed to affect a target's beliefs and attitudes in the manner described in all four perspectives on radicalization.

It is called persuasion.

∴

Common understanding of persuasion equates it with behavioral modification.[68] We generally consider someone to be "persuaded" when they either begin doing something we want them to do or stop doing something we don't want them to do. This seems to make sense.

For example, my father was diagnosed with diabetes several years ago. After his diagnosis, his doctor told him that he needs to eat healthier foods to maintain a decent weight and blood sugar level. The problem is that my stubborn dad loves pepperoni and cake – far too much. It's not uncommon to catch the old man sneaking Little Debbie treats for breakfast or wolfing down half a bag of sliced pepperoni as a "snack." So, I regularly try to persuade him to adjust his diet in the interest of his health. The persuasive attempts targeted at my dad essentially translate to my trying to get him to switch from one behavior (i.e., eating pepperoni and cake) to another (i.e., eating some damn vegetables for once).

Although we tend to equate persuasion to behavioral conversion, behaviors do not change in and of themselves. For someone to be persuaded to engage in a behavior, they also need to develop certain beliefs, attitudes, and intentions with respect to that behavior.[69] So, despite that we may be ultimately interested in changing how someone acts, persuasion also involves attempts to modify a target's beliefs, attitudes, or intentions.

Given this, we can define persuasion as a phenomenon *whereby beliefs, attitudes, intentions, or behaviors (or any combination thereof) are modified by messages that appeal to the reason and/or emotions of the message recipient(s).*[70]

With this piece of the puzzle in place, we can begin to see the larger picture of how persuasion plays a role in radicalization.

∴

We now know that persuasion relates to communicative attempts to change beliefs, attitudes, intentions, and/or behaviors. We also know that radicalization involves belief and attitude change that results, at least in part, from exposure to messages consistent with an extremist ideology.

It therefore follows that if someone is exposed to persuasive messages that induce changes in their beliefs or attitudes such that they become more closely aligned with those advocated by an extremist ideology, then *radicalization is an inherently persuasive process.*

More formally, and consistent with the elements we identified above, we can define radicalization as *an incremental social and psychological process prompted by and inextricably bound in persuasion, whereby an individual develops increased commitment to an extremist ideology resulting in the assimilation of beliefs and/or attitudes consistent with that ideology.*

You may notice that this conceptualization of radicalization does not mention terrorist behavior. This is no accident; as many terrorism researchers have noted (and incorporated into their models), radicalization of beliefs and attitudes is not perfectly correlated with violent intentions or behavior. Once again, radicalization may put someone at increased risk for engaging in violence, but it is not a perfect predictor of it.

For an individual to engage in ideologically motivated violence, he or she must undergo a psychological process that is an extension of the radicalization process as described above. This process, called *violent radicalization*, is a "social and psychological process of *increased* and *focused* radicalization through involvement with a violent non-state movement."[71] Specifically, violent radicalization includes the initial phase of becoming involved with a terrorist organization, sustained involvement with that organization, the consideration of alternatives to violence, the search for opportunities to engage in violence, and the physical engagement in violent activity.[72]

If radicalization involves a shift in beliefs and attitudes such that they are consistent with an extremist ideology, violent radicalization is a shift in intentions and behaviors such that they support an extremist ideology through physical violence.

To exemplify the connections between radicalization (and violent radicalization) and persuasion, the next section will describe three well-known cases in which individuals developed extremist beliefs, attitudes, intentions, and/or behaviors at least partially through their exposure to messages advocating extremist ideologies.

Cases of Radicalization

Colleen LaRose

Let's first consider the case of Colleen LaRose, more notoriously known as "Jihad Jane."

In 2007, LaRose was on vacation with her boyfriend in Amsterdam. While there, the couple visited a bar where LaRose became drunk and belligerent. She insulted her boyfriend until he grew impatient with her and left her alone at the bar. With her boyfriend out of the way, a Muslim man approached LaRose, and the two left the bar to spend the night together. That encounter sparked a curiosity about Islam in LaRose, leading her to develop a keen interest in the religion that she hid from her boyfriend after they returned to the United States. Her initial interest led her to seek out more information about Islam on the Internet, where she regularly visited Muslim websites and engaged in conversations with an online mentor from Turkey.[73]

She eventually converted to Islam, and although she was not devout immediately following her conversion, her continued interest in Islam led her to online videos showing the plight of Muslims around the world. She spent hours watching these videos, soaking in images of Israeli aggression, attacks against Muslim communities, and deaths of Muslim children. By the summer of 2008, LaRose had grown sufficiently angry that she began re-posting jihadist propaganda on social media sites under the pseudonym "Jihad Jane."

Soon thereafter, LaRose progressed from just posting radical jihadist material to engaging in actual conversations with jihadists online. One of these individuals, who went by the online moniker "Eagle Eye," made grand claims of involvement with infamous jihadi attacks around the world. LaRose was impressed by Eagle Eye, believing him to be a pious Muslim willing to defend Islam against those who would threaten it. She grew to trust him and did not hesitate when he requested that she send money to fellow Muslims, even to support the establishment of an al-Qaeda cell.

By 2009, LaRose had begun interacting with al-Qaeda contacts more frequently, fulfilling their requests when they made them. In February, she agreed to meet Eagle Eye, marry him, and help him gain access to the European mainland to carry out attacks there. The following month, Eagle Eye told LaRose to go to Europe to kill Lars Vilks, a Swedish illustrator who drew a cartoon of the Prophet Mohammed. Having now steeped herself in jihadist propaganda and communicated extensively with apparent jihadis, she agreed to go to Europe to kill Vilks.

She traveled to Ireland to meet Damache, another apparent jihadi she had spoken with online. Damache told LaRose that they would be joined by several other Muslims and that she would receive training to prepare her to murder Vilks. She was ready ... She was willing.

But she never received any training, and the comrades she was told about never arrived. The Muslim warriors she thought she was talking to online turned out to be weak and timid in person. Despite promises of glory and martyrdom in an operation to kill Lars Vilks, Colleen LaRose's experiences with jihadi Islam were nothing like her expectations. She returned to the United States in October of 2009 and was quickly arrested and sent to prison.

Although "Jihad Jane" never carried out the attack she hoped for, she was nonetheless seduced by a jihadi ideology communicated to her through Islamist propaganda videos and the grand claims of radical Islamists on the Internet.

Her turn to jihadi Islam was *a function of persuasion.*

Dylann Roof

At about quarter after eight on the evening of June 17, 2015, Dylann Roof walked into the Emanuel African Methodist Episcopal Church in Charleston, South Carolina, where several African-American parishioners were in the middle of Bible study. Roof approached the group and asked for the church's senior pastor, Reverend Clementa Pinckney. Pinckney was well-known and well-liked in the community; he was a South Carolina state senator and spoke out about the shooting death of an unarmed black man at the hands of a Charleston police officer two months earlier.[74]

Visitors were not uncommon to the church, so Pinckney did not hesitate; he welcomed Roof to the group and offered him a seat next to him. Roof sat.[75] The group prayed together and talked about Scripture while Roof mostly sat and listened, though he occasionally posed arguments to the group about the Bible. By all accounts, Dylann Roof was simply another summer visitor to Emanuel AME, there to enjoy the fellowship of worshippers in the oldest African Methodist Episcopal church in the American South. He later admitted that the group had been very nice to him during his visit, and he almost abandoned his plan to do what came next.[76]

Just after 9 p.m., Dylann Roof pulled a gun from a small bag and pointed it at 87-year-old parishioner Susie Jackson. Tywanza Sanders, who was Jackson's nephew, tried to get Roof to put down the gun, asking him why he wanted to attack innocent worshippers at a church. Roof told Sanders that he had to do it, claiming that "they" (African Americans) were raping "our" (whites) women and were taking over the United States. Sanders jumped in front of his aunt to protect her as the gun fired. He was the first of the victims to be killed.

Over the next six minutes, Dylann Roof shot ten members of the Bible study group, stopping to reload his pistol five times. He shouted racial slurs as he fired rounds into victim after victim. When the attack was over, Roof had killed eight members of the church group. Another later died at the hospital.

The morning after the attack, Roof was spotted in his black Hyundai Elantra more than 200 miles away on US Route 74. The woman who saw him called her boss who tipped the police about Roof's location. He was arrested at a traffic light in Shelby, North Carolina and was charged with 33 criminal offenses, including nine counts of murder and twelve hate crimes. He was found guilty of all charges in December of 2016. The following month, he was sentenced to death.

At his sentencing, prosecutors submitted evidence showing the racist motivations for Roof's attack. Part of that evidence included a white supremacist manifesto with a statement from Roof saying that he did not regret his actions. Defiant to the last, Roof said that he had "not shed a tear for the innocent people [he] killed."[77]

In the aftermath of Roof's attack, trial, and sentencing, questions emerged about what inspired Roof to kill nine innocent people at prayer. The racial epithets and statements made during and after the shooting left little doubt that his actions were racially motivated, but how he developed racist beliefs and attitudes was yet in question. Investigations of Roof's manifesto and website answered this question, revealing the kinds of information he had been absorbing in the time leading up to the attack.

Investigators found that Dylann Roof had been interacting with racists online and had developed white supremacist beliefs from messages he encountered on the Internet. He was particularly struck with information concerning crime perpetrated by African-Americans on whites that he found online, eventually adopting the belief that he needed to kill the former to protect the latter.[78] Dylann Roof grew to hate African-Americans because of content he found on the Internet, much of which was intended to cultivate or perpetuate white nationalist or white supremacist ideals.

His embrace of white supremacist beliefs and attitudes was *a function of persuasion*.

Tamerlan and Dzhokhar Tsarnaev

On the afternoon of April 15, 2013, Dzhokhar Tsarnaev and his older brother Tamerlan detonated two pressure-cooker bombs at the finish line of the Boston Marathon. The blasts sent shrapnel through the crowd gathered at the end of the race, striking spectators and runners alike. The bombs killed three people and injured more than 260. The dead were Krystle Campbell, a 29-year-old restaurateur; Lu Lingzi, a 23-year-old

Boston University graduate student; and Martin Richard, a child of only eight.

At first, Dzhokhar and Tamerlan evaded security forces. Camera footage of the bomb site shows them casually watching the carnage they created and later leaving the scene. Three days after the attack, however, the FBI released images of the brothers as suspects in the bombing. A few hours after their photos were released to the public, the Tsarnaevs tried to escape Boston.

First, they shot and killed Sean Collier, a police officer at the Massachusetts Institute of Technology. Then they carjacked a Mercedes Benz SUV with its owner, Dun Meng, still in the vehicle. Dzhokhar followed behind Tamerlan in a green Honda Civic. When the brothers stopped a gas station, Meng escaped the SUV and sprinted across the street to another gas station. In his rush to escape, Meng left his cell phone in the Mercedes, thereby allowing police to pinpoint its location. They tracked the brothers to the Watertown neighborhood of Boston, where a police officer recognized the Mercedes SUV and the Honda Civic. A shootout ensued.

When the dust cleared, Tamerlan was dead, having been run over by Dzhokhar in the Mercedes SUV as he tried to escape. Dzhokhar later abandoned the car and hid in a Watertown resident's tarp-covered boat. Watertown police surrounded the boat, eventually pulling Dzhokhar from it and taking him to Beth Israel Deaconess Medical Center for treatment of injuries he received in his gunfight with police. He survived his wounds, and later faced trial for the use of a weapon of mass destruction and malicious destruction of property resulting in death. He was found guilty of all thirty counts he faced, and on June 24, 2015, was sentenced to death.

Long after the Tsarnaevs' attacks on the Boston Marathon, questions lingered about their motivations. Yuri Zhukov from Harvard's Program on Global Society and Security argued that the brothers were motivated by "symbols and rhetoric employed by the Caucasus [Muslim] extremists."[79] An analysis of Tamerlan's laptop showed it to contain downloads of al-Qaeda in the Arabian Peninsula's English-language propaganda magazine *Inspire*, as well as videos of Anwar al-Awlaki – an American-Yemeni al-Qaeda propagandist.[80] After Dzhokhar was pulled from the boat in Watertown, investigators found a note written inside containing "[concepts from] al-Awlaki's statements and other writings from the radicalizers."[81]

Matthew Levitt, the head of the Program on Counterterrorism and Intelligence at the Washington Institute for Near East Policy, testified that the Tsarnaevs did not need to live in Iraq or Afghanistan to stage an attack on behalf of Muslims living there. They did not have to find a "world headquarters" for jihad, nor did they need to attend terrorist training camps to prepare themselves for their attack. According to Levitt, the Internet and social media gave the Tsarnaevs access to all the material they needed to motivate and carry out the bombing.[82]

Their adoption of a jihadi ideology and the bombing it inspired were *a function of persuasion*.

∴

All cases of violent extremism are unique, so not every individual who turns to terrorism will be as clearly or heavily inspired by persuasive messaging as Jihad Jane, Dylann Roof, or the Tsarnaevs. Nevertheless, these cases demonstrate that persuasion via extremist messaging can promote radicalization and violent radicalization processes that ultimately lead to violence.

Persuasion, Radicalization, and Violent Radicalization: Four Propositions

At this point, you should pause and pat yourself on the back. We've covered quite a bit of ground here, and questions surrounding definitions, explications, and conceptualizations are not always the most exciting riddles to solve. Don't worry, though. I didn't drag you through this foundational chapter for my own entertainment. Coming to a common conceptual understanding of radicalization, violent radicalization, and persuasion will prove critical as you move forward in this book.

Most importantly, by conceptualizing these terms, it becomes possible to demonstrate the importance of persuasion to the processes of radicalization and violent radicalization. Drawing from the information covered in this chapter, I offer four propositions that lay the foundation for the remainder of this book by showing how persuasion can and does play a part in the development (and abandonment) of the extremist mindset.

Let's open with the first two.

> **Proposition 1:** *Extremist groups engage in communicative processes to promote changes in beliefs, attitudes, intentions, and/or behaviors consistent with their ideologies, goals, and objectives.*

In addition to the LaRose, Roof, and Tsarnaev examples, there is a mountain of evidence to show that extremist groups distribute messages intended to affect audiences such that they come to adopt their views – i.e., promote radicalization and/or violent radicalization.[83] Given that we have defined message-prompted changes in beliefs, attitudes, intentions, and/or behaviors as "persuasion," then,

Proposition 2: *Radicalization and violent radicalization are persuasive processes.*

So, if radicalization and violent radicalization are processes that can be affected by exposure to persuasive messages, what does that mean for preventing these processes? I would wager that this is the question that has driven most of you to open this book.

Well, just as radicalization and violent radicalization can be prompted or catalyzed by persuasion, so too can *counter-radicalization*. We can use our understanding of persuasion to develop our own messages that cue social and psychological processes that direct people away from extremist ideologies, thereby reducing their risk for engaging in violence.

This brings us to the final two propositions.

Proposition 3: *Counter-radicalization is a communicative process whereby persuasive messages are intended to prevent the adoption of beliefs, attitudes, intentions, or behaviors consistent with extremist groups' ideologies, goals, and/or objectives.*

And if we adopt this as true, then taken together, the first three propositions lead us to the major thesis of this book:

Proposition 4: *Proven theories of persuasion can inform (a) our understanding of how terrorist messaging promotes radicalization and violent radicalization and (b) our development of messages intended for counter-radicalization.*

In short, if the processes of radicalization, violent radicalization, and counter-radicalization can be affected by exposure to persuasive messages, then we can apply lessons from research on persuasion to better understand these processes, and in turn, how we approach them.

∴

Jean-Paul Sartre once said that "words are loaded pistols." The implications of Sartre's statement are clear – when used strategically, language can be a powerful weapon to achieve critical goals. Words can start wars, induce subservience, inspire fighters, or deceive enemies. Words can also establish allies, form treaties, emancipate the enslaved, and make peace.

Sartre's statement certainly applies to persuasive communication and its effect on radicalization processes that increase the risk for terrorism. When strategically used by violent extremists, words can induce loyalty, encourage isolation, deconstruct identities, and promote violence.

Loaded pistols, indeed.

But just as strategic persuasion can be used to promote radicalization or violent radicalization, it can also be leveraged in attempts to prevent these processes. But before we dive into exactly how different persuasion theories can inform our approaches to counter-radicalization, it is important that we first take account of how counter-radicalization has been attempted without having been expressly based on time-tested persuasion theories. To this end, the next chapter will discuss extant counter-radicalization efforts to identify gaps in their practices and gather valuable information from their successes that can be used in future efforts. Onward.

Notes

1 Douglas Fuchs and Lynn S. Fuchs, "Inclusive Schools Movement and the Radicalization of Special Education Reform," *Exceptional Children* 60, no. 4 (1994): 294–309.
2 Richard E. Rubenstein, *Alchemists of Revolution* (New York: Basic Books, 1987).
3 Dick Blackwell, "Tune In! Turn On! Sell Out! The Dissolution of Radicalism in Analytic Psychotherapy," *European Journal of Psychotherapy & Counselling* 6 (2003): 21–34; Annamaria Silvana de Rosa, "The Boomerang Effect of Radicalism in Discursive Psychology: A Critical Overview of the Controversy with the Social Representations Theory," *Journal for the Theory of Social Behavior* 36 (2006): 161–201.
4 W. E. Douglas Creed, "Voice Lessons: Tempered Radicalism and the Use of Voice and Silence," *Journal of Management Studies* 40 (2003): 1503–1536; Ronen Shamir, "The De-Radicalization of Corporate Social Responsibility," *Critical Sociology* 30 (2004): 669–689.
5 Myra Marx Ferree, "Resonance and Radicalism: Feminist Framing in the Abortion Debates of the United States and Germany," *American Journal of Sociology* 109(2) (2003): 302–344.
6 Takis S. Pappas, "Political Leadership and the Emergence of Radical Mass Movements in Democracy," *Comparative Political Studies* 41 (2008): 1117–1140.
7 See Bruce Hoffman, *Inside Terrorism* (New York: Columbia University Press, 1998); John Horgan, "From Profiles to Pathways and Roots to Routes: Perspectives from Psychology on Radicalization into Terrorism," *Annals of the American Academy of Political and Social Science* 618 (2008): 80–94; John Horgan, *The Psychology of Terrorism* (Abingdon: Routledge, 2014); Clark McCauley and Sophia Moskalenko, *Friction: How Radicalization Happens to Them and Us* (Oxford University Press, 2011); Marc Sageman, *Leaderless Jihad* (Philadelphia, PA: University of Pennsylvania Press, 2008).
8 E.g., Frank J. Cilluffo, Sharon L. Cardash, and Andrew J. Whitehead, "Radicalization: Behind Bars and Beyond Borders," *The Brown Journal of*

World Affairs 13, no. 2 (2007): 113–122; Jerrold M. Post and Gabriel Sheffer, "The Risk of Radicalization and Terrorism in U.S. Muslim Communities," *The Brown Journal of World Affairs* 13, no. 2 (2007): 101–112; Mitchell D. Silber and Arvin Bhatt, *Radicalization in the West: The Homegrown Threat* (New York: NYPD Intelligence Division, 2007). Available at https://sethgodin .typepad.com/seths_blog/files/NYPD_Report-Radicalization_in_the_West.pdf.

9 Kurt Braddock, "Fighting Words: The Persuasive Effect of Online Extremist Narratives on the Radicalization Process," PhD dissertation, The Pennsylvania State University, 2012.

10 Anthony Stahelski, "Terrorists Are Made, Not Born: Creating Terrorists Using Social Psychological Conditioning," *Cultic Studies Review* 4, no. 1 (2005): 30–40.

11 Donelson R. Forsythe, *Group Dynamics* (Belmont, CA: Brooks/Cole, 1999).

12 Elliot Aronson, Timothy D. Wilson, and Robin M. Akert, *Social Psychology: The Heart and the Mind* (New York: HarperCollins, 2002).

13 Margaret Thaler Singer, *Cults in Our Midst: The Continuing Fight against their Hidden Menace* (San Francisco, CA: Jossey-Bass, 1995).

14 Stephen J. Morgan, *The Mind of a Terrorist Fundamentalist: The Psychology of Terror Cults* (Brussels: Institute Spiritus Vitus, 2001).

15 Stahelski, "Terrorists Are Made, Not Born."

16 Herbert Jäger, "The Individual Dimension of Terrorist Action" [in German], in *Lebenslaufanalysen*, ed. Herbert Jäger, Gerhard Schmidtchen, and Lieselotte Sullwold, 141–174 (Opladen: Westdeutscher, 1981), p. 157.

17 Salman Akhtar, "The Psychodynamic Dimension of Terrorism," *Psychiatric Annals* 29 (1999): 350–355 (p. 352).

18 Braddock, "Fighting Words."

19 Aronson et al., *Social Psychology*.

20 Morgan, *The Mind of a Terrorist Fundamentalist*.

21 Rupert Brown, "Social Identity Theory: Past Achievements, Current Problems, and Future Challenges," *European Journal of Social Psychology* 30 (2000): 745–778; Brian Mullen, "Atrocity as a Function of Lynch Mob Composition," *Personality and Social Psychology Bulletin* 12 (1986): 187–197; Stephen Reicher, Russell Spears, and Tom Postmes, "A Social Identity Model of Deindividuation Phenomena," *European Review of Social Psychology* 6 (1995): 161–198; S. Levi Taylor, Edgar C. O'Neal, Travis Langley, and Ann Houston Butcher, "Anger Arousal, Deindividuation, and Aggression," *Aggressive Behavior* 1, no. 4 (1991): 193–206.

22 Stahelski, "Terrorists Are Made, Not Born."

23 James Waller, *Becoming Evil: How Ordinary People Commit Genocide and Mass Killing* (Oxford University Press, 2002); Daniel Bar-Tal, *Shared Beliefs in a Society: Social Psychological Analysis* (Thousand Oaks, CA: Sage, 2000).

24 See Klaus Jünschke, *Spätlese: Texte zu Raf und Knast* (Frankfurt: Verlag Neue Kritik, 1988), p. 164 for an example.

25 Stahelski, "Terrorists Are Made, Not Born," paragraph 19.

26 Amit Cohen, "Hamas Dot Com," *Ma'ariv* (July 2, 2003). Available at www.tomgrossmedia.com/mideastdispatches/archives/000294.html; Hoffman, *Inside Terrorism*, p. 108.

27 Rohan Gunaratna, "Al Qaeda's Lose and Learn Doctrine: The Trajectory from Oplan Bojinka to 9/11," in *Teaching Terror*, ed. James J. F. Forest, 171–188 (Oxford: Rowman & Littlefield, 2006).

28 Cynthia C. Combs, "The Media as a Showcase for Terrorism," in *Teaching Terror*, ed. Forest, 133–154.

29 Gabriel Weimann, *Terrorism on the Internet: The New Arena, the New Challenges* (Washington, DC: United States Institute of Peace Press, 2006), p. 121.

30 James J. F. Forest, "Training Camps and Other Centers of Learning," in *Teaching Terror*, ed. Forest, 69–110.

31 Bruce Hoffman, *Al Qaeda, Trends in Terrorism and Future Potentialities: An Assessment* (Santa Monica, CA: RAND Corporation, 2003), p. 9.

32 J. Bowyer-Bell, *The Dynamics of Armed Struggle* (London: Frank Cass, 1998), p. 137.

33 Elaine Pressman, "Exploring the Sources of Radicalization and Violent Radicalization: Some Transatlantic Perspectives," *Journal of Security Studies* 2 (2008): 1–20.

34 Forest, "Training Camps and Other Centers of Learning."

35 CNN, "Controversial Cleric of UK Mosque" (April 1, 2003). Available at www.cnn.com/2003/WORLD/europe/01/20/uk.hamzaprofile/.

36 US Department of Justice, "Abu Hamza Arrested in London on Terrorism Charges Filed in the United States," Press Release #371 (May 27, 2004). Available at www.justice.gov/archive/opa/pr/2004/May/04_crm_371.htm.

37 National Commission on Terrorist Attacks Upon the United States, *9/11 Commission Report* (New York: W. W. Norton, 2004), pp. 160–165.

38 Brian A. Jackson, "Training for Urban Resistance: The Case of the Provisional Irish Republican Army," in *The Making of a Terrorist: Recruitment, Training, and Root Causes, Vol. 2*, ed. James J. F. Forest, 119–135 (Westport, CT: Praeger).

39 Ibid.

40 Marc Sageman, *Understanding Terror Networks* (Philadelphia, PA: University of Pennsylvania Press, 2004); Sageman, *Leaderless Jihad*.

41 Carlyle Alan Thayer, "Explaining 'Clean Skins': The Dynamics of Small Group Social Networks and the London Bombers." Paper presented at the Workshop on Sacrificial Devotion in Comparative Perspective: Tamil Tigers and Beyond, Adelaide, Australia, December 5–7, 2005, p. 18. Available at www.scribd.com/document/18260792/Thayer-Terrorism-Radicalization-Through-Social-Networks.

42 Thomas Hegghammer, "Terrorist Recruitment and Radicalization in Saudi Arabia," *Middle East Policy* 13, no. 4 (2006): 39–60 (p. 50).

43 Edwin Bakker, *Jihadi Terrorists in Europe: Their Characteristics and the Circumstances in Which They Joined the Jihad—An Exploratory Study* (The Hague: Clingendael Institute, 2006).

44 Donatella Della Porta, "Recruitment Processes in Clandestine Political Organizations: Italian Left-Wing Terrorism," in *From Structure to Action: Comparing Social Movement Research across Cultures*, ed. Bert Klandermans, Hanspeter Kriesi, and Sidney G. Tarrow, 155–171 (Greenwich, CT: JAI Press, 1988), p. 158.

45 Friedhelm Neidhardt, "Soziale Bedingungen Terroristischen Handelns: Das Beispiel der 'Baader-Meinhof-Gruppe' (RAF)," in *Gruppenprozesse*, ed. Wanda von Kaeyer-Katte, Dieter Claessens, Hubert Feger, and Friedhelm Neidhardt, 318–391 (Opladen: Westdeutscher, 1982).
46 Klaus Wasmund, "The Political Socialization of West German Terrorists," in *Political Violence and Terror: Motifs and Motivations*, ed. Peter H. Merkl, 191–228 (Berkeley, CA: University of California Press, 1986).
47 Bakker, *Jihadi Terrorists in Europe*; Sageman, *Understanding Terror Networks*; Thayer, "Explaining 'Clean Skins.'"
48 Stahelski, "Terrorists Are Made, Not Born."
49 Clark McCauley and Sophia Moskalenko, "Mechanisms of Political Radicalization: Pathways toward Terrorism," *Terrorism and Political Violence* 20, no. 3 (2008): 415–433.
50 Ibid., p. 418.
51 Ibid., p. 416.
52 For examples, see Helena Flam, "Anger in Repressive Regimes: A Footnote to *Domination and the Arts of Resistance* by James Scott," *European Journal of Social Theory* 7 (2004): 171–188; Jeff Goodwin, James F. Jasper, and Francesca Polletta, eds., *Passionate Politics: Emotions and Social Movements* (University of Chicago Press, 2001); Theodore D. Kemper, "Social Constructionist and Positivist Approaches to the Sociology of Emotions," *American Journal of Sociology* 87 (1981): 336–362.
53 Clark McCauley, "Jujitsu Politics: Terrorism and Response to Terrorism," in *Collateral Damage: The Psychological Consequences of America's War on Terrorism*, ed. Paul R. Kimmel and Chris E. Stout, 45–65 (Westport, CT: Praeger).
54 Fathali M. Moghaddam, "The Staircase to Terrorism: A Psychological Exploration," *American Psychologist* 60, no. 2 (2005): 161–169.
55 Andrew Silke, "Becoming a Terrorist," in *Terrorists, Victims, and Society: Psychological Perspectives on Terrorism and its Consequences*, ed. Andrew Silke, 29–53 (London: John Wiley & Sons, 2003).
56 International Criminal Court, "Warrant of Arrest Unsealed against Five LRA Commanders," ICC-CPI-20051014-110, 2005. Available at www.icc-cpi.int/Pages/item.aspx?name=warrant%20of%20arrest%20unsealed%20against%20five%20lra%20commanders.
57 David Kilcullen, *The Accidental Guerrilla* (Oxford University Press, 2009).
58 Palestinian Center for Policy and Survey Research, Palestinian Public Opinion Poll #27. Available at www.pcpsr.org/survey/polls/2008/p27e1.html.
59 John Horgan, *Walking Away from Terrorism: Accounts of Disengagement from Radical and Extremist Movements* (Abingdon: Routledge, 2009), p. 152.
60 Ibid., p. 144; see also Max Taylor and John Horgan, "A Conceptual Framework for Addressing Psychological Process in the Development of the Terrorist," *Terrorism and Political Violence* 18, no. 4 (2006): 585–601 (p. 591).
61 Clark McCauley and Sophia Moskalenko, "Understanding Political Radicalization: The Two-Pyramid Model," *American Psychologist* 72, no. 3 (2017): 205–216.
62 See Aaron T. Beck, *Cognitive Therapy and the Emotional Disorders* (New York: Plume, 1979).
63 Horgan, *Walking Away from Terrorism*, p. 143.

64 Ibid.
65 Taylor and Horgan, "A Conceptual Framework," p. 592.
66 Edward Newman, "Exploring the 'Root Causes' of Terrorism," *Studies in Conflict & Terrorism* 29, no. 8 (2006): 749–772.
67 Taylor and Horgan, "A Conceptual Framework," p. 592.
68 Gerald R. Miller, "On Being Persuaded: Some Basic Distinctions," in *The SAGE Handbook of Persuasion: Developments in Theory and Practice*, ed. James Price Dillard and Lijiang Shen, 70–82 (Thousand Oaks, CA: Sage, 2013), p. 73.
69 Martin Fishbein and Icek Ajzen, *Predicting and Changing Behavior: The Reasoned Action Approach* (New York: Routledge, 2010); Martin Fishbein and Icek Ajzen, *Belief, Attitude, Intention, and Behavior: An Introduction to Theory and Research* (Reading, MA: Addison-Wesley, 1975).
70 Miller, "On Being Persuaded," p. 73.
71 Horgan, *Walking Away from Terrorism*, p. 152.
72 Ibid.
73 John Shiffman, "From Abuse to a Chat Room, a Martyr is Made," *Reuters Special Report* (December 7, 2012). Available at http://graphics.thomson reuters.com/12/12/JihadJaneAll.pdf.
74 McClatchy, "Sen. Clementa Pinckney on Walter Scott Killing," *The State* (February 7, 2018). Available at www.thestate.com/latest-news/article2533 9573.html.
75 Wayne Drash, "Inside the Bible Study Massacre: A Mom 'Laid in Her Son's Blood,'" *CNN* (December 17, 2015). Available at www.cnn.com/2015/06/19/ us/inside-charleston-bible-study-massacre/index.html.
76 Erik Ortiz and Daniel Arkin, "Dylann Roof 'Almost Didn't Go Through' with Charleston Church Shooting," *NBC News* (June 19, 2015). Available at www.nbcnews.com/storyline/charleston-church-shooting/dylann-roof-almost-didnt-go-through-charleston-church-shooting-n378341.
77 Alan Blinder and Kevin Sack, "Dylann Roof, Addressing Court, Offers No Apology or Explanation for Massacre," *New York Times* (January 4, 2017). Available at www.nytimes.com/2017/01/04/us/dylann-roof-sentencing.html.
78 See Michael S. Schmidt, "Charleston Suspect was in Contact with Supremacists, Officials Say," *New York Times* (July 3, 2015). Available at www.nytimes .com/2015/07/04/us/dylann-roof-was-in-contact-with-supremacists-officials-say.html; Mark Berman, "Prosecutors Say Dylann Roof 'Self-Radicalized' Online, Wrote another Manifesto in Jail," *The Washington Post* (August 22, 2016). Available at www.washingtonpost.com/news/post-nation/wp/2016/08/ 22/prosecutors-say-accused-charleston-church-gunman-self-radicalized-online.
79 Lisa Wangsness and Brian Ballou, "Islam Might Have Had Secondary Role in Boston Attacks," *Boston Globe* (April 20, 2013). Available at www.boston globe.com/metro/2013/04/19/scholars-caution-against-drawing-easy-religious-conclusions-about-suspects-boston-marathon-bombings/a5Iucv4ntQHgSvXc hQqKOM/story.html.
80 Ann O'Neill, "The 13th Juror: The Radicalization of Dzhokhar Tsarnaev," *CNN* (March 30, 2015). Available at www.cnn.com/2015/03/27/us/tsarnaev-13th-juror-jahar-radicalization/index.html.

81 Richard Valdmanis, "Boston Bomb Suspect Influenced by Al Qaeda: Expert Witness," *Reuters* (March 23, 2015). Available at www.reuters.com/article/us-boston-bombings-trial/boston-bomb-suspect-influenced-by-al-qaeda-expert-witness-idUSKBN0MJ0Z620150323.

82 O'Neill, "The Radicalization of Dzhokhar Tsarnaev."

83 See Gabriel Weimann, "New Terrorism and New Media," *Wilson Center Research Series Vol. 2*, 2014. Available at www.wilsoncenter.org/sites/default/files/STIP_140501_new_terrorism_F_0.pdf; Philip Seib and Dana M. Janbek, *Global Terrorism and New Media: The Post al-Qaeda Generation* (New York: Routledge, 2010). Also see entire issue concerning terrorist propaganda on the Internet and its promotion of radicalization in *Studies in Conflict & Terrorism* 40, no. 1 (2017).

2 The Riddle of the Sphinx: Lessons from Past and Current Counter-Radicalization Efforts

For years, the Sphinx terrorized the ancient Greek city of Thebes.

Born of a three-headed, fire-breathing monster called the Chimaera, the Sphinx had a powerful physical form, possessing the colossal body of a lion (flanked on both sides by equally massive wings) and a serpent's tail in the form of a snake. In addition to the brute strength afforded to it from its bestial frame, the Sphinx also boasted a cunning intellect, owed to its human (female) head. The combined strength and intelligence of the Sphinx made her a ruthless guard of Thebes, imposing famines and droughts on the city at her leisure. The only way to defeat her was to answer a riddle correctly. If someone gave a wrong answer to the riddle, the Sphinx strangled the challenger and devoured him.

Many commoners tried to solve the Sphinx's riddle. They were all strangled and eaten.[1]

One day, Prince Haemon of Thebes confronted the Sphinx to rid his father's city of the perpetual nuisance. The Sphinx posed its question: *What is that which has one voice and yet becomes four-footed and two-footed and three-footed?*

Haemon's royal blood was of no help to him. He had no answer to the riddle. Just like the commoners who came before him, the prince was likewise killed and eaten.

Creon, Haemon's father and king of Thebes, had had enough. The Sphinx had caused him and his city enough anguish. In response to his son's death, Creon offered his entire kingdom and his daughter's hand in marriage to anyone who could correctly answer the riddle. Motivated by the rewards that would be given to whoever defeated the Sphinx, Oedipus confronted her.

The Sphinx, ever confident, again posed her riddle: *What is that which has one voice and yet becomes four-footed and two-footed and three-footed?*

Oedipus responded: *A man—for as a babe he goes on four limbs, as an adult he goes on two, and as an old man, he gets a third support from a staff.*

The Sphinx, enraged in disbelief at Oedipus's correct answer, leapt from her perch on the city's acropolis to her death upon the rocks below. Finally, Thebes was at peace.

∴

It may seem strange to encounter references to Greek mythology in a book about violent radicalization and counter-radicalization. After all, the issues that led you to pick up this book are likely rooted in psychology, sociology, political science, economics, communication, or any number of other disciplines, none of which I'd wager are ancient Greek literature.

However, the Thebans' struggles with the Sphinx are comparable to the challenges we currently face. Terrorism researchers, counterterror practitioners, analysts, and governments have tried for years to understand the persuasive appeal of terrorist messaging and discover the key to developing effective countermeasures against that messaging. And just like many Thebans were slaughtered for failing to answer the Sphinx's riddle, so too have we paid for our failures to blunt the allure of extremist ideologies.

The so-called Islamic State successfully persuaded about 30,000 fighters to join the group in Iraq and Syria from all over the world, including the United States.[2] The number of hate groups in the United States reached an all-time high in 2018, with the majority of those being white nationalist, neo-Nazi, anti-immigrant, and anti-Semitic groups.[3] Members of the alt-right performed seventeen attacks between 2014 and 2018, killing 81 and injuring more than 100.[4] These facts would suggest that despite our best efforts, the appeal of extremist groups remains a significant problem. We seem to be missing something with respect to counter-radicalization.

In this way, we have our own Sphinx to contend with, and it comes in the form of propaganda produced by violent Islamists, white nationalists, and other extremists who attempt to persuade otherwise peaceful individual to join their ranks.

So how do we go about slaying our Sphinx? How do we effectively confront the appeal of extremist ideologies? How can we learn from what we've done so far to improve our counter-radicalization efforts in the future? As a first step, we must evaluate what has already been attempted, recognize our successes, and fix what we've gotten wrong. This chapter is meant to assist in doing so.

More specifically, the next several sections will detail different kinds of counter-radicalization programs that have been implemented around the world. Although the programs listed in the next sections do not comprise a comprehensive list, they are meant to signify the various types of ways that counter-radicalization has been attempted. Following these descriptions, the chapter will close with a consideration of what we can learn from how counter-radicalization has been implemented thus far, with a focus on how persuasion theory can improve our efforts moving forward.

Past and Current Counter-Radicalization Efforts

This section offers synopses of the different kinds of counter-radicalization efforts that have been implemented in different regions around the world. But before we jump in, there are two important things to note.

First, the programs described in this section focus on *counter-radicalization* as it was defined in Chapter 1. Although some countries and organizations say their efforts are intended to promote counter-radicalization, they really engage in activities that more closely align with *de-radicalization*. This section is focused on initiatives that seek to prevent or stop the process of violent radicalization, not initiatives that seek to undo a radicalized mindset once it has been adopted (or the violent activity that results from that mindset has already been performed). The motivated reader can find references to research on de-radicalization programs in the reference material for this chapter.[5]

Second, to preserve space (and your patience), I have chosen only a sample of programs to represent each type of counter-radicalization initiative. There are countless other efforts that could be classified into the categories below, but the purpose here is just for you to gain an understanding of how different forms of counter-radicalization are enacted. For a more comprehensive listing of the programs that make up the global counter-radicalization landscape, see the outstanding work by Daniel Köhler in Chapter 10 of his book *Understanding Deradicalization*.[6]

With those issues out of the way, let's have a look at the different ways that counter-radicalization has been attempted. These attempts can be broadly placed into one of four categories. The first category is characterized by programs designed to offer training, education, or support to individuals whose lives may be affected by exposure to terrorist ideologies. The second category contains programs in which concerned individuals refer people showing initial signs of violent radicalization to specialists for treatment. The third group of programs seeks to reduce the risk of exposure to terrorist ideologies by limiting the degree to which at-risk individuals can access content that supports those ideologies (especially online). The last type of counter-radicalization initiative centers on the development and distribution of messages that challenge terrorist propaganda and the ideologies that underpin it.

The next few sections will cover each of these types of counter-radicalization efforts in turn.

Training, Education, and Support

Target: Family and Friends

Those at risk for violent radicalization and engagement in terrorist violence sometimes demonstrate signs of their changing mindset. They may seclude themselves from their normal social circles, spend an excessive amount of time on the Internet, experience drastic mood swings, or behave in several other ways that seem strange to their loved ones. Given that their families and friends are often the first to witness these changes, they can serve as a first line of defense against violent radicalization. Many organizations have developed and implemented programs to provide training and support to those who recognize these signs and wish to intervene before the at-risk individual goes too far down the path of violence.

For example, in the UK, the Institute for Strategic Dialogue's (ISD) Against Violent Extremism (AVE) program features an initiative called "Extreme Dialogue."[7] In this program, ISD personnel offer training to teachers and students on ways that they can understand the nature of violent extremism, recognize it in others, and challenge it in schools. Based largely on filmed testimonials of individuals affected by extremism, the Extreme Dialogue program is designed to foster discussion about issues surrounding extremism in school settings. In doing so, trainees are equipped to promote critical thinking among young people that will make them resilient to the appeal of violent extremist ideologies.

A similar initiative has been developed by the Active Change Foundation (ACF), also in the UK. With this program, the ACF seeks to "challenge, educate, and raise awareness to the many vulnerabilities, issues and events that can lead to radicalisation and extremism."[8] Like ISD Global, the ACF offers training to schools, universities, and local organizations that informs trainees on the signs of extremism and how to prevent it. This initiative is implemented primarily through a one-day program in which the ACF uses real-life case studies to educate "delegates" on extremism and how individuals are recruited into extremist groups.[9]

In contrast to programs that are exclusively designed to offer training intended to prevent the adoption of extremist ideologies, some programs support those whose loved ones have already succumbed to extremism. In Canada, for example, Christianne Boudreau founded "Mothers for Life," a network of parents and partner organizations that connect family members of current and budding extremists to counselors that can assist them.[10] These counselors are equipped to provide emotional support to families in which someone has begun the process of violent radicalization, has gone off to fight in support of a terrorist group, or has died while engaging in armed activity as part of a terrorist group (particularly in Iraq and Syria). In some cases, individuals can be referred to specialists that may be able to intervene before the individual engages in violent activity.

In addition to these in-person programs, several countries have made hotlines available to those who suspect that their family members are at risk for violent radicalization. In Denmark for example, the city of Copenhagen employs an administrative unit responsible for the early prevention of violent radicalization and ideological extremism. This unit, called VINK, has a dedicated phone number for individuals concerned about loved ones showing signs of radicalization. Calls are evaluated on a case-by-case basis, and serious cases (as determined by VINK personnel) are referred to the Copenhagen Coordination Unit for follow-up.[11]

The German Federal Office of Migration and Refugees has used a hotline for dealing with budding extremists as well.[12] Similar to the Danish hotline, the German hotline is intended for families of individuals who have grown concerned that their loved one is demonstrating signs of radicalization. Through the hotline, concerned individuals are connected with the Advice Centre on Radicalization, who then refers the individual to a counselor who is local to the caller. Advice Centre personnel can also put callers into contact with other families who suspect their loved ones are in the process of violent radicalization. The Austrian Family Ministry operates a hotline program very much like the German initiative.[13]

Although many of these programs are organized and implemented by government organizations, some non-governmental organizations have provided similar support. For instance, the Swedish Red Cross offers a hotline like those operating in Denmark, Germany, and Austria.[14]

Target: Security Forces and Frontline Workers

Friends and family members are likely to be the first to recognize signs of a problem in their loved ones, but others may also be well-placed to intervene if they recognize signs of violent radicalization. Regular interactions with their communities put police forces and other frontline workers in the position to step in when a member of those communities poses a risk for violence. To make the best use of these individuals to prevent violent extremism, several training programs have been developed specifically for security personnel.

The European Union, for example, has partnered with police forces in multiple countries to promote an understanding of violent extremism and how to prevent it. For instance, the EU has financed a program called "Improving Security through Democratic Participation" (ISDEP)[15] based on the EU Commission's overall counterterrorism strategy. Led by the UK Association of Chief Police Officers (but implemented in eight EU member states), the ISDEP program is designed to provide frontline police officers, practitioners, prison and probation staff, and other frontline officials with training on how to recognize indicators of violent radicalization. ISDEP training makes use of e-learning modules to instruct trainees on the use of a toolkit related to intervening in the radicalization process. The training module was designed by the Director of the German Institute on Radicalization and De-radicalization Studies, the abovementioned Daniel Köhler.

Like ISDEP, the Belgian Community Policing and Prevention of Radicalization (COPPRA) program is also funded by the EU (with co-funding coming from the Belgian Federal Police). The COPPRA program is predicated on the notion that community police officers have strong links with the communities they serve, and therefore understand their communities' problems better than any outsiders. Given this, officers are well-positioned to "spot the signs of radicalization and work in partnership with local communities to prevent or tackle it."[16] Although local police tend to be very knowledgeable about their communities and what goes on in them, the COPPRA program assumes that they are not always equipped to recognize the warning signs of violent radicalization or how to effectively respond to it. To address this gap in their knowledge, the program has produced a "pocket guide" for police officers to instruct them on terminology related to violent extremism, the radicalization process, legal frameworks concerning extremism and terrorism, and related issues.[17]

In Australia, the "All Together Now" project is dedicated to challenging racism in New South Wales through educational programs. Unlike the ISDEP and COPPRA programs, CAPE training is primarily designed for non-security frontline personnel, like social workers, community counselors, healthcare workers, and others. Part of the project – dubbed Community Action for Preventing Extremism (CAPE) – features several kinds of interventions intended to "plant a seed of doubt in the minds of young people who are attracted to white nationalism and white supremacy."[18] One element of CAPE is a training module designed to increase participants' understanding of far-right groups and ideologies. Specifically, the CAPE program helps participants to communicate with young people about complex ideological topics, engage with kids who have already shown racist tendencies, and build connections with other frontline workers who can benefit from exchanging best practices.[19]

Target: Susceptible Individuals (often Young People)

Rather than provide support for individuals in a position to help those who may be susceptible to violent radicalization, some programs offer support directly to the individuals themselves. Through educational, training, and support interventions aimed at at-risk individuals, these programs seek not only to reduce the likelihood of their violent radicalization, but also to increase overall community resilience against extremist ideologies. Though these programs are implemented in an array of different contexts, many are designed for application in school settings.

For instance, in Belgium, the Society against Violent Extremism (S.A.V.E. Belgium) considers its "priority field of action" to be school networks within the country.[20] Specifically, S.A.V.E. Belgium organizes speeches and provides general education about the Syrian conflict, and violent extremists' participation in it. As part of its educational initiatives, S.A.V.E. Belgium promotes debates, presents testimonials, and follows up with students following their interventions. Through these efforts, the group seeks to reduce the appeal of radical Islamism and promote ideologies that are not underpinned by violence.[21]

Just north of Belgium, a similar program has emerged in the Netherlands. In the Amsterdam neighborhood of Slotevaart, the Slotevaart Action Plan to Prevent Radicalization also takes an educational approach to counter-radicalization. The plan was developed because Slotevaart was thought to be a potential "hot spot" of radicalization in the Netherlands, due to the high level of unemployment and substantial population of young, second-generation immigrants from Morocco and Turkey that characterize the area. To address potential feelings of anger and frustration that may emerge in Slotevaart, program designers developed an educational initiative intended to increase young people's awareness of radicalization and the factors that put them at risk for it. Moreover, the plan seeks to channel participants' discontent away from violent activities and towards more constructive ways to express their negative feelings.[22]

Educational and support programs aimed at those susceptible to violent radicalization are not unique to school systems. The Bangladeshi military (disguised as a fake NGO) have conducted educational seminars and workshops to spread the "true spirit of Islam" (rather than violent Islamism) within the country's borders. In addition to these educational initiatives, the military has also offered vocational training to participants to provide them with opportunities to keep them from turning to violent extremism.[23]

Some countries have also used online initiatives to counter violent extremism via education and support for at-risk populations. In the United States, for example, the FBI's "Don't Be a Puppet" program[24] is centered around an online interactive tool designed to inform teens about the risks associated with extremist ideologies. By clicking through the various interfaces presented on the program's website, visitors can learn about different terrorist groups, identify markers of radicalization, recognize when an extremist group may be trying to recruit them, and reach out to others if they need help.

∴

The examples described in this section are by no means a comprehensive account of efforts that leverage education, training, or support for the purpose of counter-radicalization. Nevertheless, they provide a representative synopsis of these kinds of programs and how they are implemented. Despite their differences, these efforts are all similalrly focused on informing participants about the dangers of violent extremism and how/why they should avoid it.

Other kinds of programs include this as an element of their overall strategy, but involve it only as part of a larger process geared towards counter-radicalization. The next section describes some of these initiatives.

Identification, Referral, Assessment, and Counseling

Rather than offer support to wider audiences who may be at risk for starting – but have not yet begun – the process of violent radicalization, some initiatives are based on a more targeted approach that identifies people who may have already shown concerning signs to this effect. These kinds of programs are meant to interrupt the radicalization process at an early stage to prevent the individual from progressing to the point where they may engage in ideologically motivated violence.

Perhaps the most well-known of these programs is the UK's Channel Program.[25] Born out of the Counter-Terrorism and Security Act of 2015, Channel is designed to provide individualized treatment to those considered to be at increased risk for violent radicalization and subsequent engagement in terrorism. Specifically, the Channel Program involves four key steps:

(1) *Identification and referral of at-risk individuals* – In this first stage, local authorities build relationships with individuals who have close

contact with those who are "vulnerable to being drawn into terrorism" (e.g., social workers, teachers, etc.).[26] According to the Channel Program, vulnerability to violent extremism can be associated with peer pressure, bullying, anti-social behavior, family tensions, lack of self-esteem, political grievances, and a variety of other factors. Through the relationships they have cultivated, local authorities can be made aware of "vulnerable" individuals, who are then referred for further assessment in the program.

(2) *Initial assessment* – Following the referral, the Channel Police Practitioner (CPP; the individual responsible for implementing Channel policies in his/her area) will perform a preliminary assessment of the case. If the case does not relate to violent extremism, the CPP refers the case to other services that may benefit the individual. If the individual is determined to be at risk for violent radicalization, the case is referred to a multi-agency panel to determine the risk posed by the individual.

(3) *Assessment by multi-agency panel* – The CPP, in coordination with local authorities and partner organizations (e.g., local government officials, education organizations, social care workers), review the vulnerability of the individual and determine the support he/she needs. From here, the panel develops a plan of action to benefit the at-risk individual, and if the individual agrees to receive support, that plan of action is implemented in the next step.

(4) *Provision of support* – The at-risk individual is provided with services to reduce his/her risk for continued violent radicalization. These services can include the development of life skills, educational support, vocational training, family support, health awareness, role-model mentoring, anger management or several other constructive practices.[27]

Although the Channel Program is often criticized for being a veiled method for stigmatizing and policing certain populations (mostly Muslims),[28] its design has clearly inspired the development of similar programs around the world.

In Denmark, for example, the Aarhus Model comprises multiple initiatives intended to thwart radicalization and redirect at-risk individuals away from violent extremism.[29] Much like the Channel Program, the first step in the Aarhus Model is the referral and evaluation of individuals thought to be showing signs of radicalization. Referrals are made by social workers, teachers, parents, and others who pass information about the individual to the "InfoHouse," a small organization staffed by police from the East Jutland district of Aarhus.

Following referral, InfoHouse staff evaluate the information to determine whether it truly indicates a case of violent radicalization, or if the referred individual is experiencing some other issue (e.g., typical youth rebellion, psychological strain). If it is the latter, InfoHouse officials refer the individual to social services or counseling that can provide the assistance they need. If, however, the InfoHouse determines that the individual *does* pose a risk for violent radicalization, officials contact the individual to inform him/her of the concerns surrounding their behavior. Officials will also attempt to get in touch with members of the individual's social circle (i.e., family, friends, recreation groups) to leverage them as resources. Working together, InfoHouse staff and members of the person's social circle attempt to get him/her to "acknowledge and seek alternative ways to resolve resentment and offense" rather than resort to violence.[30]

The Municipality of Aarhus also employs ten mentors (overseen by four coordinators) who counsel the at-risk individual by highlighting the ideological shortcomings of extremist ideologies, as well as the personal and societal dangers associated with enacting those ideologies with violence. Rather than just discredit extremist ideologies, Aarhus mentors also help these individuals to better integrate into their respective communities through closer relationships with their families, employment opportunities, education, and other non-violent pursuits. Ultimately, these mentors are meant to be "well-informed, interested, and empathic sparring partner[s]" that the mentee can speak with about their ideological and personal concerns.[31]

In addition to the process outlined above, the counter-radicalization element of the Aarhus Model also involves arranging workshops in schools that warn young people about the dangers of violent extremism, organizing a network of parents of radicalized children, and engaging in open dialogue with Muslim communities in Aarhus.[32] All of these efforts are based on a Life Psychology approach, which assumes that all individuals simply want to be "good enough" to address life's challenges, and that the development of life skills can help individuals to do so. By taking this approach, practitioners of the Aarhus Model seek to avoid the over-securitization of counter-radicalization – a common criticism of the Channel Program in the UK.

These kinds of programs are not unique to Europe. In Canada for instance, Calgary's "ReDirect" program operates in much the same way as the Channel Program and the Aarhus Model. Concerned individuals refer participants to the ReDirect program, where a case planning team comprising different private and public organizations evaluate the case in terms of the individual's engagement with a radical ideology, as well as their intent and ability to cause harm. If the individual is deemed to be a risk for extremist violence, the case planning team then develops a support plan for him/her. Although the exact nature of ReDirect's interventions is unclear (the program's website says that it employs a "variety of strategies"), the initiative's efforts undergo the same degree of planning and oversight as those featured in the UK and Aarhus.[33]

∴

The counter-radicalization programs outlined in the preceding sections are meant to be enacted through engagement with different kinds of individuals. Although the education/training-based programs and the referral/intervention programs differ in terms of how they are executed, both kinds of initiatives focus on the "demand side" of violent radicalization – they are designed to reduce the appeal of terrorist ideologies through education and support. There are some programs, however, that focus on the "supply side." Rather than diminish the appeal of extremist ideologies through broad educational initiatives or the identification and treatment of specific individuals, some efforts are meant to deny individuals the possibility of engaging with terrorist ideologies in the first place. We turn to those efforts next.

Denial of Access

The oft-mentioned "War of Ideas" between terrorists and governments evokes the image of two ideologies competing for space within vulnerable individuals' heads. Although it is true that some programs are predicated on promoting ideas that challenge terrorist ideologies, some governments and organizations have attempted to remove terrorist ideologies from the psychological battlefield altogether. That is, some counter-radicalization efforts are designed to prevent individuals from engaging with the ideas that comprise terrorist ideologies by denying the possibility that those individuals would even encounter them.

This approach to counter-radicalization has grown particularly popular in the realm of online social media, where propagandists from several kinds of groups have effectively distributed content consistent with their groups' ideologies. For example, with personnel in New York and London, the Counter-Extremism Project (CEP) has called on social media companies to "stop extremists from weaponizing their networks" by spreading potentially radicalizing content on them.[34] These efforts are part of a larger program called Digital Disruption, several elements of which are intended to identify accounts that spread extremist propaganda and have them scrubbed from social networking sites. For example, in 2014, CEP launched the #CEPDigitalDisruption hashtag with which members of social media networks could expose and report accounts on several sites (e.g., YouTube, Facebook, Twitter) that have posted terrorist propaganda.[35]

Instead of having extremist content removed, other organizations have attempted to direct vulnerable individuals away from that content. In a collaboration with Google's Jigsaw program, Moonshot CVE's "Redirect Method" (not to be confused with the Calgary counter-radicalization initiative) seeks to guide vulnerable eyes away from terrorist propaganda to messages that challenge that propaganda. The Redirect Method involves identifying people vulnerable to violent extremist propaganda based on keywords they enter in their online searches.[36] When these individuals attempt to engage with content they believe is consistent with their searches, they are instead redirected to content that challenges the propaganda they would have found. For example, a user who searches for "Amaq news agency" (an organization responsible for distributing ISIS propaganda) could be directed to a YouTube playlist comprising carefully crafted messages that, despite having the look and feel of other ISIS propaganda, challenges the ISIS ideology. During an eight-week pilot, the combined English- and Arabic-language programs redirected nearly 321,000 users who watched over a half million minutes of messages that challenge the ISIS ideology.[37]

Governments have also sought to deny users' access to extremist content through legislation and political action. In 2014 for example, after a recommendation from its Anti-Terrorism Squad, the Indian government blocked its citizens from accessing thirty-two video-sharing websites, including Vimeo and Dailymotion[38] for spreading "anti-Indian" content. Other countries have taken similar actions, but rather than restrict access to content for *all* citizens by shielding that content from view, they have limited Internet access of specific individuals at risk for violent radicalization. This approach was considered in the Australian state of Victoria, though some experts believed it would only further alienate those seeking information about terrorist organizations.[39]

Messaging Efforts

Although the abovementioned three approaches to counter-radicalization involve messaging to various degrees (e.g., educational initiatives are delivered via communication between experts and "students," social support requires communication between counselors and clients, the dissemination of online hashtags to mark extremist content), the messages used in the context of these programs are not the focal point of the programs. For these initiatives, communication serves as a tool to be used in the service of a larger effort geared towards counter-radicalization.

In some cases, however, counter-radicalization programs are based *entirely* on strategic messaging. These programs are characterized by the development and distribution of messages that, by themselves, serve as the mechanisms by which counter-radicalization is attempted. Governments, NGOs, and research organizations have sought to engage in strategic communication of this type for years. And although these efforts can be tailored to the contexts in which they are enacted, they largely take one of two forms: argumentation and counter-narrative.

Argumentation

In the context of counter-radicalization, argumentation refers to the delivery of messages that overtly challenge terrorist ideologies or actions. These messages often take the form of rebukes against terrorist groups' activities, dismissals of their legitimacy, or contradictions of their claims. There is little tact used in the development of these messages; they assert, with unambiguous clarity, that terrorist groups are wrong.

For example, the French government administers a program called "Stop Jihadism" that makes use of several kinds of interventions. Some of these interventions are like the efforts outlined above, including the use of family referrals and the provision of educational support to security professionals about the threat of violent extremism.[40] In addition to these elements of Stop Jihadism, the French government also uses different social media outlets to disseminate counter-speech that "deconstructs the lies of jihadist propaganda and call[s] for rallies around [French] values."[41] To achieve this, the Stop Jihadism accounts post reminders about the laws being broken by violent extremists, spread factual information that contradicts jihadists' claims about military victories, and demonstrate the ways that terrorist groups try to appeal to potential recruits.[42]

The well-known Saudi PRAC (Prevention, Rehabilitation, and Aftercare) initiative employs a similar tactic. As a component of the Prevention element of the program, Saudi officials have developed public information and communication campaigns that make appeals to the Saudi populace. These appeals were intended to foster cooperation between Saudi civilians and security personnel responsible for tracking and capturing terrorists.[43] Other elements of the Saudi public information campaign showed the damage caused by terrorists within the Kingdom and exemplified the heroism of Saudi security forces in their struggles to protect the country from terrorist attacks.[44]

In addition to communication campaigns that primarily target civilians, other programs have involved direct engagement with violent extremists. These programs are generally intended to show witnesses to the interactions the faults in terrorist groups' arguments, thereby deconstructing their ideologies and invalidating their claims. Perhaps the most notorious of these programs was the ill-fated "Think Again Turn Away" initiative developed by the US Department of State's Center for Strategic Counterterrorism Communications (CSCC). Think Again Turn Away was initially designed in the same vein as France's Stop Jihadism and the Prevention element of the Saudi PRAC initiative (i.e., counter-messaging intended to dissuade non-combatants to adopt terrorist ideologies), but it rapidly morphed into something completely different.

When it was first implemented, Think Again Turn Away involved the compilation of media stories that highlighted the threats posed by ISIS and the development of media material intended to demonstrate the brutal nature of the group. This content was then disseminated via social media accounts that were officially affiliated with the Department of State. However, these postings quickly devolved into online arguments in which ISIS supporters would make fun of the CSCC postings. CSCC personnel would respond, trying to defend their communicative attacks on ISIS. What originated as a standard counter-messaging campaign turned into an embarrassing flame-war, and the back-and-forth between Think Again Turn Away accounts and terrorist supporters removed any semblance of legitimacy that the program may have had. Evaluations of the program judged it to be an abject failure.[45]

Despite their intentions, programs that involve direct argumentation have not been shown to be terribly effective. Their efficacy has ranged from ambiguous (as in the case of Stop Jihadism) to counter-productive (as in the case of Think Again Turn Away). Unsurprisingly, it seems that direct arguments comprised without nuance or tact persuades very few members of one's audience.

Another popular form of strategic counter-radicalization messaging is characterized by more implicit – and assumedly, more effective – persuasive arguments. This strategy involves the use of counter-narratives.

Counter-Narratives

Before discussing counter-narratives, it is first important to understand what we mean by "narratives." This will be addressed in much greater detail in Chapter 3, but for now, let narratives be defined as *any cohesive and coherent account of events with an identifiable beginning, middle, and end about characters engaged in actions that result in questions or conflicts for which answers or resolutions are provided.*[46] So, given this definition, what are counter-narratives?

In past work, I have argued that counter-narratives are generally defined as "narratives comprised of content that challenges the themes intrinsic to other narratives."[47] When being used for the purpose of countering violent extremism, counter-narratives comprise content that challenges the themes in terrorist narratives that promote the group's ideology. Because violent extremist groups extensively use narratives to achieve strategic communicative goals, many governments, analysts, researchers, and organizations have looked for ways to reduce the persuasive effectiveness of those narratives with counter-narratives.

For example, consider the counter-narrative efforts of ISD Global. In addition to their efforts outlined in the preceding sections, ISD Global has also developed a toolkit for practitioners meant to guide the development of counter-narratives. In this toolkit, they offer strategies for identifying target audiences, broad recommendations for producing content, and suggestions for how to evaluate the effectiveness of counter-narratives.[48]

EuRad, a European project funded by Agenfor Italia, has also attempted to leverage the potential for counter-narratives to challenge terrorist ideologies.[49] Developed in 2012, the EuRad project was meant to "develop horizontal, Shari'ah-based methods to prevent religious radicalization within European civil societies through the mass-media." More specifically, the project sought to highlight the anti-jihad narratives that emerged among Muslim activists during the Arab Spring uprising. Using these narratives as a blueprint, EuRad personnel developed counter-narrative media messages to be spread through EU media outlets and Islamic religious centers. A similar program was also implemented in Kenya, where the Building Resilience against Violent Extremism (BRAVE) Initiative used the stories of returning fighters as counter-narratives to be distributed through Kenyan media and social media platforms.[50]

One of the fundamental issues associated with the creation and distribution of counter-narratives relates to the source from which they come. In my previous work with John Morrison on counter-narratives and trust,[51] I've argued that source credibility is a cornerstone of counter-narrative effectiveness (see also Chapter 3). If audiences do not trust the source of a counter-narrative, they are unlikely to believe its content. In this vein, and based on the assumption that former extremists are the most credible agents of counter-radicalization, some counter-narrative programs use these individuals' stories to illustrate the dangers of violent extremism.

In the United States for example, the Life After Hate program is designed to "interrupt violence committed in the name of ideological or religious beliefs" through multiple efforts.[52] To achieve this mission, Life After Hate uses several tools for the purpose of counter-radicalization. One of these tools – the development and distribution of counter-narratives by former extremists – is one of the more well-known. Life After Hate's "Against Violent Extremism Network" (AVE) is populated by former violent extremists who "push back against extremist narratives and prevent the recruitment of at-risk youths."[53] This is often achieved through stories told by the former extremists, with an emphasis on the factors that led to the abandonment of their former ideologies. Several prominent ex-white supremacists – including Sammy Rangel and Tony McAleer – are active contributors to Life After Hate's programs.

The extent to which counter-narratives have been used for counter-radicalization makes a comprehensive listing of counter-narrative initiatives impossible to put in a single chapter. Someone could easily write an entire book on counter-narratives and the contexts in which they have been implemented. If you'd like to read more on this popular strategy, see the notes section for this chapter.[54] There, I have listed several articles that serve as a foundation for the literature on counter-narratives and their effectiveness. And, of course, be sure to see Chapter 3 in this book where I offer a more detailed account of counter-narratives and how they should be developed and disseminated to maximize their effectiveness.

∴

As evidenced by the examples in the last few sections, experts have used several methods to challenge terrorist ideologies and reduce the incidence of violent radicalization among vulnerable target audiences. The differences between these methods are clear. Guiding online users away from terrorist content is substantially different than engaging with vulnerable youths. Developing and distributing counter-narratives that challenge terrorist ideologies is distinct from the provision of counseling prompted by referrals from family members. Educating students on white supremacist groups will yield different outcomes than teaching security personnel to recognize indicators of violent radicalization. The differences are many, and their effects are varied.

In the final section of this chapter, though, we'll focus on one feature that cuts across all these categories – a feature that serves as the basis for the rest of the book. Specifically, to conclude the chapter, we will see that all these interventions are founded on the tenets of persuasion. In reading this section, you will come to recognize a critical opportunity that has been missed thus far: these programs are regularly developed without guidance from long-supported persuasion theory.

Conclusions

To refine our counter-radicalization efforts moving forward, it is important to understand what's already been done. As such, one of the goals of this chapter has been to describe how researchers, government workers, and security experts have tried to prevent individuals from adopting beliefs, attitudes, intentions, or behaviors consistent with terrorist ideologies. By examining these efforts, we can learn from our past mistakes and develop stronger counter-radicalization practices.

In this spirit, there are three key lessons that can be learned from the discussions above.

(1) *Although all counter-radicalization programs differ in some ways, strategic persuasive communication plays a role in all of them.*

In education and support programs, warnings about extremist organizations and their propaganda efforts are communicated from experts to program participants. Programs like UK's Channel and the Aarhus Model require referrals to be communicated from concerned parties to program personnel, and the treatments that program participants receive often take the form of communication intended to change their beliefs and attitudes (e.g., counseling). Some efforts intended to restrict access to extremist propaganda include communicative elements that can be used to mark radicalizing content (e.g., hashtags). Direct argumentation and counter-narrative campaigns are based entirely on the persuasive efficacy of the messages they feature.

Just as the radicalization process is inherently communicative, so too are efforts to fight it. Given the central role of communication in all counter-radicalization programs, it is imperative to know how the content, style, and delivery of the messages used in those programs psychologically affect those to whom they are directed. This brings us to the second lesson to be taken from past programs.

(2) *There is little understanding about the exact nature of the communication used in some interventions or empirical evaluation of the psychological processes that are being triggered by them.*

Despite the central role of persuasive communication in counter-radicalization, there is little understanding about the form that communication takes, or its implications. Of course, privacy issues surrounding the interventions and their participants requires some secrecy, but some programs are characterized by vague descriptions about how the programs are implemented, as well as how the messages that form the basis of the programs are devised. For example, the counter-narrative toolkit developed by ISD Global is one of the more comprehensive guides available. But when describing the kinds of content that counter-narratives should employ, it is a bit broad in its assertions, saying that "there are no strict rules for creating counter-narrative content. Campaigners should seek to be as creative, bold and open-minded as possible."[55] Though the suggestions in the toolkit are reasonable, some of the broad assertions found in it (as well as other counter-narrative efforts) suggest that the psychological effects of specific message types, styles, features, and contexts are not being given due consideration. This leads to the third lesson to be gleaned from extant counter-radicalization efforts. This lesson serves as the basis for the remainder of the book.

(3) *Neither persuasion theory, nor an understanding of the persuasive implications of certain forms of strategic communication, seem to have played a central part in the development of the programs, leading to assumptions about best practices in the context of counter-radicalization.*

In 1988, Alex Schmid and Berto Jongman famously lamented the state of terrorism studies, claiming that "there are probably few areas in the social science literature in which so much is written on the basis of so little research."[56] Decades later, experts still recognize the lack of viable social scientific theory in the study of violent extremism. In a particularly scathing rebuke, Lisa Stampnitzky noted that even researchers of terrorism described its study as "poorly conceptualized, lacking in rigor, [and] *devoid of adequate theory* [emphasis added]."[57]

Unfortunately, this still seems to be true with respect to counter-radicalization. Many of the efforts outlined above (as well as those that are not included in this chapter) are well-intentioned and decently conceptualized, but are not scientifically rigorous. They seem to be based on assumptions of effectiveness rather than empirically validated social scientific theories that have been successfully applied in other contexts for decades.

The counter-messages featured in the EuRad program are based on the assumption that anti-jihad narratives that emerged during the Arab Spring would be the most effective to use. This assumption seems commonsensical, but there is no theory-based evidence to support it, nor does there seem to be a consideration about what kinds of psychological effects might be prompted by these kinds of counter-narratives. EXIT USA assumes that stories from former extremists are effective counter-radicalization messages. Again, this seems to make a lot of sense, but social scientific theory tells us that it may be useful in some cases but not others. Extant counter-radicalization programs have made an excellent start to the communicative battle against violent extremism, but we can do better.

Namely, we can systematically apply theories of persuasion that have been mainstays of communication research for years to inform how we confront the threats posed by violent radicalization. By developing a more thorough understanding of how persuasion works in the context of violent extremism, we can get a better grasp on (a) how different kinds of extremist messages influence audiences, and (b) how to develop and deliver messages that effectively challenge terrorist ideologies.

∴

According to the legend, scores of people were devoured by the Sphinx before Oedipus solved her riddle. Challenger after unprepared challenger approached her with confidence, sure that they would be the one to pull Thebes out from under her yoke. And sure enough, challenger after unprepared challenger were unceremoniously killed and eaten. These brave, but uninformed individuals assumed that they would know the answer to the Sphinx's riddle without a careful consideration of what she might ask. Their ignorance ultimately cost them their lives and left Thebes under the constant threat of ruin.

We cannot afford to go into our battle of wits unprepared, waiting for a mythical hero to save us. Whereas the Sphinx and her victims are mythical characters, the challenges associated with violent extremism are very real. How we confront the threats posed by extremist ideologies has serious implications for our security. We must know how to answer the riddle we now face, and a thorough understanding of persuasion can assist us in doing so.

To this end, the next segment of the book turns to several persuasion theories that can equip us with the knowledge needed to help cast our own monster – the threat posed by violent radicalization – into the proverbial sea.

Notes

1 Sir James George Frazer, ed., *Apollodorus Library*, 3.5.8. Available at www.perseus.tufts.edu/hopper/text?doc=Apollod.+3.5.8&redirect=true; Mark Cartwright, "Sphinx," *Ancient History Encyclopedia* (September 8, 2012). Available at www.ancient.eu/sphinx/.
2 Efraim Benmelech and Esteban F. Klor, "What Explains the Flow of Foreign Fighters to ISIS?" NBER Working Paper Series 22190 (2016), National Bureau of Economic Research. Available at www.nber.org/papers/w22190.pdf.
3 Heidi Beirich, "The Year in Hate: Rage Against Change," *Southern Poverty Law Center Intelligence Report* (February 20, 2019). Available at www.splcenter.org/fighting-hate/intelligence-report/2019/year-hate-rage-against-change.

4 Bill Morlin, "The 'Alt-Right' is Still Killing People," *Southern Poverty Law Center Intelligence Report* (February 20, 2019), pp. 6–7. Available at www.splcenter.org/sites/default/files/intelligence_report_166.pdf

5 John Horgan and Kurt Braddock, "Rehabilitating the Terrorists? Challenges in Assessing the Effectiveness of De-radicalization Programs," *Terrorism and Political Violence* 22, no. 2 (2010): 267–291; John Horgan and Mary Beth Altier, "The Future of Terrorist De-Radicalization Programs," *Georgetown Journal of International Affairs* 13, no. 2 (2012): 83–90; Darcy M. E. Noricks, "Disengagement and Deradicalization: Processes and Programs," in *Social Science for Counterterrorism*, ed. Paul K. Davis and Kim Cragin, 299–322 (Santa Monica, CA: RAND Corporation, 2009).

6 Daniel Köhler, *Understanding Deradicalization: Methods, Tools and Programs for Countering Violent Extremism* (London: Routledge, 2017).

7 Institute for Strategic Dialogue, *Extreme Dialogue* [brochure]. Available at https://extremedialogue.org/sites/isd.hocext.co.uk/files/2018-03/ISD-Brochure-Web.pdf.

8 Zahra Qadir, "Preventing Extremism." Available at www.activechange foundation.org/blog/blog-post-3.

9 Active Change Foundation, "Preventing Extremism: One-Day Prevent Extremism Training." Available at www.activechangefoundation.org/Event/preventing-extremism.

10 Mothers for Life Network, "About the Mothers for Life Network." Available at www.mothersforlife.org/en/about-us.

11 VINK, "Are You Worried about Someone You Know?" [in Danish]. Available at https://vink.kk.dk/indhold/er-du-bekymret-en-du-kender.

12 Bundesamt für Migration und Flüchtlinge, *Faith or Extremism? Help for Relatives: The Advice Centre on Radicalisation* [brochure]. Available at www.bamf.de/SharedDocs/Anlagen/EN/Publikationen/Broschueren/glaube-oder-extremismus.pdf.

13 The Local, "'Extremism Hotline' Swamped with Calls," *The Local – Austria* (January 21, 2015). Available at www.thelocal.at/20150121/austrian-extremism-hotline-swamped-with-calls.

14 The Local, "Swedish Extremism Hotline Prepares to Open," *The Local – Sweden* (October 29, 2015). Available at www.thelocal.se/20151029/swedish-extremism-hotline-prepares-to-open.

15 Agenfor International, "ISDEP: Improving Security by Democratic Participation." Available at www.agenformedia.com/international-projects/isdep.

16 Institute for Strategic Dialogue, *Case Study Report: Community Policing and the Prevention of Radicalisation, Belgium*. Available at www.counterextremism.org/download_file/88/134/117/.

17 Ibid.

18 All Together Now, "CAPE: About Us." Available at https://cape.allto gethernow.org.au/about-us/.

19 All Together Now, "Responding to Far-Right Extremism: Training for Frontline Workers." Available at https://cape.alltogethernow.org.au/wp-content/uploads/2017/03/CAPE Training-Program-2.jpg.

20 Society against Violent Extremism Belgium, "The Actions" [in French]. Available at www.savebelgium.org/#about.
21 Ibid.
22 Institute for Strategic Dialogue, *Case Study Report: Slotevaart Action Plan to Prevent Radicalisation.* Available at www.counterextremism.org/download_file/205/134/508/.
23 Jane Harrigan, "The Rise of Religious-Based Radicalism and the Deradicalisation Programme in Bangladesh," in *Deradicalising Violent Extremists: Counter-Radicalisation and Deradicalisation Programmes and their Impact in Muslim Majority States,* ed. Hamed El-Said and Jane Harrigan, 50–73 (London: Routledge, 2013).
24 Federal Bureau of Investigation, *Don't Be a Puppet.* Available at https://cve.fbi.gov/home.html.
25 HM Government, *Channel Duty Guidance: Protecting Vulnerable People from Being Drawn into Terrorism* (London: Crown Copyright, 2015). Available at www.gov.uk/government/publications/channel-guidance.
26 Ibid., p. 10.
27 Ibid., p. 17.
28 Paul Thomas, "Failed and Friendless: The UK's 'Preventing Violent Extremism' Programme," *The British Journal of Politics and International Relations* 12 (2010): 442–458; Paul Thomas, "Youth, Terrorism and Education: Britain's Prevent Programme," *International Journal of Lifelong Education* 3, no. 2 (2016): 171–187.
29 Preven Bertelsen, "Danish Preventative Measures and De-radicalization Strategies: The Aarhus Model," *Panorama* 1 (2015): 241–253. Available at http://psy.au.dk/fileadmin/Psykologi/Forskning/Preben_Bertelsen/Avisartikler_radikalisering/Panorama.pdf.
30 Ibid.
31 Ibid., p. 244.
32 Ibid.
33 Calgary Police Service, "ReDirect: About Us." Available at www.redirectprogram.ca/.
34 Counter Extremism Project, "Digital Disruption: Fighting Online Extremism." Available at www.counterextremism.com/digital-disruption.
35 Ibid.
36 *The Redirect Method: Targeting.* Available at https://redirectmethod.org/pilot/#targeting.
37 *The Redirect Method: Results.* Available at https://redirectmethod.org/pilot/#results.
38 Government of India Ministry of Communications, "Website Blocked Following Court Order" (December 31, 2014). Available at http://pib.nic.in/newsite/mbErel.aspx?relid=114259.
39 Melissa Davey, "Victoria's Deradicalisation Plan: A 'Soviet-Style' Idea that Will Only Alienate—Expert," *The Guardian* (June 8, 2015). Available at www.theguardian.com/australia-news/2015/jun/08/victorias-deradicalisation-plan-a-soviet-style-idea-that-will-only-alienate-expert.

40 Stop Djihadisme, "How to Prevent and Fight against the Radicalization of Minors?" [in French]. Available at www.stop-djihadisme.gouv.fr/lutte-contre-terrorisme-radicalisation/prevention-radicalisation/comment-prevenir-lutter-contre.

41 Stop Djihadisme, "Fight against Jihadist Propaganda on the Internet" [in French]. Available at www.stop-djihadisme.gouv.fr/que-faire/relayer-contre-discours/lutter-contre-propagande-djihadiste-internet.

42 Ibid.

43 Christopher Boucek, "Saudi Arabia's 'Soft' Counterterrorism Strategy: Prevention, Rehabilitation, and Aftercare," *Carnegie Papers* 97 (2008). Available at https://carnegieendowment.org/files/cp97_boucek_saudi_final.pdf.

44 Ibid., p. 11.

45 Rita Katz, "The State Department's Twitter War with ISIS is Embarrassing," *Time* (September 16, 2014). Available at http://time.com/3387065/isis-twitter-war-state-department/; Greg Miller and Scott Higham, "In a Propaganda War against ISIS, the U.S. Tried to Play by the Enemy's Rules," *The Washington Post* (May 8, 2015). Available at www.washingtonpost.com/world/national-security/in-a-propaganda-war-us-tried-to-play-by-the-enemys-rules/2015/05/08/6eb6b732-e52f-11e4-81ea-0649268f729e_story.html.

46 Kurt Braddock and John Horgan, "Towards a Guide for Constructing and Disseminating Counternarratives to Reduce Support for Terrorism," *Studies in Conflict & Terrorism* 3, no. 5 (2016): 381–404 (pp. 382–383).

47 Ibid., p. 386.

48 Henry Tuck and Tanya Silverman, *The Counter-Narrative Handbook* (Washington, DC: ISD Global, 2016). Available at www.isdglobal.org/wp-content/uploads/2018/10/Counter-narrative-Handbook_1_web.pdf.

49 Agenfor International, "EuRad: Shari'ah Based Counterradicalization." Available at www.agenformedia.com/international-projects/eurad.

50 Centre for Sustainable Conflict Resolution, *BRAVE: Building Resilience against Violent Extremism* (August 25, 2017). Available at http://braveprogram .org/; Anthony Langat, "Muslim Leaders Are Trying to Change the Way Kenya Fights Terrorism," *Agence France-Presse* (August 23, 2015). Available at www.pri.org/stories/2015-08-23/muslim-leaders-are-trying-change-way-kenya-fights-terrorism.

51 Kurt Braddock and John F. Morrison, "Cultivating Trust and Perceptions of Source Credibility in Online Counternarratives Intended to Reduce Support for Terrorism," *Studies in Conflict & Terrorism* (in press).

52 Life After Hate, "Who We Are." Available at www.lifeafterhate.org/about-us-1.

53 Life After Hate, "Our Programs." Available at www.lifeafterhate.org/programs.

54 Braddock and Horgan, "Towards a Guide for Constructing and Disseminating Counternarratives"; Christian Leuprecht, Todd Hataley, Sophia Moskalenko, and Clark McCauley, "Winning the Battle but Losing the War? Narrative and Counter-Narratives Strategy," *Perspectives on Terrorism* 3, no. 2 (2009): 25–35; William D. Casebeer and James A. Russell, "Storytelling and Terrorism: Towards a Comprehensive 'Counter-Narrative' Strategy," *Strategic Insights* 4, no. 3 (2005). Available at https://apps.dtic.mil/dtic/tr/fulltext/u2/a521449.pdf

55 Tuck and Silverman, The Counter-Narrative Handbook, p. 17.
56 Alex Schmid and Albert Jongman, *Political Terrorism: A New Guide to Actors, Authors, Concepts, Databases, Theories and Literature* (Amsterdam: North Holland Publishing, 1988), p. 179.
57 Lisa Stampnitzky, "Disciplining an Unruly Field: Terrorism Experts and Theories of Scientific/Intellectual Production," *Qualitative Sociology* 34, no. 1 (2011): 1–19 (p. 3).

Part II

The Weapons
Theories of Persuasion and their Application to
Radicalization and Counter-Radicalization Processes

3 Extremist Narratives and Counter-Narratives

It was barely after ten in the morning, and Highway Patrolman Charles Hanger was already having a busy day. About an hour before, an explosion had rocked the city, and he was ordered to connect with his command post there. But shortly after beginning his drive south, he was re-ordered to turn around and head back north; the command post in the city had all the help it needed. Hanger complied and turned around. There would be plenty more to do that morning.

Driving back up Interstate 35, he took notice of an old, pale yellow Mercury Marquis. The car was unremarkable except for one detail that happened to catch Hanger's eye as he sped past it – it was missing a rear license plate. After nearly cruising past the Marquis, Patrolman Hanger slowed to match its speed. Once alongside it, Hanger looked over and nodded courteously at the driver. The person behind the wheel – a young, clean-shaven man of no more than 30 – nodded back. Hanger slowed even more, pulled behind the Marquis, and turned on his flashers.

After the Marquis settled to a stop on the side of the Interstate, Hanger pulled his car behind it. He opened the door and emerged from his vehicle. Hanger noticed that the man he pulled over was also getting out of his car. This made him nervous – people who get pulled over typically wait in their cars for officers to approach. Given that another patrolman had been shot at during a routine stop just weeks before, Hanger was wary. He stayed behind his open car door, placing a barrier between himself and the man, who was now moving towards him.

After a few seconds, Hanger left the safety of his car door and approached the man. Moving forward steadily, he announced the reason for the stop, "You don't have a license plate."

"Huh," the man said, turning to look at his rear bumper. "No."

In the short discussion that followed, Hanger discovered that the otherwise-unremarkable Mercury Marquis was not insured or registered, and the man he pulled over was carrying a loaded pistol for which he had no in-state license. Hanger led the man to the backseat of his patrol car and went about the business of searching the Marquis.

In the front seat, Hanger found a baseball cap, a sign that read PLEASE DO NOT TOW, and a large, white, sealed envelope. He took note of these items and returned to his prisoner, preparing to transport him to the county jail about twenty miles away. Hanger asked the man if he wanted to get anything from his car before they left – just in case there was something valuable in the envelope the man might need. The man was short in his response.

"No," he said. "Leave it there."

∴

Investigators would later examine the contents of the envelope, finding written quotes by the likes of Patrick Henry and Thomas Jefferson, a copy of the Declaration of Independence, a justification for war against those that restrict liberty, and a long passage from William Luther Pierce's *The Turner Diaries*. The passage read:

The real value of our attacks today lies in the psychological impact, not in the immediate casualties. More important, though, is what we taught the politicians and the bureaucrats. They learned this afternoon that not one of them is beyond our reach. They can huddle behind barbed wire and tanks in the city, and they can hide behind the concrete walls of their country estates, but we can still find them and kill them.

The Turner Diaries is a novel that describes an armed resistance against a government that seeks to outlaw firearms and restrict liberty among its people. In the story, this resistance – which promotes the killing of blacks and Jews – culminates in bomb attacks against FBI headquarters and other government buildings. Investigators found that *The Turner Diaries* was a personal favorite of the driver that Patrolman Hanger pulled over on Interstate 35.

The man was Timothy McVeigh. When he was stopped with an excerpt from *The Turner Diaries* in his front seat, he was driving away from his attack on a federal building in Oklahoma City. Just an hour before he was pulled over, McVeigh murdered 168 people in that attack, including 19 children.

∴

Leaving a passage from *The Turner Diaries* in his car was no accident; McVeigh wanted those pages to be found. They told the story that inspired and justified the largest domestic terror attack in the history of the United States. They weren't just part of a random anti-government narrative. They were his manifesto. They explained why.

The subsequent investigation and testimony provided at McVeigh's trial showed the extent to which *The Turner Diaries* shaped his beliefs and attitudes, as well as how much they inspired his plot to bomb the Murrah Building. McVeigh first encountered the book in his early days as a US Army infantryman. Consistent with the book's central theme, he came to believe that the United States was threatened by a collective of "money-grubbing liberals, multiculturalists, and Jews intent on stripping citizens of their basic rights."[1] Of great concern to McVeigh was the possibility that the US government would eventually come to take away citizens' guns, just like in *The Turner Diaries*. McVeigh gave the book to several people whom he thought shared his concerns and his worldview, including Terry Nichols – his key partner in the Oklahoma City bombing. The pair were struck by the book's revolutionary tone, and believed it foreshadowed the future of the United States.

McVeigh and Nichols came to believe that the plot of *The Turner Diaries* was playing out in real life in September of 1994, when President Clinton approved a ten-year ban on assault weapons. Immediately after the ban was enacted, McVeigh began to search for the bags of ammonium nitrate that would be used to construct the bomb that tore a hole in Oklahoma City. What began as a grudge against the United States government for its sieges at Ruby Ridge and Waco came into deadly focus when real-world events mimicked a story that McVeigh identified with.

∴

How was this possible? How could a story – even one as politically charged and hate-filled as *The Turner Diaries* – help motivate someone to kill dozens of his fellow citizens? How could *any* story help shape beliefs and attitudes that promote violence? And if stories can push someone towards violence, can stories be used to pull someone away from violence?

The answers to these difficult questions can be found in an area that has been studied by communication experts for decades. Research has shown that stories are strong tools for persuading people to adopt certain beliefs and attitudes, or even engage in certain behaviors. Most of this research has not focused on political violence, but as issues related to terrorism and national security have become increasingly prominent around the world, experts have come to realize the capacity for narratives to carry terrorist ideologies and motivate terrorist violence.

Luckily, some communication researchers have realized that it is possible to beat terrorists at their own narrative game. Just as terrorist groups distribute their ideologies and motivate would-be terrorists through their stories, counter-narratives can be used to challenge those ideologies and promote peace over violence. For these reasons, it is critical to understand how narratives are used in the context of terrorism. This chapter achieves that goal.

More specifically, this chapter discusses the nature of narrative persuasion, how it has been used to promote violent radicalization, and how it can be used for counter-radicalization. To these ends, this chapter describes the mechanisms through which narrative persuasion occurs and demonstrates how terrorists have used narratives to achieve their objectives. Most importantly, however, this chapter explains how counter-terrorists and analysts can use their own narratives (called counter-narratives) to challenge terrorist propaganda.

But first, it is important to clarify what we mean when we talk about narratives and narrative persuasion. The next section will define these terms and lay the foundation for effective narrative persuasion that may help keep the next Timothy McVeigh from acting out a violent story of his own.

Foundations of Narrative Persuasion

What Are Narratives?

Social science researchers have debated the definition for "narrative" for years. These debates have not produced a consensus definition, but there are some common elements across existing definitions. For example, all definitions argue that at the simplest level, narratives are representations of an event or a series of events.[2] This definition implies that narratives must contain at least one action. Without representing an event (or series of events), one could produce a description, an exposition, or an argument, but not a narrative.

Others have argued that a narrative must contain at least two events, suggesting that a narrative's defining feature is its serial nature.[3] French literary theorist and narrative expert Gérard Genette adopted this point of view, arguing that narratives are essentially sequences of events.[4]

Still others have claimed that narratives are characterized by not only the number of events that comprise them, but also how they are interpreted by those that consume them. Walter Fisher – who brought narratives to communication theory and science – contended that the sequential nature of narrative is only one of its features. He argued that narratives consist of symbolic actions that have meaning for those that create or interpret them.[5]

More recent narrative experts have gone even further. They've argued that although narratives do, indeed, consist of sequentially ordered events that make sense to those that create or consume them, the events in the narrative must also be causally related. That is, events presented in a narrative must be meaningfully connected in cause–effect relationships to move the plot forward.[6]

Although these different definition types provide some information about the inherent nature of narratives, none are sufficiently comprehensive to capture exactly what a narrative is. In response to this, Marie-Laure Ryan developed a list of characteristics that collectively define narratives. She argued that the degree to which a message can be called a "narrative" is based on eight key propositions:[7]

- Narratives are about worlds populated with individual entities.
- Narrative worlds must experience changes in time.
- Changes to narrative worlds must be caused by physical events that aren't habitual to that world.
- At least some of the narrative event participants must be intelligent beings.
- At least some of the narrative events must be purposeful actions by those beings.
- The narrative events must be causally linked and lead to closure in the narrative.
- At least one of the narrative events must be a fact in the story world.
- The narrative must be meaningful to the audience in some way.

By using Ryan's "toolkit" and drawing from past research on narratives, it becomes possible to develop a definition for our purposes here. Based on my past work on terrorist messaging, I have found it useful to define narratives as *cohesive, causally linked sequences of events that take place in dynamic worlds subject to conflict, transformation, and resolution through non-habitual, purposeful action performed by characters.* By using this definition as we move forward through the chapter, it becomes easier to understand what kinds of terrorist communication can be called "terrorist narratives," and what kinds of counter-narratives can be produced to challenge terrorist messaging.

Before turning to examples of terrorist groups' narratives or how analysts can develop their own narrative messages to challenge violent extremism, we first need to address two fundamental questions related to narratives. First, to consider whether terrorist narratives contribute to violent radicalization (or if counter-narratives can prevent it), it is important to determine whether narratives are persuasive at all. Then, we must understand *how* narratives persuade individuals that are exposed to them. The following sections address these basic questions.

Are Narratives Persuasive?

Given the incredible amount of research on the topic, one could be forgiven for assuming that communication experts had settled whether narratives can change people's minds. But despite a thirty-year history of research on narrative persuasion, we have only just begun to get a clear idea about how persuasive narratives can be. This is largely due to the fact that past studies of narrative persuasion have produced mixed evidence.

Some studies have shown that exposure to a narrative has a positive persuasive effect. That is, these studies have produced evidence to show that when someone reads or watches a narrative, he/she adopts beliefs, attitudes, intentions, or behaviors that are consistent with arguments embedded in it. For example, some research has shown that being exposed to a narrative with content that warns about health-related issues has caused individuals to adopt positive attitudes about things like exercise,[8] seat-belt use,[9] vaccination,[10] and other health-conscious outcomes. Other work has shown that people also sometimes adopt intentions[11] or engage in behaviors[12] that they encountered in a narrative.

In contrast to these findings, some other studies have shown that exposure to a narrative can have a boomerang effect. This means that researchers found that being exposed to a narrative caused individuals to adopt perspectives that were *opposite* to those that appeared in the narrative. For instance, in one study, researchers found that being exposed to a narrative intended to increase acceptance of overweight individuals caused audience members to develop negative attitudes towards those individuals and have less intention to make friends with anyone who is overweight.[13] Another study showed that exposure to a narrative designed to reduce apprehension about dying actually *increased* participants' fear of death.[14]

Further confusing matters, communication experts have used different methods to determine how persuasive narratives can be. Many studies have compared narratives to other kinds of evidence (e.g., statistics, lists) to determine which is more persuasive.[15] These kinds of studies have been useful, but they don't tell us whether narratives are persuasive in and of themselves. They haven't shown whether being exposed to a narrative significantly affects audience members' opinions.

To address this long-standing confusion, I worked with an accomplished researcher of social influence, Dr. James Dillard, to perform a series of meta-analyses on the decades of research concerning narratives and persuasion.[16] In doing so, Dillard and I analyzed thousands of research participants across dozens of papers, all while controlling for the sampling and measurement error that inevitably affect individual studies. These meta-analyses produced a definitive conclusion: narratives induce a positive persuasive effect on individuals that consume them, regardless of the context in which they are presented. Of course, there may be some factors that affect a narrative's persuasiveness (i.e., moderators), but our findings showed that if an individual reads a book, watches a movie, attends a play, or experiences a narrative via any other medium, he/she is likely to adopt perspectives consistent with those that are advocated in the narrative, at least to some degree.

If narratives are persuasive independent of context, it follows that narratives that promote a terrorist ideology have the potential to promote violent radicalization among audience members. However, to fully understand how terrorists use narratives for violent radicalization (and how counter-narratives can be used to challenge the effects of terrorist propaganda), it is not enough to know only that terrorist narratives are persuasive. It is also important to recognize and understand the factors and psychological processes that drive their persuasiveness.

How Do Narratives Persuade?

Even with the relatively new research showing narratives to be persuasive, there are still several questions concerning the psychological processes that drive their persuasiveness. For their part, communication researchers and psychologists have continued to explore these persuasive processes and mechanisms, offering some insight into how narratives induce change in audience members' beliefs, attitudes, intentions, or behaviors.

Rick Busselle and Helena Bilandzic proposed that a narrative's persuasiveness depends on the degree to which it causes the reader to construct three types of "mental models": character models, story world models, and situation models.[17] Character models refer to the identities, traits, and goals of individual characters in a story; story world models describe the spatial and temporal setting of the story, and establish its logic; and situation models combine character models and story world models to track the actions of characters to cue the story forward. To illustrate how audiences construct these mental models, consider Lewis Carroll's *Alice's Adventures in Wonderland*. In reading this story, an audience member would develop a character model for the Queen of Hearts that identifies her as a rage-prone antagonist to Alice. The reader would also develop a story world model that identifies Wonderland as a place outside Alice's normal world where seemingly nonsensical things can occur. Finally, the reader would combine character models and the story world model to make sense of events in the story (e.g., why the Queen of Hearts wishes to decapitate anthropomorphized playing cards).

To understand a story's events in this way, audience members must shift their focus from the actual world to the story world. In doing so, they undergo *psychological transportation*, a process whereby they lose awareness of the actual world around them due to psychological immersion in the fictional world. The experience of psychological transportation opens the door to several mechanisms of persuasion.

For instance, some researchers have claimed that psychological transportation resulting from absorption into a narrative can render audience members less likely to critique a narrative's messages[18] or counter-argue against the points that comprise it.[19] Other research similarly shows that regardless of a narrative's content, psychological transportation into a narrative is associated with enjoyment of that narrative. This means that psychological transportation can be useful in motivating an individual to attend to topics they may have otherwise avoided.[20]

Other researchers have shown that narratives can help get around a persistent barrier to persuasion – psychological reactance.[21] Psychological reactance theory contends that individuals have a basic need to choose their own opinions and actions. Threats to this freedom cause a negative form of arousal that motivates individuals to re-assert their power. So, when a persuasive message is perceived as a threat to an individual's freedom to choose his/her own opinions or actions, that individual may re-assert their freedom by dismissing the persuasive message or engaging in a behavior opposite to the one that is advocated.[22]

Less intrusive messages are less likely to be rejected by their audiences,[23] and narratives (e.g., fictional stories, television dramas) are generally thought to be designed for entertainment, not persuasion. So, narrative forms of persuasion have the potential to avoid arousing psychological reactance, making them more effective than overt persuasive messages in some contexts.

More recently, communication experts have argued that what makes narratives persuasive is their capacity to prompt audience members to adopt characters' perspectives. This process, called *identification*, often leads audience members to experience an increased willingness to think about ideas or imagine behaviors that they would not otherwise consider.[24] Narratives can also induce persuasion by increasing audience members' perceptions of similarity with characters. For instance, some individuals may maintain psychological biases whereby they believe they are at lesser risk than others for negative consequences associated with violent behaviors (e.g., "I know that people who join ISIS are often killed, but they were unprepared. That will never happen to me"). Because of this perceived invulnerability, individuals may dismiss persuasive messages that warn against engaging in violent behavior.[25] However, if an individual perceives a character in a narrative that *does* experience negative consequences from engaging in violent behavior as similar to him/her, then the narrative may effectively dissuade participation in that behavior.

It is also possible for audience members to encounter characters they perceive as similar that engage in more prosocial behaviors (e.g., "I never thought I could abandon my violent friends, but that character is like me and walked away from violence. I can too.").[26] If an individual recognizes that a similar character engages in behaviors that the individual previously thought impossible, it can increase the individual's self-efficacy and prompt more constructive behavior.

Research on *parasocial relationships* and persuasion has produced similar results. Parasocial relationships are feelings of connection between a spectator (an audience member) and performer (a narrative character). These relationships develop when audience members come to like and trust the character because of the character's perspectives and behaviors in the context of the story he/she inhabits. Of course, a character in a narrative cannot develop any feelings of connection to an audience member; parasocial relationships are intrinsically one-sided. Regardless, the feelings of association felt by the audience member are a strong mechanism for persuasion. Burgoon and colleagues argued that persuasion can occur via parasocial interaction because individuals tend to perceive peers as less authoritative or controlling.[27] As a result, audience members are unlikely to treat persuasive messages delivered by liked or trusted characters (whom they perceive as de facto peers) as overt attempts to control their beliefs, attitudes, or behaviors. This circumvents the problem of psychological reactance that hinders most persuasive attempts.

Finally, the development of parasocial relationships with narrative characters can alter audience members' impressions about social norms regarding a particular belief, attitude, or behavior. When a message recipient parasocially interacts with a character, that character is perceived as being part of the recipient's social network.[28] Individuals derive their understanding of social norms from members of their social networks, so the inclusion of a parasocially interactive character that holds a certain belief or engages in a certain behavior can change the message recipient's perceptions of the norms surrounding that belief or behavior. In short, when someone likes and/or trusts a character within a narrative, the things that the character says and does can exert a strong influence on that person.

∴

The research described in this section shows the variety of ways that narratives can be persuasive. They can prompt psychological transportation, distracting us from embedded messages intended to change our beliefs, attitudes, or behaviors. They can feature characters we perceive as similar to ourselves, causing us to identify with those characters and open ourselves to perspectives and behaviors we hadn't previously considered. They can bring us to like or trust those characters, inducing us to make them influential "members" of our social circles. These are powerful mechanisms for persuasion, and they have been exploited by individuals and groups in all kinds of contexts.

Unfortunately, terrorist organizations have leveraged the persuasive power of narratives to their advantage. The next section explores how some terrorists have used narratives to achieve their objectives. Once we understand how terrorist groups use narratives to persuade their audiences, we begin to think about how to use counter-narratives to fight back.

Terrorist Narratives

Since the early days of terrorism research, analysts have attempted to highlight how terrorist behavior is somehow different than "normal" behavior.[29] However, closer inspection of the factors surrounding the use of terrorism shows that there is little evidence to suggest that it is a "special" kind of behavior. It may be considered special because it is statistically and socially abnormal, but the practice of terrorism and the processes that precede it are governed by the same social and psychological dynamics that drive all human behavior. For example, there is no evidence to suggest that politicians motivate, persuade, or mobilize their constituents any differently than terrorist groups do. Of course, the content of the messages that are delivered may be different, but the dynamics and mechanisms for persuasion are similar across these (and other) contexts.

When influence over an audience is a strategic objective, narratives can be (and are) used to change beliefs and attitudes so they are more consistent with the persuader's goals. This is true even for terrorist groups. Although terrorist and extremist groups use a wide array of communicative strategies to encourage audiences to adopt their ideologies, support their actions, or engage in violent behavior, the development and distribution of narratives that promote the group's ideology is one of the more popular.

Consider the number of extremist organizations that use narratives. On the popular Stormfront online discussion forms, radical white nationalists post stories related to fictional race wars, interactions with members of other races, and the exploits of the group's role models. The Animal Liberation Front maintains an online archive of sympathetic narratives created by adherents to its ideology. Several jihadi groups tell the story of the Meccans' defeat at the hands of Muhammad in the Battle of al-Badr in their statements to the public.[30] ISIS's sophisticated social media presence features stories of current and former combatants who have come to fight for the glory of the Islamic State. The list goes on and on.

Although the exact strategic objectives of these and other terrorist narratives are rarely disclosed by the groups that distribute them, communication researchers have shown that they have the potential to promote the adoption of beliefs, attitudes, intentions, and behaviors consistent with those of the group.[31] That said, the potential for narratives to promote support for terrorism among their audiences is heavily contingent on (a) the themes that make up the terrorist narratives, and (b) the extent to which they trigger the psychological processes that facilitate persuasion (i.e., identification, transportation, parasocial interaction). It is likely impossible to determine the quantitative degree to which a specific terrorist narrative may have induced an individual to engage in violent activity, but the potency of narratives as tools for persuasion, coupled with the presence of narrative themes that spur psychological processes that contribute to radicalization,[32] suggests that being exposed to a terrorist narrative can at least theoretically increase the likelihood that an individual may come to support terrorism.

There are certainly some cases in which narratives seem to have played a part in individual trajectories towards terrorism. In addition to Timothy McVeigh's widely reported admiration for *The Turner Diaries*, several other domestic terrorists have also shown an affinity for the book and its messages. For example, in April of 2007, anti-abortion extremist Paul Evans planted a bomb in the parking lot of an Austin, Texas women's health center, along with four mail bombs to other targets. After Evans was arrested, a search of his apartment produced a copy of *The Turner Diaries*.

Anti-government extremists, white nationalists, and anti-abortion terrorists are not unique in their attraction to stories and adherence to the themes contained in them. Jihadi groups have enjoyed similar success in using narratives to get others to adopt their ideologies. ISIS's most prominent narrative seems to have been extremely persuasive. This narrative, outlined in detail by Graeme Wood,[33] describes a final apocalyptic battle in a town called Dabiq between the devout Muslim fighters of ISIS and soldiers of "Rome" (thought to mean Western forces). After winning this battle, the Islamic caliphate will expand until Dajjal (an anti-Messiah character) will emerge from Iran and kill all but 5,000 cornered Muslim fighters. As Dajjal moves to destroy the remaining fighters, Jesus (who is the second-most important prophet in Islam) will return, kill Dajjal, and open the way to the new caliphate. Despite the ostensible irrationality of this narrative, many individuals have been seduced by it, leaving their homes to fight for ISIS and bring it to fruition. Consider Musa Cerantonio, an Australian national who was caught trying to emigrate to Syria by way of the Philippines in June of 2014. Described by terrorism expert Peter Neumann as a "new spiritual authority" in service of ISIS, Cerantonio has championed the group's efforts to re-establish the caliphate described in the Dajjal narrative and spoken with great hope about the signs of the imminent Islamic apocalypse.[34]

Cerantonio is not the only one who has proven susceptible to persuasion via ISIS narratives; in 2015 alone, more than 25,000 fighters from 100 countries left their homes to fight for the group in Iraq and Syria.[35] The US House Homeland Security Committee on Combating Terrorist and Foreign Fighter Travel noted the importance of ISIS narratives in driving this trend, claiming that rank-and-file members of the group have become central in recruiting new members by documenting stories from the battlefield.[36] Narratives are clearly useful to terrorist groups for their ability to persuade individuals to adopt their ideologies and/or engage in violence.

Luckily, as has been argued by some communication researchers, we can "beat terrorists at their own narrative game." Just as terrorist groups can develop persuasive narratives with the potential to prompt radicalization and engagement in violent activity, it is also possible to construct and distribute narratives designed to challenge the radicalizing themes that make up terrorist narratives. These are called counter-narratives. Although some researchers have discussed the possibility of developing and distributing counter-narratives to prevent and counter violent extremism, it has not been explored in great depth. The vital work headed by researchers at Arizona State's Consortium for Strategic Communication (CSC) has discussed the importance of systems of stories for deterring terrorism.[37] Some other communication experts have also discussed the importance of using systems of stories to contradict dominant extremist perspectives.[38] Still others have talked about the development of counter-narratives generally,[39] without providing a theoretical basis for the counter-narratives' construction and/or distribution. Despite the steps made in the production of effective counter-narrative strategy, detailed guidance on how to develop and disseminate counter-narratives has long been missing from the strategic counter-terrorist toolkit.

The remainder of this chapter provides this guidance.

Using Counter-Narratives to Reduce Support for Terrorism

Before turning to the strategic development and distribution of counter-narratives, it is important to discuss (a) exactly what counter-narratives are and (b) why they can be useful for reducing support for terrorism. Generally speaking, counter-narratives are narratives comprising content that contradicts the themes that make up other narratives. Stated more obviously, the content in a counter-narrative is designed to *counter* the content in another narrative. In the context of violent extremism, counter-narratives are narratives that challenge the themes that can be found in terrorist groups' narratives. For instance, some ISIS narratives advocate martyrdom as a glorious way to serve not only ISIS, but all Muslims around the world. Counter-narratives intended to challenge this claim might contain content that depicts martyrdom in the service of ISIS to be an empty act that serves no moral, social, or spiritual purpose.

As outlined earlier in this chapter, my work on the effectiveness of narratives has shown them to be persuasive, independent of context.[40] In addition, established communication theory has identified certain features of narratives (and by extension, counter-narratives) that determine how persuasive they are. For example, Moyer-Gusé argued that narratives are persuasive because they reduce psychological reactance, counter-arguing, and selective avoidance, as well as increasing audience members perceptions of vulnerability and self-efficacy.[41] To achieve these outcomes, authors of counter-narratives must attempt to mask their persuasive intent by promoting identification, transportation, and parasocial interaction (see above). Counter-narratives should be effective in challenging the themes that comprise terrorist narratives to the extent that they can arouse these key psychological processes.[42]

That said, it does not matter how well a counter-narrative is constructed if the message is dismissed because its intended target discounts it as untrustworthy. A long history of research on source credibility strongly suggests that a counter-narrative's effectiveness depends not only on the content that comprises it, but also the manner in which it is distributed.[43] It is critical for analysts to deliver counter-narratives so audience members believe they were constructed by credible entities.

Given the importance of both construction *and* dissemination of counter-narratives, the remainder of this chapter takes the form of a guide that includes instructions concerning both processes. Obviously, a counter-narrative must be developed before it can be distributed, so we first turn to the process of counter-narrative construction.

Constructing Counter-Narratives

There are two fundamental steps involved in constructing counter-narratives meant to challenge violent extremism. The first step involves the analysis of terrorist narratives intended to bolster support for terrorist groups, ideologies, or activities. The second step involves using the results from the analysis of terrorist narratives to guide the development of counter-narratives.

Identifying Themes that Comprise Terrorist Narratives

To effectively develop counter-narratives intended to reduce support for terrorism, it is vital to first understand the thematic content that comprises the targeted terrorist narrative(s).[44] Without identifying and comprehending the themes embedded in terrorist narratives, counternarratives will be developed arbitrarily and without targets to aim for, making them ineffective. So, it is important for developers of counternarratives to use a systematic method for analyzing terrorist narratives and chronicling the thematic content that comprises them. Content analysis – a group of techniques used to describe the elements of messages – can be useful in this regard.

The complexity of content analysis techniques varies, with the least complex version of content analysis involving the simple counting of message characteristics (e.g., words, phrases). However, a more sophisticated content analytic method is necessary to account for the higher-order concepts in terrorist narratives that contribute to violent radicalization. *Theme analysis* represents one of these more complex (and useful) content analytic methods.

Researchers have used the term "theme analysis" to describe several different kinds of qualitative methods. However, all kinds of theme analysis involve reading, listening to, or watching a message (or series of messages) and recognizing patterns within the message(s) that provide some insight about the meaning of the words that comprise them. The patterns that emerge from the communicative data are called "themes."

Theme analysis helps the analyst to understand the latent meaning of text through the identification of intrinsic higher-level concepts within language-based data.[45] As such, it is uniquely suited for identifying the themes in terrorist narratives that counter-narratives can attack.[46] More specifically, theme analysis allows the analyst to make inferences about the objectives of terrorist narratives. This, in turn, allows the analyst to understand how terrorist narratives may be interpreted by their intended audiences. Once the analyst has a grasp of the themes that comprise the terrorist narrative(s), he/she can then embed opposing themes in the counter-narratives intended to reduce support for terrorism.

There are several ways that an analyst can perform a theme analysis. In a previous article,[47] I used a theme analytic method that combined the systematic labeling of communicative excerpts[48] and the organization of these excerpts[49] to identify higher-order, latent concepts within terrorist narrative data. This method includes four fundamental steps:[50]

Step 1: *Obtain a general feel for the tone, style, and meaning of the terrorist narratives by carefully reading them at least twice.* Before beginning the process of formally analyzing the terrorist narrative data, analysts should first read or watch the narratives to become generally familiar with them. When the analyst reads or watches the narratives for a second time, he/she should more carefully note the language used in them and how that language may promote the terrorist group's ideology or actual engagement in violence. By immersing oneself in terrorist narratives before systematically analyzing them, analysts can develop a nuanced understanding of the narratives and what the terrorist group hopes to accomplish with them.

Step 2: *Read the terrorist narratives a third time and generate an initial list of codes that relate to excerpts that relate to the terrorist group's ideology (or are otherwise important).* Codes are labels attached to portions of narrative data that allow the analyst to organize that data in a meaningful way.[51] Codes can be used to categorize excerpts of any length, provided every excerpt classified under a code are all similar somehow. For instance, if an analyst was reading ISIS stories about the aforementioned battle in Dabiq, that analyst may encounter a single sentence describing a fighter's use of a rocket-propelled grenade, as well as an entire paragraph describing another fighter's use of a Kalashnikov assault rifle. Although these excerpts are different in terms of length, they both relate to ISIS fighters' use of weapons to repel enemy forces. As such, they could both be placed in a category called "Weapon Use."

Step 3: *If some of the codes are similar, consolidate them to reduce their overall number.* After generating a preliminary list of codes that categorize the language within the terrorist narratives, the analyst may find that some codes are somewhat similar in terms of the content they describe. For example, analyzing ISIS narratives may produce three different codes, respectively advocating for the execution of homosexuals, Jews, and Shi'ite Muslims. Depending on the research questions guiding the analysis of the narratives, the analyst may reasonably consolidate these three separate codes (i.e., "Execution of Homosexuals," "Execution of Jews," and "Execution of Shi'ite Muslims") into a single code called "Execution of 'Undesirables.'" Merging the codes in this way makes the terrorist narrative data more manageable and easier to interpret before organizing them into overarching themes.

Step 4: *Sort the remaining codes into overarching themes to identify higher-order concepts within the terrorist narratives.* Once all overlapping codes have been consolidated, the analyst can then evaluate the remaining codes to determine which fit together in a meaningful way. These codes are then placed into conceptual categories; these categories are the themes that comprise the terrorist narrative data. The analyst should make sure that (a) all the codes within each theme are conceptually similar, and (b) all the themes have identifiable differences.

Once the analyst has completed these four steps, he/she will have generated a useful set of themes that describe the fundamental ideas embedded in the terrorist narratives. Depending on the analyst's goals, however, it might be useful to quantify the data to illustrate which ideas are most prevalent within the narrative data. By determining which themes are most strongly represented within narratives, the analyst can develop counter-narratives that target those themes. In this case, the analyst should also perform the following:

Step 5 (Optional): *Quantify the thematic elements of the terrorist narratives.* To identify the themes that the terrorist group emphasizes most heavily in their narratives, the analyst can tally the number of times each theme appears within them. The analyst can do this him/herself, but a more reliable method involves the use of two independent coders. If the analyst opts to use coders to quantify the themes in the terrorist narratives, he/she should provide the coders with the codes identified in Step 2 (and possibly Step 3) and instruct the coders to find excerpts of text within the narratives that correspond to those codes (and therefore the themes under which those codes are categorized). After both coders have made their decisions, these decisions should then be compared for consistency (Cohen's kappa[52] is a good indicator of intercoder reliability). Disagreements between coders can be resolved by reviewing the discrepancies, discussing the reasoning behind the coders decisions, and making a mutual decision about the presence of a code/theme in the narratives.[53]

After completing these four (or five) steps, the analyst will have generated a list of themes. The analyst will also have a general idea about the extent to which each theme appears in the terrorist narratives. These themes represent the central ideas represented within the terrorist narratives. The next section contains guidelines for constructing counter-narratives that challenge these ideas.

Developing Counter-Narratives Based on Identified Themes

Ultimately, the goal of this chapter is to describe a comprehensive method for developing individual narratives that deter support for terrorism. Although past work in terrorism and communication studies has not previously provided such a method, some researchers (led by the Consortium for Strategic Communication at Arizona State University) have provided some insight into how we can fight "systems of stories" that underpin terrorist ideologies.[54] As one of the foremost authorities on counter-narratives, communication expert Bud Goodall once argued that systems of stories can be useful for contradicting politically extremist messages by providing ideological counterpoints to those messages.[55] Jeffry Halverson and his colleagues similarly described ways that "master narratives" that promote terrorist ideologies can be attacked.[56] However, whereas this past work focused on "systems of stories" as viable tools for promoting (or inhibiting) radicalization, this chapter focuses on the effectiveness of more localized, individual narratives for these purposes. That said, existing research related to the former has significant implications for the pursuit of the latter. As John Horgan and I argued in the article on which this chapter is based, "the ideas that comprise both localized terrorist narratives and master narratives are similar, and can therefore be attacked similarly, but at different levels of abstraction."[57] Therefore, we can draw from past work on "systems of stories" and "master narratives" to offer some logical recommendations for developing counter-narratives intended to challenge terrorist narratives.

Recommendation 1: *Do not reinforce the themes that appear in the terrorist narratives.* Although this recommendation may seem obvious, it can be very easy to unintentionally reinforce the themes that appear in terrorist narratives through careless language use.[58] For example, before the emergence of ISIS as the most potent source of terrorist propaganda in the Middle East, al-Qaeda dominated the narrative landscape. One of the central themes in the al-Qaeda narratives is the notion that Muslims are under attack everywhere in the world.[59] By invoking this idea in their narratives, al-Qaeda intends to communicate to Muslims that non-Muslims in general (and American forces in particular) seek to wage war on Islam itself. In the days following the 9/11 terrorist attacks on the United States, then-President George W. Bush laid the foundation for the impending fight against al-Qaeda by claiming that "this *crusade* ... is going to take a while."[60] Though this statement was not presented in a counter-narrative, it nonetheless illustrates how careless language can inadvertently strengthen the arguments intrinsic to terrorist narratives. In making this seemingly innocuous statement about the effort needed to combat terrorism, Bush may have suggested to Muslims that the fight against al-Qaeda would be akin to the historical wars between Muslims and Christians – one of the very themes that drives the al-Qaeda ideology.

To avoid reinforcing the themes that comprise the targeted terrorist narratives, the analyst should carefully review the results of the theme analysis to determine which themes should be avoided in the counter-narratives.

Recommendation 2: *Disrupt analogies that equate elements of terrorist narratives to real-world events.* One of the most enduring characteristics of terrorist narratives is their tendency to connect elements of terrorist ideologies to events that occur in the real world. Although terrorist groups often frame their narratives as accurate reflections of real-world events, there is often significant deviation between what they say and what actually occurs. These inconsistencies represent opportunities to emphasize the hollowness of the terrorist narratives and the predictions they make. That said, whether counter-narratives are effective at disrupting analogies in terrorist narratives depends on the nature of the analogy. In his work on analogical argumentation, Cameron Shelley developed a taxonomy to guide what kind of counter-arguments can be made against specific analogical claims.[61] Shelley's work suggests that counter-arguments made against terrorist messages that liken narrative events to real-world events should be based on two questions. First, is the analogy

Table 3.1 *Counter-narrative strategies in response to analogies in terrorist narratives*

Counter-narrative strategy	Counter-argument	Strategy objective
False analogy	Although the terrorist analogy seems legitimate, it falls apart under closer inspection	Demonstrate the differences between the objects in the terrorist narrative and the real world
Misanalogy	The terrorist analogy is wrong, and there is another analogy that has a stronger basis in reality	Develop a better analogy that directly challenges that analogy in the terrorist narrative
Disanalogy	The terrorist analogy appears true, but there are demonstrable facts that contradict its structure	Highlight the characteristics that the objects being compared *would* share if the analogy were valid, but do not
Counter-analogy	Although the terrorist analogy seems to be legitimate, there is another analogy that more accurately describes the same scenario	Use a different comparison point to make a claim about the target that contradicts the original claim

in the terrorist narrative valid? This question relates to whether a terrorist narrative accurately describes real-world occurrences. Second, is the analyst's goal to destroy the terrorist narrative's analogical argument outright, or replace the terrorist narrative with a different idea? Based on the answers to these questions, the developer of a counter-narrative should use one of four strategies: highlighting a false analogy, using a misanalogy, attacking a disanalogy, or offering a counter-analogy. Table 3.1 describes these four strategies and how to employ them.

With these strategies in mind, we can begin to consider which would be the most effective. To this end, Figure 3.1 offers guidelines for determining which strategy to use. Halverson and his colleagues used this taxonomy to recommend methods for challenging systems of stories presented by terrorist groups.[62] It can be equally useful for challenging singular narratives.

Using an earlier example, ISIS narratives have long contended that the group would engage in a real-world battle with enemy forces in Dabiq, Syria, and that the battle would precipitate an apocalypse out of which a new Islamic caliphate would rise.[63] There was a time when it seemed that this prophecy was coming to fruition. In October of 2016, Syrian rebels backed by the Turkish military entered Dabiq and engaged in a short

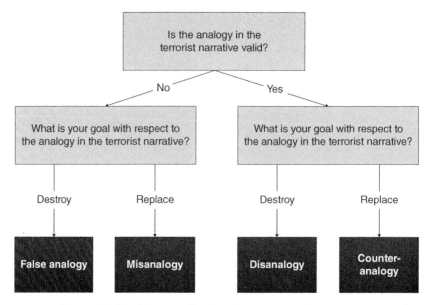

Figure 3.1 Decision-tree for choosing a strategy in response to terrorist narrative analogies

battle against ISIS forces there. Despite ISIS narratives likening the battle to the start of Armageddon and the new Islamic caliphate, Dajjal did not appear, the apocalypse did not occur, and the group was quickly routed from its positions. These outcomes showed the analogy in the ISIS apocalypse narrative to be invalid. Depending on the goals of the analyst, effective counter-narratives designed to challenge this narrative could (a) highlight the differences between the ISIS narrative and what actually happened in Dabiq (i.e., the false analogy strategy), or (b) liken ISIS's losses in Dabiq to another case of catastrophic failure that will resonate with the target audience (i.e., the misanalogy strategy).

Recommendation 3: *Disrupt thematic binaries that appear in the terrorist narratives.* Another consistent feature of terrorist narratives is the presence of binary comparisons that place the group's ideology and/or members in direct conflict with another group or institution.[64] When a terrorist narrative describes the terrorist group and its members as the opposite of some sinister "enemy," it characterizes the group as being on the unmistakable side of good. For instance, many jihadist groups describe their terrorist activities as a necessary struggle between *mu'minūn* (true believers of Islam) and *kuffār* (non-believers, including non-jihadist Muslims). In these narratives, members of the jihadist groups are portrayed as soldiers dedicated to the defense of Islam, while the non-believers they target with violence are depicted as threats to the truth. In this way, these jihadist narratives frame the group's activities as part of a rightful struggle against lies, falsehood, and apostasy. This kind of simple binary comparison is not unique to jihadist narratives. They also appear in the narratives of white supremacists (e.g., whites vs. minorities), sovereign citizens (freedom vs. government control), left-wing revolutionaries (e.g., the benefits of socialism vs. the evils of capitalism), anti-abortionists (e.g., soldiers of God vs. murderers of the innocent), and many other types of terrorist groups.

Despite the attractive simplicity of these kinds of binary comparisons, they "ignore, repress, or obscure the diverse 'micronarratives' that were a real part of history and resist[ed] or contested such a characterization."[65] In other words, the binary comparisons that appear in terrorist narratives deliberately omit information that would show the comparison to be false. Terrorist groups benefit from characterizing their actions in binary terms because it prevents their audiences from sympathizing or identifying with their enemies, which would in turn reduce support for the group. Given this, counter-narratives that reveal some "gray areas" in the binary portrayals presented by terrorist groups can help to discredit those portrayals, the narratives in which they appear, and the terrorist group(s) that designed them.

For instance, counter-narratives designed to challenge the dominant binary comparison in white supremacist narratives could contain scenes that highlight similarities between the struggles of white and black middle-class families. This depiction would weaken the "white vs. black" motif by showing that "villains" of the terrorist narrative (i.e., African Americans) are not as different from audience members (i.e., white readers) as the group would have them believe. This, in turn, can reduce audience support for the terrorist group's characterization of its purported enemies and the violent actions it takes against them.

Recommendation 4: *Comprise counter-narratives with themes that provide an alternative representation of the terrorist narrative's target(s).* As with any other narratives, terrorist narratives often feature characters portrayed as villains. By describing specific characters in this way, terrorist narratives are designed to cast real-world individuals and organizations as enemies of the group, its cause, and its supporters. To garner support for the group's actions, terrorist narratives often depict their villains as threats to innocents, thereby justifying the group's fight against them. For instance, on the website of the Animal Liberation Front is a link to an image from a book entitled *Animal Liberation: A Graphic Guide.* The image is a stylized, comic-book-based narrative that depicts a scientist cutting into a living dog for research purposes.[66] In this narrative, animal researchers are cast as bloodthirsty monsters who take pleasure in the suffering of innocent animals. By illustrating animal researchers in this way, the ALF justifies its violent actions against vivisectors and animal research.

To challenge the negative portrayals of the "villains" in terrorist narratives, counter-narratives should provide audiences with alternative views of those villains to cast them in a more positive light. One method for doing so involves dismissing the characterization of villain characters by having those characters perform more compassionate actions. Although this strategy may be somewhat useful, it is unlikely to be persuasive by itself. Instead, counter-narratives should also leverage the persuasive power of identification and parasocial interaction (see above) to promote a more positive assessment of the terrorist group's described enemies. To do so, developers of counter-narratives should depict villain characters in terms that highlight their similarities with audience members. This can make the audience more sympathetic to those characters, thereby undermining the terrorist group's justifications for their actions.

Recommendation 5: *Comprise counter-narratives with themes that highlight the contradictions in the terrorist narratives and how the terrorists act with respect to those narratives.* Terrorist communication expert Steve Corman once argued that there are two ways that terrorist narratives can be contested on the basis of how they deviate from the group's actions.[67] First, a terrorist narrative can be attacked for having poor coherence; that is, counter-arguments against the terrorist narrative can show that it makes no structural sense. Counter-narratives that use this strategy would show, for example, how the cause–effect relationships depicted in the terrorist narrative are not realistic. The second strategy involves challenging the themes in the terrorist narrative on the basis of its *fidelity* – the degree to which the events in the narrative would seem realistically consistent with the group's ideology. Messages intended to challenge a terrorist narrative based on its lack of fidelity may describe how the group's actions actually deviate from the ideals the group claims to live by.

For instance, the Army of God (AOG) – a Christian, anti-abortion terrorist group – has engaged in several violent attacks against abortion clinics, doctors, and police since 1982.[68] The group's narratives are based on claims that the group's violent actions are intended to protect human life and to carry out the will of God. To support these claims, many of the messages (including narratives) on the AOG's website are flanked by biblical verses.[69]

It is clear from the group's website, as well as the propaganda contained on it, that the AOG puts great stock in the Bible as a guide for proper behavior. With this in mind, it becomes possible to demonstrate the hypocrisy of the group. There are several Bible verses that advocate forgiveness[70] and love[71] for one's fellow man, regardless of the sins he is guilty of. Counter-narratives intended to challenge messages produced by the AOG would do well to reference such verses. Although biblical references are surely open to interpretation, showing how the group's own source for guidance speaks out against its actions can reveal the contradictions between the AOG's ideals and actions.

Some programs designed to reduce the risk of violent radicalization have adopted this approach with some success. For example, Imam Mohamed Magid of the All Dulles Area Muslim Society has used verses from the Qur'an to reveal the inconsistencies in ISIS's interpretation of Islam. His efforts have been useful in keeping young Muslims from traveling to Syria or Iraq to join the group.[72]

∴

This list of recommendations should not be considered the final word on how to properly develop counter-narratives meant to challenge terrorist propaganda. Depending on the nature of the terrorist narratives being targeted, effective counter-narratives can take several different forms and be characterized by several different features. As the study of terrorist narratives moves forward, our knowledge about the form and style of effective counter-narratives will continue to evolve. Still, these five recommendations provide a foundation on which counter-narratives of all types can be built.

As mentioned above, however, constructing effective counter-narratives is only half of the process for challenging terrorist narratives. An analyst could develop a counter-narrative that is perfectly tailored to the narrative and audience it targets, but without an effective method for distributing that counter-narrative, it would be worthless. The next section offers some suggestions for disseminating counter-narratives so they are most likely to have their desired counter-radicalizing effects.

Disseminating Counter-Narratives

As evidenced by the variety of chapters in this book, there are several ways to use communication as a tool for preventing or countering violent extremism (P/CVE). However, a specific strength of counter-narratives is the ability for the author to control perceptions of the counter-narrative's source. In some cases, it may be useful for a counter-narrative to come from an ideological expert. In other cases, it may be beneficial to hide the source of the counter-narrative altogether. Which dissemination strategy to use depends on a number of factors, perhaps the most important of which is the culture in which the message is disseminated.

Some cultures hold independence, individualism, and responsibility for one's own actions in high regard (e.g., the United States, some Western European nations).[73] As such, individuals in these cultures are more likely to be persuaded by counter-narratives that are not dictated to them by authority figures. In contrast, other cultures place value on authoritative leadership and the strong bonds that form between leaders and followers (e.g., East Asia, Muslim cultures).[74] Individuals in these cultures value the guidance provided by authority figures, and are therefore more likely to be influenced by counter-narratives communicated to them by respected leaders.[75] Given that cultures differ in their reverence for (and obedience to) authority figures, it is critical for analysts to first recognize the cultural environment the target audience inhabits before deciding on a strategy for disseminating a counter-narrative.

In this section, I offer a few methods for distributing counter-narratives to different kinds of audiences. The first method, which relates to using online communication tools to cultivate trust among Web users exposed to terrorist narratives, would be more useful for distributing counter-narratives in cultures that value independence. The lack of an identified author for the counter-narrative or a specified authority figure preserves the independence and autonomy of the target audience. The second strategy concerns efforts to make a counter-narrative "go viral." Like the first strategy, viral messages tend not to have authority figures associated with them. So, the second method presented here can also be useful for target audiences in cultures that value self-reliance and independence. The final method relates to working with trusted others to distribute counter-narratives. In communities that value guidance from established authority figures, ideological leaders can be powerful partners in distributing counter-narratives, as the authority granted to these leaders makes them particularly influential. This influence can be leveraged to provide credence to the counter-narratives they assist in distributing.

With this in mind, consider the following methods for disseminating counter-narratives to audiences at risk for violent radicalization.

Cultivating Trust Online

Research into how terrorists use the Internet has recently turned towards how they use social media (e.g., Facebook) to contact potential followers or use secure communication channels (e.g., Telegram) to recruit others and discuss operations.[76] As the nature of terrorist communication continues to evolve, this kind of work is critical. But, there are still many groups that maintain websites for communicating terrorist ideologies to would-be recruits and the public at large.

For instance, the white nationalist Stormfront website comprises discussion forums on which active members of hate groups can directly interact with other white nationalists and neo-Nazis. Individuals who are not hardliners, but are simply curious about these ideologies can register for the site and interact as well. As Horgan and I argued, the popularity of Stormfront and the sheer number of narratives on its forums make it a "ground-zero" where counter-narratives might be effective.[77] The websites of many other terrorist groups (as well as some social media sites) offer similar communicative channels on which visitors to the sites can interact.

Although counter-narratives that appear "behind enemy lines" are unlikely to persuade the hardcore believers of the ideology, this limitation does not completely temper the usefulness of counter-narratives in these contexts. In many cases, casual browsers – visitors to the site that do not overtly express any dedication to the group's ideology – comprise the majority of a terrorist site's users. Consider that as of early 2016, about 296,000 users had contributed to discussions on the Stormfront forums since the site's creation in 1996. That may seem like a large number until you consider that more than two million users visited the site *in 2014 and 2015 alone*. Put plainly, only a very small proportion of visitors to Stormfront comment in the forums, and an even smaller proportion express overtly racist or nationalist views. Though it is impossible to gauge an individual's attitudes because of an activity they did *not* engage in (i.e., espousing a terrorist ideology), casual browsers and benign posters are likely to be more susceptible to persuasion by counter-narratives than hardliners.

For counter-narratives to be persuasive, however, they must be presented as if they are coming from a legitimate source. This means that in the context of online communication channels organized by terrorist groups, they should be presented as if from a genuine member of the online community in which it is distributed. If a counter-narrative is presented by someone perceived as an outsider, or worse, an enemy, it will likely arouse psychological reactance and its message will be dismissed. So, officials and analysts that use these online communication channels to distribute counter-narratives would do well to cultivate trust with some members of the community by developing friendly relationships with them while maintaining the anonymity that online communication channels afford. After developing these relationships with other members of the forums, it might become possible to respond to overt terrorist narratives with subtle counter-narratives that gently refute the points in the terrorist narrative.[78] This will require a careful consideration of the dynamics of the community, the relationships among its members, and estimations of how well-trusted the counter-narrative distributor is within that community.

As mentioned above, hardline members of online community are probably unlikely to be persuaded by any counter-message presented within it. In fact, there is likely to be pushback against the counter-narrative and the person that presented it. However, casual browsers, benign posters, and the mildly curious might be more prone to persuasion, making them the true targets of the counter-narrative.

Despite the usefulness of this approach, it comes with significant risk. Posing as a member of an online community to distribute counter-messaging material is entirely contingent on the message distributor maintaining anonymity. If the counter-narrative distributor is revealed as having ulterior motives, it risks confirming the group's messages about supposed enemies of the group, particularly if part of the group's ideology relates to secretive government forces, covert enemy agents, or other sneaky or nefarious outgroups. Worse, the revelation of "enemy" forces working within the group's own communication medium could cause strong psychological reactance among those the counter-narrative is meant to persuade. If this happens, audiences could be put at greater risk for violent radicalization than if no counter-messaging strategy was attempted at all.

For these reasons, the use of this strategy should only be considered if the developer of the counter-narrative (a) has a strong grasp on the nature of the communication medium within which the community interacts, and (b) is absolutely certain that their identity will not be revealed. Given that these two requirements are often difficult to guarantee, this strategy is the least promising of the three presented here.

Luckily, there are two other strategies that do not require cloak-and-dagger tactics related to message sourcing. One of these strategies is based on disconnecting a counter-narrative from its source altogether and letting the infinite space of the Internet reveal the message to those at risk for violent radicalization. In short, this strategy promotes a counter-narrative's online virality.

Encouraging Counter-Narratives to "Go Viral"

The degree to which contemporary terrorist groups and their supporters communicate online[79] demands that any strategy for distributing counter-narratives should seek to spread the messages through online interfaces. It follows that the effectiveness of counter-narratives distributed via online channels at least partially depends on how much Web users choose to engage with and/or share those counter-narratives – that is, whether and how much the counter-narrative(s) go "viral." Communication experts, statisticians, and probability researchers have only recently begun to explore message virality, but their early findings provide insight into the factors that render a message more likely to go viral.

Work on message virality has generally shown that there are three elements that affect whether something is shared online: message characteristics, audience characteristics, and socio-structural factors. First, several studies have shown that a message's content influences whether it goes viral. These studies have demonstrated that viral content tends to be practically useful, interesting to its initial audiences,[80] or contain messages with unexpected or surprising information.[81] Other research shows that content that features multiple pictures, has a famous author, or is released early in the day on Fridays or Saturdays is more likely to go viral than content that does not.[82]

Second, many researchers have shown that certain message recipients are more likely to spread messages online and/or promote their virality. For instance, individuals who are prone to "high-activation emotions" like awe, anger, happiness, or anxiety are more likely to share messages that arouse these emotions.[83] In addition, individuals who are motivated to use social media outlets like Facebook or Twitter for social interaction are more inclined to share content than individuals who use those outlets for other reasons.[84]

Finally, there are several factors related to the social contexts in which a message is distributed that affects whether it goes viral. Research on these factors has shown that the features of the communication medium in which a message appears influences whether others will share it. For example, messages that appear close in proximity to mechanisms for sharing them (e.g., "share" buttons) or provide the opportunity for online communities to engage with the messages[85] are more likely to go viral than messages that do not have these characteristics. In addition, the size of the social network in which a message initially appears[86] and the number of social networks for which the message is important[87] also affect the likelihood that a message will go viral.

Although the research findings related to online virality are bound by the methods that produce them and the contexts in which they were performed, they give us some preliminary insight into how developers and distributors of counter-narratives can increase the likelihood that the messages "go viral." These studies collectively suggest that counter-narratives should:

- Include practically useful information (e.g., instructions for non-violent political activity) presented in a novel or surprising storyline;
- Be distributed early in the day on Fridays and Saturdays;
- Be initially distributed among those with a proclivity for strong emotions, use social media websites primarily to interact with others, or have large online social networks (this will require the use of audience analysis techniques[88]); and/or
- Be presented in close proximity to mechanisms for sharing the counter-narratives (e.g., "share" buttons).

Despite the potential utility of these preliminary suggestions, there remains significant uncertainty surrounding the possibility of *causing* a message to "go viral." In addition, predicting whether a certain audience will share a counter-narrative depends heavily on that audience's characteristics. It follows that any developer/distributor of a counter-narrative will need to analyze its audiences very carefully. This can require significant time and resources.

Because of these potential hurdles to counter-narrative virality, it remains important that developers of counter-narratives seek out other methods for distributing their messages. One of the most promising avenues for doing so involves working with individuals who are well-trusted within the communities in which the counter-narratives are to be distributed.

Partnering with Credible Others

The two previous strategies may be effective for distributing counter-narratives in response to groups that operate within cultures that value independence and free thought. Consuming a counter-narrative that was obtained of one's own volition – whether through online interactions with others or by engaging with a viral message – does not threaten a person's sense of freedom to act as he/she sees fit. However, to challenge the narratives of terrorist groups that operate in cultures that value leadership and authority, it might be more useful to distribute counter-narratives with the assistance of sources that are respected by target recruits.

In these cases, it might be beneficial to partner with individuals with expertise regarding the terrorist group's ideology, familiarity with the community the group claims to defend, respect among the group's targeted recruits, or experience with the group's operations. These kinds of individuals can serve as "vessels through which to distribute counter-narratives."[89] Examples of these kinds of individuals include past extremists that have maintained relationships with active members of their former groups; those who have experienced disillusionment and disappointment as a result of supporting the group; members of the community that the terrorist group claims to represent; and ideological experts that may support the group's ideas, but not its violent methods.

First, former members of terrorist groups that have maintained social relationships with still-active members can be valuable links between the developers of counter-narratives and those at which they are targeted.[90] Many former terrorists have revealed that despite having become disillusioned with the terrorist group's ideology, they have maintained relationships with individuals who are still involved. This is unsurprising, given that for many individuals, their introduction to the group is through close friends, mutual acquaintances, or family members.[91] These links are difficult to sever; leaving an organization (even a violent one) does not necessarily diminish an individual's affinity for his/her comrades.

In addition, many former members of terrorist groups have expressed the desire to help other members quit the group or prevent new recruits from joining the group altogether.[92] Individuals who have maintained social relationships with active members and are sympathetic to counter-radicalization efforts would be well positioned to distribute counter-narratives to reduce support for the terrorist group. Given their previous experiences, they may be perceived as more credible and trustworthy than other potential counter-narrative sources.[93] There are already some institutionalized programs in which former extremists work to promote disengagement from violent groups (e.g., Life After Hate);[94] these may be valuable avenues for distributing counter-narratives tailored to their intended audiences.

Related to this, there is a smaller group of disillusioned individuals who have been seduced by the group's promises, though perhaps not recruited as fighters. Many extremist groups – particularly those that seek to build communities governed by their ideologies (e.g., ISIS) – recruit individuals to support the group in roles other than fighting. These individuals are just as susceptible to disillusionment by participating in the group's activities as active fighters. For example, many women in Western nations (e.g., France, the UK) have left their home countries to support ISIS in Iraq and Syria. When recruited, these women were promised a pure caliphate – an Islamic paradise in which they could help Muslim children through charity work, receive free healthcare, or start families away from the *kuffār*. However, in contrast to the utopian Islamic caliphate they were promised, their lives in Iraq and/or Syria were anything but beautiful. ISIS provided little to no infrastructure to support them or their needs. They were expected to marry ISIS fighters after a 20-minute conversation. Some women were even used purely as sex slaves for the group's male members.[95] After experiencing the "caliphate" firsthand, these women wished to flee Iraq and Syria and return to their homes.

Though these women were not recruited as traditional members of ISIS (i.e., fighters), their firsthand experience and deep disillusionment with the realities of supporting ISIS makes them powerful conduits through which counter-narratives can be told. These kinds of "formers" – individuals who were victimized by the group after being recruited – have great potential for counter-narrative distribution. They were there; they know the horrors of supporting a terrorist group. Given their firsthand experiences, their stories may be useful in helping others from making the same mistakes they did.

Second, respected members of the community that the group claims to represent are critical for the rejection of terrorist narratives and the acceptance of counter-narratives that advocate against violence. The importance of community support in challenging terrorist narratives has been known to researchers for some time. For instance, Corman and Schiefelbein recognized that the success of any strategy intended to challenge terrorist messaging would require the inclusion of the Muslim community from which jihadist groups recruit.[96] They argued that members of the Muslim community are in prime position to recognize the elements of Islam that jihadist strategies and actions contradict. In this way, peaceful members of Muslim communities can identify the hypocrisies of terrorist narratives better than nearly anyone.

Many ideological leaders in some communities have already spoken out against terrorists and their narratives. For example, the aforementioned Imam Magid – director of the All Dulles Area Muslim Society – has been active in speaking to Muslim communities about the dangers of ISIS messaging. His counter-radicalization work involves organizing conferences and speaking one-on-one with individuals who are targeted by ISIS for recruitment. Imam Magid is well respected in the Muslim community in Washington, and has successfully persuaded several young men from being seduced by ISIS propaganda.[97] Developers of counter-narratives should work closely with individuals like Imam Magid not only as conduits through which their messages can be delivered to communities at risk for violent radicalization, but also because these individuals are intimately familiar with those targeted by terrorist narratives. This familiarity makes them experts about what content will resonate most strongly with target audiences.

Finally, there may be cases in which it is necessary to reveal the distributor of a counter-narrative to its intended audience. In these cases, it would be advisable to work with individuals who may agree with the tenets of the ideology that comprises terrorist narratives, but not the violent means by which they are realized.[98] In addition to being well known within the community in which the counter-narrative is to be distributed, these individuals have the added credibility of supporting the terrorist group's goals, if not its methods. Their philosophical consistency with those at risk for radicalization can disarm resistance to persuasion among target audiences. However, it must be certain that the counter-narrative distributor is clear in his/her rejection of violence as a valid form of pursuing ideological objectives. Failure to be clear in this regard risks validating the terrorist narrative, theoretically increasing the chances that target audiences will accept it.

∴

As with the guidelines for developing counter-narratives, this list of recommendations should not be considered the final word on message distribution. As the study of violent radicalization and communication moves forward, researchers may identify factors that influence the effectiveness of these recommendations or develop other distribution methods altogether. Still, these recommendations are reinforced by empirical evidence and represent a good starting point for effectively disseminating counter-narratives. Terrorism experts should continue to conduct systematic research to develop recommendations like these. Otherwise, we risk using time and resources to tailor counter-narratives for individuals that will never bother listening to them – essentially leaving us to scream stories into a void.

Conclusions

Timothy McVeigh was strapped to a gurney and executed by lethal injection on the morning of June 11, 2001. He can't write any more letters;[99] he can't give any more interviews to inquisitive journalists;[100] he can't provide any more justifications for his terrible actions. McVeigh is gone, and in his wake, he has left a legacy of violence and hate. But beyond the destruction McVeigh caused, there are lessons to be learned for the ongoing fight against violent extremism.

McVeigh was put to death for actions that were, in part, inspired by a story. His reading of *The Turner Diaries* contributed to the adoption of an ideology that led to his massacre of 168 innocent people. Earlier, I asked a seemingly simple question: How could reading a book inspire violence of that magnitude? The answer to this question can be found in communication research.

Stated very plainly, narratives are persuasive. They affect our belief systems,[101] our emotional states,[102] our behavioral patterns,[103] our health,[104] and our responses to the world around us.[105] Unfortunately, they also have the power to impart dangerous beliefs and attitudes to those that would use those ideas for violent ends. However, just as narratives can be used to spread ideas that are consistent with terrorist ideologies, they can also be used to challenge those same ideas.

Terrorism researchers have come to recognize the potential of counter-narratives for preventing or countering violent radicalization. That said, we are still very early in our efforts at using counter-narratives to fight terrorist propaganda, and so far, these attempts have not been based on scientific evidence. This chapter is meant to change that pattern. The recommendations that appear here are based on years of scientific investigation. In the future, analysts, policymakers, and academics can use these recommendations to construct and disseminate counter-narratives that help prevent the next Timothy McVeigh from hurting others because of a story told by terrorists.

Notes

1 Andrew Gumbel and Roger G. Charles, *Oklahoma City: What the Investigation Missed – and Why It Still Matters* (New York: William Morrow, 2012), p. 170.
2 H. Porter Abbott, *The Cambridge Introduction to Narrative*, 2nd edition (New York: Cambridge University Press, 2008).
3 Roland Barthes, "Introduction to the Structural Analysis of Narrative," in *A Barthes Reader*, ed. Susan Sontag, 251–295 (New York: Hill & Wang, 1982); Shlomith Rimmon-Kenan, *Narrative Fiction: Contemporary Poetics* (London: Routledge, 1996).
4 Gérard Genette, *Figures of Literary Discourse* (New York: Columbia University Press, 1982), p. 127.
5 Walter R. Fisher, *Human Communication as Narration: Toward a Philosophy of Reason, Value, and Action* (Columbia, SC: University of South Carolina Press, 1987), p. 24.
6 Susana Onega and José Ángel Garcia Landa, eds., *Narratology* (New York: Routledge, 2014), p. 6; Brian Richardson, *Narrative Dynamics: Essays on Time, Plot, Closure, and Frames* (Columbus, OH: Ohio State University Press, 2002).
7 Marie-Laure Ryan, "Toward a Definition of Narrative," in *The Cambridge Companion to Narrative*, ed. David Herman, 22–36 (New York: Cambridge University Press, 2007), p. 29.
8 Jennifer B. Gray and Nancy G. Harrington, "Narrative and Framing: A Test of an Integrated Message Strategy in the Exercise Context," *Journal of Health Communication* 16, no. 3 (2011): 264–281.
9 Dean C. Kazoleas, "A Comparison of the Persuasive Effectiveness of Qualitative versus Quantitative Evidence: A Test of Explanatory Hypotheses," *Communication Quarterly* 4, no. 1 (1993): 40–50.

10 Gabriele Prati, Luca Pietrantoni, and Bruna Zani, "Influenza Vaccination: The Persuasiveness of Messages Among People Aged 65 Years and Older," *Health Communication* 2, no. 5 (2012): 413–420.

11 For examples, see Gray and Harrington, "Narrative and Framing"; Holley A. Wilkin, Thomas W. Valente, Sheila Murphy, Michael J. Cody, Grace Huang, and Vicki Beck, "Does Entertainment-Education Work with Latinos in the United States? Identification and the Effects of a Telenovela Breast Cancer Storyline," *Journal of Health Communication* 1, no. 5 (2007): 455–469. Also see Kurt Braddock and James P. Dillard, "Meta-Analytic Evidence for the Persuasive Effect of Narratives on Beliefs, Attitudes, Intentions, and Behaviors," *Communication Monographs* 83, no. 4 (2016): 446–467 (pp. 459ff.) for meta-analytic data regarding narrative's effect on intentions.

12 For examples, see Kathryn Greene and Laura S. Brinn, "Messages Influencing College Women's Tanning Bed Use: Statistical versus Narrative Evidence Format and a Self-Assessment to Increase Perceived Susceptibility," *Journal of Health Communication* 8, no. 5 (2003): 443–461; Marijke Lemal and Jan Van den Bulck, "Testing the Effectiveness of a Skin Cancer Narrative in Promoting Positive Health Behavior: A Pilot Study," *Preventative Medicine* 51, no. 2 (2010): 178–181. Also see Braddock and Dillard, "Meta-Analytic Evidence for the Persuasive Effect of Narratives," p. 460 for meta-analytic data regarding narrative's effect on behaviors.

13 Anat Gesser-Edelsburg and Ronit Endevelt, "An Entertainment-Education Study of Stereotypes and Prejudice against Women: An Evaluation of *Fat Pig*," *Health Education Journal* 70, no. 4 (2011): 374–382.

14 Edward Schiappa, Peter B. Gregg, and Dean E. Hewes, "Can a Television Series Change Attitudes about Death? A Study of College Students and *Six Feet Under*," *Death Studies* 28, no. 5 (2004): 459–474.

15 For examples, see Mike Allen and Raymond W. Preiss, "Comparing the Persuasiveness of Narrative and Statistical Evidence using Meta-Analysis," *Communication Research Reports* 14 (1997): 125–131; E. James Baesler and Judee K. Burgoon, "The Temporal Effects of Story and Statistical Evidence on Belief Change," *Communication Research* 21, no. 5 (1994): 582–602; Jenifer E. Kopfman, Sandi W. Smith, James K. Ah Yun, and Annemarie Hodges, "Affective and Cognitive Reactions to Narrative versus Statistical Evidence Organ Donation Messages," *Journal of Applied Communication Research* 26, no. 3 (1998): 279–300; Richard F. Yalch and Rebecca Elmore-Yalch, "The Effect of Numbers on the Route to Persuasion," *Journal of Consumer Research* 11 (1984): 522–527.

16 Kurt Braddock, "Fighting Words: The Persuasive Effect of Online Extremist Narratives on the Radicalization Process," PhD dissertation, The Pennsylvania State University, 2012, pp. 76–119; Braddock and Dillard, "Meta-Analytic Evidence for the Persuasive Effect of Narratives."

17 Rick Busselle and Helena Bilandzic, "Fictionality and Perceived Realism in Experiencing Stories: A Model of Narrative Comprehension and Engagement," *Communication Theory* 18 (2008): 255–280.

18 Emily Moyer-Gusé, "Toward a Theory of Entertainment Persuasion: Explaining the Persuasive Effects of Entertainment-Education Messages," *Communication Theory* 18 (2008): 407–425.

19 Melanie C. Green and Timothy C. Brock, "In the Mind's Eye: Transportation-Imagery Model of Narrative Persuasion," in *Narrative Impact: Social and Cognitive Foundations*, ed. Melanie C. Green, Jeffrey J. Strange, and Timothy C. Brock, 315–341 (Mahwah, NJ: Lawrence Erlbaum Associates, 2002).

20 Howard Levanthal, "Findings and Theory in the Study of Fear Communications," in *Advances in Experimental Social Psychology*, Volume 5, ed. Leonard Berkowitz, 119–186 (New York: Academic Press, 1970); Moyer-Gusé, "Toward a Theory of Entertainment Persuasion."

21 Jack W. Brehm, *A Theory of Psychological Reactance* (New York: Academic Press, 1966).

22 Michael Burgoon, Eusebio Alvaro, Joseph Grandpre, and Michael Voloudakis, "Revisiting the Theory of Psychological Reactance," in *The Persuasion Handbook: Theory and Practice*, ed. James Price Dillard and Michael Pfau, 213–232 (Thousand Oaks, CA: Sage, 2002).

23 Wendy L. McGrane, Eric B. Allely, and Frank J. Toth, "The Use of Interactive Media for HIV/AIDS Prevention in the Military Community," *Military Medicine* 155, no. 6 (1990): 235–240.

24 Moyer-Gusé, "Toward a Theory of Entertainment Persuasion."

25 Luc Goossens, Wim Beyers, Mieke Emmen, and Marcel A. G. Van Aken, "The Imaginary Audience and Personal Fable: Factor Analyses and Concurrent Validity of the 'New Look' Measures," *Journal of Research on Adolescence* 12, no. 2 (2002): 193–215.

26 Albert Bandura, "Social Cognitive Theory in Cultural Context," *Applied Psychology* 51, no. 2 (2002): 269–290.

27 Burgoon et al., "Revisiting the Theory of Psychological Reactance."

28 Jane D. Brown, Kim Walsh Childers, and Cynthia S. Waszak, "Television and Adolescent Sexuality," *Journal of Adolescent Health Care* 11 (1990): 62–70.

29 John Horgan, *The Psychology of Terrorism*, 2nd edition (London: Routledge, 2014).

30 R. Bennett Furlow and H. L. Goodall, "The War of Ideas and the Battle of Narratives," *Cultural Studies* ←→ *Critical Methodologies* 11, no. 3 (2011): 215–223.

31 Kurt Braddock, "The Utility of Narratives for Promoting Radicalization: The Case of the Animal Liberation Front," *Dynamics of Asymmetric Conflict* 8, no. 1 (2015): 38–59; Braddock and Dillard, "Meta-Analytic Evidence for the Persuasive Effect of Narratives."

32 Kurt Braddock, "The Talking Cure? Communication and Psychological Impact in Prison De-Radicalisation Programmes," in *Prisons, Terrorism, and Extremism: Critical Issues in Management, Radicalisation and Reform*, ed. Andrew Silke, 60–74 (London: Routledge, 2014); Steven R. Corman, "Understanding the Role of Narrative as Extremist Strategic Communication," in *Countering Violent Extremism: Scientific Methods and Strategies*, ed. Laurie Fenstermacher and Todd Levanthal, 36–43 (Washington, DC: Air Force Research Laboratory,2011) Available at www.psychologytoday.com/files/attachments/95226/ucounterviolentextremismfinalapprovedforpublic

release28oct11.pdf; H. L. Goodall Jr., *Counter-Narrative: How Progressive Academics can Challenge Extremists and Promote Social Justice* (Walnut Creek, CA: Left Coast Press, 2010); Jeffry R. Halverson, H. L. Goodall Jr., and Steven R. Corman, *Master Narratives of Islamic Extremism* (New York: Palgrave Macmillan, 2011).

33 Graeme Wood, "What ISIS Really Wants," *The Atlantic* (March 2015). Available at www.theatlantic.com/magazine/archive/2015/03/what-isis-really-wants/384980/.

34 Ibid.

35 Homeland Security Committee Task Force on Combating Terrorist and Foreign Fighters Travel, *Final Report* (Washington, DC: Homeland Security Committee, 2015), p. 11.

36 Ibid.

37 Corman, "Understanding the Role of Narrative as Extremist Strategic Communication"; Goodall Jr., *Counter-Narrative*

38 Christian Leuprecht, Todd Hataley, Sophia Moskalenko, and Clark McCauley, "Winning the Battle but Losing the War? Narrative and Counter-Narrative Strategy," *Perspectives on Terrorism* 3, no. 2 (2009): 25–35. Available at www.terrorismanalysts.com/pt/index.php/pot/article/view/68/html.

39 Omar Ashour, "Online De-Radicalization? Countering Violent Extremist Narratives: Message, Messenger and Media Strategy," *Perspectives on Terrorism* 4, no. 6 (2010). Available at www.terrorismanalysts.com/pt/index.php/pot/article/view/128/html.

40 Braddock, "The Utility of Narratives for Promoting Radicalization"; Braddock and Dillard, "Meta-Analytic Evidence for the Persuasive Effect of Narratives."

41 Moyer-Gusé, "Toward a Theory of Entertainment Persuasion."

42 See Busselle and Bilandzic, "Fictionality and Perceived Realism in Experiencing Stories"; Jonathan Cohen, "Defining Identification: A Theoretical Look at the Identification of Audiences with Media Characters," *Mass Communication and Society* 4, no. 3 (2001): 245–264; Melanie C. Green, "Narratives and Cancer Communication," *Journal of Communication* 56 (2006): S163–S183; Michael D. Slater and Donna Rouner, "Entertainment-Education and Elaboration Likelihood: Understanding the Processing of Narrative Persuasion," *Communication Theory* 12, no. 2 (2002): 173–191.

43 For example, see Carl I. Hovland and Walter Weiss, "The Influence of Source Credibility on Communication Effectiveness," *Public Opinion Quarterly* 15, no. 4 (1951): 635–650.

44 Daniel Leonard Bernardi, Pauline Hope Cheong, Chris Lundry, and Scott W. Ruston, *Narrative Landmines: Rumors, Islamist Extremism, and the Struggle for Strategic Influence* (New Brunswick, NJ: Rutgers University Press, 2012), p. 156.

45 Bernard Berelson, *Content Analysis in Communication Research* (New York: Free Press, 1952).

46 Kurt Braddock and John Horgan, "Towards a Guide for Constructing and Disseminating Counternarratives to Reduce Support for Terrorism," *Studies in Conflict & Terrorism* 39, no. 5 (2016). 381–404 (p. 387).

47 Braddock, "The Utility of Narratives for Promoting Radicalization," pp. 44–45.

48 Richard E. Boyatzis, *Transforming Qualitative Information: Thematic Analysis and Code Development* (Thousand Oaks, CA: Sage, 1998).

49 Michael Quinn Patton, *Qualitative Research & Evaluation Methods* (Thousand Oaks, CA: Sage, 2002).

50 Braddock and Horgan, "Towards a Guide for Constructing and Disseminating Counternarratives," pp. 387–388.

51 Boyatzis, *Qualitative Research & Evaluation Methods.*

52 For a detailed account of how to calculate Cohen's kappa, see Jacob Cohen, "A Coefficient of Agreement for Nominal Scales," *Educational and Psychological Measurement* 20, no. 1 (1960): 37–46. For an illustration of Cohen's kappa in the analysis of qualitative data, see Braddock, "Fighting Words," pp. 145, 156–159.

53 This method for resolving disagreements between coders is common in the analysis of qualitative data. See Margrit Screier, *Qualitative Content Analysis in Practice* (London: Sage, 2012).

54 Corman, "Understanding the Role of Narrative."

55 Goodall Jr., *Counter-Narrative,* pp. 160–162.

56 Halverson et al., *Master Narratives of Islamic Extremism.*

57 Braddock and Horgan, "Towards a Guide for Constructing and Disseminating Counternarratives," p. 389.

58 Halverson et al., *Master Narratives of Islamic Extremism.*

59 Tom Quiggin, "Understanding al-Qaeda's Ideology for Counter-Narrative Work," *Perspectives on Terrorism* 3, no. 2 (2009). Available at www.terrorism analysts.com/pt/index.php/pot/article/view/67/html.

60 Peter Waldman and Hugh Pope, "Crusade Reference Reinforces Fears War on Terrorism is Against Muslims," *The Wall Street Journal*, September 21, 2001. Available at www.wsj.com/articles/SB1001020294332922160.

61 Cameron Shelley, "Analogical Counterarguments: A Taxonomy for Critical Thinking," *Argumentation* 18 (2004): 223–238.

62 Halverson et al., *Master Narratives of Islamic Extremism.*

63 Wood, "What ISIS Really Wants."

64 Halverson et al., *Master Narratives of Islamic Extremism.*

65 Ibid, p. 202.

66 Original comic appeared in Lori Gruen and Peter Singer, *Animal Liberation: A Graphic Guide* (London: Camden Press, 1987), see also in Kurt Braddock, "Fighting Words," pp. 128, 224.

67 Corman, "Understanding the Role of Narrative."

68 See, for example, "3 Men Charged in Bombings of Seven Abortion Facilities," *New York Times*, January 20, 1985. Available at www.nytimes.com/1985/01/20/us/3-men-charged-in-bombings-of-seven-abortion-facilities.html; Pierre Thomas, "Army of God Letters Claim Responsibility for Clinic Bombing," *CNN*, February 2, 1998. Available at www.cnn.com/US/9802/02/clinic.bombing.530pm/index.html?_s=PM:US.

69 www.armyofgod.com.

70 For example, Leviticus 19:18 of the New International Version: "Do not seek revenge or bear a grudge against anyone among your people, but love your neighbor as yourself."

71 For example, Proverbs 10:12, of the New International Version: "Hatred stirs up conflict, but love covers all wrongs."

72 Laurie Goodstein, "U.S. Muslims Take on ISIS' Recruiting Machine," *New York Times*, February 19, 2015. Available at www.nytimes.com/2015/02/20/us/muslim-leaders-in-us-seek-to-counteract-extremist-recruiters.html.

73 Groups in these cultures often include white nationalists, white supremacists, sovereign citizens, and others.

74 Groups in these cultures often include Muslim jihadists, Asian apocalyptic cults (e.g., Aleph/Aum Shinrikyō), and others.

75 Bernard M. Bass, "Leadership: Good, Better, Best," *Organizational Dynamics* 13, no. 3 (1985): 26–40; Ricarda B. Bouncken, Aim-Orn Imcharoen, and Wilma Klaasen-van-Husen, "What Does Collectivism Mean for Leadership and Teamwork Performance? An Empirical Study in Professional Service Firms," *Journal of International Business and Economics* 7, no. 2 (2007): 5–9.

76 Mia Bloom, Hicham Tiflati, and John Horgan, "Navigating ISIS's Preferred Platform: Telegram," *Terrorism and Political Violence* (forthcoming). doi:10.1080/09546553.2017.1339695.

77 Braddock and Horgan, "Towards a Guide for Constructing and Disseminating Counternarratives," p. 392.

78 Ibid.

79 See Maura Conway, "Terrorism and the Internet: New Media – New Threat?" *Parliamentary Affairs* 59, no. 2 (2006): 283–298; Majeed Khader, Neo Loo Seng, Gabriel Ong, Eunice Tan Mingyi, and Jeffry Chin, eds., *Combating Violent Extremism and Radicalization in the Digital Era* (Hershey, PA: IGI Global, 2016); Paul Gill, Emily Corner, Maura Conway, Amy Thornton, Mia Bloom, and John Horgan, "Terrorist Use of the Internet by the Numbers," *Criminology and Public Policy* 16, no. 1 (2017): 99–117.

80 Jonah Berger and Katherine L. Milkman, "Emotion and Virality: What Makes Online Content Go Viral?" *GfK Marketing Intelligence Review* 5, no. 1 (2013): 19–23.

81 Kevin Allocca, "Why Videos Go Viral," *TED Talks* [video]. Available at www.ted.com/talks/kevin_allocca_why_videos_go_viral/up-next; Berger and Milkman, "Emotion and Virality," pp. 20–21; Chip Heath and Dan Heath, *Made to Stick: Why Some Ideas Survive and Others Die* (New York: Doubleday, 2007).

82 Irina Heimbach, Benjamin Schiller, Thorsten Strufe, and Oliver Hinz, "Content Virality on Online Social Networks: Empirical Evidence from Twitter, Facebook, and Google+ on German News Websites," *Proceedings of the 26th ACM Conference on Hypertext & Social Media* (2015): 39–47. Available at http://dynamic-networks.org/publications/papers/papers/content-virality.pdf.

83 Berger and Milkman, "Emotion and Virality," p. 20; Heimbach et al., "Content Virality on Online Social Networks," Table 4; Hyun Suk Kim, Sung-kyoung Lee, Joseph N. Capella, Lisa Vera, and Sherry Emery, "Content

Characteristics Driving the Diffusion of Antismoking Messages: Implications for Cancer Prevention in the Emerging Public Communication Environment," *Journal of the National Cancer Institute Monographs* 47 (2013): 182–187; Owen Carter, Robert Donovan, and Geoffrey Jalleh, "Using Viral E-mails to Distribute Tobacco Control Advertisements: An Experimental Investigation," *Journal of Health Communication* 16 (2011): 698–707; Petya Eckler and Paul Bolls, "Spreading the Virus: Emotional Tone of Viral Advertising and its Effect on Forwarding Intentions and Attitudes," *Journal of Interactive Advertising* 11, no. 2 (2011): 1–11.

84 Saleem Alhabash and Anna R. McAlister, "Redefining Virality in Less Broad Strokes: Predicting Viral Behavioral Intentions from Motivations and Uses of Facebook and Twitter," *New Media & Society* 17, no. 8 (2015): 1317–1339.

85 Allocca, "Why Videos Go Viral."

86 Adam J. Mills, "Virality in Social Media: The SPIN Framework," *Journal of Public Affairs* 12, no. 2 (2012): 162–169; Alhabash and McAlister, "Redefining Virality in Less Broad Strokes"; Allocca, "Why Videos Go Viral."

87 Lilian Weng, Filippo Menczer, and Yong-Yeol Ahn, "Virality Prediction and Community Structure in Social Networks," *Scientific Reports* 3, no. 2522 (2013). Available at www.nature.com/articles/srep02522.pdf.

88 See Michael D. Slater, "Choosing Audience Segmentation Strategies and Methods for Health Communication," in *Designing Health Messages: Approaches from Communication Theory and Public Health Practice*, ed. Edward Maibach and Roxanne Louiselle Parrott, 186–198 (Thousand Oaks, CA: Sage, 1995).

89 Braddock and Horgan, "Towards a Guide for Constructing and Disseminating Counternarratives," p. 393.

90 Kurt Braddock, "Developing and Disseminating Narratives for Countering Violent Extremism: The Utility of Former Offenders," presentation at the Understanding Terrorism and Political Violence Conference, Cork, Ireland, March 30, 2015.

91 Marc Sageman, *Understanding Terror Networks* (Philadelphia, PA: University of Pennsylvania Press, 2004),

92 Citation currently classified. To be populated once the data is published.

93 Kurt Braddock and John Morrison, "Cultivating Trust and Perceptions of Source Credibility in Online Counternarratives Intended to Reduce Support for Terrorism," *Studies in Conflict & Terrorism* (under review).

94 Christina Couch, "Life After Hate: Recovering from Racism," Master's thesis, Massachusetts Institute of Technology, 2015. See also Life After Hate's website: www.lifeafterhate.com.

95 Nick Paton Walsh, Salma Abdelaziz, Mark Phillips, and Mehamed Hasan, "ISIS Brides Flee Caliphate as Noose Tightens on Terror Group," *CNN* (July 17, 2017). Available at www.cnn.com/2017/07/17/middleeast/raqqa-isis-brides/index.html.

96 Steven R. Corman and Jill S. Schiefelbein, "Communication and Media Strategy in the Islamist War of Ideas." Consortium for Strategic Communication Report #0601, Arizona State University, April 20, 2006. Available at http://csc.asu.edu/wp-content/uploads/2012/06/119.pdf.

97 Goodstein, "U.S. Muslims Take on ISIS' Recruiting Machine."
98 Braddock and Horgan, "Towards a Guide for Constructing and Disseminating Counternarratives," p. 393.
99 Tracy McVeigh, "The McVeigh Letters: Why I Bombed Oklahoma," *The Guardian* (May 6, 2001). Available at www.theguardian.com/world/2001/may/06/mcveigh.usa.
100 CBS News Staff, "McVeigh Vents on '60 Minutes,'" *CBS News* (March 13, 2000). Available at www.cbsnews.com/news/mcveigh-vents-on-60-minutes/.
101 See Melanie C. Green and Timothy C. Brock, "The Role of Transportation in the Persuasiveness of Public Narratives," *Journal of Personality and Social Psychology* 79, no. 5 (2000): 701–721; Deborah A. Prentice, Richard J. Gerrig, and Daniel S. Bailis, "What Readers Bring to the Processing of Fictional Texts," *Psychonomic Bulletin & Review* 4, no. 3 (1997): 416–420.
102 See Patrick Colm Hogan, *The Mind and its Stories: Narrative Universals and Human Emotion* (New York: Cambridge University Press, 2003).
103 See Leslie J. Hinyard and Matthew W. Kreuter, "Using Narrative Communication as a Tool for Behavior Change: A Conceptual, Theoretical, and Empirical Overview," *Health Education & Behavior* 34, no. 5 (2007): 777–792.
104 See James W. Pennebaker and Janet D. Seagal, "Forming a Story: The Health Benefits of Narrative," *Journal of Clinical Psychology* 55 (1999): 1243–1254.
105 See Michael F. Dahlstrom, "The Role of Causality in Information Acceptance in Narratives: An Example from Science Communication," *Communication Research* 37, no. 6 (2010): 857–875.

4   Vaccinating against the Enemy: Attitudinal Inoculation, Radicalization, and Counter-Radicalization

On a summer afternoon in July of 2011, Anders Breivik drove a white Volkswagen Crafter into the heart of the Oslo government district.[1] He stopped the vehicle at the H Block of Grubbegata – at the main entrance to the office of Norway's Prime Minister. He exited the van and walked down Grubbegata towards a gray Fiat Dobló, where witnesses described him getting into the car and driving the wrong way down Møllergata. This may have seemed strange to those that saw it occur, but the man was wearing a black helmet with a lowered visor and carrying a pistol in his right hand. Perhaps he was a police officer with urgent matters to attend to. Breivik was not a police officer, but he did have other plans for the day.

Though the Oslo government district was bustling throughout the entire year, people typically left work early during the summer months. At a different time of year, it would be common for nearly 2,000 people to be working in the district in the mid-afternoon. But because it was the end of July, only about 250 people were in the buildings and fewer than 100 were walking around in the streets surrounding the H Block. Still, there was some activity around the Volkswagen Crafter that Breivik left on Grubbegata. Two young lawyers at the Ministry of Justice stood directly behind the van. Another lawyer, Jon Vegard Lervåg, walked through the lobby of H Block, also moving towards the Volkswagen parked outside. They had no idea that the innocuous white van contained a 2,000-pound bomb made of fertilizer, ammonium nitrate, and number-2 fuel oil.

At 3:25 p.m., the massive bomb exploded in a flash of white light. Lervåg was instantly torn to pieces, his body scattered across the front of the buildings on Grubbegata. The two women behind the van were also killed instantly when they were thrown into the air and enveloped by fire. A shockwave tore through the government district, repositioning cars as if they were weightless and tossing other pedestrians to the pavement. Searing hot glass, wood, and metal passed through H Block and the surrounding buildings. The lower floors of the buildings were decimated. Fires sparked by the blast raged at street level and holes were blown into the pavement itself. Several individuals lay on the ground, bloody and burned.

Breivik never heard the explosion. He only learned that his bomb had successfully detonated after hearing reports on the radio while he was sitting in traffic in the gray Fiat Dobló he used to get out of the city.

He was going west. He was going to Utøya.

At 5:17 p.m., Anders Breivik landed on Utøya Island, ten miles northwest of the spot where his bomb tore through the heart of Oslo. Disguised as a member of the Norwegian Police Security Service (PST), Breivik arrived at the island on the *MS Thorbjørn* ferry. He was carrying a heavy case containing ammunition, fuel, smoke grenades, and other weapons. Also on the ferry was Monica Bøsei, the manager of a summer camp held on the island for a political youth organization affiliated with the Norwegian Labour Party. More than 600 teenagers and young adults were on the island when Breivik arrived.

Bøsei introduced Breivik (who was calling himself Martin Nilsen) to a security guard near the pier where the ferry had docked. The guard, a police officer named Trond Berntsen, asked Breivik which district he came from. Breivik responded that he was from the Grønland station of the PST, and that he had been sent to secure Utøya after the bomb attack in Oslo. Unsatisfied, Berntsen asked when other members of the PST would be arriving at Utøya.

"They'll be here later," Breivik responded.

Berntsen asked Breivik if he knew Jørn, who presumably worked at the Grønland station. Realizing that Berntsen was suspicious of him, he was wary of giving the wrong answer. He only shrugged. To avoid being exposed, Breivik suggested that they go to the main building, only a few yards from the dock. Berntsen agreed, and they began walking towards the building.

Upon reaching a steep part of the hill that led to the main building, Breivik drew his pistol and pointed it at Berntsen. Bøsei screamed, "No, you mustn't point it at him like that!" Breivik pulled the trigger, shooting Berntsen in the head at point-blank range. Monica Bøsei tried to run but was too close to Breivik to escape. He shot her as well. Bøsei and Berntsen fell next to one another. Breivik moved close to their bodies and fired two more shots into each of their heads.

Another guard on the island, Rune Havdal, turned to run to a group of trees. Breivik shot him in the back to disable him and as he did to Bøsei and Berntsen, executed him with a follow-up shot to the head.

Campers and counselors who saw the murders screamed and ran in every direction.

For the next hour and a half, Anders Breivik hunted the children on Utøya.

∴

Breivik executed thirteen campers in the island's main building, many of whom were cowering against the walls. He pumped bullets into several terrified campers on a hill behind the camp's café, careful to finish off his targets with shots to the head. Their bodies twitched while they lay dying. He shot several children hiding on the edge of a cliff overlooking the water at the end of the island. Those he didn't kill, he left to bleed at the water's edge.

He paused only to call emergency services to report himself as "Commander Anders Behring Breivik of the Norwegian Anti-Communist Resistance Movement" and his desire to give himself up. Then, he continued his mission, killing more campers as he waited for police to arrive.

The first members of the Norwegian Emergency Response Unit (code name Delta) arrived at Utøya at 6:27 p.m. As the Deltas stormed the island, they could hear heavy gunfire in the distance.

They moved around a red schoolhouse and spotted Breivik moving brushwood 50 meters away. They announced themselves, shouting "Delta! Delta!" and commanded that Breivik put his hands in the air. He set down his rifle and approached the Deltas with his arms at his sides. As he advanced, the Deltas ordered him to lie face-down on the ground. He complied. Officer Håvard Gåsbakk pounced on him, driving his midsection downward into the grass. The officers bound his hands and feet, and disarmed him of the Glock he still had in its holster. Gåsbakk demanded to know if there were any other attackers on Utøya.

Breivik responded, "There is only me."

At around 6:30 p.m., just over three hours after it began, Anders Breivik's attack on Norway was over. Seventy-seven individuals were dead and more than 300 were injured. Fifty of the dead were 18 years old or younger.

Despite the horror of his action, Breivik had no intention of letting it speak for itself. Hours before the bomb exploded in downtown Oslo, he uploaded a video to YouTube describing his justifications for the attack and e-mailed a 1,500-page manifesto to hundreds of recipients. Both the video and the manifesto warned of the sacrifice of European purity on the altar of political correctness and the hollow arguments of domestic enemies that made that sacrifice possible.

Breivik's manifesto (and the video it was based on) described the Western world as being under attack. According to Breivik, political correctness had run rampant, forcing white, Christian Europeans to accept the destruction of their culture via the acceptance of Muslims, homosexuals, feminists, and other minorities. As part of this argument, Breivik likened political correctness and liberalism to "Cultural Marxism," a system where equality among cultures is forced and the virtues of non-white, non-Christian, non-heterosexual people are assumed. He argued that Cultural Marxism was a pervasive ideology – one that appeals to large segments of Europe. And because of how persuasive the arguments for Cultural Marxism are, the annihilation of Christian Europe was imminent unless actions were taken against the leftists that allowed it to happen.

Breivik's manifesto paints the picture of a narcissist. Through his attacks in Oslo and on Utøya, he thought of himself as a Christian soldier acting in the tradition of past heroes of Christendom – another warrior in the line of Charles Martel, El Cid, Richard the Lionheart, and Oliver Cromwell. He justified the murder of 77 people with the idea that he bore the responsibility of preventing the contamination of Norway and greater Europe by cultural minorities. Anders Breivik wanted the world to think of him as a knight.

Despite the manifesto's central focus on Breivik's actions in the context of his imagined crusade, some of his claims may have had other persuasive effects. Before the segments of the manifesto where Breivik depicts himself as a heroic Christian soldier, his warnings of politicians' advocacy of Cultural Marxism are meant to prepare audiences to resist these arguments when they encounter them. By warning of imminent persuasive arguments made by his enemies, Breivik may have strengthened some audience members' ability to resist those arguments.

He may not have known it, but this communicative technique – *attitudinal inoculation* – has a long history of success in persuasion research. Generally speaking, it involves warning a message target of an impending threat to their beliefs and attitudes, and then providing that target with the tools needed to fend off those threats.

It's simple. It's straightforward. And it works.

Unfortunately, the simplicity and effectiveness of attitudinal inoculation means that violent extremist actors like Anders Breivik can easily apply it. Terrorist groups often warn audiences that their enemies are going to try to convince them of something. They try to "get ahead of the game" and preempt any chance to demonstrate the faults in their ideologies.

It can be disheartening to think that terrorist groups can thwart our attempts to challenge their ideas before we can even join the debate. However, it is important to realize that like other persuasive strategies, *we* can also use attitudinal inoculation to undercut *their* arguments to audiences. As one of the strongest and most reliable methods of counter-persuasion, inoculation holds huge promise in this regard. We just need to develop effective inoculation messages and target them at the right audiences.

This chapter describes how we can do so.

∴

Anders Breivik is sitting in a prison cell 60 miles southwest of Oslo. He does not have access to other prisoners, and only sees a prison chaplain every two weeks. His mother is dead, and she only visited him five times before she died.

He is not a knight. He is not a warrior. He is not a cultural defender. He is alone. Still, the ideas that Breivik espoused before his attacks in Norway have a dangerous appeal. Inoculation can help defend against those ideas and assist in preventing another nightmare like the one that occurred in the mild Norwegian summer of 2011.

Foundations of Attitudinal Inoculation

The history of work on attitudinal inoculation has been one of seemingly implausible success within the social sciences. Since the 1960s, inoculation has been tested countless times, across many disciplines, and with respect to several behaviors. Time and time again, the results of these studies have demonstrated its effectiveness. The continuous stream of studies illustrating the effects of inoculation have caused it to be celebrated as one of the "most consistent and reliable method[s] for conferring resistance to persuasion."[2] In short, decades of research have produced resounding evidence to confirm a basic fact – inoculation messages work.[3]

To understand inoculation's potential as a tool for counter-radicalization more fully, the following section will describe what inoculation is, the elements that comprise inoculation messages, and the psychological mechanisms by which those messages are effective. The chapter will then turn to how extremist groups attempt to inoculate potential recruits against messages that might deter their willingness to support those groups. Finally, the chapter will show how violent radicalization – an inherently persuasive process – can be prevented with the use of attitudinal inoculation.

What Is Attitudinal Inoculation?

Every autumn, moms and dads march reluctant children into their local doctors' offices. The kids cry, pout, and stamp their feet because they know what's waiting for them there. They know that the doctor will ask them to hop up on the table covered in weird, crumply paper before she pulls a sharp metal tube filled with strange liquid out of her pocket. They know that she will tell them to look across the room at a cartoon picture of a smiling puppy with a Band-Aid on its tail. And they know that while they are looking at that puppy, they are going to feel a sudden sting in their shoulder as the doctor sticks them with that sharp metal tube. The child may begin to cry, but the trauma is quickly alleviated when he gets a lollipop. The parents, though, get something much more valuable; they get the peace of mind from knowing that their child is protected from the flu for another school year.

Most people are familiar with the concept of inoculation because of their experience with this very episode. There's a good chance that you have even had a vaccine in the last few years. Vaccinations for influenza, hepatitis, measles, mumps, whooping cough, human papilloma virus, and several other diseases have effectively reduced the incidence of their occurrence. Some deadly diseases (e.g., polio) have even been largely eradicated because of the vaccinations developed for them. These successes have made it clear that medical inoculation is one of the modern world's greatest strategies for preventing disease in populations vulnerable to illness.

In 1961, William McGuire[4] proposed that the usefulness of inoculation was not limited to our immune systems. He said that just as an individual's body can be inoculated against attacks by unwanted viruses, so too can their minds be inoculated against attacks by unwanted ideas.[5] Consistent with this analogy, McGuire's inoculation theory says that people can be made resistant to persuasion if they are (a) warned that a third party will attempt to change their current beliefs and attitudes, and (b) provided with information that can be used to argue against the impending persuasive attempt.[6]

When an individual is medically inoculated, they are exposed to a weakened form of the virus to be protected against. This weakened virus is strong enough to activate the immune system, but not so strong as to make the inoculated person sick.[7] Through this exposure, the inoculated person's immune system naturally produces antibodies that make the person resistant to stronger attacks by the virus in the future. It seems counterintuitive, but exposing a person to a virus can prevent that person from catching that virus in the future.

Attitudinal inoculation works in the same way. When individuals have "healthy" beliefs and attitudes about an issue, they can be exposed to messages that trigger the development of psychological defenses that prepare them to reject persuasive attempts to change their positions on that issue.[8] In the context of violent extremism, "healthy" beliefs and attitudes would be those that are not yet supportive of violence in support of an extremist ideology.

The degree to which inoculation messages can prevent change in an individual's current beliefs and/or attitudes largely depends on how well the preempting message describes the threat posed by future attempts to persuade them. When message recipients recognize a threat to their current positions, they become motivated to counter-argue against any attempts to change the beliefs or attitudes they currently hold.[9]

Because successful inoculation hinges on message recipients' perceptions of impending threats to their positions, it's critical that those threats are effectively conveyed. So, inoculation messages should have two elements that encourage resistance to future persuasive attempts. First, inoculation messages should contain a *clear, unambiguous warning* of a future attack against the target's beliefs and attitudes.[10] This cautions them that although they may *feel* secure in what they believe, their beliefs and attitudes are vulnerable to being changed by crafty groups and individuals.[11]

After presenting this threat, inoculation messages then feature their second element – *refutational preemption*. In this part of the message, inoculation messages offer weakened versions of the arguments that future persuasive attempts may contain. This serves as a minor challenge to individuals' current beliefs and attitudes. This portion of the inoculation message also includes information that can be used to refute these kinds of persuasive threats when the inoculated person encounters them.[12]

The threat component of the inoculation message triggers perceptions of vulnerability and concern about defending one's positions. The refutational preemption component provides the target with the psychological tools needed to successfully mount such a defense. The question remains, though: Why does the knowledge of imminent threats to our beliefs (and exposure to weakened versions of those threats) motivate us to "dig in" and maintain our current attitudinal positions?

Psychological Antibodies: Reactance and Resistance against
Future Persuasion

Most people – particularly in the Western world – have a deep-seated need for autonomy and independence. Basically, we really don't like it when someone tries to tell us what to do or think. We want to make our own decisions, and when we think someone is trying to affect those decisions, we get angry and counter-argue against the messages we think are aimed at us.[13] Based on this, some researchers have identified a psychological process that occurs when an individual is exposed to messages they think are trying to persuade them. This process – which is an intertwined combination of anger and counter-arguing – is commonly referred to as *reactance*.

Founded by Jack Brehm, reactance theory contends that when someone perceives a threat to their freedom (like when someone is trying to persuade them), they respond in ways that reestablish their lost freedom and reassert their independence to make their own decisions.[14] For example, when a parent tells their teenage son that he should not drink, reactance theory would predict that the teenager would be *more* inclined to drink because he would want to assert his independence.

Remember that inoculation messages warn individuals of imminent threats to their beliefs and attitudes. In this way, they tell message targets that their freedom to make their own decisions will be challenged by someone in the future. By doing this, inoculation messages prime message targets to feel reactance against a message *that they haven't encountered yet.*[15]

Also remember that when people encounter threats to their autonomy, they get angry and counter-argue against those threats.[16] Research has shown that inoculation messages trigger these very responses.[17]

In short, inoculation messages generate all kinds of psychological, emotional, and cognitive reactions that cause people to resist messages that inoculation treatments warn against. If inoculation messages are vaccines, then reactance is the immune system pumping out antibodies.

How Well Does Inoculation Work?

At the beginning of this chapter, I mentioned how past experts have celebrated inoculation as a useful strategy for preventing persuasion. Where most persuasion theories tend to cause researchers to debate, argue, and squabble, they seem to be largely united in their praise of attitudinal inoculation. Rather than take these experts at their word about how effective it can be, let's look at some past research that has tested how well inoculation has prevented people from being persuaded.

As a first step in evaluating how effective inoculation is, it's useful to look at a meta-analysis on the topic.[18] In 2010, John Banas and Stephen Rains took a comprehensive look at research that tested the tendency for inoculation to protect against persuasion. They evaluated forty-one studies (including more than 10,000 research participants) in their analysis and found that inoculated people are more likely to resist persuasion than individuals who were not inoculated. They also showed that people who are exposed to inoculation messages are more likely to resist future attempts to persuade them than individuals who are exposed to messages that support the attitudes they already have. In short, Banas and Rains's study provided strong support for the notion that inoculation messages promote resistance to future persuasive attempts.[19]

This is a good start in understanding how effective inoculation can be, but let us also consider the contexts in which inoculation has been tested and proven useful. Since the 1960s, communication experts have produced inoculation messages meant to protect against persuasive messages of different types. Almost without fail, these messages have caused research subjects to resist later persuasive messages aimed at them.

For example, in the context of politics, many researchers have shown the effectiveness of inoculation for shoring up support among constituents. As far back as 1990, Michael Pfau and Henry Kenski showed that individuals exposed to inoculation messages are more likely to resist messages that attacked the image of a political candidate, thereby leading to an increased likelihood of their continued support of that candidate.[20] Later researchers (some of whom also worked with Pfau) provided additional support for the usefulness of inoculation for keeping voters' attitudes from changing as a result of political attacks aimed at supported politicians.[21]

In addition to defending attitudes about *politicians*, attitudinal inoculation also helps protect beliefs and attitudes about highly charged political *topics*. For instance, in his later work, Pfau evaluated how people responded to inoculation messages intended to arouse negative reactions to messages about the Iraq War. Working with several researchers, he showed that when individuals were exposed to messages and images about the war, their pride in the United States wavered. But, when those messages and images were preceded by an inoculation message, the loss of pride was mitigated among some people.[22]

Related to its effectiveness in the political sphere, attitudinal inoculation has also been shown to be an effective means of protecting beliefs and attitudes on other social issues.

Inoculation has proven useful for helping message targets resist persuasive messages that advocate against societal equality,[23] promote censorship in films,[24] justify plagiarism,[25] include manipulative content or disinformation,[26] and seek to influence people about many other topics of societal importance.[27]

One of the most active strands of inoculation research has evaluated how well it helps individuals resist engaging in risky health behaviors. Once again, Michael Pfau's influence is unmistakable; his work has shown that attitudinal inoculation can reduce alcohol consumption[28] and intention to smoke[29] among individuals exposed to messages that advocate these behaviors. Other researchers have produced similar findings, showing that inoculation can also help protect attitudes regarding safe sex practices[30] and the safety of vaccinations.[31]

In addition to these more traditional medical topics, Alicia Mason and Claude Miller demonstrated that attitudinal inoculation is a valuable tool in an era of disinformation about health knowledge. They showed that by using attitudinal inoculation to warn consumers about misleading information about some food products, message designers could induce them to be more skeptical about sketchy claims of those products' nutritional value.[32]

A final group of studies have shown how inoculation can be used in the commercial context. One subset of these studies has focused on how firms can use inoculation to retain customer bases. In this line of research, researchers have demonstrated that by inoculating people against persuasive messages from rival companies, message designers can prevent targets from changing their brand preferences[33] or losing their positive attitudes about the company's products.[34]

On the other hand, inoculation can also be useful for protecting consumers. For example, when people are exposed to inoculation messages before seeing different kinds of advertisements, they are more resistant to messages that try to induce them to buy various products[35] or sign up for credit cards.[36] Attitudinal inoculation has even made people more perceptive to "front group stealth ads" that corporations develop and distribute through parties that do not appear to be commercial entities.[37]

There is even evidence to show that if a person is inoculated about one topic, they will resist messages related to *other, related topics*. In one study on this phenomenon, Kim Parker and her colleagues showed that when college students were inoculated against messages that advocate for unprotected sexual activity, they (predictably) reported less intention to engage in risky sex. Interestingly, these students also reported less intention to engage in another risky health behavior – binge drinking – despite *not being inoculated against it*.[38] Attitudinal inoculation, it seems, confers a "blanket of protection" around all kinds of related behaviors.[39]

More research on inoculation and the kinds of behaviors it can prevent is being produced every day. But as this small sample of studies suggests, widespread enthusiasm for it as a communicative method for preventing persuasion is warranted. Put simply – attitudinal inoculation works.

Terrorist Propaganda and Attitudinal Inoculation

The overwhelming evidence in support of inoculation's efficacy leads us to a bit of an unfortunate question. If the strategy works so well, does that mean extremist groups can use it to achieve their own persuasive goals? Sadly, the answer to this is yes. Extremist groups regularly use inoculation messages as part of their propaganda, primarily to preempt future messages that may turn individuals away from their ideologies. This section reviews some of the ways that this occurs. Although extremists can develop attitudinal inoculation messages intended to defend against messages from any source, they primarily develop them to promote resistance to messages that come from their enemies, their message target's valued others (e.g., friends, family), and former members of the extremist group.

Inoculation against Messages from Enemies

There is a common refrain among analysts, practitioners, and journalists concerning the way we talk about political violence. This catchphrase has been used so regularly in the last several decades that it can now safely be called a cliché. Without fail, when talking about a political violence performed by a group that claims to represent some victimized constituency, someone will offer the following platitude:

"One man's terrorist is another man's freedom fighter."

The banality of this statement has stripped it of any real value. However, it does reveal a truth about how extremists seek to frame their identities to those they attempt to bring to their side by undercutting the messages of their enemies.

Specifically, extremist groups regularly seek to inoculate their audiences against messages that would characterize them using negative terminology. In doing so, they try to ensure that those negative portrayals do not take hold in their target audiences, thereby circumventing the shame associated with those portrayals that may serve as a barrier to extremist activity. One of the more popular methods by which extremists do this is by warning those who support them that some enemy is likely to refer to them as evil figures.

For instance, in the months following an attack in Australia by a man who dedicated allegiance to "the caliph of Muslims,"[40] there was a surge in anti-Muslim sentiment in the country.[41] This increase in hostility towards the Muslim community emboldened the far-right in Australia, including the United Patriots Front (UPF), a neo-Nazi, nationalist, anti-immigration organization.

At a UPF rally in 2015, Blair Cottrell – chairman of the organization – forewarned supporters that as anti-Muslim sentiment grew in Australia, enemies would seek to disgrace them with derogatory labels.[42]

Said Cottrell:

> They will call you racists [and] bigots, they will put pressure on you, but in order to rise above it, you need to not care.

This statement and others like it prepare targets for messages they will encounter that may be designed to shame them into rethinking their loyalty to a group. By warning message targets of these kinds of imminent arguments, Cottrell can strengthen the resolve of his group's members.

Recall that an effective inoculation message also includes some counter-arguments upon which audiences can elaborate, thereby allowing them to defend against the messages they were warned about. Cottrell does this in his speech as well. Although the counter-arguments he offers are not terribly sophisticated, they provide a basis on which his followers can respond to those who would characterize them as racists or bigots:

> You need to … stand up to defend the history of our great nation … You will see our movement grow. You will see us blossom, you will see us advance into the greatest upheaval this country has ever known.

Here, Cottrell suggests that the UPF's future is one of growth and legitimacy, and that its members cannot be dismissed as simple racists or bigots.

This is a common strategy employed by extremist groups. By claiming that "they will call us terrorists" and providing counter-arguments to refute that characterization, extremist groups can effectively undercut any message produced by its enemies that does, indeed, characterize them as terrorists.

Inoculation against Messages from Valued Others

Recall from Chapter 1 that Stahelski's model of identity negotiation emphasizes isolation from valued others as a crucial element of radicalization. The model explains that as an individual is cut off from valued social ties unaffiliated with the extremist group, they are more likely to adhere to the values of the group, bringing them into closer attitudinal alignment with the group's ideology. Of course, physical isolation can be fundamental to this process; as individuals physically remove themselves from the company of others, they grow more reliant on their remaining affiliation (i.e., the extremist group) to define who they are.

In addition to physical isolation, extremist groups often attempt to psychologically isolate target recruits by preempting messages that might deter them from abandoning their social ties.

Imam Mohamed Magid, the Executive Imam of the All Dulles Area Muslim Society, has experienced this phenomenon firsthand.[43] As an Islamic scholar and leader, he has seen the strategies used by ISIS to recruit young Muslims. Magid explains that during the recruitment process, ISIS would seek to socially isolate target recruits by stripping away what Magid called their "social safety nets" – buffers that protect them from being exposed to and persuaded by ideas that are not consistent with their values. Consistent with Stahelski's model, these social safety nets include affiliations with different groups that build the foundation of the individual's identity: family, friends, classmates, teammates, and so on.

One strategy that ISIS would use to psychologically isolate targets involved telling them that individuals who might argue against the extremists' ideology – including their parents, local imams, or religious scholars – could not be trusted. ISIS recruiters would claim that the arguments made by anyone who might talk to them about Islam would fail to address the real problems facing Muslims and that ISIS was the only viable source for addressing those problems. In this way, ISIS would attempt to inoculate targets' attitudes against persuasive messages delivered by trusted others. If successful, the inoculation messages would diminish the capacity of the protective messages delivered by trusted others (e.g., family, friends) to protect against the acceptance of ISIS-congruent beliefs and attitudes.

This pattern of messaging is relatively commonplace; extremist groups will often preemptively challenge messages from other sources by referencing the arguments in those messages as part of a warning (eliciting threat). Extremists will then offer rebuttals to those arguments, positioning them as the only entity capable of resolving the individual's needs (refutational preemption). This communicative pattern is entirely consistent with efforts geared towards attitudinal inoculation in more traditional contexts.

Inoculation against Messages from Former Members

In recent years, researchers and practitioners have championed former extremists as credible sources of messages intended to deter vulnerable individuals from being radicalized by extremists. This is an unsurprising conclusion; former extremists have experienced the realities of engagement with their respective groups (which often fall short of their expectations) and have often left those groups of their own volition. It makes sense that potential recruits would ascribe credibility to those who have lived the experiences they seek.

Empirical research in this regard has provided some support for the importance of credibility on the radicalization and counter-radicalization processes. In my work with John Horgan based on source credibility research within communication studies, I have argued that former terrorists are a promising route through which counter-radicalization messages can be deployed.[44] I later extended the conclusions I drew with Horgan to the online domain, where Dr. John Morrison and I developed guidelines for cultivating trust and perceptions of source credibility among those targeted by counter-radicalization messages.[45]

Seminal research on the social nature of radicalization also provides insight into how former extremists can be viable channels through which counter-radicalization messages can be distributed. Recall from Chapter 1 that the social-network approach to understanding radicalization shows that individuals often get involved with extremist groups because of their preexisting social affiliations with established members.[46] When people leave extremist groups, however, those social affiliations are not always cut off. People often retain social ties with the members with whom they were affiliated before they got involved.

For example, let's suppose that an individual is drawn to the Aryan Nations (a white nationalist organization) because his brother is an active member. However, after joining the organization, this individual becomes disillusioned with the realities of engagement[47] and decides to leave the group. Just because this individual leaves the group does not mean the relationship with his brother is dissolved. On the contrary, interview data have suggested that when individuals leave extremist organizations and are exposed to different messages and experiences, they express a desire to *help others leave those organizations as well.*[48]

Taken together, these facts would suggest that former members of extremist organizations have the potential to be persuasive deliverers of counter-radicalization messages.

Extremist groups seem to recognize the threat posed by their former members in this regard. Recruitment and radicalization efforts would be more difficult if former members share their knowledge about the disappointing realities of engagement, the poor treatment they received at the hands of their "comrades," or the otherwise unsatisfying experiences associated with joining such groups. So, it is not uncommon for members of extremist groups to undercut the messages that their former members deliver to rob them of their persuasive strength. Whether by derogating the source[49] or claiming that the former members was never "true" believers in the cause,[50] extremists attempt to inoculate their targets against messages that would prevent their radicalization.

For example, on the Stormfront online forums – a widely known haven for supporters of white nationalism and supremacy – these kinds of inoculation messages are widespread. In several threads, members of the forums attempt to blunt messages delivered by former white nationalists by preemptively disparaging them or otherwise explaining away the statements that the extremists expect them to make.

A common target of these kinds of inoculation messages is Christian Picciolini, a former white supremacist and leader of the Chicago Area Skinheads (CASH).[51] Picciolini left the white nationalist movement in the late 1990s and has since become an advocate for helping right-wing extremists abandon their violent ideologies. Derogation of Picciolini on Stormfront is common, particularly when he is featured in the media for his efforts. Members of the Stormfront forums have claimed that he has "mental issues" and is a race traitor.[52] Some members seek to undercut the credibility of Picciolini's credibility by claiming that he was never a "true" white nationalist to begin with. So, commenters warn visitors to the forums about Picciolini by mentioning his faults before referencing the arguments he is expected to make (eliciting threat). They then shoot down those arguments with defensive communication meant to disprove his claims (refutational preemption).

In another example on Stormfront, Don Black – the founder of the forums – describes how his son (Derek) left the white nationalist movement.[53] He explains his belief that Derek's change of heart was not attributable to the development of genuine beliefs, but rather due to "Stockholm Syndrome" resulting from his immersion with non-racist people. By describing his son's transition away from white nationalism in this way, Black could communicate to others that Derek's opinions could be dismissed as nonsensical. After all, if Derek's statements were a function of Stockholm Syndrome (identifying with his "captors"), they were not based on objective truth. This could have had significant implications at the time, as Derek Black was getting significant media attention following his abandonment of white nationalism.

∴

So far, this chapter has argued two key points. First, attitudinal inoculation is an effective strategy for preventing persuasion. Second, extremists regularly use attitudinal inoculation to remove psychological defenses that targets for radicalization might have. Together, these facts paint a bleak picture about the role of attitudinal inoculation in the realm of violent extremism.

It's important to remember, however, that we have the knowledge and the tools to construct effective messages that work in the *opposite* direction. Just as countless researchers in other domains have used inoculation to prevent message targets from engaging in all sorts of unwanted behaviors (e.g., smoking, binge drinking, risky sex) or changing their minds about a person or policy, we can use attitudinal inoculation to prevent vulnerable individuals from assimilating beliefs and attitudes consistent with extremist ideologies.

Preventing Radicalization through Attitudinal Inoculation

This section of the chapter describes how to develop inoculation messages intended to prevent the adoption of extremist beliefs and attitudes. Although the chapter will review the elements of attitudinal inoculation messages that were covered earlier (explicit forewarning and refutational preemption), the first segment discusses some things that must be considered before even beginning to think about inoculation as a strategy for counter-radicalization.

Considerations before Designing Inoculation Messages for Preventing Radicalization

Though past research has overwhelmingly supported the notion that attitudinal inoculation is a viable strategy for boosting resistance to persuasion, constructing an effective inoculation message requires a consideration of a few factors that can influence their effectiveness. Most importantly, message designers should consider the modality through which the inoculation treatment is presented and the kinds of content that specific target audiences would be most responsive to.[54]

Different audiences tend to have different preferences for the media through which they receive messages. This is no different for inoculation messages. In this regard, Michael Pfau found that when younger adolescents were exposed to inoculation treatments intended to increase their resistance to smoking intentions, they responded most favorably to video-based messages.[55] But when older adolescents and teenagers were exposed to inoculation treatments, text- and video-based messages were equally effective at conferring resistance to persuasion.[56]

These empirical findings would suggest that when counter-radicaliza-tion-focused inoculation messages are targeted at young children, they would be most effective if presented in a video format. In contrast, if the messages are targeted at older children, teenagers, or adults, a text- or video-based format would be appropriate. In the latter case, where either form of inoculation message would be effective, inoculation message designers may consider issues related to cost and ease of transmission, both of which can be affected by the funding available for counter-radicalization programs that include inoculation treatments.

In addition to the modality preferences of target audiences, the nature of the content that gets incorporated into counter-radicalization inocula-tion messages should also be considered. While it is true that the con-struction of inoculation messages of all types follow the same general formula – elicit threat, present weakened arguments, and provide defen-sive measures – the content embedded in inoculation messages can differ in focus. Specifically, message designers can ground their inoculation treatments in logic or emotion, both of which can be persuasive under different conditions.

Ivanov argues that the decision as to whether emotion or logic should be the focus of an inoculation message depends on two things: (1) the age/cognitive processing abilities of the target audience and (2) the nature of the attitude that the inoculation treatment is designed to protect from change.[57] Because of limitations on their ability to process hard facts, younger targets are likely to be more responsive to inoculation messages couched in emotional content. So, inoculation messages embedded in emotional testimony or anecdotes might be more effective for young people than statistics or empirical evidence.[58] This would suggest that counter-radicalization-based inoculation messages aimed at youngsters would likely be effective if they were presented as a video-based story that includes emotionally charged scenes and/or testimony.

In contrast, older message recipients have the cognitive capacity to understand deductive logic, statistics, and empirical data. This would suggest that either emotional or logical content would be appropriate for inclusion in inoculation messages aimed at them. While this would be true if there were no other factors to consider, recall that the base of the attitude being protected is another determinant of how the inoculation treatment should be constructed.

Generally, past research has suggested that the nature of the inocula-tion message should match the nature of the attitude to be protected. That is, when a person's attitude is based in logic (e.g., joining an extremist group is bad because I may be put in jail), the most effective inoculation message targeted at that person would likewise be based on logic. In contrast, when a person's attitude is based in emotion (e.g., joining an extremist group is bad because I love my family and don't want to disappoint them), the most effective inoculation treatment would be emotional in kind.[59]

Finally, the success of attitudinal inoculation hinges on the recognition of the kinds of messages that will pose a threat to targets' extant attitudes. As such, message designers should be sure to do preliminary research on the strongest threats that message recipients are likely to face that will challenge their current attitudes, as well as the sources of those threats (i.e., which people will try to challenge them). Once these threats are identified, it becomes possible to construct inoculation treatments that incorporate content tailored towards defending against those threats. Ivanov argues for the use of interviews and focus groups in populations of interest to address this issue.[60]

For example, let's suppose that we want to develop inoculation messages intended to dissuade children in an elementary school from being persuaded by white supremacist propaganda that has been posted around their town by teenage members of a white nationalist group. We know that because of their age and cognitive abilities, a video-based inoculation message delivered as part of an emotionally charged story would be most effective. In addition to these format- and style-based considerations, we must also identify the attitudinal threats that we need to inoculate against. To do so, it might be useful to hold discussions with teachers and students in the school to ask them which aspects of the white supremacist propaganda has been noticed and/or has resonated with the kids (if any). Through this basic formative research, message designers can begin to develop the content of the inoculation treatments.

Designing Inoculation Messages for Preventing Radicalization

After analyzing the audience and identifying the salient threats to their current attitudes, it is possible to begin constructing the counter-radicalization inoculation messages to be disseminated. As I mentioned earlier, regardless of context, inoculation messages typically follow a specific format with distinct communicative elements. These elements involve:

(1) Eliciting the perception that current attitudes are under threat and vulnerable to changing,
(2) Exposing message targets to weakened forms of the arguments they are likely to encounter, and

(3) Refuting the arguments raised in Step 2 to provide message targets with cognitive resources needed to defend against future threats.

The next few sections will cover these steps in turn.

Eliciting Threat and Perceptions of Attitudinal Vulnerability

The first step in the construction of an effective inoculation message involves drawing message recipients' attention to an impending threat to their current attitudes. To do so, the first paragraph of the inoculation message should feature an explicit warning that the targets' attitudes are likely to be challenged and the challenges they are likely to use to persuade them to change their current attitudes or behaviors. To reinforce the threat to their current attitudes or behaviors, the inoculation treatment should also tell recipients that others have already been exposed to the messages that they will face, and that those individuals were successfully persuaded by it.[61] By explicitly warning of the impending challenges to targets' current attitudes, the inoculation message will motivate message recipients to psychologically reinforce those attitudes, thereby increasing their resistance to change.

The formative research from the last section should inform how this first paragraph is constructed. Using the example referenced above (i.e., protecting young children from persuasion via right-wing extremist propaganda), let's consider how the first part of the inoculation message might look. Here are some salient factors related to the audience we are targeting and the context in which the message will be delivered:

- Young children targeted
- Intend to protect against persuasion via white supremacist propaganda
- Teenage white nationalists in the area are likely to confront elementary school kids to promote messages on posted propaganda

Using these factors as a framework around which to build an inoculation message, the first part of the message – which would be delivered in a video testimonial format – could say the following:

Getting involved with racist groups who want to hurt people different than them is a dangerous idea. You can get in trouble with your teachers or your parents. You could be asked to hurt your friends. You could even be forced to do things that will get you put in jail. Even though you don't want to get in trouble or hurt anybody, kids just like you are often persuaded **[elicitation of threat/ vulnerability of current attitude]** to join these groups by other kids who are older than them **[reference to likely source of attitudinal challenge]**. Just last year, a fourth-grader from a school nearby started hanging out with kids from one of these groups. His new group asked him to beat up one of his oldest friends, just because he is African-American. Even though he was sad to do it, he listened to his group and attacked his friend. Afterward, he got in trouble with the police and was kicked out of school **[reinforcement of threat with emotional-laden story about a person similar to the target audience]**. Are you prepared to resist those groups when their members try to convince you to join them? Are you brave enough to tell an older kid that you're not interested in hanging out with people who hurt others? You might not be as prepared as you think ... **[reinforced vulnerability of current attitude]**.

Having made our message targets feel that their attitudes are susceptible to change, it is time to give them the small dose of the challenges they may experience. The next part is what puts the "inoculation" in inoculation theory.

Message Exposure and Refutational Preemption

After eliciting threat and priming feelings of attitudinal vulnerability, it is necessary to expose message recipients to weakened versions of the most potent challenges to their existing attitudes and behaviors. The nature of the threats that message targets will face will have been identified via the foundational research conducted prior to the construction of the inoculation message. These threats are then refuted, thereby giving message targets the content they need to make their own counter-arguments in the future, as well as the experience of seeing how those counter-arguments can be presented.

Pfau argued that when exposing message recipients to the weakened versions of the attitudinal challenges they will face, it is most effective to present and refute those challenges in order of decreasing potency.[62] So, the argument that is most likely to change targets' attitudes and behaviors is presented and refuted first, then the second-most likely, the third-most, and so on.

Given this, the second part of the inoculation message could say:

One of the ways that racist groups will try to persuade you to join them and hurt other people is by telling you that the people they want to hurt are dangerous. Without any proof, they will tell you that your African-American friends break the law and that you would be protecting America by fighting them. They will even tell you fake stories about African-Americans, saying things like "White people are more peaceful than Black people," and "White people should be separate from Black people" **[raising weakened versions of common white-supremacist propaganda]**.

This statement is meant to show the white supremacist arguments in a weakened form – with only vague, unconvincing claims as support. Following this, the weakened arguments are then soundly refuted. Recall that our target audience here comprises young children, so refuting the white supremacist claims with detailed emotional anecdotes is likely to be the most effective. If our audience comprised older children, teens, or adults, statistical evidence showing the inaccuracy of the propaganda's claims may be more appropriate.

With this in mind, the refutation portion of the inoculation message could say:

These statements are as silly and wrong as it gets **[strong refutation]**. Kids of all races and cultures can come together and have fun! In your school, black students and white students grow and learn with each other without any problems. They compete together on sports teams, work together on schoolwork, and play together after school. Sometimes, these groups of friends grow up together, and they become best friends – always happy and having fun, and never hurting each other **[brief, emotion-laden examples refuting propaganda claims]**.

Whereas the challenges to attitudes are presented in weak, vague format, the refutational message is characterized by detailed, emotional language that shoots down the arguments in the previous paragraph. The use of anecdotes and emotional language in the refutational preemption paragraph is appropriate given the limited processing capabilities of the target audience. It is also likely that young children's attitudes about race would be emotional in kind, given that they would be too young to comprehend data or figures related to race, crime statistics, biases in the criminal justice system, or other related issues.

From here, the message designer would repeat the process of presenting weakened versions of attitudinal challenges and refuting them. Perhaps the next paragraph would present weakened versions of arguments derived from popular, but inaccurate, stereotypes of African-Americans emphasized by the propaganda posted around town (e.g., laziness). Once again, these claims would be most effectively refuted with brief emotion-laden anecdotes (e.g., a short story about a hard-working African-American teacher in the school). Inoculation experts have demonstrated that the process of presenting arguments and refuting them need only repeated two or three times to successfully confer resistance to persuasion.[63]

There is some evidence to suggest that the strength of the attitudinal inoculation declines over time. As time passes, message recipients may need "booster messages" (i.e., subsequent inoculation treatments) to reinforce their resistance to the messages that were inoculated against.[64] Pfau and his co-researchers said that the potential for booster messages to reestablish resistance to persuasion is dependent on the timing of the booster's administration.[65] Research in this regard has identified several potential timing windows that would optimize the booster's effectiveness,[66] but more work needs to be done to pin down the optimal time frame in which to administer booster messages (and the factors that influence this).[67]

Conclusions

There is a common analogy used in the popular media that likens violent extremism to a virus.[68] The implications of this metaphor are obvious; it can spread from person to person, it can cause harm, and if left unchecked, it can kill.

Anders Breivik did not try to fight the virus; he embraced it. He cultivated his racist, xenophobic ideology like germs in a Petri dish, intensifying violent beliefs and attitudes about those he thought to be his enemies until eventually, he performed one of the most heinous acts of violence in the last several decades.

A less obvious implication of the virus metaphor concerns how violent extremism can be defended against. Though ideas associated with extremist ideologies can infect those who are left unprotected, it is possible to defend individuals against infection. This chapter has shown not only that attitudinal inoculation can be useful in this respect, but also how inoculation treatments can be effectively administered. If violent ideologies are viruses, attitudinal inoculation can provide the antibodies that kill them.

In the next chapter, we move on to a theory that explains how beliefs and attitudes translate to behavior. An understanding of this process can help us recognize not only the kinds of inoculation messages that might be useful, but also how to develop *other* kinds of messages that are geared towards counter-radicalization.

Notes

1 For complete accounts of the Breivik attack and its aftermath, see the carefully researched *One of Us: The Story of a Massacre in Norway and its Aftermath* by Åsne Seierstad (New York: Farrar, Straus & Giroux, 2016) and *A Norwegian Tragedy: Anders Behring Breivik and the Massacre on Utøya* by Aage Borchgrevink (Cambridge: Polity Press, 2013).

2 Claude H. Miller, Bobi Ivanov, Jeanetta Sims, Josh Compton, Kylie J. Harrison, Kimberly A. Parker, James L. Parker, and Joshua M. Averbeck, "Boosting the Potency of Resistance: Combining the Motivational Forces of Inoculation and Psychological Reactance," *Human Communication Research* 39 (2013): 127–155.

3 Bobi Ivanov, William J. Burns, Timothy L. Sellnow, Elizabeth L. Petrun Sayers, Shari R. Veil, and Marcus W. Mayorga, "Using an Inoculation Message Approach to Promote Public Confidence in Protective Agencies," *Journal of Applied Communication Research* 44, no. 4 (2016): 381–398.

4 William J. McGuire, "The Effectiveness of Supportive and Refutational Defenses in Immunizing and Restoring Beliefs against Persuasion," *Sociometry* 2, no. 2 (1961): 184–197; William J. McGuire and Demetrios

Papageorgis, "The Relative Efficacy of Various Types of Prior Belief-Defense in Producing Immunity against Persuasion," *Journal of Abnormal and Social Psychology* 62 (1961): 327–337; William J. McGuire and Demetrios Papageorgis, "Effectiveness of Forewarning in Developing Resistance to Persuasion," *Public Opinion Quarterly* 26, no. 1 (1962): 24-34.

5 Ivanov et al., "Using an Inoculation Message Approach to Promote Public Confidence in Protective Agencies," p. 383; William J. McGuire, "Inducing Resistance to Persuasion: Some Contemporary Approaches," in *Advances in Experimental Social Psychology 1*, ed. Leonard Berkowitz, 191–229 (New York: Academic Press, 1964).

6 John A. Banas and Stephen A. Rains, "A Meta-Analysis of Research on Inoculation Theory," *Communication Monographs* 77, no. 3 (2010): 281–311; Michael Pfau, Bobi Ivanov, Brian Houston, Michel Haigh, Jeanetta Sims, Eileen Gilchrist, Jason Russell, Shelley Wigley, Jackie Eckstein, and Natalie Richert, "Inoculation and Mental Processing: The Instrumental Role of Associative Networks in the Process of Resistance to Counterattitudinal Influence," *Communication Monographs* 72, no. 4 (2005): 414–441; Adam Richards and John A. Banas, "Inoculation against Resistance to Persuasive Health Messages," *Health Communication* 30 (2015): 451–460.

7 Bobi Ivanov, "Designing Inoculation Messages for Health Communication Campaigns," in *Health Communication Message Design: Theory and Practice*, ed. Hyunyi Cho, 73–93 (Thousand Oaks, CA: Sage, 2012).

8 Ivanov et al., "Using an Inoculation Message Approach to Promote Public Confidence in Protective Agencies," p. 383; Kimberly A. Parker, Stephen A. Rains, and Bobi Ivanov, "Examining the 'Blanket of Protection' Conferred by Inoculation: The Effects of Inoculation Messages on the Cross-Protection of Related Attitudes," *Communication Monographs* 83, no. 1 (2016): 49–68.

9 McGuire, "Inducing Resistance to Persuasion."

10 Banas and Rains, "A Meta-Analysis Research on Inoculation Theory," p. 285; Josh Compton, Ben Jackson, and James A. Dimmock, "Persuading Others to Avoid Persuasion: Inoculation Theory and Resistant Health Attitudes," *Frontiers in Psychology* 7 (2016): article 122.

11 McGuire and Papageorgis, "The Relative Efficacy of Various Types of Prior Belief-Defense in Producing Immunity against Persuasion."

12 Banas and Rains, "A Meta-Analysis of Research on Inoculation Theory"; Compton et al., "Persuading Others to Avoid Persuasion"; Parker et al., "Examining the 'Blanket of Protection' Conferred by Inoculation"; Pfau et al., "Inoculation and Mental Processing"; Josh Compton and Michael Pfau, "Use of Inoculation to Foster Resistance to Credit Card Marketing Targeting College Students," *Journal of Applied Communication Research* 32 (2004): 343–364; Michael Pfau, Kyle James Tusing, Ascan F. Koerner, Waipeng Lee, Linda C. Godbold, Linda J. Penaloza, Violet Shu-huei Yang, and Yah-Huei Hong, "Enriching the Inoculation Construct: The Role of Critical Components in the Process of Resistance," *Human Communication Research* 24, no. 2 (1997): 187–215.

13 James Price Dillard and Lijiang Shen, "On the Nature of Reactance and its Role in Persuasive Health Communication," *Communication Monographs* 72 (2005): 144–168; Brian L. Quick and Michael T. Stephenson, "Further

Evidence that Psychological Reactance Can Be Modeled as a Combination of Anger and Negative Cognitions," *Communication Research* 34, no. 3 (2007): 255–276; Richards and Banas, "Inoculation against Reactance to Persuasive Health Messages"; Stephen A. Rains and Monique Mitchell Turner, "Psychological Reactance and Persuasive Health Communication: A Test and Extension of the Intertwined Model," *Human Communication Research* 33 (2007): 241–269.

14 Jack Williams Brehm, *A Theory of Psychological Reactance* (New York: Academic Press, 1966); Sharon S. Brehm and Jack W. Brehm, *Psychological Reactance: A Theory of Freedom and Control* (New York: Academic Press, 1981).

15 Kurt Braddock, "Vaccinating against Hate: Using Inoculation to Confer Resistance to Persuasion by Extremist Propaganda," *Journal of Communication* (in press).

16 See Note 12.

17 Dillard and Shen, "On the Nature of Reactance"; Miller et al., "Boosting the Potency of Resistance"; Parker et al., "Examining the 'Blanket of Protection' Conferred by Inoculation."

18 A meta-analysis is a study of studies; it looks at the average effect that one variable has on another variable across several studies. Meta-analyses are useful because they correct for errors in how those variables were measured and how the samples for the individual studies were selected. As such, they provide a corrected estimate of the magnitude between two variables.

19 Banas and Rains, "A Meta-Analysis Research on Inoculation Theory."

20 Michael Pfau and Henry C. Kenski, *Attack Politics: Strategy and Defense* (Santa Barbara, CA: Praeger, 1990); see also Michael Pfau, Henry C. Kenski, Michael Nitz, and John Sorenson, "Efficacy of Inoculation Strategies in Promoting Resistance to Political Attack Messages: Application to Direct Mail," *Communication Monographs* 57, no. 1 (1990): 25–43.

21 Chasu An, "Efficacy of Inoculation Strategies in Promoting Resistance to Political Attack Messages: Source Credibility Perspective," dissertation, University of Oklahoma, 2003; Chasu An and Michael Pfau, "The Efficacy of Inoculation in Televised Political Debates," *Journal of Communication* 54, no. 3 (2004): 421–436.

22 Michael Pfau, Michael Haigh, Andeelynn Fifrick, Douglas Holl, Allison Tedesco, Jay Cope, David Nunnally, Amy Schiess, Donald Preston, Paul Roszkowski, and Marlon Martin, "The Effects of Print News Photographs of the Casualties of War," *Journalism & Mass Communication Quarterly* 83, no. 1 (2006): 150–168.

23 Mark M. Bernard, Gregory B. Maio, and James M. Olson, "The Vulnerability of Values to Attack: Inoculation of Values and Value-Relevant Attitudes," *Personality and Social Psychology Bulletin* 29, no. 1 (2003): 63–75.

24 Stewart Bither, Ira J. Dolich, and Elaine B. Nell, "The Application of Attitude Immunization Techniques in Marketing," *Journal of Marketing Research* 8 (1971): 56–61.

25 Josh Compton and Michael Pfau, "Inoculating against Pro-Plagiarism Justifications: Rational and Affective Strategies," *Journal of Applied Communication Research* 36, no. 1 (2008): 98–119.

26 Joon Soo Lim and Eyun-Jung Ki, "Resistance to Ethically Suspicious Parody Video on YouTube: A Test of Inoculation Theory," *Journalism and Mass Communication Quarterly* 84, no. 4 (2007): 713–728.

27 See Banas and Rains, "A Meta-Analysis of Research on Inoculation Theory" for synopses of these topics.

28 Linda C. Godbold and Michael Pfau, "Conferring Resistance to Peer Pressure among Adolescents: Using Inoculation Theory to Discourage Alcohol Use," *Communication Research* 27, no. 4 (2000): 411–437; Richards and Banas, "Inoculating against Reactance to Persuasive Health Messages."

29 Michael Pfau, Steve Van Bockern, and Jong Geun Kang, "Use of Inoculation to Promote Resistance to Smoking Initiation among Adolescents," *Communication Monographs* 59, no. 3 (1992): 213–230; Michael Pfau and Steve Van Bockern, "The Persistence of Inoculation in Conferring Resistance to Smoking Initiation among Adolescents: The Second Year," *Human Communication Research* 20, no. 3 (1994): 413–430.

30 Kimberly A. Parker, Bobi Ivanov, and Josh Compton, "Inoculation's Efficacy with Young Adults' Risky Behaviors: Can Inoculation Confer Cross-Protection over Related but Untreated Issues?" *Health Communication* 27, no. 3 (2012): 223–233.

31 Norman C. H. Wong and Kylie J. Harrison, "Nuances in Inoculation: Protecting Positive Attitudes toward the HPV Vaccine & the Practice of Vaccinating Children," *Journal of Women's Health, Issues and Care* 3, no. 6 (2014).

32 Alicia M. Mason and Claude H. Miller, "Inoculation Message Treatments for Curbing Noncommunicable Disease Development," *Pan American Journal of Public Health* 34, no. 1 (2013): 29–35.

33 E.g., Joseph Abramson, "Comparing Advertising, Inoculation Theory, and the Prevention of Attitude Change among Brand Loyal Consumers: A Laboratory Experiment," dissertation, Louisiana State University, 1977.

34 E.g., Michael Pfau, "The Potential of Inoculation in Promoting Resistance to the Effectiveness of Comparative Advertising Messages," *Communication Quarterly* 40, no. 1 (1992): 26–44.

35 Michael A. Kamins and Henry Assael, "Two-Sided Versus One-Sided Appeals: A Cognitive Perspective on Argumentation, Source Derogation, and the Effect of Disconfirming Trial on Belief Change," *Journal of Marketing Research* 24 (1987): 29–39.

36 Compton and Pfau, "Use of Inoculation to Foster Resistance to Credit Card Marketing Targeting College Students."

37 Michael Pfau, Michael Haigh, Jeanetta Sims, and Shelley Wigley, "The Influence of Corporate Front-Group Stealth Campaigns," *Communication Research* 34, no. 1 (2007): 73–99.

38 Parker et al., "Inoculation's Efficacy with Young Adults' Risky Behaviors."

39 Parker et al., "Examining the 'Blanket of Protection' Conferred by Inoculation."

40 Michael Safi, "Sydney Siege: Anonymous Warning about Man Haron Monis Followed Up, Says PM," *The Guardian* (December 21, 2014). Available at www.theguardian.com/australia-news/2014/dec/21/sydney-siege-anonymous-warning-about-man-haron-monis-followed-up-says-pm.

41 Kylie Simmonds, "Sydney Siege: Police Respond to Anti-Muslim Sentiment in Wake of Lindt Café Shootout," *Australian Broadcasting Corporation* (December 16, 2014). Available at www.abc.net.au/news/2014-12-17/anti-muslim-sentiment-sydney-siege-auburn-mosque-threat/5972784.

42 Christine El-Khoury, "Anti-Muslim Extremists: How Far Will They Go?" *Australian Broadcasting Corporation* (November 22, 2015). Available at www.abc.net.au/radionational/programs/backgroundbriefing/anti-muslim-extremists-how-far-will-they-go/6954442.

43 Interfaith Voices, "Losing a Child to Extremism, Stopping Others" [podcast]. Available at http://interfaithradio.org/Archive/2016-June/Losing_a_Child_to_Extremism__Stopping_Others.

44 Kurt Braddock and John Horgan, "Towards a Guide for Constructing and Disseminating Counternarratives to Reduce Support for Terrorism," *Studies in Conflict & Terrorism* 39, no. 5 (2016): 381–404; Kurt Braddock, "Developing and Disseminating Narratives for Countering Violent Extremism: The Utility of Former Offenders," presented at the Understanding Terrorism and Political Violence Conference, Cork, Ireland (March 2015).

45 Kurt Braddock and John Morrison, "Cultivating Trust and Source Credibility in Online Counternarratives Intended to Reduce Support for Terrorism," *Studies in Conflict & Terrorism* (in press).

46 See also Marc Sageman, *Understanding Terror Networks* (Philadelphia, PA: University of Pennsylvania Press, 2004); Marc Sageman, *Leaderless Jihad* (Philadelphia, PA: University of Pennsylvania Press, 2008).

47 John Horgan, *Walking Away from Terrorism: Accounts of Disengagement from Radical and Extremist Movements* (Abingdon: Routledge, 2009).

48 John Horgan classified interviews with former white nationalist extremist offenders.

49 Josh Compton, "Inoculation Theory," in *The SAGE Handbook of Persuasion: Developments in Theory and Practice*, ed. James Price Dillard and Lijiang Shen, 220–236 (Thousand Oaks, CA: Sage, 2013), p. 229; Miller et al., "Boosting the Potency of Resistance."

50 For instance, ISIS would refer to Muslims who did not adhere to their brand of Islam as *kufar* – non-believers in Islam altogether. By branding non-ISIS Muslims as *kufar*, the group would (1) seek to undermine their religious arguments against the group's statements and actions (i.e., attitudinal inoculation), and (2) justify targeting them with terrorist attacks. See John L. Esposito, *The Oxford Dictionary of Islam* (Oxford University Press, 2003), p. 312. See also Alex P. Schmid, "Challenging the Narrative of the 'Islamic State,'" ICCT Research Paper (June 2015). Available at https://icct.nl/wp-content/uploads/2015/06/ICCT-Schmid-Challenging-the-Narrative-of-the-Islamic-State-June2015.pdf.

51 Christian Picciolini, *Romantic Violence: Memoirs of an American Skinhead* (Chicago: Goldmill Group, 2015).

52 www.stormfront.org/forum/t1187696/.

53 www.stormfront.org/forum/t981157/.

54 Ivanov, "Designing Inoculation Messages for Health Communication Campaigns," pp. 78–79.

55 Pfau et al., "Use of Inoculation to Promote Resistance to Smoking Initiation among Adolescents."

56 Pfau and Van Bockern, "The Persistence of Inoculation in Conferring Resistance to Smoking Initiation among Adolescents."

57 Ivanov, "Designing Inoculation Messages for Health Communication Campaigns," p. 79.

58 Ibid.; Pfau et al., "Use of Inoculation to Promote Resistance to Smoking Initiation among Adolescents."

59 Michael Pfau, Shane M. Semmler, Leslie Deatrick, Alicia Mason, Gwen Nisbett, Lindsay Lane, Elizabeth Craig, Jill Underhill, and John Banas, "Nuances about the Role and Impact of Affect in Inoculation," *Communication Monographs* 76, no. 1 (2009): 73–98.

60 Ivanov, "Designing Inoculation Messages for Health Communication Campaigns."

61 Ibid.; Bobi Ivanov, Michael Pfau, and Kimberly A. Parker, "The Attitude Base as a Moderator of the Effectiveness of Inoculation Strategy," *Communication Monographs* 76, no. 1 (2009): 47–72; Michael Pfau, R. Lance Holbert, Stephen J. Zubric, Nilofer H. Pasha, and Wei-Kuo Lin, "Role and Influence of Communication Modality in the Process of Resistance to Persuasion," *Media Psychology* 2, no. 1 (2000): 1–33.

62 Michael Pfau, "Designing Messages for Behavioral Inoculation," in *Designing Health Messages: Approaches from Communication Theory and Public Health Practice*, ed. Edward Maibach and Roxanne Louiselle Parrott, 99–113 (Thousand Oaks, CA: Sage, 1995).

63 Ivanov et al., "The Attitude Base as a Moderator of the Effectiveness of Inoculation Strategy"; Pfau et al., "Inoculation and Mental Processing"; Parker et al., "Inoculation's Efficacy with Young Adults' Risky Behaviors."

64 James B. Stiff and Paul A. Mongeau, *Persuasive Communication* (New York: Guilford Press, 2002).

65 Michael Pfau, Joshua Compton, Kimberly A. Parker, Elaine M. Witenberg, Chasu An, Monica Ferguson, Heather Horton, and Yuri Malyshev, "The Traditional Explanation for Resistance Versus Attitude Accessibility: Do They Trigger Distinct or Overlapping Processes of Resistance?" *Human Communication Research* 30, no. 3 (2004): 329–360.

66 Pfau et al., "Use of Inoculation to Promote Resistance to Smoking Initiation among Adolescents"; Pfau and Van Bockern, "The Persistence of Inoculation in Conferring Resistance to Smoking Initiation among Adolescents"; Michael Pfau, "The Inoculation Model of Resistance to Influence," in *Progress in Communication Sciences: Advances in Persuasion, Vol. 13*, ed. George Barnett and Franklin J. Bostner, 133–171 (Greenwich, CT: Ablex, 1997).

67 Josh Compton and Michael Pfau, "Inoculation Theory of Resistance to Influence at Maturity: Recent Progress in Theory Development and Application and Suggestions for Future Research," in *Communication Yearbook 29*, ed. Pamela J. Kalbfleisch, 97–145 (Mahwah, NJ: Lawrence Erlbaum, 2005).

68 For recent examples connected to the Christchurch Mosque attack, see News Corp Australia, "Australian Man Brenton Tarrant Named as Christchurch Gunman as Four Taken into Custody," *The West Australian* (March 15,

2019). Available at https://thewest.com.au/news/terrorism/australian-man-brenton-tarrant-named-as-christchurch-gunman-as-four-taken-into-custody-ng-b881137083z; Reuters, "'Islamophobic Terrorism Must Stop': World Reacts in Horror to New Zealand Mosque Attacks," *News18* (March 15, 2019). Available at www.news18.com/news/world/islamophobic-terrorism-must-stop-world-reacts-in-horror-to-new-zealand-mosque-attacks-2067551 .html.

5 The Reasoned Action of Radicalization and Counter-Radicalization

Well-mannered and handsome, 24-year-old Muhammad Dakhlalla couldn't help but smile when asked about what attracted him to his former girlfriend.

"Looks, one thing," he bashfully admits before laughing softly to himself. He blushes a little.

Muhammad (or Mo, as he is known to friends) can hardly be blamed for smiling when he recalls what he describes as his first real relationship. Jaelyn Young is a stunning, bright young woman who had been studying to become a doctor at Mississippi State University (MSU). Mo met her at MSU, where the two began dating. They were on the cusp of adulthood, with seemingly endless potential to succeed in any way they wanted to.

But as Mo reflects on Jaelyn and what the two of them had done, his expression fades. Coy happiness gives way to regret, and he looks down at the tan jumpsuit he is required to wear as an inmate at the Oklahoma City Federal Transfer Center. Muhammad was arrested and imprisoned for conspiracy to support ISIS, and Jaelyn Young was a big reason why.

∴

Jaelyn had been a model student at Warren Central High School in Vicksburg, Mississippi. She was easy to get along with and had friends within virtually every social circle.[1] A teacher at Warren Central described her as "one of the top students" she'd ever taught, and an "unusual combination" of beauty, charisma, and intelligence. Various members of the community remembered her fondly as well. She was a regular attendee at Triumph Church, where the pastor described her as a "precious, well-mannered" girl. Nobody had reason to doubt that Jaelyn was happy.

By senior year, however, Jaelyn's interests seemed to shift. She quit the cheerleading squad to focus on academic studies.[2] Her mother claimed that she had been bullied by other girls at school. Despite her early popularity at Warren Central, her mother said she only had one real friend by twelfth grade, and that friend tragically died after succumbing to a lung infection. Jaelyn became even more isolated after the death of her friend, thinking that people at the school disliked her. Her fellow students had no idea about Jaelyn's unhappiness; they assumed she lived the charmed life that only high-school popularity can bring to a teenager.

After graduating from Warren Central in 2013, Jaelyn enrolled at Mississippi State, where she befriended several international students. Their impression of Jaelyn was similar to how she was described in high school. Sweet. Friendly. Kind.

But by the end of her freshman year at MSU, Jaelyn's life had changed dramatically. Despite years of attendance at Triumph Church in her native Vicksburg, Jaelyn began to explore other faiths, including Buddhism and Hinduism. She rented an apartment, but didn't tell her parents about it. She began dating a boy named Matthew, but the two fought a lot.

After a summer-long break from the relationship with Matthew, Jaelyn began speaking to one of Matthew's friends – a charming, handsome boy. His buddies called him Mo.

∴

After Matthew learned of how much time his girlfriend had been spending with Mo, he and Jaelyn split up. By November of 2014, Jaelyn and Mo had begun dating, and the two almost immediately isolated themselves from their previous friends. Mo's friends distrusted Jaelyn, citing her insistence that Mo get her permission to socialize with others. They also claimed that Jaelyn would get angry if Mo stayed out late without letting her know of his whereabouts. Even when the couple would meet up with other people, they would keep to themselves.

At the same time, Jaelyn's search for spirituality was assisted by her association with Mo. By March of 2015, she had converted to Islam, reciting the *shahada* at Mo's parents' house. She quickly abandoned more traditional clothes worn by college-aged women in favor of a black hijab.

Surprising many in Mo's family, as well as the Starkville Muslim community at large, Mo and Jaelyn were married in June of 2015. Jonathan, a friend of Mo's brother, called the marriage a "bit fishy." To be sure, things seemed a bit hurried about the union between Jaelyn and Mo. There was no marriage contract, nobody to perform the ceremony, and no witnesses to the marriage. Said Jonathan, "we were told [about the wedding] the day of, and that it would be a potluck dinner."

The couple's friends and family were suspicious of the decisions they had been making. What the couple kept private from others, however, was far more troubling.

In the months before her marriage to Mo, Jaelyn had taken to watching videos produced by Anjem Choudary, a British radical Islamist who would later be imprisoned for swearing allegiance to ISIS. She began asking questions about ISIS leadership, distributing articles about the duty of Muslims to support ISIS, and downloading English-language ISIS propaganda. Mo became involved as well. After moving in with Jaelyn, he watched ISIS propaganda videos with her and downloaded ISIS material providing information on how to move overseas.

Jaelyn and Mo gradually became more active in their online support of ISIS. Through interactions with other ISIS supporters online, Jaelyn claimed that she wanted to travel to ISIS territory where she could raise children according to ISIS's brand of Islamic law. She celebrated the murder of a sailor and four Marines in Tennessee. Mo's enthusiasm seemed to grow as well. He began to refer to Jaelyn using an Arabic name and expressed a willingness to fight for ISIS. In one of his posts online, he said that he wanted to "be taught what it really means to have a heart in battle."

Together, they planned to leave the United States, but did not tell family members about their desire to join ISIS. Instead, they wrote letters to loved ones telling them that they saw no future for themselves in the United States and that they should not come looking for them.

The stories they told their families to justify their departure didn't matter. The other "ISIS supporters" that they had been interacting with online were FBI agents. When the pair arrived at Golden Triangle Regional Airport to leave for ISIS territory, they were arrested with little more than clothes, candy, and video games in their possession. Grossly underprepared and ignorant of the implications of what they were trying to do, Jaelyn Young and Muhammad Dakhlalla's jihad ended before it began.

For months following their arrest, Jaelyn wrote notes to Mo while the two waited in jail. She was concerned that Mo was cooperating with prosecutors, and continuously reminded him of their plan to travel to the Middle East to expose "un-Islamic states." Even after being arrested, Jaelyn maintained the illusion that her plan could still be carried out. Mo had no such illusions; in March of 2016, he handed over every letter Jaelyn had written him and pleaded guilty to conspiracy to provide material support to ISIS.

It seems that Mo was not nearly as dedicated to living a life consistent with ISIS values as Jaelyn. She was far more active than him in overt support for the group, and he was quick to abandon the pair's plan following their arrest. In an interview with CNN, Mo even admitted that he should have slowed down and thought about what he and Jaelyn were doing before it had gone too far.[3] Given Mo's modest enthusiasm for ISIS, what could have motivated him to come so close to traveling to the Middle East to support the group?

To hear Mo tell it, his lukewarm support for ISIS was amplified by his love for Jaelyn. He said that love can "blind out your intelligence, your reasoning. Without that love there, I don't believe I would be [jailed] today. I wouldn't have even considered [joining ISIS] at all."

Although Mo may have claimed that he was "blinded" by love, his path towards supporting ISIS was anything but irrational. It was paved with carefully considered decisions based on his beliefs about what he would be doing for ISIS and how he wanted Jaelyn to view him. Love didn't blind Mo, but it did motivate him.

∵

Mo's feelings for Jaelyn and their influence on his decision-making were part of a mental calculus that has been studied by communication and psychology researchers since the mid-1970s. This research has shown that most decisions are made because of individuals' beliefs and attitudes about the behaviors they are considering and how they believe *others* think about those behaviors.

In Mo's case, he developed beliefs about the sorts of things he would be doing with ISIS through his engagement with the propaganda that he consumed alongside Jaelyn. Additionally, Jaelyn's enthusiasm for supporting ISIS led Mo to believe that she would be pleased by his support of the group. Mo may not have been passionate about the ISIS ideology, but he loved Jaelyn, and was keen on helping the group in his own way. Mo's mental calculus – misguided though it was – ultimately led him to attempt to travel to the Middle East and join one of the most ruthless terrorist groups in recent memory.

Although the behavior that Mo attempted to perform (i.e., support ISIS) can be considered extreme, the psychological processes he engaged in to develop that intention was not. Many researchers have shown how individuals consider the costs and benefits of engaging in terrorism before ultimately deciding to do so.

Fortunately, this reasoning process can be interrupted and exploited to prevent an individual's movement towards terrorism. We can use messages that target specific beliefs about terrorism to dissuade individuals' potential support for it. This chapter shows how.

Specifically, this chapter will show how *reasoned action theory* explains some individuals' support for terrorist groups. More importantly, this chapter will also identify specific vulnerabilities in the reasoning process that, when effectively targeted by strategic communicative interventions, can dissuade support for terrorist groups or activity.

Before discussing how we can intervene in reasoning processes that lead to support for terrorism, it is critical that we first develop an understanding of decision-making and reasoned action more generally. To this end, the next section will explain reasoned action theory. The chapter will then turn to how the perspectives that comprise reasoned action theory can be used to target specific points in the decision-making process that can interrupt violent radicalization.

Mo eventually realized that the path he took was wrong. This chapter will show how we can construct mental detours so others can reach similar conclusions about supporting terrorism before it is too late to turn back.

Reasoned Action Theory and Persuasion

The architects of reasoned action theory, Martin Fishbein and Icek Ajzen, argued that an individual's beliefs about a behavior are the driving force behind their decision to engage in that behavior.[4] These beliefs can be affected by any number of factors, but regardless of how an individual develops these beliefs, they affect whether the individual will perform that action. The process by which beliefs translate to behaviors is characterized by a series of relationships relating beliefs to attitudes, attitudes to intentions, and intentions to manifest behavior. This series of relationships serves as the basis for reasoned action theory (see Figure 5.1 for a visual representation).

What is Reasoned Action Theory?

Reasoned action theory is an evolved series of relationships between beliefs, attitudes, norms, perceptions of control, and intentions that describe how different factors lead to a person's engagement in a behavior. I say "evolved" because the current state of reasoned action theory is based on the evolution of three other theories: the theory of reasoned action (yes, I know it sounds very similar),[5] the theory of planned behavior,[6] and the behavioral prediction model.[7] Going over each of these theories and models in detail is beyond the scope of this chapter (and would likely make the chapter much longer than you'd like), so for the sake of simplicity, I will follow Marco Yzer and "refer to the current formulation of the theory and to propositions that apply to all formulations of the theory" as reasoned action theory.[8] Stated more simply, reasoned action theory is a combination of three other theories that all relate to how individuals come to engage in behaviors.

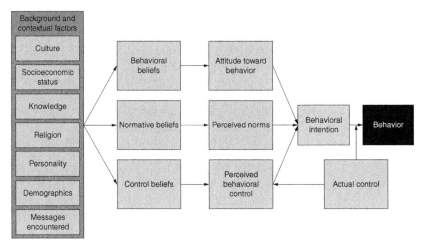

Figure 5.1 Reasoned action theory

As Fishbein and Ajzen theorized, reasoned action theory says that a person's beliefs about a behavior will affect whether the person engages in that behavior. They argued that no matter how a person develops these beliefs – learning them from their family, being exposed to them on television, pulling them from the Internet – they ultimately guide that person's decision to engage (or not to engage) in the behavior.[9]

That's all well and good, but if you look at Figure 5.1 you'll see that different kinds of beliefs do not *directly* affect a person's behavior. Instead, those beliefs respectively influence their attitudes, perceived norms, and perceptions of the control they have over performing the behavior. These factors then influence the person's intention to engage in a behavior, which then determines whether the behavior is performed. Developing beliefs about a behavior is only the first step on the road to performing that behavior.

To show how beliefs about an extremist group can lead to an individual's supporting that extremist group, we need to dig a bit deeper into the theory and go through all its elements.

Illustrating the Elements of the Reasoned Action Process:
"Mark" and the White-Power Group

I realize I just threw you into the deep end of a conceptual pool, submerging you in terms specific to reasoned action theory. Sorry about that, I didn't mean to scare you. But I promise I did it for a good reason.

To understand how to influence the behaviors of those targeted by terrorists for radicalization and recruitment, it is important that we understand each of these terms (and their meaning in relation with one another) in the context of reasoned action theory. So, before we discuss the theory with respect to general persuasion, radicalization, and counter-radicalization, I will provide you with definitions for the different elements that comprise the theory. For the sake of clarity (and your sanity), the definitions will appear in the order that the theory unfolds (from left to right in Figure 5.1).

Background and Contextual Factors

Remember that Fishbein and Ajzen said that people develop beliefs about behaviors from a seemingly infinite number of factors.[10] Reasoned action theory calls these *background and contextual factors*. For example, consider a person who watches a local news program that reports heavily on domestic terrorism cases in her region of the country ("messages encountered" in the theory model). Because of the messages the individual receives from the program every day, she may believe that she is at risk for being victimized in a terrorist attack. Consider another example where a white teen is raised in a family where the parents use racist epithets to describe African-Americans ("culture" in the theory model). By being raised in a culture where African-Americans are derogated, insulted, and dehumanized, that teenager may come to develop beliefs consistent with those of his racist parents.

In both examples, different beliefs held by the individuals are derived from things that characterize them as individuals with unique background characteristics (i.e., the messages they consume and family culture, respectively).

Beliefs, Attitudes, Norms, and Perceived Control

Beliefs are our unvalenced ideas about the nature of the reality in which we exist.

Now that I have gotten the technical definition out of the way, let me speak a little more plainly. Beliefs are our understanding about what *is* versus what *is not* in the world around us. Beliefs are not good, bad, favorable, unfavorable, pleasant, unpleasant, happy, sad, or described by any other words that indicate value. If I accept the notion that "the world is round," it simply indicates my belief about the shape of the Earth. There is no value attached to this statement; it just represents my understanding of the nature of the planet we live on.

But, if I accept that "people who think the world is flat are foolish," reasoned action theory would not characterize this as a belief. "Foolish" is an adjective that indicates value attached to the idea – the theory would treat this statement as an *attitude*. More on that later.

For now though, let's go over the three different kinds of beliefs that are affected by background and contextual factors and in turn, influence other outcomes: beliefs about a behavior, beliefs about norms associated with the behavior, and beliefs about one's control to perform the behavior. To properly illustrate these elements of the theory in the context of radicalization, I will use one of the examples from earlier – a teenager raised in a racist family (let's call him Mark) who is thinking about joining a local white-power group.

Behavioral Beliefs Predict Attitude about a Behavior

Behavioral beliefs represent an individual's unbiased ideas about performing a behavior and the consequences of doing so. Reasoned action theory predicts that over time and experiences, an individual will develop a large set of beliefs about the behavior in question. This large set of beliefs will eventually develop into a sense of how favorable it would be to engage in the behavior (i.e., *attitude about the behavior*). This process occurs as an individual develops expectations about the consequences of his performing the behavior and how favorable or unfavorable those consequences would be.[11]

In the process of considering joining a white-power group, Mark may initially believe that if he joins up, he will have the opportunity to directly protest African-American cultural influence in the United States. Note that at this point in the model, Mark's belief about joining the group has no evaluations associated with it. He simply believes that joining the group will give him opportunities for political expression that he wouldn't have had otherwise.

Over time, as he continues to think about potentially joining the group, Mark may develop a larger set of beliefs about the consequences of his doing so beyond his initial belief about protest opportunities. For example, he may believe that joining the group would provide him with a larger group of like-minded friends, give him access to white-power punk rock shows, and protect him from bullying by African-American students at his school. As these beliefs develop, Mark is likely to judge these outcomes to be favorable for him, resulting in his developing a positive attitude about joining the white-power group.

Let's start to illustrate this process using the reasoned action theory model (see Figure 5.2).

At this point, Mark has developed a substantial set of beliefs about joining a local white-power group and the implications of his doing so. That said, whether he joins the group is dependent on several other factors as well. One set of these relates to how he thinks others will judge him if he actually goes through with it.

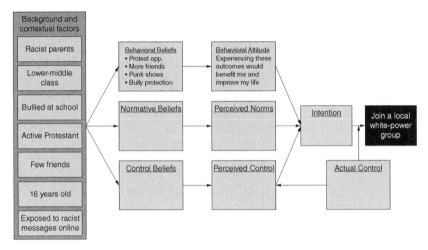

Figure 5.2 Mark's behavioral beliefs and behavioral attitude related to joining a local white-power group

Normative Beliefs Predict Perceived Norms

Normative beliefs represent an individual's notions about others' stances on a behavior being considered. Although original conceptualizations of the theory of reasoned action[12] called this element of the theory "subjective norms," later researchers realized that norms are multifaceted and can't be reduced to one set of factors. Specifically, they found that subjective norms were relatively unstable predictors of behavioral intention by themselves,[13] so they tested different kinds of normative pressure on whether someone will engage in a behavior. This research showed that there are two different kinds of norms that exert pressure on someone's intention to engage in a behavior – injunctive norms and descriptive norms.

Beliefs about *injunctive norms* indicate whether a person thinks other people would approve (or disapprove) of his behavior. In our example, when deciding whether to join a white-power group, Mark may consider whether his parents, friends, or teachers think doing so would be a good idea. Beliefs about *descriptive norms* indicate whether a person thinks other people engage in the behavior themselves. For instance, Mark may think about whether his parents or teachers were affiliated with a white-power group when they were his age, or whether his friends engage in any secret white supremacist behavior he doesn't know about.

Mark may think about these other people as he debates joining the white-power group, but they will not all have the same influence on him.

The potential for injunctive norms and/or descriptive norms to exert normative pressure on someone to engage in a behavior depends on the person being thought about. Generally, individuals consider how much they value another person's opinion in conjunction with that opinion to determine how much weight they give to it.

So, suppose that Mark thinks that his parents would be extremely pleased if they found out that he joined a local white-power group. On the other hand, he is confident that his teachers would be extremely disappointed if they found out he joined the group. If Mark valued his parents and teachers to the exact same degree, these two beliefs would cancel each other out. However, let's imagine that Mark hates his teachers and loves his parents. Because of this, his parents' expected approval will carry much more weight in his decision to join (or not join) the white-power group than his teachers' expected disappointment.

Perceived norms are the combination of injunctive and descriptive norms, and are a kind of collective pressure felt by an individual in considering how others would judge their behavior. Mark's perceived norms would be his cumulative perceptions about what valued others would think about his joining the white-power group (see Figure 5.3).

Regardless of how Mark thinks others would react to his joining the group (or whether he thinks others have been part of similar groups), there is one last set of factors that will influence whether he intends to join the group. All the psychological pressure in the world will not get

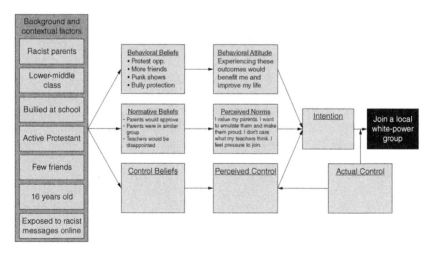

Figure 5.3 Mark's behavioral beliefs, behavioral attitude, normative beliefs, and perceived norms related to joining a local white-power group

him to take action towards joining the white-power group if he doesn't believe he can physically do so. That's where control beliefs and perceived behavioral control come in.

Control Beliefs Predict Perceived Behavioral Control

Control beliefs are an individual's perceptions of how likely it is that she will have the resources and opportunities to perform a certain behavior, as well as the degree to which those resources and opportunities will help the person to engage in the behavior.[14]

The history of research on *perceived behavioral control* is a bit more complex. It was originally defined as an individual's perception of the ease with which they could perform a behavior.[15] In this way, it was often thought of as nearly synonymous with self-efficacy. However, this definition was unsatisfying to several researchers, many of whom analyzed scales that respectively measured someone's confidence or control in performing a specific action. These analyses showed that an individual's confidence in their ability to perform an action and the degree to which they believe they have control over performance of that action are distinct factors.[16]

Not to be corrected, Fishbein and Ajzen were displeased with researchers theorizing that perceived behavioral control and self-efficacy were conceptually distinct.[17] They instead argued instead that it was a multifaceted construct defined by individuals' perceptions of their capacity (i.e., how certain someone is they can perform a behavior) and autonomy (how much freedom someone believes they have to perform a behavior).[18]

Mark's control beliefs would be his perceptions concerning the resources he would use and the opportunities he would have to join the local white-power group. Let's assume that the group demands that its members attend meetings twice a month in a bar across town from where Mark lives. To meet the group's membership requirements, Mark will need a reliable means of transportation to bring him to the meetings (i.e., a necessary resource). Luckily for Mark, he just bought a new car with no mechanical problems, so he believes that his car will suit this need. Transportation will not pose a problem.

Let's also assume that Mark believes that if he attends a single meeting, established members of the group will invite him to attend future meetings (i.e., an opportunity for engagement).

Because Mark believes that his new car and his initial attendance at a meeting will facilitate his movement towards the group, his perceptions of the control he has over joining the group strengthen. In Fishbein and Ajzen's language, Mark will believe himself to have the capacity and the

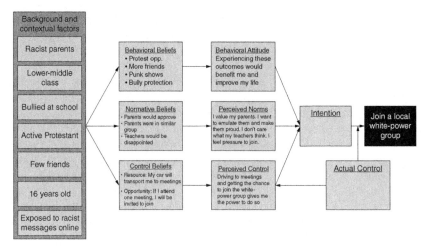

Figure 5.4 Mark's behavioral beliefs, behavioral attitude, normative beliefs, perceived norms, control beliefs, and perceived behavioral control related to joining a local white-power group

autonomy to join the group, thereby increasing the likelihood that he will do so. Let's have a look at how this would play out in reasoned action theory (Figure 5.4).

∴

At this point, we have covered how background factors affect different kinds of beliefs, and how those beliefs respectively affect attitudes, perceptions of norms, and perceptions of control with respect to a specific behavior. However, these latter outcomes do not have a direct effect on whether someone decides to engage in a behavior. Instead, researchers have found that the closest predictor of someone's doing something is their intention to do it. So, we now turn to behavioral intention.

Behavioral Intention

When Ajzen conceived of behavioral intention as the most proximal predictor of a behavior, he conceptualized it as a collective variable that encapsulates all the different factors that influence whether someone will engage in that behavior. He further argued that the behavioral intention variable indicates how much effort someone is willing to exert to successfully perform the behavior in question.[19]

Since the creation of the theory of reasoned action and the theory of planned behavior, other researchers have offered more refined definitions and alternate propositions for what is the closest predictor of someone's behavior. Some individuals have argued that the best predictor of an individual's behavior is their belief of how likely it is that they will, in fact, perform that behavior. These researchers, beginning with Warshaw and Davis around the same time Ajzen was arguing for behavioral intention, called this factor behavioral expectation.[20] They claimed that expectation was a better predictor of behavior because it accounted for factors outside the individual's control that might prevent them from engaging in the behavior. Later studies showed that these authors may have been a bit presumptuous with their assumption; behavioral expectation was shown to be better at predicting manifest behavior than behavioral intention (as conceptualized by Ajzen).[21]

Other researchers claimed that behavioral willingness – intention to act under certain conditions – would predict behavior better than the classic intention variable.[22] These authors argued that someone may intend to do something, but will in fact do something else if the opportunity arises. Fishbein and Ajzen rejected this idea, arguing that behavioral willingness is not conclusively different than behavioral intention; the former is just a conditional version of the latter.[23]

Despite numerous variations proposed on the intention construct, it has generally retained a widely understood meaning. Specifically, *behavioral intention* represents an individual's readiness to engage in a behavior. Moreover, reasoned action theory dictates that an individual's attitude about a behavior (behavioral attitude), the pressure exerted on the individual to engage in the behavior (perceived norms), and the individual's perceptions of their control to perform the behavior (perceived behavioral control) directly influence whether the individual will develop a state of readiness to perform that behavior.

Let's review Mark's case to evaluate whether he would develop an intention to join a white-power group in his community. First, he has concluded that joining the group would likely lead to outcomes that would have a positive effect on his life. Second, he feels pressure to join the white-power group because he believes his parents – whom he values very much – would approve of his doing so. Third, he knows that he has the resources he needs to join the group and will likely be given the opportunity to do so if he makes use of those resources (i.e., uses his car to transport him to mandatory meetings). Reasoned action theory would predict that taken together, these three factors would lead Mark to develop a readiness to join the group.

That is, at this point, Mark would have a positive intention to affiliate himself to the white-power group. Figure 5.5 shows this continued trajectory.

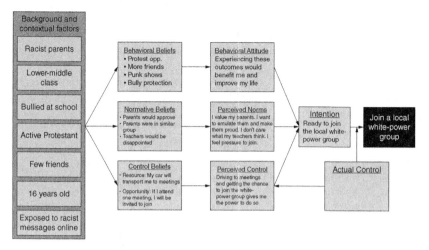

Figure 5.5 Mark's behavioral beliefs, behavioral attitude, normative beliefs, perceived norms, control beliefs, perceived behavioral control, and intention related to joining a local white-power group

Actual Control

It's important to note that even when someone has a strong intention to perform a behavior, there may be factors that constrain their ability to do so. So, before discussing the final element of the reasoned action theory model (how intentions predict behavior), we must account for these potential restraints. Fishbein and Ajzen explain that despite developing beliefs regarding their ability to engage in a behavior, an individual may, in reality, lack the skills to do so. In addition, environmental barriers may prevent them from engaging in the intended behavior.

More simply, an individual can be wrong about how much control they have over the performance of a behavior. As a result, they may not be able to perform that behavior despite intending to. If they fail to perform the behavior despite their intentions, they are likely to develop a new estimation of their perceived behavioral control, which will influence their intention to attempt the behavior in the future.[24]

Let's turn back to Mark and his consideration of joining a white-power group. Recall that one of the stipulations of joining the hypothetical white-power group is attendance at meetings. Mark believes that this will not be a problem (i.e., he has high perceived behavioral control). He believes that his car will carry him to the meetings without a problem, and when he arrives at the first meeting, the opportunity to officially join the group will be made available to him.

However, on the day of the first meeting Mark plans to attend, his car fails to start. He curses as he slams his fists down on the steering wheel, frustrated that despite his best intentions, he will not get to the bar on time for his first meeting with the group. Mark was ready and willing to put himself in a position to join the white-power group, but an environmental factor – a faulty spark plug – prevented him from doing so.

Behavior

The final segment of reasoned action theory is the simplest. After background factors contribute to different kinds of beliefs; those beliefs respectively affect behavioral attitudes, norms, and perceptions of behavioral control; and these factors influence intention, the only remaining relationship is the one for which intention leads to manifest behavior. If the preceding variables lead the individual to have an intention to engage in the behavior, then he is likely to do so (assuming environmental factors do not negatively affect the person's ability to perform the action).

We have finally reached the final stage of Mark's decision-making process. Following the development of his attitudes about joining the white-power group, his perceptions of normative pressure on him to do so, and his notions of the control he has over doing so, he has the intention of joining the white-power group in his town. Reasoned action theory contends that because he has this intention – a psychological readiness to affiliate himself with a racist social group – he is likely to do so. Mark's radicalization has been completed as a function of a reasoned action process.

See Figure 5.6 for a complete reasoned-action-based account of our fictional teenager's radicalization trajectory.

⁙

We now have a complete conceptualization of the process by which decisions are made via reasoned action. We've also grappled with a hypothetical example of how reasoned action applies to the psychological development of a budding extremist. However, the purpose of this book is not only to help you understand the psychological developments that contribute to violent extremism, but also how different kinds of persuasive messages can influence those developments.

With the knowledge of reasoned action theory and how persuasive messages can influence the process that defines it, we can use that knowledge to craft successful messages and distribute them effectively. To that end, the following section offers some recommendations for using reasoned action theory to inform the development of messages for the purpose of counter-radicalization.

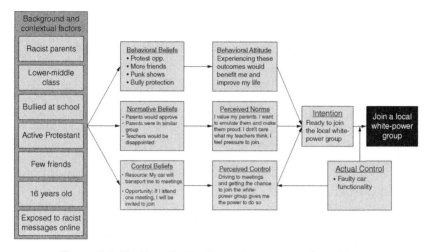

Figure 5.6 Mark's radicalization trajectory towards a white-power group via reasoned action

Using the Reasoned Action Process to Prevent Radicalization

Reasoned action theory dictates that if we can identify message targets' attitudes, perceived norms, and perceived control over performing a behavior, we can predict their attitudes, intentions, and performance of that behavior. It follows that if we can influence the beliefs that underpin those attitudes, perceived norms, and perceptions of control, we can similarly influence these outcomes, ultimately shaping the behavior of message targets. In this way, reasoned action theory guides us to target different kinds of beliefs that can, in theory, have different implications for whether message targets eventually engage in (or avoid) a desired (or undesired) behavior.

But before a message designer can even consider developing an intervention intended to affect message targets' beliefs, attitudes, intentions, or behaviors surrounding an extremist ideology, several other steps must be taken to improve the chances of the intervention's success. The first of these seems obvious but is often overlooked – we must identify the specific behavior that we hope to promote or suppress.

Step 1: Identifying Radicalization-Related Behaviors Targeted for Reinforcement or Change

In the general model for reasoned action theory, all belief-, attitude-, and intention-related variables ultimately lead to one outcome – behavior.

This seems simple enough, but in developing communicative interventions based on the reasoned action process, there are several ways that this final outcome can be conceptualized. Let's use our earlier example – Mark, the budding white supremacist – to illustrate these different outcomes.

First, message designers can seek to change beliefs associated with specific behaviors in a clear, measurable way. In the case of an intervention aimed at young, vulnerable individuals like Mark, we would want to change beliefs related to a *specific* behavior that might result in a closer affiliation with the nationalist organization he is considering joining. An intervention based on this kind of behavioral outcome might attempt to persuade Mark to attend two fewer white-power punk rock shows per month or spending six more hours per week engaging in activities unrelated to white-power politics. Note that these behavioral outcomes are specific and measurable.

Second, message designers might attempt to change beliefs related to more general behavioral categories. These outcomes have less defined boundary conditions and can encapsulate any number of specific behaviors. Communicative interventions aimed at Mark and based on this category might seek to persuade him to engage in less illegal activity, protest legally, or talk to individuals from other cultures. These outcomes could be useful in pushing Mark away from the white-power group, but do not provide him with tangible guidance about how to implement the behaviors.

Finally, message designers can seek to change beliefs related to goals that are consistent with the designers' persuasive objectives. If message designers wanted to dissuade Mark (and other vulnerable individuals) from gravitating towards the white-power group, they may seek to promote beliefs associated with goals that would, by their very nature, pull them away from the group. An intervention designed in this way might encourage beliefs consistent with Mark's growing more popular outside the context of the white-power group (a social goal) or learning to defend himself from bullies on his own (a self-esteem goal).

All three of these behavioral outcomes can be useful to target via reasoned action theory under different circumstances. However, over decades of work on the theory of reasoned action and the theory of planned behavior, Martin Fishbein found that interventions based on the first category – changing specific behaviors – are the most likely to be effective.[25]

With this in mind, communicative interventions based on reasoned action theory will be most useful if they *target specific behaviors that would reduce support for an extremist group or terrorist behavior.*

For our purposes, let us suppose that Mark has already begun to attend white-power events and getting deeper into the white nationalist ideology. To challenge the ideology into which Mark has begun to descend, we have decided to develop a communicative intervention that promotes engagement in non-white-power activities for six more hours per week. This, by extension, will reduce the number of hours per week that Mark (and other vulnerable individuals) will have available to spend on supporting the white nationalist group.

Step 2: Distinguishing Targets at Risk for Radicalization by Intention

Having identified a specific behavior that a message designer wishes to target, it becomes necessary to determine why a message target is (or is not) engaging in the behavior in question. The theory of reasoned action indicates that a person's engagement in a behavior hinges on two factors: (1) they have the intention to perform the behavior and (2) they have the skills and opportunity to perform the behavior. In the absence of either factor, the behavior will not be performed. So, among those who do not engage in a behavior, there are two types of message targets:

- People who have the intention to perform the behavior, but not the skills/opportunity.
- People who have the skills and opportunity to perform the behavior, but have no intention to do so.

Given that there are two subsets of the target audience, message designers will need to develop different respective interventions to influence those with intention but not ability and those with ability but not intention. To determine the degree to which the population being targeted is primarily characterized by the former or latter category, *message designers should obtain measures of targets' beliefs, attitudes, norms, self-efficacy, and intentions in relation to the behavior in question.*

Getting back to our example, recall that Mark has only just begun to gravitate towards the local white-power group and we want to challenge this movement by getting him involved in other activities. A first step in developing an intervention aimed at Mark (and other individuals vulnerable to persuasion by white-power propaganda) would involve surveying this population to determine what they think and how they feel about engaging in different kinds of non-white-power activities. This will reveal whether these individuals do not engage in more traditional activities because they have no intention to or because they do not see any possibility of doing so (due to a lack of skills or opportunity).

Suppose that after we survey our population of interest, including Mark, we find that the vast majority feel as though they have the skills and opportunity to engage in non-white-power activities, but they simply have no intention to do so. At this point, we must assume that the white-power group has gotten its persuasive claws into our message targets, and we'll need to increase their intentions to engage in activities away from that group.

Luckily, reasoned action theory provides us with guidance on how to go about doing so. Remember that an individual's intention to engage in a behavior depends on their attitudes about the behavior, their perceptions of norms associated with the behavior, and their perceptions of control over performing the behavior. In addition to telling us whether our audience fails to perform a behavior because of a lack of intention or lack of skills/opportunity, our survey will also tell us which of the three predictors (attitudes, norms, or control) is the strongest determinant of their intention (or lack thereof). These data provide critical information about which specific belief to target in a communicative intervention.

Let's suppose that our survey data show that most of the vulnerable individuals in our audience of interest are very much like Mark; most respondents say that they strongly value their parents' opinions about them and the activities they engage in. This would suggest that in our case, perceived norms are the strongest predictor of behavioral intentions.

Now, we are getting somewhere. First, we know that we want to promote six more hours of engagement in non-white-power activities per week to reduce the time our target audience can spend with the local extremist group. Second, we know that our target audience generally lacks the intention to engage in six more hours of non-white-power activities per week. Third, we know that our target audience's behavioral intentions are most strongly influenced by what their parents think about the activities they engage in.

With these facts in mind, we can now move on to designing the intervention itself.

Step 3: Selecting Radicalization-Related Beliefs to Target

As indicated in Step 2, appropriate use of reasoned action theory demands that a message designer determine whether an intention is primarily determined by their audience's attitudes, perceived norms, or self-efficacy related to a behavior. This is not the only condition we need to consider in determining which belief to construct our communicative intervention around. In a domain where the success or failure of an intervention hinges on other tangible factors, research spearheaded by Robert Hornik identified other things that message designers should consider when determining how to persuade message targets to engage in behaviors.[26]

First, they argued that *the targeted belief should be strongly correlated with the behavior that the message designer wishes to change.* Though the message designer should have already chosen to develop a communicative intervention based on the strongest predictor of message targets' intentions, reasoned action theory indicates that attitudes, perceived norms, and self-efficacy are only indirectly related to behavior via mediation through intention. To ensure the salience of the belief being targeted, message designers can evaluate the degree to which the belief and behavior are related with data from the survey administered in Step 2.

In our example, this would involve evaluating our survey data to see how closely our population's beliefs associated with their parents' opinions associated with engaging in non-white-power activities are correlated with actual engagement in non-white-power activities. If we see that this correlation is statistically significant, we have further evidence to suggest that an intervention that references parental approval might be effective.

Second, Hornik and Woolf said that for an intervention to be successful, there need to be enough people in the target audience that do *not* hold the belief that the intervention promotes. That is, message designers must *consider whether the development of a communicative intervention intended to change audience beliefs will affect enough people to make it worth the time, effort, and in some cases, resources.* This is particularly important in the domain of violent extremism, where monetary resources are often restricted to efforts that yield substantial effects.

Let's turn again to our hypothetical intervention aimed at Mark and his teenage cohort. Thus far, we know that we want to include references to parents' opinions in our intervention, given that perceived norms are the strongest predictor of behavior. Here, to maximize the intervention's impact, it might be useful to identify a non-white-power activity that (1) most respondents' parents would approve of and (2) most respondents do not yet engage in. This would get us the most "bang for our buck" in developing a norm-based intervention intended to promote alternate behaviors among those at risk for radicalization.

As a final consideration in choosing which belief to target, Hornik and Woolf made a critical, if obvious claim. *Any targeted belief must be capable of changing.* As succinctly argued by Fishbein and Yzer, "not all beliefs are equally amenable to change, and relatively little will be accomplished by attacking a belief that is very difficult, if not impossible, to change."[27]

This is largely a subjective evaluation on the part of the message designer, but beliefs based on experience tend to be more resistant to influence than beliefs based on information received via communication from others.

Taking this into consideration with respect to our intervention aimed at Mark and other teenagers vulnerable to white nationalist propaganda, we would need to consider what beliefs about parental norms our target audience developed via experience with their parents rather than via other means (e.g., assumption, persuasive communication from others). Once we have a reasonable idea about which normative beliefs our target audience developed about non-white-power activities via the latter, we could target them with a communicative intervention intended to persuade message recipients that their parents approve of those activities.

Developing a Counter-Radicalization Communicative Intervention Using Reasoned Action Theory: A Synopsis

We have now gone through reasoned action theory in its entirety and considered various factors that might influence target audiences via different routes to intention and behavior. To bring this discussion full-circle, let's review the steps here:

(1) Choose a *specific* behavior to target with the intervention. This behavior should be consistent with your goals as message designer, but sufficiently detailed as not to be a vague behavioral category (e.g., improve your education).

(2) Distinguish target audiences via intention. This involves using a survey to determine targets' beliefs, attitudes, intentions, norms, and self-efficacy in relation to the behavior identified in Step 1.

  (2a) Some individuals will have the intention to perform the advocated behavior, but not the skills or opportunity. Interventions aimed at these individuals should emphasize self-efficacy or provide pathways to opportunities to engage in the desired behavior.

  (2b) Some individuals will have the skills and opportunity to perform the advocated behavior, but not the intention. Interventions aimed at these individuals should identify which of the three key predictors of intention (attitudes, norms, or control) is the strongest determinant of audience intentions.

(3) Select a specific belief to target with the intervention that is associated with the targeted behavior. This belief should meet three criteria:

- Correlated with the behavior
- Underrepresented within the target audience
- Capable of being affected via persuasion

With these factors in mind, we can develop the framework for a persuasive intervention intended to pull Mark and similar individuals away from the white-power extremist group in their town.

(1) We want to advocate that Mark engage in six additional hours of non-white-power activities per week. The assumption is that this will reduce the amount of time that Mark will spend with the white-power group, thereby weakening its hold on his identity, and hopefully, his interest in it.

(2) We administer a survey to Mark and others in his school to determine his beliefs, attitudes, intentions, norms, and perceived efficacy regarding his non-white-power activities. From this survey, we know that Mark has the skills and opportunity to engage in six more hours of non-white-power activities per week but does not have the intention to do so. To promote this intention, we refer to the survey data to see that most respondents' intentions are strongly influenced by their perceived norms (which themselves are affected by their perceptions of their parents' opinions).

(3) To identify which beliefs to target with our intervention, we again refer to our survey data to identify beliefs that are correlated with engaging in six additional hours of non-white-power activity per week, are not overly prevalent within our target audience, and are capable of being changed or reinforced. With these data, we determine that the following beliefs meet all these conditions:

> "Parents are proud of kids who go to college, and kids who work after-school jobs, play after-school sports, or join after-school activities are more likely to go to college."

While it is true that some of our audience will be more difficult to persuade due to parental norms regarding racism and extremist activity, this belief will be largely universal to the entire target audience. Moreover, it will be relatively easy to provide evidence for the claim in the intervention itself.

Taking this into account, we could develop reasoned action-based persuasive messages that advocate specific activities away from the extremist group with the promise of parental approval.

Conclusions

In the time since his arrest, Muhammad Dakhlalla has come to recognize how his decisions led him to federal prison. By all accounts, he regrets the decisions he has made, and is in near disbelief that he let himself go so far astray. Reasoned action theory can help us understand what Mo experienced; the immense pressure he faced due to perceived norms related to Jaelyn which pushed him on a trajectory toward ISIS – a trajectory that he thanks the FBI for interrupting.[28] Mo almost died because of choices that he now finds absurd, a testament to the predictive power of reasoned action theory when one is subject to the forces identified in the model.

Despite its many strengths, reasoned action theory is almost entirely cerebral in character and assumes that we act rationally with respect to our behavioral intentions. While it is true that our inherent rationality often drives us to optimize benefits and reduce costs in a systematic way, we often respond to other stimuli when we engage with different kinds of messaging. We do not always assimilate information and logically react. We are not cyborgs. We are humans.

And as humans, we have emotions – emotions that play a massive role in how we think and what we do. This is doubly true in the realm of radicalization and counter-radicalization, where dueling elements seek to elicit reactions that drive audiences towards or away from politically charged actions, including violence. In the next chapter, we explore how these dueling elements – violent extremists and counterterrorists – exploit our emotions ... and the behavioral consequences that occur when they succeed.

Notes

1 Emma Green, "How Two Mississippi College Students Fell in Love and Decided to Join a Terrorist Group," *The Atlantic* (May 1, 2017). Available at www.theatlantic.com/politics/archive/2017/05/mississippi-young-dakhlalla/524751/.
2 Ibid.
3 Scott Bronstein and Drew Griffin, "Young ISIS Recruit: I was Blinded By Love," *CNN* (December 6, 2016). Available at www.cnn.com/2016/12/02/us/mississippi-isis-muhammad-dakhlalla-interview/index.html.
4 Martin Fishbein and Icek Ajzen, *Predicting and Changing Behavior: The Reasoned Action Approach* (New York: Routledge, 2010).
5 Martin Fishbein and Icek Ajzen, *Belief, Attitude, Intention, and Behavior: An Introduction to Theory and Research* (Reading, MA: Addison-Wesley, 1975).

6 Icek Ajzen, "From Intentions to Actions: A Theory of Planned Behavior," in *Action Control: From Cognition to Behavior*, ed. Julius Kuhl and Jürgen Beckman, 11–39 (Heidelberg: Springer, 1985). See also Icek Ajzen, "The Theory of Planned Behaviour: Reactions and Reflections," *Psychology & Health* 26, no. 9 (2011): 1113–1127.

7 See Martin Fishbein, "The Role of Theory in HIV Prevention," *AIDS Care* 12 (2000): 273–278.

8 Marco Yzer, "Reasoned Action Theory: Persuasion as Belief-Based Behavior Change," in *The SAGE Handbook of Persuasion: Developments in Theory and Practice*, ed. James Price Dillard and Lijiang Shen, 120–136 (Thousand Oaks, CA: Sage, 2013), p. 120.

9 Fishbein and Ajzen, *Predicting and Changing Behavior*.

10 Ibid.

11 Yzer, "Reasoned Action Theory," p. 127.

12 Icek Ajzen and Martin Fishbein, "Attitudinal and Normative Variables as Predictors of Specific Behavior," *Journal of Personality and Social Psychology* 27 (1973): 41–57; Martin Fishbein, "Attitude and the Prediction of Behavior," in *Readings in Attitude Theory and Measurement*, ed. Martin Fishbein, 477–492 (New York: Wiley, 1967).

13 Dolores Albarracín, Blair T. Johnson, Martin Fishbein, and Paige A. Muellerleile, "Theories of Reasoned Action and Planned Behavior as Models of Condom Use," *Psychological Bulletin* 127, no. 1 (2011): 142–161; Richard Cooke and David P. French, "How Well Do the Theory of Reasoned Action and Theory of Planned Behaviour Predict Intentions and Attendance at Screening Programmes? A Meta-Analysis," *Psychology & Health* 43 (2008): 745–765. However, subjective norms did have some effect in different kinds of populations; see M. Giles, C. Liddell, and M. Bydawell, "Condom Use in African Adolescents: The Role of Individual and Group Factors," *AIDS Care* 17, no. 6 (2005): 729–739; Bas Van den Putte, "On the Theory of Reasoned Action," dissertation, University of Amsterdam, 1993.

14 Icek Ajzen, "The Theory of Planned Behavior," *Organizational Behavior and Human Decision Processes* 50 (1991): 179–211; Ajzen, "From Intentions to Actions."

15 Ajzen, "The Theory of Planned Behavior," pp. 183–184.

16 See, for example, Deborah J. Terry and Joanne E. O'Leary, "The Theory of Planned Behaviour: The Effects of Perceived Behavioural Control and Self-Efficacy," *British Journal of Social Psychology* 34, no. 2 (1995): 199–220; M. M. Pertl, David Hevey, Kent Steven Thomas, Agnella Craig, Siobhan Ní Chuinneagáin, and Laura Maher, "Differential Effects of Self-Efficacy and Perceived Control on Intention to Perform Skin Cancer-Related Health Behaviours," *Health Education Research* 25 (2010): 769–779.

17 Fishbein and Ajzen, *Predicting and Changing Behavior*.

18 Ibid.

19 Ajzen, "From Intentions to Actions," p. 181.

20 Paul R. Warshaw and Fred D. Davis, "Disentangling Behavioral Intention and Behavioral Expectation," *Journal of Experimental Social Psychology* 21, no. 3 (1985): 213–228.

21 See, for example, Martin Fishbein and Mark Stasson, "The Role of Desires, Self-Predictions, and Perceived Control in the Prediction of Training Session Attendance," *Journal of Applied Social Psychology* 20 (1990): 173–198.

22 See, for example, Frederick X. Gibbons, Meg Gerrard, Hart Blanton, and Daniel W. Russell, "Reasoned Action and Social Reaction: Willingness and Intention as Independent Predictors of Health Risk," *Journal of Personality and Social Psychology* 74 (1998): 1164–1180.

23 Fishbein and Ajzen, *Predicting and Changing Behavior*.

24 Ibid.; also Ajzen, "From Intentions to Actions."

25 Martin Fishbein, "Developing Effective Behavior Change Interventions: Some Lessons Learned from Behavioral Research," in *Reviewing the Behavioral Sciences Knowledge Base on Technology Transfer*, ed. Thomas E. Backer, Susan L. David, and Gerald Saucy, 246–261 (Rockville, MD: National Institute on Drug Abuse, 1995). Available at https://archives.drugabuse.gov/sites/default/files/monograph155.pdf; Fishbein, "The Role of Theory in HIV Prevention."

26 Robert Hornik and Kimberly Duyck Woolf, "Using Cross-Sectional Surveys to Plan Message Strategies," *Social Marketing Quarterly* 5 (1999): 34–41; Robert C. Hornik, Allyson, C. Volinsky, Shane Mannis, Laura A. Gibson, Emily Brennan, Stella J. Lee, and Andy S. L. Tan, "Validating the Hornik & Woolf Approach to Choosing Media Campaign Themes: Do Promising Beliefs Predict Behavior Change in a Longitudinal Study?" *Communication Methods and Measures* 13, no. 1 (2019): 60–68.

27 Martin Fishbein and Marco C. Yzer, "Using Theory to Design Effective Health Behavior Interventions," *Communication Theory* 13, no. 2 (2003): 163–183 (p. 175).

28 "Mississippi ISIS Recruit: 'The FBI, They Really Saved My Life,'" *CBS News* (August 25, 2016). Available at www.cbsnews.com/news/mississippi-isis-recruit-muhammad-dakhlalla-fbi-saved-my-life/.

6   Terrorism is Theater: Emotion in Extremist Propaganda and Counter-Propaganda

A young voice begins to sing as the black screen fades to show an inquisitive child walking through a ruined city. The singing continues as the child – no older than 12 – paces between destroyed buildings. Images appear in the rubble. An injured baby crying uncontrollably. Muslim men pulling a critically injured infant from beneath the remains of a large, stone structure. Destruction. Chaos.

The pacing child continues his walk as the song's lyrics are translated for English-speaking audiences and superimposed on the scene.

> *You grant yourselves the right to massacre us in the name of your so-called precious freedoms.*

The boy walks down the hallway of another bombed-out building as images continue to appear around him. An image of US President Obama shaking hands with Russian President Vladimir Putin dissolves to reveal a baby with blood smeared on its face struggling to breathe through an oxygen mask. The young protagonist peers into an empty room before turning away from it with a melancholy look on his face.

As the child walks slowly out of the building, the song quickens, and images of various world leaders appear in turn. Bashar al-Assad of Syria, former President Obama, former US Secretary of State John Kerry, and Russian Foreign Minister Sergey Lavrov all appear next to unambiguous accusations against them: murderers, manipulators, liars.

The scene changes, showing the child sitting quietly in a small grove of trees. He is peering downward at a small Qu'ran, studying diligently. Despite the tranquility around him, images again begin to materialize. Children dressed in camouflage with automatic rifles resting against their shoulders. Children awaiting orders while dutifully lined up in front of an adult commander. Children practicing their skills with pistols – taking cover behind trees, and then pointing the guns menacingly. All the while, the march-like song carries on.

*Beware, we have what we need to defend ourselves; well-armed soldiers are
ready to kill you.*

The walking child has left the grove and has returned to what remains
of his city. As he continues his tour of the carnage, images continue to
come into view. A bomb explodes, sending dust and debris hundreds of
feet into the air. Blood pours from a dead dove that is lying in the rubble
of one of the destroyed buildings. The corpses of two toddlers lie parallel
to one another, each one scarred black from fire and smoke.

The boy stops in the rubble and leans down to pick up a small stone
that had been part of one of the demolished buildings. He kneels to study
the stone more closely, rotating it between his little fingers the way a child
might inspect a bug or a small toy.

The scene changes to show a different child sitting in the same grove of
trees from earlier. Instead of observing a stone, however, this child is
rotating a bullet between his fingers. With a curious look on his face, the
child loads the round into a magazine, which he then attaches to an
assault rifle. After the rifle is loaded, the child assumes a crouching
position, and aims the rifle into the distance.

The song continues.

*You fool the world with your eloquence while legalizing your delinquency.
Beware, we are ready to fight back; our swords are sharpened to slice necks.*

As this line is sung, an image is superimposed over the crouching child-
soldier; a man in an orange jumpsuit is beheaded in slow motion.

The scene shifts again. No longer do we see a single child walking
through a destroyed city. Nor do we see anyone sitting quietly in a grove.
Instead, we see multiple boys of various ages wearing desert camouflage
in different stages of preparation for battle. One olive-skinned child
straps combat gloves to his hands. Another boy – pale-faced and blue-
eyed – slides extra ammunition into his pockets. A dozen barefoot
children pay close attention to mock battle plans being drawn on the
ground with stones and sand.

Finally, the group of boys are shown lined up. Organized. Ready. Each
of them is armed with a rifle, dutifully pointed downward as they have
been trained. Their faces are shown individually. One boy with soft,
innocent features looks upward with a slight smile. Another boy furrows
his brow and looks straight ahead.

A final boy – different from the others – stares blankly into the distance
with no sign of malice. He looks as though he is about to cry.

The children begin to march in unison, and the black flag of ISIS is
held skyward by one of the children. The song concludes, its final lyrics
fading out in a gradually quietening echo.

Your goods, your lives – to us, none of it is sacred;
Your blood will flow for your heinous crimes.

∴

These scenes are part of an ISIS propaganda video called *Blood for Blood*, and it is not exceptional. Since ISIS first emerged as a global terror threat, it has been adept at producing and distributing propaganda just like this video – propaganda that has proven quite effective at drawing individuals to Iraq and Syria to fight on behalf of the group.

This raises several questions about how the group uses propaganda to persuade audiences. After all, the *Blood for Blood* video (and many others like it) don't contain overt appeals to audiences. There are no ISIS members explaining why they feel the group deserves a caliphate. There are no narrators describing the facts surrounding their campaign. In short, much of the group's propaganda abandons logical argument as a strategic persuasive weapon. How, then, are ISIS videos like these so persuasive?

Although there are multiple reasons why a propaganda video might be persuasive to different audiences, ISIS videos like *Blood for Blood* evoke a reaction that can be more powerful than any response to a rhetorical argument, logical proof, or ethical claim. These videos are designed to evoke *emotion*.

For years, researchers have shown the potential of arousing different kinds of emotions to achieve persuasive goals. With foundations in Richard Lazarus's work on stress-coping mechanisms[1] and Carroll Izard's research on human emotion,[2] much of this research has focused on how different emotions can promote or prevent different kinds of activities. Carl Hovland's early work on fear suggested that scaring people about negative outcomes can persuade them to avoid behaviors that make those outcomes more likely.[3] Marketing specialists argue that by making consumers feel hope about their products, they can increase the likelihood that the consumers will purchase those products.[4] Political researchers like Ted Brader have shown that politicians can affect voter behavior by exploiting the voters' emotions.[5] Emotions often drive our behavior, and communicators have taken advantage of this.

Unfortunately, terrorist groups have also recognized the potential for emotions to motivate different audiences to behave how they want. *Blood for Blood* was clearly produced to make audiences feel anger about the victimization of Muslims and pride in Muslim children for choosing to fight back against their attackers. Both emotions can be incredibly useful for motivating viewers to support ISIS, to attack the source of their anger, and to feel pride in doing so.

As with other communicative perspectives and strategies, emotions can also be used to challenge terrorist messaging, prevent the adoption of terrorist ideologies, and dissuade the use of terrorism itself. However, to effectively harness the persuasive power of emotions, it is important to recognize why emotions are persuasive and how different emotions can be evoked in the proper contexts.

So, this chapter will discuss the evolution of *discrete emotions*, their capacity for motivating behavior (i.e., action tendencies), and the ways in which terrorist groups use emotions to achieve strategic objectives consistent with their respective ideologies. Then, the chapter will offer specific guidance on the development of messages that evoke emotions designed to turn individuals away from violent radicalization.

First, however, it is important to clarify our understanding about the very nature of emotions. With this understanding, we can move on to recognize how they can be strategically leveraged to counter violent extremism.

Emotions and Persuasion

Researchers have long sought to understand how individuals process information and ultimately make decisions based on that information. In the middle of the twentieth century, researchers were proposing advanced theories and making groundbreaking discoveries regarding the power of computers and the kinds of information they process. Around this time, Norbert Wiener's research on cybernetics[6] and McCarthy and Minsky's work on artificial intelligence[7] began to emerge, inspiring many to adopt a cognitive approach to information processing. This perspective assumed that human minds are like desktop computers – using stored memory and processing power to calculate the best perspective to adopt or behavior to engage in.

Rational. Logical. Precise.

Of course, *some* decision-making processes are comparable to tasks carried out by computers. When we are presented with basic information, we can absorb the data, process it, and experience some output in the form of beliefs, attitudes, intentions, or behaviors. Later this week, you may look out the window before leaving your home and notice that the sky is full of dark clouds, small droplets of water are falling, and the ground is wet. You could process this information quickly to conclude that it's raining, and unless you want to get soaked, you had better bring an umbrella with you. You will have objectively processed visual data to form an intention that suits your needs.

However, human beings are not computers and not all scenarios trigger such dispassionate responses. We all have our own subjective experiences, memories, and biochemistries that computers can't mimic, and these factors can activate responses that are unique to the human condition. We don't just think; we feel.

We experience *emotions*, and they can exert a powerful influence on what we believe and how we act.

What Are Emotions?

Before determining what emotions are, it is first necessary to understand the concept of *affect*, which refers to all the different kinds of feelings that we experience, emotions included. Dillard and Seo contend that the simplest conception of affect treats it as essentially bimodal, whereby our feelings can be mapped on a continuum with "good" on one end and "bad" on the other.[8] This model suggests that the more "good" a person feels, the less "bad" they feel (and vice versa). This may be the simplest and most convenient way to think about affect, but as any teenager with raging hormones can tell you, it ignores the complexity inherent in how we experience things.

A more complex model of affect, used in the 1990s by David Watson and Lee Anna Clark to measure how individuals feel,[9] suggests that good and bad feelings can be felt independently and simultaneously. For this model, you can feel some good and some bad at the same time.

Still, though, our subjective experience of emotions is more complex than "good" and "bad." Researchers like James Russell and Lisa Barrett considered some feelings can be more intense than others. So, these researchers developed yet another model that considers our feelings to be defined by how much they stimulate us and how much pleasure we gain from them.[10] In this model, different emotions can be mapped on a grid where the x-axis represents how much energy the emotion arouses in a person (high vs. low) and the y-axis indicates the amount of pleasure that person gains from it (unpleasurable vs. pleasurable). For example, sadness would be mapped in the quadrant represented by low arousal and low pleasure and fear would be mapped in the quadrant represented by high arousal and low pleasure.

Although this model does better to distinguish emotions based on how they feel subjectively, there are several problems with it. Most notably, it runs the risk of characterizing different emotions as feeling similar. For instance, anger and fear are both characterized by high stimulation and unpleasant sensation, but they feel different. Being angry at someone feels quite different than being afraid of them.

Another model is necessary to understand how distinct emotions are not only experienced, but how they influence responses to different stimuli, including communication. This brings us to the *discrete emotions* perspective.

Discrete Emotions

The discrete emotions perspective contends that emotions are physical and psychological reactions to cognitive appraisals – judgments of the degree to which environmental factors facilitate or inhibit our goals. If environmental factors are consistent with our goals, we experience a positive emotion. If the environment prevents us from achieving our goals, we experience a negative emotion. The specific emotion felt depends on the nature of the environmental stimulus and the type of goal being assisted or restricted.

Based on how an individual appraises their environment and how it relates to salient goals, different emotions are defined via different criteria:

- Qualitative "feel" – Emotions feel subjectively different from one another. Anger feels different from sadness; sadness feels different from hope; hope feels different from happiness; happiness feels different from envy; and so on.
- Physiological changes – Different emotions will trigger physical changes in the body. For example, highly stimulating emotions (e.g., anger, fear) can increase adrenaline output, spike blood pressure, and ready muscles for quick use. In contrast, mood-depressing emotions (e.g., sadness) can cause us to feel weary and motivate us to rest.
- Neurological stimulation – Different emotions are associated with increased neural activity in different parts of the brain.[11]
- Manifest expression – Different emotions prompt involuntary changes in facial and body expressions. For example, whereas sadness is associated with frowning and slouched posture, disgust is associated with clenched lips and a wrinkled nose.
- Cognitive changes – Different emotions trigger changes in the ways in which the individual addresses their environment cognitively. For instance, fear "narrows the perceptual field and focuses attention on the threatening stimulus."[12]

Although these five qualities effectively differentiate various kinds of emotions, perhaps the most important distinguishing characteristic of different emotions is the behavioral motivation that the emotion provokes. These motivations – called *action tendencies* – are generally geared towards approaching or avoiding the emotion-arousing stimulus in specific ways. For instance, when we see something that scares us, we tend to run away from it. When something in our environment causes us happiness, we go towards it to continue feeling happy.

Some theorists, including our friends Richard Lazarus and Carroll Izard, have identified a handful of discrete emotions based on (a) how

Table 6.1 *Discrete emotions, appraisals, and action tendencies*

Emotion	Appraisal	Action Tendency
Anger	Unwarranted obstruction of a goal	Approach: Attack, remove, or reject the source of the obstruction
Fear	Probability of harm to one's body	Avoidance: Retreat from or acquiesce to a threat
Disgust	Probability of harm to one's health	Avoidance: Abstain from interacting with or consuming material that can make oneself ill
Guilt	Violation of personally held moral	Approach: Redress the moral violation
Sadness	Irrevocable failure to achieve a salient goal	Avoidance: Review plan for continued pursuit of goal; regain strength and resources
Envy	Recognition that one's goal (performance or possession of an object) has been achieved by another	Approach: Seek to obtain that which rival possesses; dispossess rival of that which he/she has
Happiness	Acute movement towards a goal	Approach: Bask in continued success towards a valued goal
Hope	Change in probability of goal achievement	Approach: Renew and strengthen efforts towards achieving a valued goal
Pride	Recognition of credit for an achievement by oneself or a group with which one identifies	Approach: Bask in celebration of completion of goal

Note: Adapted from Dillard and Peck's Table 1, as well as different works by Lazarus, Izard, and Frijda and Kuipers.

they manifest, and (b) the action tendencies associated with them.[13] Table 6.1 lists these emotions, the appraisals that prompt them, and the specific action tendencies they provoke.[14]

Having identified different discrete emotions, we can now explore how those emotions affect the process of persuasion. From there, we can consider how different terrorist groups exploit message targets' emotions to promote beliefs, attitudes, and behaviors consistent with their ideologies.

Communication and the Persuasiveness of Emotions

Anger

Anger is an emotional experience triggered by the recognition that one's goals – especially goals consistent with the preservation of a person's ego have been threatened or prevented.[15] Physically, anger causes increased blood pressure and muscle capacity, making individuals more motivated and capable of removing physical barriers that block them from achieving their goals. These physiological responses can push individuals to take control of a threatening situation[16] or assist in self-defensive survival activities by directing mental and physical energies.[17] The increased strength a person feels when they are angry is no illusion; the body is preparing to remove obstacles from its path.

Anger is an intense emotion that can result in negative behavioral tendencies, like increased aggression, antisocial behavior, and punishing those that caused the anger.[18] Although the physical responses to anger-inducing stimuli can prompt these kinds of negative outcomes, anger can also trigger cognitive processes that help a person solve problems without a physical response. Specifically, anger can cause focus a person's thinking, allowing them to consider a problem more analytically. By doing so, anger can help a person to resolve the issues causing them to feel angry and prevent them from recurring.[19]

For example, researchers have shown that people sometimes feel angry when they believe that another person is being treated unfairly or victimized. In these situations, anger has been linked with prosocial behaviors intended to compensate the victimized person for their unfair treatment.[20] Others have even shown that individuals who feel anger about others' disadvantages are more likely to help them fix those disadvantages or donate to charity than people who feel guilt or sympathy.[21] In short, despite the fact that anger can lead to destructive behaviors in some cases, it can also yield positive results – even when audiences feel other emotions at the same time.[22]

Given the strong motivations associated with feeling anger, some experts have studied how it works in the context of persuasion. This line of research suggests that the effectiveness of anger appeals – persuasive messages that are designed to elicit anger on the part of audiences – depends on several factors.

First, whether an anger appeal will lead to destructive or proactive outcomes largely depends on audience perceptions of their own efficacy.[23] That is, if an anger appeal is designed to motivate target audiences to do something, those audiences must believe that (a) they are able to perform some sort of behavior that will alleviate their anger, and (b) the behavior being recommended would be effective. Moreover, these perceptions must outweigh any fear they might feel from seeing the message.[24] If an individual's anger outweighs their belief that they can resolve it, they won't process the message in a helpful way and will instead ignore the issue to alleviate their angry feelings.[25]

Second, the intensity with which a person feels anger can affect how they react to it. For example, Melvyn Fein showed that when a message

Table 6.2 *Turner's Anger Activism Model*

	Anger Intensity	
	Low	High
High Efficacy	Empowered	Activist
Low	Disinterested	Angry

makes someone *too* angry, they are more likely to become aggressive against the object responsible for their anger.[26] But if a message elicits only a moderate amount of anger, it's more likely to lead to more constructive responses, like analytical thinking and problem solving.[27]

Finally, target audiences' prior attitudes about the response recommended in the anger appeal are likely to affect whether they will react favorably to the message. Specifically, anger appeals are likely to be most effective for individuals who are already somewhat predisposed to agreeing with the message but have not yet acted in accordance with what the message says. As such, anger "can aid in persuading people to do behaviors that they typically would find too difficult" to perform.[28]

Based on these conditions, Monique Turner proposed the Anger Activation Model to identify audiences that might be receptive to anger appeals.[29] Specifically, Turner suggested that audiences can be distinguished based on their anger intensity and perceptions of efficacy. Table 6.2, which is adapted from Turner's work, shows these distinctions.

According to the Anger Activation Model and research associated with it,[30]

• Activists will have the most positive attitudes about the topic, will be most likely to engage in recommended behaviors, and will engage in the most systematic processing in response to the message;
• Empowered individuals do not feel as though the topic of the message is terribly important, but that the recommended behaviors are likely to resolve the problem; these individuals are only likely to commit to behaviors that aren't too inconvenient or difficult;
• Angry individuals are upset about an issue and don't think there is much that can be done to resolve it; they are unlikely to engage to engage in behaviors that require much commitment; and
• Disinterested people don't care about the topic of the message, nor do they think anything can (or should) be done about the current state of affairs; these individuals are unlikely to engage in any behavior in response to an anger appeal.

Message designers using anger appeals should recognize the differences between these audience types and how they might result in different responses by audience members.

Fear

Fear appeals are persuasive messages that highlight dangers to an individual's well-being if they fail to adhere to the messages' recommendations. These messages are typically designed to warn target audiences of physical harm that may befall them so they (a) avoid behaviors that increase the likelihood of their experiencing harm, or (b) proactively engage in behaviors that mitigate their chances of experiencing harm.[31]

To promote (or prevent) the behavior discussed in the message, fear appeals generally elicit three responses: fear, perceived threat, and perceived efficacy. First, fear appeals should elicit a visceral response consistent with the recognition that an environmental stimulus may cause an individual harm. Stated more simply (and obviously), fear appeals should contain content that elicits fear in its audience. Second, fear appeals should intensify audience members' perceptions of the threat posed by failing to adhere to the messages' recommendations. To do so, effective fear appeals highlight the audience's susceptibility to the harm described in the message, as well as the severity of that harm. Third, fear appeals contain elements that empower message recipients to engage in (or avoid) behaviors that reduce the likelihood of their experiencing harm. Specifically, fear appeals contain content that increases target audiences' perceptions that they have the ability to engage in the recommended behavior and that doing so would actually reduce the likelihood of their experiencing harm.[32]

These kinds of persuasive messages have been used in advertising, political campaigns, public health initiatives, and other contexts for decades. For instance, many campaigns designed to reduce the incidence of drunk driving have raised the possibility of hurting oneself or others as a consequence of getting behind the wheel after drinking too much. Campaigns like these are often characterized by vivid language and imagery that depicts the nature of the harms that might occur if the message's recommendations are not adhered to. Almost everyone can remember the videos they were forced to watch in high school illustrating the disastrous (and often bloody) results of drinking and driving. The question remains though – are these kinds of messages persuasive?

Unfortunately, early research on fear appeals was largely inconsistent. In the first empirical study of how fear-based messages affect behavior, Irving Janis and Seymour Feshbach showed that as individuals received messages that showed increasingly scary messages about dental hygiene, they became *less* likely to improve their brushing behavior or use proper dental equipment.[33] Other early studies found similar results. In one of these studies, Janis and Robert Terwilliger tested how message-induced fear affects attitudes towards smoking. Their results showed that when participants were exposed to greater threat (i.e., when they were told more gruesome details about lung cancer), they were less likely to develop anti-smoking attitudes than people who weren't exposed to such threatening language.[34] In a similar study, Howard Leventhal and Jean Watts found that when participants were exposed to increasingly scary content (in this case, a video of lung-cancer surgery), they were less likely to get a chest X-ray than those who were not exposed to the scary content.[35] These and other studies suggested that when a message designer arouses fear in an audience, it can have a counter-productive effect.

At the same time, other researchers were finding that eliciting fear had a *positive* effect on persuasion. Even more confusing, these findings were emerging for research on the same topics that produced evidence for a negative relationship between fear and persuasion. In direct contrast to Janis and Feshbach's study from 1953, Leventhal (yes, the same Leventhal that found a negative relationship between fear and persuasion) and Robert Singer found that when individuals were exposed to materials that induced greater fear about tooth decay, they were *more* likely to follow proper dental hygiene recommendations.[36] In the same vein (and again in contrast to other studies of the same era), Chester Insko and his colleagues found that when participants were exposed to a fear-inducing message that told them that smoking could make them personally vulnerable to cancer, heart disease, and emphysema, they had less intention to smoke in the future than people who were not made to feel personally susceptible to these diseases.[37]

Clearly, early work on fear appeals and persuasion was all over the place. To get an idea about just how inconsistent this research was, see a paper by Kenneth Higbee that evaluated the first fifteen years of research on the topic.[38] In that paper, he looked at dozens of papers on fear appeals published between 1953 and 1968. As indicated by the small sample above, there was no consistency in the findings. Confusion abounds.

After 1968, though, the literature became a bit more consistent in showing that fear is positively related to persuasion. Still, there remained a few studies that produced other results. Some studies have suggested that fear appeals have no effect on audiences,[39] or worse, persuaded them to do the opposite of what the message advocated in some cases.[40]

It is likely that the past inconsistency in research on fear appeals was due to the different ways that the researchers induced fear in participants. Obviously, inducing fear in participants in different ways is likely to produce different results. It was not until 1975 that a commonly accepted explication for fear appeals emerged,[41] after which it is possible that results would have become more consistent.

To test this possibility, Melanie Tannenbaum and her co-authors recently performed the largest and most comprehensive meta-analysis of research on fear appeals and their usefulness for persuasion to date.[42] By analyzing dozens of studies populated by thousands of participants, they concluded that fear appeals are, in fact, powerful tools for influencing audiences' attitudes, intentions, and behaviors, and that this effect is consistent in most cases.

Despite a shaky early history, research and practice has shown fear to be one of the strongest tools for inducing changes in target audiences' behaviors such that they are consistent with a communicator's goals.

Disgust

Though it has not been extensively studied as a mechanism for persuasion, there has been some literature to suggest that eliciting disgust can induce changes in audiences' attitudes or behaviors. Generally, disgust results from objects or ideas that are considered repulsive or potentially damaging to one's health (e.g., bodily fluids, rotting meat). In this way, disgust is similar to fear in its capacity to affect an individual's perceptions about their own well-being. However, there are some key things that distinguish the two emotions. First, in terms of physiological effects, fear is associated with an increased heart rate and body temperature; disgust lowers these measures.[43] Second, fear relates to an individual's perception that they are at risk for physical harm; disgust is primarily related to an individual's perception that they are at risk for illness.

Despite these differences, the action tendencies associated with fear and disgust are similar. Specifically, both emotions motivate movement away from the emotion-inducing object or idea.[44] Some researchers have even demonstrated that when exposed to messages that elicit disgust, message recipients can also experience fear, showing the two emotions to be closely linked.[45]

That said, disgust appeals are not employed very often, and there is little empirical evidence about its persuasive efficacy. Nevertheless, the demonstrated link between fear and disgust suggests that messages that elicit the latter can be effective at motivating individuals to avoid behaviors that lead to disgusting outcomes.

Guilt

Guilt typically results from situations in which individuals fail to meet their own standards of conduct.[46] For instance, individuals can feel guilt when they fail to adhere to an exercise plan, are unable to quit smoking, or cheat on their romantic partners.[47] Past research has shown that when individuals remember experiences that caused them to feel guilty, they often say they feel like they violated some moral standard they had for themselves, and wish that they had reacted to the situation differently.[48] In this way, feeling guilt is often related with a sense of failed responsibility that drives a person to rectify their actions, thereby reducing their guilt.[49]

Guilt appeals are persuasive messages that exploit this action tendency by arousing feelings of remorse and failed responsibility in their audiences. Typically, guilt appeals seek to arouse these feelings in two ways. First, these messages can highlight how an individual's behaviors are inconsistent with their extant values. For instance, a message designer may assume that audience members adhere to the attitude that they should not harm their sexual partners. Based on this assumption, a guilt appeal may assert that failing to get tested for HIV violates audience members' values by potentially endangering the health of those they have sex with.[50] Second, a guilt appeal can create an inconsistency for audience members by giving them the impression that their behavior violates a value that they *should* have.

Research on these kinds of messages has shown that eliciting *moderate* guilt can be persuasive, but arousing *intense* feelings of guilt (perhaps caused by the explicitness of the appeal) can cause audience members to resist persuasion.[51] This is likely because when audience members are made to feel too guilty, they get angry at the source of the message for making them feel that way. In turn, they resist the message's persuasiveness.[52]

In addition to eliciting a moderate amount of guilt among message recipients, effective guilt appeals should also offer them suggestions for repairing the perceived violation of personal values.[53] This provides audience members with specific avenues for making their behaviors consistent with their values, thereby reducing their guilt.

Sadness

Sadness is a negative emotion resulting from the loss of important objects or the failure to achieve important goals.[54] Although the persuasion literature has focused heavily on how messages can elicit negative emotions like fear and anger, there has been surprising little work on how sadness functions as a persuasive emotion.

The few studies that *have* evaluated the persuasive effectiveness of sadness appeals have produced conflicting results. Early research performed by emotion experts like Nico Frijda considered sadness to promote inaction, allowing people to retreat from the public and remain stationary. By doing so, these people can regather strength and resources to function normally.[55] This can include taking part in emotionally reparative behaviors (e.g., eating unhealthy "comfort food").[56]

Later work showed that when individuals observe someone else's sadness, they can be motivated to assist those who feel sad and repair any damages that those individuals may have suffered.[57] This latter experience of sadness is common in the media and advertising domains, where another individual's loss is often depicted to persuade individuals to engage in some reparative behavior on behalf of the afflicted. As anyone who has seen the ASPCA commercial featuring Sarah McLachlan and scores of homeless animals knows, this kind of sadness can be extremely persuasive.[58]

Though the literature is inconsistent in its descriptions of how individuals respond to sadness, there have been several studies to show that it can be persuasive. Lu demonstrated that sadness appeals effectively persuade message recipients to seek information about the environment, support policies that protect the environment, and engage in behaviors that preserve the environment.[59] Dillard and colleagues similarly showed that in some cases, sadness was associated with audience perceptions of a message's persuasiveness.[60] Finally, some studies have shown the persuasiveness of sadness to be dependent on the nature of the message being delivered. For example, one study showed that message recipients believed a sad message was persuasive if it had a high "message sensation value" (e.g., lots of edits, music, bright colors).[61]

In short, sadness appears to be a motivating emotion, but the jury is out on the nature of the motivation. Some research has shown it to promote inaction, while other work has shown it to promote prosocial behaviors under certain conditions.

Envy

Envy is an unpleasant emotional experience defined by feelings of inferiority about one's own circumstances, particularly in relation to others.[62] An individual feels envious when they perceive someone else to be better off than they are, causing them to desire what the other person has.[63] To be sure, the desire for an admired object or outcome can motivate individuals to work harder, foster healthy competition between colleagues, or prompt positive change within individuals or organizations.[64] However, the experience of envy is more than admiration for something and the drive to obtain it; there is a darker side to it.

In addition to motivating a drive to better one's own circumstances, envy also motivates a desire to *worsen* another person's circumstances.[65] Specifically, researchers have shown that envy is related to feelings of ill will and resentment towards individuals who possess coveted objects. This can lead to several negative outcomes including a feeling of pleasure when another person experiences misfortune (*schadenfreude*),[66] aggression and conflict within groups,[67] and aspirations to "bring down" those of whom we are envious.[68]

Research on messages and media that elicit envy have shown that it can be very effective at motivating different kinds of behavior. In one study, researchers demonstrated that benign envy – feelings of frustration coupled with a motivation to better oneself – motivated individuals to study for more hours so they could emulate the success of a famous scientist.[69] However, malignant envy – feelings of frustration coupled with a desire to see another person fail – were related to negative thoughts and the desire for another person to lose what they had.[70] Other research showed that individuals who compared themselves to reality TV stars felt greater envy about the way those people looked than people who did not compare themselves to others. These feelings were so strong that envious people reported greater intention to get self-enhancement surgical procedures, like breast implants or facelifts.[71]

There exists substantially less research on the persuasive power of envy relative to emotions like fear and guilt. However, the literature that does exist clearly shows that the desire for what others have can be a potent motivating force for action.

Happiness

Happiness is a positive emotional response to making progress towards a valued goal.[72] There are several cultural and personality factors that influence when we feel happy, but there also seem to be multiple things that elicit happiness across contexts. Familiar objects, achievement of sought-after goals, and experiences that reduce negative emotion seem to consistently increase the degree to which individuals feel happy.[73] Because the experience of happiness is associated with positive expectations about the future, it can produce feelings of confidence and openness, and promote feelings of trust in others, which itself can induce sharing behaviors.[74]

There has been a significant amount of research on the persuasive power of happiness, but this work has largely treated it as a general mood instead of a discrete emotion. Still, this research provides some insight about the psychological effects of happiness. For instance, some experts have shown that a happy mood is related to more simplified information processing with little attention to the details that make up messages.[75]

Despite the substantial focus on happiness as a general mood, advertising research has evaluated the elicitation of happiness through humor. This line of work has suggested that messages that use humor to elicit happiness are likely to be persuasive for everyday products in which consumers are not psychologically invested or products that are feeling-oriented.[76] Others suggested that humor-induced happiness is persuasive because it effectively distracts consumers from the negative elements of the issue under consideration.[77] Regardless, happiness seems to have a moderate persuasive effect on audiences, but that effect is unstable and short-lived.[78]

Hope

Hope is a positive emotion that arises from recognizing that outcomes consistent with one's goals are possible, but not necessarily certain.[79] Through this recognition, individuals sense an opportunity to pursue those outcomes. Hope is a high-arousal emotion, causing increases in heart rate and skin conductance. When an individual feels hopeful, they tend to have an alert body posture, an open facial expression, and a heightened focus on the issue at hand, leading to an overall experience of eager attention towards desired outcomes.

In addition to these physical responses, hope also motivates people to take advantage of the opportunity before them.[80] In this way, hope triggers behaviors that individuals believe will help them achieve goals that will be beneficial to them in the future. Message developers can leverage this action tendency through hope appeals that create a sense of opportunity to achieve salient goals and recommend behaviors that help them take advantage of that opportunity.

Research on the effectiveness of hope appeals has shown that the emotion can be very persuasive across several contexts. Different studies have respectively shown that messages that elicit hope among audiences can affect interest in climate preservation,[81] improve attitudes about (and the likelihood of using) a healthcare provider,[82] and intentions to discuss medical procedures with one's doctor.[83]

Pride

Pride is a positive emotion that results from evaluating one's capability or effort exerted in achieving a valued goal.[84] Feeling pride involves a sense of self-achievement and capacity for doing things on one's own.[85] Researchers have shown that this increased sense of autonomy can expand an individual's attention to other activities, thereby pushing them to pursue other achievements in the future.[86]

Although pride is often thought of as an individual-level emotion, people can also feel pride on behalf of groups of which they consider themselves a part. Cialdini and his colleagues called this phenomenon "basking in reflected glory."[87] Other researchers have argued that because individuals are driven to maintain positive social identities within their groups, they engage in behaviors consistent with their groups' norms to build self-esteem among the group members.[88]

This pursuit of pride and self-esteem in a group with which one identifies can have a motivating effect on individuals' behaviors. To illustrate, Kemp and Kennett-Hensel showed that pride for an organization, entity, or cause (which serve as proxies for the individual him/ herself) can induce an individual to assist the organization, entity, or cause in achieving their goals.[89] In this way, an individual can feel pride not only in the effort they exert for the sake of an ingroup, but also through the ingroup's successes. This phenomenon explains every sports fan that gloats to their co-workers the day after their team wins a big game. I'm looking at you, New England Patriots fans!

Other Emotions

In addition to the nine emotions discussed here, there are also several other emotions that can affect audiences. These emotions are often considered to be variations of the emotions described in this chapter, eliciting similar responses and having similar action tendencies. Table 6.3 lists some of these variations and the discrete emotions they are associated with.

To this point, we have established what emotions are and how they can affect people who feel them. Now, let's turn to the ways that terrorist groups exploit their audiences' emotions to achieve strategic goals.

Emotional Appeals in Terrorist Propaganda

All the emotions described in this chapter have long traditions within the persuasion literature, as they can all have powerful effects on message targets. Although all emotions are important (and are occasionally targeted in terrorist propaganda), research on terrorist messaging suggests that terrorist actors primarily seek to arouse four emotions: fear, anger, guilt, and pride. This section will discuss what terrorist groups hope to achieve by arousing these emotions and provide some real-world examples as to how they have gone about inducing these emotions in their audiences.

Fear

In 1975, terrorism expert Brian Jenkins said that "Terrorists want a lot of people watching, not a lot of people dead." Although terrorist attacks have grown deadlier since the mid-1970s, Jenkins's contention remains

Table 6.3 *Variations of discrete emotions*

Anger	Fear	Disgust	Guilt	Sadness	Envy	Happiness	Hope	Pride	Others
Rage	Anxiety	Aversion	Shame	Sorrow	Jealousy	Joy	Nervousness	Relief	Surprise
Annoyance	Startled	Repulsion	Regret	Disappointment		Love			Boredom
Contempt	Distrust	Revulsion		Upset		Contentment			Indifference
Hatred						Enthusiasm			
						Compassion			

true with respect to terrorist propaganda. One of the fundamental objectives of terrorist communication is to promote and spread fear to as many
people as possible to facilitate the achievement of political goals.

This can occur in one of two ways. First, terrorist groups seek to
induce fear about individuals or organizations that the terrorist group
identifies as enemies. Because fear has an avoidance-oriented action
tendency, by arousing fear about enemy groups, terrorists seek to characterize them as dangerous entities to be avoided or attacked. By inducing fear about enemies, terrorist groups can also characterize themselves
as being well-positioned to protect target audiences from the "dangerous" enemies, thereby justifying the use of violence.

For example, consider the video posted by Anders Breivik only hours
before his 2011 attacks that killed seventy-seven and injured more
than 300 in Norway (we covered the video and its persuasive power in
Chapter 4). In the video, which was based on his manifesto, Breivik
warned of the destruction of mainland Europe by those he called "Cultural Marxists." He argued that Europe was losing its cultural identity
due to open immigration and the "Islamization" of major European
cities. All these problems, he argued, were derived from a failure to reject
multiculturalism in Europe – a problem he equated with a new Crusade.
And of course, this new Crusade would require armed resistance.

The manifesto was littered with references to shady enemies that wish
to undo the true-and-pure (i.e., white) culture in Europe. Figure 6.1
illustrates one of the enemies that appeared in the video on which the
manifesto was based, a Marxist doctor strapping on a rubber glove,
suggesting he is preparing to violate Europe. With this image and others

Cultural Marxist rape of Europe, 1968-2011

Figure 6.1 Image from Breivik video

like it, Breivik wishes to communicate the threat posed by those he perceives as enemies to white Europe. By doing so, he can arouse fear among audience members, thereby justifying his action as a needed response to a dangerous threat.

In a similar example, The Daily Stormer – an anti-Semitic, neo-Nazi website – regularly produces propaganda highlighting elements of its white supremacist ideology. Much of this propaganda is designed to elicit some of the same emotions as those targeted by Breivik. Specifically, The Daily Stormer emphasizes that the United States is under attack and at risk for losing its cultural identity. Whereas Breivik blamed "Cultural Marxism" for the degeneration of white culture in Europe, The Daily Stormer identifies Jews as dangerous agents of change, intent on altering the cultural fabric of the United States. By characterizing Jews in this way, The Daily Stormer seeks to elicit fear among white men about the potential "destruction of their country," thereby justifying their extremist rhetoric and violent behavior against Jews.[90]

Although terrorist groups often develop messages intended to induce fear about their enemies, they can also use fear to their own benefit by distributing messages that demonstrate their willingness to engage in violence if their demands are not met (or as a form of punishment). By doing so, terrorist groups exploit the avoidance tendency associated with fear by coercing target audiences to "escape" potential violence by acquiescing to the group's demands. Specifically, terrorist groups seek to arouse fear that induces audiences to pressure governments (or other entities) to make changes consistent with the terrorist group's goals.

One infamous form of terrorist messaging that can be used to induce fear in target audiences are execution videos. Videos depicting the execution of enemies are distributed for several reasons, among them being to weaken the resolve of their opponents or arousing fear in the public by demonstrating the group's commitment to barbaric violence.[91] Between 2013 and 2016, ISIS produced and distributed many such videos with the intention of demonstrating how the group treats those they perceive as traitors, enemies, and spies.

For instance, in 2014, ISIS released a video in which an American freelance journalist, James Foley, was executed. Like many other videos depicting ISIS executions, Foley was required to read a statement expressing regret for his action in Iraq. The executioner, Mohammed Emwazi, then warned of bloodshed in response to continued aggression by the United States in Iraq. Although the actual beheading is not shown in the video, Foley's decapitated body appears near the end of the video to leave no doubt about those that would dare challenge ISIS.

Like Anders Breivik's manifesto or The Daily Stormer's propaganda, the ISIS execution video was designed, in part, to instill fear. Unlike Breivik or The Daily Stormer, however, ISIS meant to arouse fear about the group's actions in response to efforts to challenge it. Whereas the first two examples are meant to promote movement away from enemy agents (and towards those that can protect against those agents), the final example is meant to promote movement away from actions that might interfere with ISIS operations.

Regardless of the strategy employed by terrorist groups to elicit fear among message recipients, the avoidance-orientation associated with the emotion's action tendency can be a powerful driver of audience responses. When carefully harnessed, the power of fear can push audience members away from outcomes the terrorist group seeks to avoid and towards outcomes the group seeks to achieve.

Anger

Anger is similar to fear in that they both cause negative reactions. Unlike fear, however, anger has a strong *approach*-oriented action tendency that can push individuals to engage in aggressive behaviors against the source of their anger. Terrorist groups take advantage of this action tendency by developing persuasive messages intended to arouse anger that will motivate audiences to lash out at the terrorists' enemies.

This is a common propaganda tactic among terrorist groups, who often depict the victimization of those they claim to represent. For example, in my earlier research, I showed that one of the major themes embedded in the online narratives of the Animal Liberation Front is the victimization of innocent animals. In their narratives, ALF authors depicted animals as innocent victims and those who kill animals (hunters, meat-eaters) as barbaric murderers. In doing so, the ALF attempts to make its audience angry at the villains in their narratives.[92] This can activate the approach-oriented action tendency to either strike back at the enemies of the group or accept the violent tactics used by the group as legitimate.

Other groups have similarly sought to arouse anger in their audiences by highlighting the crimes of their enemies. On its website, Hamas maintains a repository of news stories relating to Israeli aggression against Palestinian civilians. In one of these stories, Hamas describes a story in which an Israeli soldier shoots a Palestinian and leaves him to bleed in the street. The story goes on to describe how other Israeli soldiers were standing around ignoring the pain filled cries of the wounded Palestinian until one soldier turns to shoot him in the head, executing him. To further enflame anger that might result from reading this story, Hamas included a picture of the killed Palestinian, bleeding in the street.

Anger can be a particularly dangerous emotion to contend with, should terrorist groups be successful in evoking it. In other contexts, anger's approach-oriented action tendency has been shown to arouse hostility and engagement in activities that they perceive as self-defense against an aggressor. In the context of political violence, this can translate to support for or engagement in violence against those depicted as the source of the anger. This very phenomenon is often referenced in discussions with former terrorists, who claim that their decision to get involved with terrorism was at least partially influenced by the anger they felt against those they perceived as enemies.[93]

Guilt

As evidenced by the fear and anger appeals referenced above, a significant amount of terrorist messaging is meant to induce emotions in audience members by focusing on the actions of others. To elicit fear, tell the audience they are in danger from some imminent threat. To provoke anger, tell the audience about the atrocities perpetrated by enemies. Although referencing actions by others can elicit powerfully motivating emotions, so too can highlighting the things that the audience *themselves* fail to do.

To this end, terrorist groups often attempt to motivate their audiences to engage in behaviors consistent with the group's goals by framing the audience's actions (or lack of actions) as a moral failure. In doing so, the terrorist group seeks to induce guilt among its audience. Recall that the action tendency associated with guilt is a drive to redress the perceived moral failing. Therefore, if the terrorist group is successful in making audiences believe they have failed a moral imperative, they can motivate them to engage in behaviors that resolve that failure in a manner consistent with the group's suggestions.

Examples of guilt appeals within terrorist propaganda are pervasive. Many of these appeals characterize the preservation of the terrorists' ideology as a duty incumbent on audience members. By framing their arguments in this way, terrorist groups can impose on audiences that the group's recommendations for action may be communicated by the group, but are based on a much larger moral standard.

For example, the propaganda distributed by American Vanguard, a white supremacist, neo-Nazi organization, emphasizes that the defense of white culture is nothing to apologize for. Instead, the group's propaganda suggests that a white person's failure to defend his/her people (other whites) is a moral failure. This can induce guilt on the part of those who do not yet support the American Vanguard ideology, particularly if they identify strongly with their race.

In an illustration of the American Vanguard's attempts to sow feelings of guilt among audiences they target, in April of 2017, the group's name was included on a sign that was posted around the University of Texas at Arlington.[94] Like its earlier propaganda, this poster imposed on white Americans that it is their "civic duty" to report illegal aliens to US Immigration and Naturalization Services. Again, by describing the reporting of illegal aliens as a duty to be performed, American Vanguard seeks to communicate that failing to report illegal aliens is immoral. The guilt that can result from this may motivate individuals to redress the perceived moral oversight by behaving in a manner consistent with American Vanguard's wishes.

Pride

So far, we have discussed how negative emotions have the potential to motivate audience members to act in accordance with a terrorist group's ideology. However, it is important to note that terrorist groups often seek to elicit a positive emotion through their propaganda as well. Whereas fear, anger, and guilt orient audiences to the group's enemies and imbue them with action tendencies geared towards striking back at those enemies in some way, pride is more closely related to cultivating group identity and feeling good about the direction the group is headed. Specifically, pride has the tendency to induce actions geared towards renewing and strengthening efforts towards achieving goals the terrorist group claims are valuable.

By cultivating pride through their propaganda, terrorist groups achieve two complementary goals. First, they communicate to audiences that they remain steadfast in their adherence to the ideology driving their violent actions; they demonstrate the ongoing resolve of the group and its certainty in the ideology it fights for. Second, pride appeals tend to demonstrate the group's strength and capacity for continuing its violent actions.

Let's consider the propaganda video referenced at the beginning of this chapter – ISIS's *Blood for Blood*. This video is full of imagery meant to instill feelings of pride among those who agree – even if only philosophically – with the ISIS ideology. The video also includes many images of children who are characterized as being brave enough to fight for ISIS, an indication that the viewer should be proud of what these children have accomplished.

Figure 6.2 Still from ISIS propaganda video *Blood for Blood*
Source: Video posted on Aaron Zelin's repository for online content available to researchers, *Jihadology*. Available at www.jihadology.net (password-gated).

Here, let's focus on a still image from one of the closing scenes of the video (see Figure 6.2). As the video nears its conclusion, a group of children are lined up carefully, beginning a military-style march. The scene is backlit with a setting sun against which it is clear to see the child-soldiers carrying their weapons. One child raises the black flag of ISIS and raises it high as inspirational music echoes.

The feelings of pride that this propaganda (and other propaganda like it) musters have multiple effects. Most notably, feelings of pride towards a group with which one identifies can induce the individual to support that group in some manner.[95] Most people who see this video will not be a member of ISIS – they will not have engaged in violence on behalf of the group. From the perspective of ISIS, however, that's perfectly fine. The intended audience for this kind of message are those who agree with the group's arguments, if not their tactics. By instilling pride in these individuals due to what Cialdini called "basking in reflective glory," this ISIS propaganda can promote helping behaviors on the part of audience members.

∴

To be sure, terrorist groups can exploit many other emotions through their propaganda. Propaganda that highlights relative deprivation between the terrorist group's constituents and those they perceive as enemies can trigger envy in their audiences, which in turn can lead to support for violence.[96] There is a long history of terrorist groups eliciting disgust towards enemies on the part of their audiences by describing those enemies as dirty vermin, animals, and pests. By eliciting disgust in this way, the terrorist groups can facilitate audience aversion and dehumanization of those enemies.[97] These represent only two examples. Terrorists have run the gamut when it comes to the emotions they try to exploit through their messages.

However, of all the emotional reactions that terrorists attempt to evoke through their propaganda, fear, anger, guilt, and pride are the most pervasive. This section has discussed the kinds of goals that terrorists hope to achieve by arousing these emotions and offered some real-world examples of these efforts.

Now, we turn to how the motivational nature of emotions can be used to challenge terrorist propaganda and drive individuals away from the appeal of terrorist groups.

Developing Emotional Appeals for Countering Violent Extremism

Terrorist groups clearly expend significant effort to arouse emotions geared towards motivating belief, attitude, or behavior change in potential supporters. But the strength of emotions and their capacity for promoting persuasion are not tools that are uniquely available to terrorist groups. Research on discrete emotions and their persuasive effects suggests that researchers, practitioners, and analysts can develop their own messages that evoke emotions that *challenge* terrorist ideologies.

Whereas terrorist groups have primarily relied on fear, anger, guilt, and pride in their messaging, those who would seek to use emotions for countering violent extremism (CVE) could viably provoke other useful emotions. Of course, analysts should seek to arouse some of the same emotions that terrorist groups target; anger and pride can be extremely powerful instruments when pointed in the right direction. However, counterterror practitioners could also seek to evoke hope – a potent emotion that can be used to offer audience members a positive alternative view about a future without the terrorist group.

Given the potential for emotions to support goals related to CVE, this section describes how we can develop and distribute messages that respectively evoke anger, hope, and pride. In doing so, this section will outline not only how some efforts have already sought to exploit these emotions, but also the sorts of beliefs, attitudes, and behaviors that might result from evoking them. Following each brief discussion, I will offer some practical guidance on how to elicit these emotions via messages intended to challenge terrorist ideologies.

Anger

As indicated above, anger is generally aroused in response to things that unjustifiably keep us from achieving our goals. When we experience anger, we are motivated to remove the obstacles that block our progress. To make use of this motivational tendency for the purpose of counter-radicalization, it is necessary to develop and distribute messages that show how targeted terrorist groups obstruct audiences from their goals.

Before developing such messages, however, it is necessary to *identify and understand the nature of target audiences' valued goals*. Although different audiences will inevitably prioritize some goals over others, many goals are likely to be common to most audiences. For example, regardless of culture, most audiences will value the safety and security of their loved ones and themselves. Therefore, it can be useful to arouse anger in response to danger that terrorist groups pose to local populations, despite claims that they are acting in support of those populations. This can be particularly useful if terrorist groups engage in activity that is unpopular among those the groups mean to persuade.

For instance, in November of 1987, the Provisional Irish Republican Army carried out a bombing in Enniskillen, Northern Ireland (Figure 6.3). The attack occurred during a Remembrance Day ceremony intended to honor those who had been killed in service of the British military. The attack killed ten civilians, most of whom were elderly. A police officer was also killed in the blast. In addition to the eleven killed, sixty-three were injured by the explosion and the collapse of buildings in the surrounding area.[98]

The PIRA apologized for the attack, claiming that the targets of the bomb were soldiers from the Ulster Defence Regiment (UDR) – infantry soldiers in the British military tasked with assisting the Royal Ulster Constabulary with peacekeeping in Northern Ireland.[99] The apology didn't matter.

Politicians in the United Kingdom and Ireland condemned the bombing, describing it as a "desecration"[100] and an "outrage."[101] Other politicians spoke for their constituents, claiming that people felt revulsion in response to the attack.[102]

Regardless of the PIRA's intentions with the Remembrance Day bombing, people on both sides of the Ireland/Northern Ireland border were angry. The Provos recognized the fallout caused by their attack; one unnamed senior leader conceded that following the attack, the PIRA's support among sympathizers would be "totally devastated."[103]

A similar response occurred in the wake of ISIS's execution of Jordanian pilot Muath al-Kasasbeh.[104] In December of 2014, al-Kasasbeh's

Figure 6.3 Aftermath of the Enniskillen bombing
Source: Image sourced from "Revulsion in Government at Enniskillen Bomb Outrage Revealed," *Irish Independent* (December 29, 2017). Available at www.independent.ie/irish-news/revulsion-in-government-at-enniskillen-bomb-outrage-revealed-36443145.html (accessed December 2, 2018). Reprinted with permission from Peacemaker Press International.

F-16 experienced mechanical issues while executing a bombing raid in ISIS territory. He ejected and was captured by ISIS militants near Raqqa, Syria. In the days that followed al-Kasasbeh's capture, ISIS took to social media to crowdsource ways to execute him.[105] Twitter produced several gruesome suggestions, including being eaten by a crocodile, dissolved with acid, or stung to death by scorpions.[106] In the subsequent weeks, several negotiations and rescue missions were attempted, but none were successful.

On February 3, 2015, ISIS released a 22-minute propaganda video through their al-Furqan Media Foundation.[107] The video showed a battered al-Kasasbeh being marched through the rubble of Syrian towns at gunpoint and reading statements to the camera. Near the end of the video, al-Kasasbeh is shown trapped in a cage with a trail of accelerant leading to a group of ISIS militants. One of the militants lights the liquid, causing fire to creep towards the cage, eventually reaching al-Kasasbeh as he stands quietly. When the fire reaches him, his orange jumpsuit immediately becomes engulfed in flame and he reaches to his face, trying to shield it. Al-Kasasbeh swings his arms and jumps several times, trying in vain to extinguish the flames. Within a few seconds, his entire body is burning, and he collapses to his knees at the side of the cage where he stops moving, flesh melting off his body.[108]

Following the release of the video, public outcry showed a fresh hatred of ISIS and its acts among Jordanians. Massive demonstrations erupted in Amman, indicating an intense desire for revenge against the Islamic State.[109] Surveys of public opinion within Jordan also showed that following the execution, angry Jordanians overwhelmingly supported military action against ISIS (which had previously not had such strong support). These surveys further indicated that 95 percent of Jordanians considered ISIS to be a terrorist organization after the attack – an increase in 23 percent from just two months earlier.[110]

This anger was not confined to Jordan. Political leaders, religious figures, and news outlets in Egypt, Saudi Arabia, Qatar, Bahrain, the Palestinian territories, Syria and other countries condemned the attack, expressing disgust at ISIS's actions. Even al-Qaeda fighters denounced the barbaric execution of al-Kasasbeh.[111]

∴

Though unquestionably tragic, events like the Remembrance Day bombing and the execution of Muath al-Kasasbeh represent opportunities for the development of strategic messages that further diminish support for the terrorists through the perpetuation of anger in response to the events. The PIRA's botched effort to attack the British military aroused anger in Irish, Northern Irish, and British citizens alike. ISIS sought to pressure Jordan into abandoning the coalition of countries attacking the group in Syria, but its execution of al-Kasasbeh sparked such anger that Jordanians and other Middle Easterners expressed increased commitment to stamp out the group entirely.

These examples are expressly related to anger elicited in response to the obstruction of valued goals – the safety of noncombatants and the limitation of suffering on the part of valued others, respectively. When the PIRA and ISIS violated people's pursuits of these goals (or at least their perceptions of their goals being respected), the people's anger affected their beliefs and attitudes towards the terrorist groups and their activities.

In this way, these examples are instructive; they show that *highlighting terrorist groups' obstructions of audiences' goal pursuits (or the terrorist groups' disrespect of those goals)* can induce anger that influences their perceptions of the terrorist groups themselves.

Although we might assume that all audience members will react to these kinds of anger-inducing stimuli in the same way, it is important to remember that different audience members respond to anger appeals in various ways. So, the development of effective messages intended to arouse anger against terrorist organizations demands that we understand how different kinds of audiences are attitudinally oriented with respect to those organizations and their activities. Turner's Anger Activation Model is useful for this.

According to Turner, audiences targeted by anger appeals should be categorized along two dimensions – the intensity with which they experience anger in response to a stimulus, and the degree to which they think a suggested course of action will resolve the situation responsible for their anger.[112]

Individuals who are already predisposed to agree with a message communicated by an anger appeal would be most likely to act in accordance with that message if it pushes them "over the edge" in terms of their anger. For example, individuals who were already inclined to thinking the PIRA put innocent individuals in danger with their activities would be prime targets for anger appeals related to the Enniskillen bombing. By highlighting the innocent civilians killed in that attack, message designers could elicit intense anger on the part of these audiences. Moreover, suggestions for behaviors that challenge PIRA objectives (e.g., "attend a march in protest of the PIRA") could provide these audiences with increased perceptions of efficacy, indicating that the proposed solutions would effectively combat the PIRA. For these individuals, message designers have the option to propose behaviors that require significant effort, as individuals with high levels of anger and high perceptions of efficacy will likely be motivated to engage in these behaviors, regardless of their complexity. Turner called this group of audience members "activists" (high anger, high efficacy).

Another group of individuals – those for whom anger appeals are unlikely to arouse much anger – should be targeted with different kinds of messages. For these individuals, message designers should emphasize simple behaviors that do not require much effort or otherwise inconvenience them. Staying with the PIRA example, let us assume that some of our audience is not terribly angry about the group's activities or its attack in Enniskillen. However, these individuals believe that something should be done about the group, given the pain they are causing others. These individuals are not terribly angry, and are therefore not too motivated to act. But, they *would* be willing to engage in behaviors to mitigate the problems caused by the PIRA as long as they are not too taxing (e.g., "do not let your children interact with known PIRA members"). Turner called these individuals "empowered" (low anger, high efficacy).

The key to motivating behavior among any individuals in a set audience is either *highlighting or fostering perceptions of efficacy*. Regardless of how angry a message makes someone, if they do not believe they can act in a way that will help resolve a situation, they are unlikely to be persuaded to engage in any such behaviors. Using the Anger Activation Model's language, these individuals would be "disinterested" (low anger, low efficacy) or simply "angry" (high anger, low efficacy).

Given the above, I offer seven specific recommendations regarding the development of anger appeals intended to challenge terrorist propaganda and ideologies:

(1) Before developing a message about a terrorist group intended to induce anger, identify the valued goals of audiences targeted by terrorist propaganda.
(2) Highlight events performed by the terrorist group that obstruct the audience's ability to achieve those valued goals.
(3) Target "activists" (individuals predisposed to agree with the content of a message and believe that their anger can be resolved with specific activities) with messages that seek to elicit high levels of anger.
(4) Optimize behavioral outcomes of "activists" by recommending behaviors that require a significant amount of effort.
(5) Target "empowered individuals" (individuals with no predisposition to agree with the content of a message, but nonetheless believe that certain activities can resolve a problematic issue) with messages that emphasize the importance of challenging terrorist behaviors and ideologies.
(6) Optimize behavioral outcomes of "empowered individuals" by recommending behaviors that do not require a significant amount of effort.
(7) Incorporate content into anger appeals that communicate the ease with which behaviors that challenge the terrorist group can be performed (i.e., emphasize the efficacy of recommended behaviors).

Hope

Hope is aroused by the recognition that one's goals are *possible* to achieve but are not a foregone conclusion. When individuals feel hopeful, they are motivated to take advantage of opportunities that they perceive will be helpful in achieving their goals. To leverage this tendency in the context of counter-radicalization, message designers should produce and disseminate hope appeals that highlight opportunities audience members could pursue to facilitate the achievement of goals that challenge terrorist ideologies.

As with anger, the development of such messages first requires that message designers *identify target audiences' valued goals*. Then, it is then necessary to *identify specific behaviors that represent opportunities for audience members to achieve these goals*. By (a) identifying audience goals that run contrary to terrorist ideologies and objectives, and (b) recommending behaviors that can help them achieve those goals, it becomes possible to elicit hope such that individuals who desire outcomes that are contrary to terrorist groups' objectives will be motivated to engage in suggested behaviors to those ends.

For instance, consider disenfranchised, young, white individuals who are targeted for recruitment by white extremist right-wing organizations. White supremacists, national socialists, and the alt-right often target these individuals, many of whom lack a feeling of identity or a place to belong. Through promises of belonging and a sense of purpose – critical goals for developing young minds – these groups persuade white youth that they are at risk for victimization by minority criminals, replacement by foreign workers, or marginalization by an emerging demand for social justice. In this way, right-wing extremists weaponize these individuals' failure to achieve important social goals (i.e., identity, purpose, belonging) to draw them towards their groups.

To counter the persuasive efficacy of these kinds of messages, it would be useful to offer message recipients hope about achieving these goals without having to join extremist groups to do so. One example of a program that specializes in these kinds of messages is Exit USA, itself part of the Life After Hate organization.[113] Originally founded by several former white supremacists, including Christian Picciolini, Sammy Rangel, and Frank Meeink, Life After Hate offers individuals who are part of (or are on the path towards) extremist groups avenues for leaving those groups behind. Unfortunately, these individuals often fear abandoning their social circle or suffering repercussions from their former comrades. As a result, they rarely see how they can leave their extremist lives.

Exit USA recognizes this inner conflict and offers hope to these individuals. Specifically, Exit USA emphasizes that current and budding extremists can achieve their social and psychological goals without maintaining racist beliefs and attitudes. Through public awareness campaigns, educational programs, job training, and community partnerships, Exit USA personnel emphasize not only that leaving extremism is possible, but also that doing so will lead to a better life. Even the website is designed to provide hope to individuals, explicitly stating that the group offers "no judgment, just help" and that "it is possible to leave."[114]

Through its communicative strategies and programming, Exit USA *builds the efficacy of those who wish to achieve important social goals*. By doing so, the organization offers these individuals hope for achieving these goals while simultaneously undercutting extremist groups' capacities for doing so.

Given the nature of hope and how it motivates individuals to engage in goal-oriented behaviors, there are four guidelines that message designers should consider in how they attempt to elicit hope through counter-radicalization messaging:

(1) Before developing a message about a terrorist group intended to induce hope, identify valued goals that the audience possesses and how they have pursued those goals.
(2) Identify specific behaviors that audience members can perform that (a) help them achieve their valued goals, and (b) run contrary to terrorist propaganda/objectives.
(3) Indicate how recommended behaviors are superior to those advocated by terrorists for achieving valued goals.
(4) Highlight the feasibility with which recommended behaviors can be performed to build the efficacy of message targets.

Pride

The sections above explain that anger and hope are respectively related to the degree to which an individual's pursuit of a goal is blocked or its success becomes more possible through assistance. In contrast to these emotions, pride is based on the notion that one can bask in the glory of having completed a valued goal. So, whereas anger and hope relate to goal *pursuit*, pride relates to reflecting on the *completion* of a goal.

Achievement-induced pride does not result only from the completion of goals that one has set for oneself, but also for *goals achieved by those with whom individuals consider themselves affiliated*. Recall that extremist messages are intended to induce pride "by proxy." That is, extremist groups often attempt to make audience members feel pride about the group's actions, particularly if audience members identify with that group in some way (e.g., culturally, ideologically). By stressing (a) the affiliation between the audience member and the group, and (b) the goals that the group has achieved, extremist groups seek to elicit helping behaviors on the part of the audience members resulting from the pride those individuals feel.

Just as feelings of affiliation and the resulting feelings of pride can be used to motivate behavior consistent with terrorist ideologies, they can also be elicited by counter-radicalization messages to prevent such behaviors. Specifically, highlighting audience affiliations with *non-violent* entities can be an effective method for challenging extremist messaging through the elicitation of pride. Some messaging campaigns have attempted this very strategy.

For example, though its authorship and origins are somewhat mysterious,[115] the Say No to Terror campaign has developed several video messages and other kinds of counter-propaganda intended to challenge terrorist ideologies in the Middle East. The website that serves as a repository for these counter-messages says that they are intended to expose the hypocrisies and crimes of terrorist agitators and calls on "those who have a conscience" to reject terrorism as a viable strategy for political change.[116] The videos produced for the campaign are developed around several themes, including the hopelessness of terrorist activity, the victimization of innocent civilians by terrorist groups, and terrorists' exploitation of children to perform violence.

One video, however, has elements that may be useful for eliciting pride among its viewers. In this video, Muslim extremists storm a peaceful market in an unnamed Middle Eastern town. They arrive in force, firing machine guns into the air, knocking children to the ground, and sending innocent bystanders ducking behind any cover they can find. After terrorizing the local population, they turn their guns towards a Muslim man looking at the terrorists with an intense stoicism.

The man does not scream; he does not run. Instead, he stares at the group of terrorists, boldly standing his ground in the face of intense violence. As he stands quietly, two other men approach him until they are standing on either side of him. More men stand adjacent to the newcomers. Then more men approach. Then more. Eventually, dozens of Muslims are standing in the street, defiantly staring at the terrorists. The men in the front row of the group link arms, and the entire crowd begins to walk towards the outnumbered terrorists. As they begin walking, a young boy picks up an Iraqi flag that had been knocked to the ground and raises it skyward.

The camera pans overhead, showing that the group of terrorists is being approached not only by the group in front of them, but by other groups of peaceful Iraqi citizens on all sides. They are surrounded by proud Iraqis who are determined to rid themselves of the terrorists ruining their country.[117]

Messages like the one communicated in this video provide viewers with a source of pride that (a) they can identify with and (b) challenge terrorist ideologies and actions. A similar example is that of Abdullah X, a YouTube personality who speaks out against Islamist terrorism, but makes no apologies for his being a Muslim in the Western world.[118] Through slickly animated videos, he expresses pride in his culture and background, and advocates for other Muslims doing the same. All the while, he highlights the contradictions inherent to ISIS's ideology. Abdullah X, who describes himself as having the "mind of a scholar" and the "heart of a warrior," shows young Muslims targeted by ISIS propaganda that they can be proud of their Muslim heritage, but need not affiliate with ISIS to do so.

Both the Say No to Terror campaign and the videos produced by Abdullah X clearly communicate to Muslims that there are affiliations that they can rightfully be proud of, and violent extremism has nothing to do with it.

Discrete emotion theory and the examples outlined above suggest a few guidelines for effectively eliciting pride for the purpose of counter-radicalization:

(1) Find different kinds of groups that audience members can identify with who do not engage in activities consistent with the targeted terrorist ideology.
(2) Highlight goals that these groups have achieved.
(3) Highlight that the goals have been achieved without resorting to violence or supporting those who engage in violence.
(4) Emphasize similarities between target audiences and the non-violent groups with which they identify.
(5) If possible, highlight activities performed by the non-violent group that run contrary to or challenge the terrorist ideology.
(6) Highlight activities that target audiences can engage in to support the non-violent group with which they identify.

Conclusions

In the pages above, I have tried to describe the processes that drive our emotions and the behavioral tendencies we have in response to them. I've tried to explain how terrorist groups have sought to exploit the emotions of vulnerable individuals to bring them into closer alignment with the groups' ideologies. Finally, I offered some recommendations for how we might elicit emotions to cultivate beliefs, attitudes, and behaviors that oppose terrorist ideologies.

In trying to do all these things, my nice, neat chapter segments may have given you the impression that messaging intended to arouse emotional responses is a simple endeavor. That's not the case. To be sure, emotions are messy. But they are also powerful.

The guidelines presented in the previous section represent some initial recommendations for harnessing that power and pointing it in a direction that steers our audiences clear of ideological violence. It may be tricky to do so, but it is a worthwhile goal if it helps us to negate the awesome persuasive appeal of terrorist propaganda.

∴

In the ISIS video described at the beginning of this chapter, a song is continuously playing over the scenes that comprise the video's narrative. At one point, the lyrics threaten the viewer:

Beware, we have what we need to defend ourselves …

With an understanding of emotions and how they might be elicited in response to counter-radicalization messaging, we have part of what we need to defend ourselves as well.

Notes

1 Richard Lazarus, *Emotion and Adaptation* (New York: Oxford University Press, 1991); see also R. S. Lazarus, "From Psychological Stress to the Emotions: A History of Changing Outlooks," *Annual Review of Psychology* 44 (1993): 1–21.

2 Carroll E. Izard, *Human Emotions* (New York: Plenum Press, 1977).

3 Carl I. Hovland, Irving L. Janis, and Harold H. Kelley, *Communication and Persuasion: Psychological Studies of Opinion Change* (New Haven, CT: Yale University Press, 1953).

4 Deborah J. MacInnis and Gustavo E. de Mello, "The Concept of Hope and its Relevance to Product Evaluation and Choice," *Journal of Marketing* 69, no. 1 (2005): 1–14.

5 Ted Brader, "Striking a Responsive Chord: How Political Ads Motivate and Persuade Voters by Appealing to Emotions," *American Journal of Political Science* 49, no. 2 (2005): 388–405.

6 Norbert Weiner, "Cybernetics," *Scientific American* 179, no. 5 (1948): 14–19.

7 See John McCarthy, Marvin Minsky, Claude E. Shannon, and Phyllis Fox, "Artificial Intelligence," Computation Center, Massachusetts Institute of Technology. Available at https://dspace.mit.edu/bitstream/handle/1721.1/53496/RLE_QPR_060_XVI.pdf.

8 James Price Dillard and Kiwon Seo, "Affect and Persuasion," in *The SAGE Handbook of Persuasion: Developments in Theory and Practice*, ed. James Price

Dillard and Lijiang Shen, 150–166 (Thousand Oaks, CA: Sage, 2013), pp. 150–151.

9 David Watson and Lee Anna Clark, *The PANAS-X: Manual for the Positive and Negative Affect Schedule*. Available at https://ir.uiowa.edu/cgi/viewcontent .cgi?referer=https://www.google.com/&httpsredir=1&article=1011&context= psychology_pubs/.

10 James A. Russell and Lisa Feldman Barrett, "Core Affect, Prototypical Emotional Episodes, and other Things Called Emotion: Dissecting the Elephant," *Journal of Personality and Social Psychology* 76, no. 5 (1999): 805–819.

11 K. Luan Phan, Tor Wager, Stephan F. Taylor, and Israel Liberson, "Functional Neuroanatomy of Emotion: A Meta-Analysis of Emotion Activation Studies in PET and fMRI," *NeuroImage* 16, no. 2 (2002): 331–348.

12 Dillard and Seo, "Affect and Persuasion," p. 152.

13 Lazarus, *Emotion and Adaptation*; Carroll E. Izard, "Emotion Theory and Research: Highlights, Unanswered Questions, and Emerging Issues," *Annual Review of Psychology* 60 (2009): 1–25; James Price Dillard and Robin L. Nabi, "The Persuasive Influence of Emotion in Cancer Prevention and Detection Messages," *Journal of Communication* 56, no. S1 (2006): S123–S139.

14 See: James Price Dillard and Eugenia Peck, "Persuasion and the Structure of Affect: Dual Systems and Discrete Emotions as Complementary Models," *Human Communication Research* 27, no. 1 (2001): 38–68 (p. 41); Lazarus, *Emotion and Adaptation*; Izard, *Human Emotions*; Nico H. Frijda, Peter Kuipers, and Elisabeth ter Schure, "Relations among Emotion, Appraisal, and Emotional Action Readiness," *Journal of Personality and Social Psychology* 57, no. 2 (1989): 212–228.

15 Lazarus, *Emotion and Adaptation*; Richard S. Lazarus and Bernice N. Lazarus, *Passion and Reason: Making Sense of Our Emotions* (Oxford University Press, 1994); Christa Reiser, *Reflections on Anger: Women and Men in a Changing Society* (Westport, CT: Praeger, 1999).

16 Michael Pfau, Erin Alison Szabo, Jason Anderson, Joshua Morrill, Jessica Zubric, and Hua-Hsin Wan, "The Role and Impact of Affect in the Process of Resistance to Persuasion," *Human Communication Research* 27, no. 2 (2001): 216–252.

17 Monique Mitchell Turner, "Using Emotion in Risk Communication: The Anger Activism Model," *Public Relations Review* 33 (2007): 114–119; Carroll E. Izard, *The Psychology of Emotions* (New York: Plenum Press, 1991); Clarissa Pinkola Estés, *Women Who Run with the Wolves: Myths and Stories of the Wild Woman Archetype* (New York: Ballantine Books, 1992).

18 Janne van Doorn, Marcel Zeelenberg, and Seger M. Breugelmans, "The Impact of Anger on Donations to Victims," *International Review of Victimology* 23, no. 3 (2017): 303–312.

19 Turner, "Using Emotion in Risk Communication," p. 115; Reiser, *Reflections on Anger*.

20 Van Doorn et al., "The Impact of Anger on Donations to Victims"; N. J. Raihani and Katherine McAuliffe, "Human Punishment is Motivated by Inequity Aversion, Not a Desire for Reciprocity," *Biology Letters* 8, no. 5 (2012): 802–804.

21 Leo Montada and Angela Schneider, "Justice and Emotional Reactions to the Disadvantaged," *Social Justice Research* 3, no. 4 (1989): 313–344.
22 Van Doorn et al., "The Impact of Anger on Donations to Victims."
23 Albert Bandura, *Social Foundations of Thought and Action* (Englewood Cliffs, NJ: Prentice Hall, 1986).
24 Kim Witte, "Fear Control and Danger Control: A Test of the Extended Parallel Process Model (EPPM)," *Communication Monographs* 61, no. 2 (1994): 113–134.
25 Robin L. Nabi, "A Cognitive Functional Model for the Effects of Discrete Negative Emotions on Information Processing, Attitude Change, and Recall," *Communication Theory* 9, no. 3 (1999): 292–320.
26 Melvyn Fein, *I.A.M.: A Common Sense Guide to Coping with Anger* (Westport, CT: Praeger, 1993); Pfau et al., "The Role and Impact of Affect."
27 Sandra P. Thomas, "Anger and its Manifestation in Women," in *Women and Anger*, ed. Sandra P. Thomas, 40–67 (New York: Springer, 1993); James R. Averill, "Studies on Anger and Aggression: Implications for Theories of Emotion," *American Psychologist* 38, no. 11 (1983): 1145–1160.
28 Turner, "Using Emotion in Risk Communication," p. 116.
29 Ibid.
30 Turner, "Using Emotion in Risk Communication"; Monique Turner, Elena Bessarabova, Kathryn Hambleton, Maribeth Weiss, Sanja Sipek, and Kristen Long, "Does Anger Facilitate or Debilitate Persuasion? A Test of the Anger Activism Model," paper presented at the annual meeting of the International Communication Association, Dresden, Germany, 2006.
31 Melanie B. Tannenbaum, Justin Hepler, Rick S. Zimmerman, Lindsey Saul, Samantha Jacobs, Kristina Wilson, and Dolores Albarracín, "Appealing to Fear: A Meta-Analysis of Fear Appeal Effectiveness and Theories," *Psychological Bulletin* 161, no. 6 (2015): 1178–1204; James Price Dillard, Courtney A. Plotnick, Linda C. Godbold, Vicki S. Freimuth, and Timothy Edgar, "The Multiple Affective Outcomes of AIDS PSAs: Fear Appeals Do More than Scare People," *Communication Research* 23, no. 1 (1996): 44–72; Eric J. Meczkowski and James Price Dillard, "Fear Appeals in Strategic Communication," in *The International Encyclopedia of Media Effects*, ed. Patrick Rössler (Hoboken, NJ: John Wiley & Sons, 2017).
32 Kim Witte and Mike Allen, "A Meta-Analysis of Fear Appeals: Implications for Effective Public Health Campaigns," *Health Education & Behavior* 27, no. 5 (2000): 591–615; Kim Witte, "Fear as Motivator, Fear as Inhibitor: Using the EPPM to Explain Fear Appeal Successes and Failures," in *Handbook of Communication and Emotion*, ed. Peter Andersen and Laura Guerrero, 423–450 (New York: Academic Press, 1998).
33 Irving L. Janis and Seymour Feshbach, "Effects of Fear-Arousing Communications," *Journal of Abnormal and Social Psychology* 48, no. 1 (1953): 78–92.
34 Irving L. Janis and Robert F. Terwilliger, "An Experimental Study of Psychological Resistance to Fear Arousing Communications," *Journal of Abnormal and Social Psychology* 65 (1962): 403–410.
35 Howard Leventhal and Jean C. Watts, "Sources of Resistance to Fear-Arousing Communications on Smoking and Lung Cancer," *Journal of Personality* 34 (1966): 155–175.

36 Howard Leventhal and Robert P. Singer, "Affect Arousal and Positioning of Recommendations in Persuasive Communications," *Journal of Personality and Social Psychology* 4, no. 2 (1966): 137–146.

37 Chester A. Insko, Abe Arkoff, and Verla M. Insko, "Effects of High and Low Fear-Arousing Communications upon Opinions toward Smoking," *Journal of Experimental Social Psychology* 1 (1965): 256–266.

38 Kenneth L. Higbee, "Fifteen Years of Fear Arousal: Research on Threat Appeals 1953–1968," *Psychological Bulletin* 72, no. 6 (1969): 426–444.

39 Natascha de Hoog, Wolfgang Stroebe, and John B. F. de Wit, "The Impact of Fear Appeals on Processing and Acceptance of Action Recommendations," *Personality and Social Psychology Bulletin* 31, no. 1 (2005): 24–33.

40 Gyalt-Jorn Ygram Peters, Robert A. C. Ruiter, and Gerjo Kok, "Threatening Communication: A Critical Re-Analysis and a Revised Meta-Analytic Test of Fear Appeal Theory," *Health Psychology Review* 7, no. S1 (2013): S8–S31.

41 Ronald W. Rogers, "A Protection Motivation Theory of Fear Appeals and Attitude Change," *Journal of Psychology* 91, no. 1 (1975): 93–114.

42 Tannenbaum et al., "Appealing to Fear."

43 Paul Ekman, Robert W. Levenson, and Wallace V. Friesen, "Automatic Nervous System Activity Distinguishes among Emotions," *Science* 221, no. 46416 (1983): 1208–1210.

44 Elizabeth A. Krusemark and Wen Li, "Do All Threats Work the Same Way? Divergent Effects of Fear and Disgust on Sensory Perception and Attention," *Journal of Neuroscience* 31, no. 9 (2011): 3429–3434.

45 Hanneke Hendriks, Bas van den Putte, and Gert-Jan de Bruijn, "Changing the Conversation: The Influence of Emotions on Conversational Valence and Alcohol Consumption," *Prevention Science* 15, no. 5 (2013): 684–693; Sheila R. Woody and Bethany A. Teachman, "Intersection of Disgust and Fear: Normative and Pathological Views," *Clinical Psychology: Science and Practice* 7, no. 3 (2000): 291–311.

46 Daniel J. O'Keefe, "Guilt as a Mechanism of Persuasion," in *The Persuasion Handbook: Developments in Theory and Practice*, ed. James Price Dillard and Michael Pfau, 329–344 (Thousand Oaks, CA: Sage, 2002); Zhan Xu and Hao Guo, "A Meta-Analysis of the Effectiveness of Guilt on Health-Related Attitudes," *Health Communication* 33, no. 5 (2018): 519–525.

47 O'Keefe, "Guilt as a Mechanism of Persuasion."

48 June Price Tangney, Rowland S. Miller, Laura Flicker, and Deborah Hill Barlow, "Are Shame, Guilt, and Embarrassment Distinct Emotions?" *Journal of Personality and Social Psychology* 70, no. 6 (1996): 1256–1269.

49 Daniel O'Keefe, "Guilt and Social Influence," *Annals of the International Communication Association* 23, no. 1 (2000): 67–101; O'Keefe, "Guilt as a Mechanism of Persuasion."

50 Vanessa Boudewyns, Monique M. Turner, and Ryan S. Paquin, "Shame-Free Guilt Appeals: Testing the Emotional and Cognitive Effects of Shame and Guilt Appeals," *Psychology & Marketing* 30, no. 9 (2013): 811–825.

51 Chun-Tuan Chang, "Guilt Appeals in Cause-Related Marketing," *International Journal of Advertising: The Review of Marketing Communications* 30,

no. 4 (2011): 587–616; Paolo Antonetti, Paul Baines, and Shailendra Jain, "The Persuasiveness of Guilt Appeals Over Time: Pathways to Delayed Compliance," *Journal of Business Research* 90 (2018): 14–25; O'Keefe, "Guilt and Social Influence."

52 Robin Higie Coulter and Mary Beth Pinto, "Guilt Appeals in Advertising: What Are Their Effects?" *Journal of Applied Psychology* 80, no. 6 (1995): 697–705; Robin L. Nabi, "Discrete Emotions and Persuasion," in *The Persuasion Handbook*, ed. Dillard and Pfau, 289–308.

53 O'Keefe, "Guilt and Social Influence," p. 80.

54 Lazarus, *Emotion and Adaptation.*

55 John Bowlby, *Attachment and Loss*, 3 vols. (New York: Basic Books, 1980); Nico H. Frijda, *The Emotions* (Cambridge University Press, 1986).

56 Nabi, "Discrete Emotions and Persuasion."

57 Robert B. Cialdini, Stephanie L. Brown, Brian P. Lewis, Carol Luce, and Steven L. Neuberg. "Reinterpreting the Empathy–Altruism Relationship: When One into One Equals Oneness," *Journal of Personality and Social Psychology* 73, no. 3 (1997): 481–494.

58 Hyo J. Kim and Glen T. Cameron, "Emotions Matter in Crisis: The Role in Anger and Sadness in the Publics' Response to Crisis News Framing and Corporate Crisis Response," *Communication Research* 38, no. 6 (2011): 826–855; Josef Nerb and Hans Spada, "Evaluation of Environmental Problems: A Coherence Model of Cognition and Emotion," *Cognition and Emotion* 15, no. 4 (2011): 521–551.

59 Hang Lu, "The Effects of Emotional Appeals and Gain Versus Loss Framing in Communicating Sea Star Wasting Disease," *Science Communication* 38, no. 2 (2016): 143–169.

60 Dillard et al., "The Multiple Affective Outcomes of AIDS PSAs."

61 Yahui Kang and Joseph N. Capella, "Emotional Reactions to and Perceived Effectiveness of Media Messages: Appraisal and Message Sensation Value," *Western Journal of Communication* 72, no. 1 (2008): 40–61.

62 Richard H. Smith and Sung Hee Kim, "Comprehending Envy," *Psychological Bulletin* 133, no. 1 (2007): 46–64; Geir Thompson, Lars Glasø, and Øyvind Martinson, "Antecedents and Consequences of Envy," *Journal of Social Psychology* 156, no. 2 (2016): 139–153.

63 W. Gerrod Parrott and Richard H. Smith, "Distinguishing the Experiences of Envy and Jealousy," *Journal of Personality and Social Psychology* 64, no. 6 (1993): 906–920.

64 Thompson et al., "Antecedents and Consequences of Envy."

65 Yochi Cohen-Charash, "Episodic Envy," *Journal of Applied Social Psychology* 39, no. 9 (2009): 2128–2173; Jan Crusius and Jens Lange, "What Catches the Envious Eye? Attentional Biases within Malicious and Benign Envy," *Journal of Experimental Social Psychology* 55 (2014): 1–11.

66 Susan T. Fiske, "Envy Up, Scorn Down: How Comparison Divides Us," *American Psychologist* 65, no. 8 (2010): 698–706.

67 Michelle K. Duffy, Kristin L. Scott, Jason D. Shaw, Bennett J. Tepper, and Karl Aquino, "A Social Context Model of Envy and Social Undermining," *Academy of Management Journal* 55, no. 3 (2012): 643–666.

68 Kenneth Tai, Jayanth Narayanan, and Daniel J. McAllister, "Envy as Pain: Rethinking the Nature of Envy and its Implications for Employees and Organizations," *Academy of Management Review* 37, no. 1 (2012): 107–129.
69 Neils van de Ven, Marcel Zeelenberg, and Rik Pieters, "Leveling Up and Down: The Experience of Benign and Malicious Envy," *Emotion* 9, no. 3 (2009): 419–429.
70 Niels van de Ven, "Envy and Admiration: Emotion and Motivation Following Upward Social Comparison," *Cognition and Emotion* 31, no. 1 (2017): 193–200.
71 Robin L. Nabi and Lauren Keblusek, "Inspired by Hope, Motivated by Envy: Comparing the Effects of Discrete Emotions in the Process of Social Comparison to Media Figures," *Media Psychology* 17, no. 2 (2014): 208–234.
72 Carroll E. Izard, *Differential Emotions Theory* (New York: Springer Science + Business Media, 1977), pp. 43–66; Lazarus, *Emotion and Adaptation.*
73 Silvan S. Tomkins, *Affect, Imagery, Consciousness: The Complete Edition* (New York: Springer, 1962).
74 Nabi, "Discrete Emotions and Persuasion."
75 Alice M. Isen, "Positive Affect and Decision Making," in *Handbook of Emotions*, ed. Michael Lewis and Jeanette M. Haviland, 261–277 (New York: Guilford Press, 1993); Diane M. Mackie and Leila T. Worth, "Feeling Good, but Not Thinking Straight: The Impact of Positive Mood on Persuasion," in *Emotion & Social Judgments*, ed. Joseph P. Forgas, 201–220 (New York: Pergamon Press, 1991).
76 Marc G. Weinberger and Charles S. Gulas, "The Impact of Humor in Advertising: A Review," *Journal of Advertising* 21, no. 4 (1992): 35–59.
77 Dorothy Markiewicz, "Effects of Humor on Persuasion," *Sociometry* 37, no. 3 (1974): 407–422; Brian Sternthal and C. Samuel Craig, "Humor in Advertising," *Journal of Marketing* 37, no. 4 (1973): 12–18.
78 Nabi, "Discrete Emotions and Persuasion."
79 MacInnis and de Mello, "The Concept of Hope and its Relevance to Product Evaluation and Choice"; Amy E. Chadwick, "Toward a Theory of Persuasive Hope: Effects of Cognitive Appraisals, Hope Appeals, and Hope in the Context of Climate Change," *Health Communication* 30 (2015): 598–611.
80 Chadwick, "Toward a Theory of Persuasive Hope."
81 Ibid.
82 Elyria Kemp, My Bui, Anjala Krishen, Pamela Miles Homer, and Michael S. LaTour, "Understanding the Power of Hope and Empathy in Healthcare Marketing," *Journal of Consumer Marketing* 34, no. 2 (2017): 85–95.
83 Matthew C. Sones, "Fear vs. Hope: Do Discrete Emotions Mediate Message Frame Effectiveness in Genetic Cancer Screening Appeals," Doctoral dissertation, Georgia State University, 2017.
84 Colin Wayne Leach, Nastia Snider, and Aarti Iyer, "'Poisoning the Consciences of the Fortunate': The Experience of Relative Advantage and Support for Social Equality," in *Relative Deprivation: Specification, Development and Integration*, ed. Iain Walker and Heather J. Smith, 136–163 (Cambridge University Press, 2002).
85 Elyria Kemp, Pamela A. Kennett-Hensel, and Jeremy Kees, "Pulling on the Heartstrings: Examining the Effects of Emotions and Gender in Persuasion Appeals," *Journal of Advertising* 42, no. 1 (2013): 69–79.

86 Maria J. Louro, Rik Pieters, and Marcel Zeelenberg, "Negative Returns on Positive Emotions: The Influence of Pride and Self-Regulatory Goals on Repurchase Decisions," *Journal of Communication Research* 31, no. 4 (2005): 833–840.

87 Robert B. Cialdini, Richard J. Borden, Avril Thorne, Marcus Randall Walker, Stephen Freeman, and Lloyd Reynolds Sloan, "Basking in Reflected Glory: Three (Football) Field Studies," *Journal of Personality and Social Psychology* 34, no. 3 (1976): 366–375.

88 Henri Tajfel and John Turner, "An Integrative Theory of Intergroup Conflict," in *Intergroup Relations*, ed. Michael A. Hogg and Dominic Abrams, 71–90 (Philadelphia, PA: Psychology Press, 2001).

89 Kemp et al., "Pulling on the Heartstrings."

90 In one example, a white supremacist hacker known as "Weev" remotely printed propaganda in support of The Daily Stormer at several college campuses. This propaganda contained several of the themes discussed here, including the threat of the "country's destruction." See Carl Straumsheim, "Stop the Presses," *Inside Higher Ed* (March 29, 2016). Available at www.insidehighered.com/news/2016/03/29/simple-potentially-serious-vulnerability-behind-anti-semitic-fliers.

91 Kasun Ubayasiri, "Virtual Hostage Dramas and Real Politics," *ejournalist* 4, no. 2 (2004): 1–25; Lisa J. Campbell, "The Use of Beheadings by Fundamentalist Islam," *Global Crime* 7, no. 3–4 (2006): 583–614.

92 Kurt Braddock, "Fighting Words: The Persuasive Effect of Online Extremist Narratives on the Radicalization Process," PhD dissertation, The Pennsylvania State University, 2012, pp. 120–161.

93 Andrew Silke, "Becoming a Terrorist," in *Terrorists, Victims, and Society: Psychological Perspectives on Terrorism and its Consequences*, ed. Andrew Silke, 29–54 (Chichester: Wiley & Sons, 2003).

94 See Claire Z. Cardona, "Turn in 'Illegal Aliens': Posters Call on UT-Arlington Campus to Do So as 'Civic Duty,'" *Dallas Morning News* (April 24, 2017). Available at www.dallasnews.com/news/higher-education/2017/04/24/turn-illegal-aliens-ut-arlington-students-urged-fliers-found-campus.

95 Kemp et al., "Pulling on the Heartstrings."

96 Barbara Franz, "Europe's Muslim Youth: An Inquiry into the Politics of Discrimination, Relative Deprivation, and Identity Formation," *Mediterranean Quarterly* 18, no. 1 (2007): 89–112.

97 Anthony Stahelski, "Terrorists Are Made, Not Born: Creating Terrorists Using Social Psychological Conditioning," *Cultic Studies Review* 4, no. 1 (2004): 30–40 (p. 30); James Waller, *Becoming Evil: How Ordinary People Commit Genocide and Mass Killing* (Oxford University Press, 2007).

98 David Hearst, "Ulster Terrorist Bomb Kills 11," *The Guardian* (November 9, 1987). Available at www.theguardian.com/uk/1987/nov/09/northernireland.davidhearst; Dominic Crossley-Holland, *Age of Terror (Episode 2): 10 Days of Terror*, BBC.

99 Howell Rains, "With Latest Bomb, I.R.A. Injures its Own Cause," *New York Times* (November 15, 1987). Available at www.nytimes.com/1987/11/15/weekinreview/the-world-terrorism-with-latest-bomb-ira-injures-its-own-cause.html.

100 "1987: Bomb Kills 11 at Enniskillen," *BBC* (November 8, 1987). Available at http://news.bbc.co.uk/onthisday/hi/dates/stories/november/8/newsid_251 5000/2515113.stm.

101 Tom King, *House of Commons Official Report* (November 9, 1987), Column 19.

102 Maurice Manning, *Senead Eireann*, Volume 17 Column 1346 (November 11, 1987).

103 Rains, "With Latest Bomb."

104 Associated Press (Baghdad), "Muslim Clerics Denounce 'Savage' ISIS Murder of Jordanian Pilot," *The Guardian* (February 6, 2015). Available at www.theguardian.com/world/2015/feb/06/muslim-clerics-denounce-jordan ian-pilot-execution-kasasbeh; Alice Su, "It Wasn't Their War," *The Atlantic* (February 5, 2015). Available at www.theatlantic.com/international/archive/ 2015/02/jordan-isis-pilot-response/385199/.

105 Andrew Griffin, "ISIS Militants Using Twitter to Ask for Suggestions on How to Kill Jordanian Pilot," *The Independent* (December 30, 2014). Available at www.independent.co.uk/life-style/gadgets-and-tech/news/isis-polls-twitter-for-gruesome-suggestions-of-how-to-kill-jordanian-pilot-9949550 .html.

106 Duncan Gardham and John Hall, "Was Jordanian Pilot Burned Alive after Sick Twitter Campaign among ISIS Supporters to Name His Method of Death?" *Daily Mail* (February 4, 2015). Available at www.dailymail.co.uk/ news/article-2939196/Was-Jordanian-pilot-burned-alive-sick-Twitter-cam paign-ISIS-supporters-method-death.html.

107 Martin Chulov and Shiv Malik, "ISIS Video Shows Jordanian Hostage Being Burned to Death," *The Guardian* (February 3, 2015). Available at www.theguardian.com/world/2015/feb/03/isis-video-jordanian-hostage-burdning-death-muadh-al-kasabeh.

108 Fox News, "ISIS Burns Hostage Alive," *Fox News* (February 3, 2015). Available at https://video.foxnews.com/v/4030583977001/#sp=show-clips.

109 BBC News, "Jordan Pilot Hostage Moaz al-Kasasbeh 'Burned Alive'" (February 3, 2015). Available at www.bbc.com/news/world-middle-east-31121160.

110 Center for Strategic Studies, University of Jordan, "Public Opinion Survey: Some Current National Issues – February 2015 Main Findings." Available at http://jcss.org/Photos/635608078830183108.pdf.

111 Rod Nordland and Anne Barnard, "Militants' Killing of Jordanian Pilot Unites the Arab World in Anger," *New York Times* (February 4, 2015). Available at www.nytimes.com/2015/02/05/world/middleeast/arab-world-unites-in-anger-after-burning-of-jordanian-pilot.html.

112 Turner, "Using Emotion in Risk Communication."

113 Life After Hate, Inc., *Exit USA*. Available at www.lifeafterhate.org/exitusa.

114 Ibid.

115 In an analysis of the "Say No to Terror" website from which all campaign messages originated, Anne Aly and her colleagues said that "attempts to identify the source of the website have not yielded any significant insights – a domain search reveals that the domain is shielded behind a Washington-based anonymity protection service" and that the site is hosted in

Montenegro, possible to "circumvent attitudes of mistrust of American-sponsored communication the Arab world." Anne Aly, Dana Weimann-Saks, and Gabriel Weimann, "Making 'Noise' Online: An Analysis of the Say No to Terror Online Campaign," *Perspectives on Terrorism* 8, no. 5 (2014): 33–47 (p. 37).

116 Say No to Terror, "Who We Are" [in Arabic]. Available at www.sntt.me/our-message/.

117 Say No to Terror, "Know Your Enemy" [in Arabic]. Available at www.youtube.com/watch?v=2NpEXoCjsKE.

118 Abdullah X, "Abdullah X." Available at www.youtube.com/user/abdullahx.

Part III

The War
Future Challenges and Ways Forward in the Battle over Strategic Influence

7   The Coming Persuasion Wars: Three Future Challenges in Radicalization and Counter-Radicalization

The previous section of the book was written with the intention of describing how we might be able to influence the psychological processes that contribute to terrorism. To that end, Chapters 3–6 each contribute something different to our understanding of how violent extremists seek to persuade their audiences and how we can produce our own persuasive communication that challenges extremist messaging.

Useful though this might be, violent extremism and terrorism are ever-evolving phenomena. They require us to be vigilant about emerging trends in how extremist groups operate and the sorts of communicative strategies they employ. A cursory evaluation of the shifting political, social, and technological landscapes shows us that there are several challenges on the horizon that will need to be addressed. In some cases, these challenges are similar to those we have experienced in the past. History, as they say, tends to repeat itself.

However, the exponential growth and proliferation of new communication technologies has facilitated the emergence of threats from extremists that we have yet to face. These new technologies provide extremist groups with the capacity to tailor their messaging strategies to wider audiences in a shorter amount of time. In short, these technologies help extremist groups get their messages out. We must adapt.

To begin developing strategies for contending with future challenges related to extremist communications, we must first identify what those challenges are and the effects they might have. This chapter considers these very issues. Although the three challenges identified in this chapter hardly comprise an exhaustive list of the new communicative threats that extremists pose, they represent some of the most immediate future obstacles that counter-radicalization researchers and practitioners will need to overcome.

First, online disinformation has become problematic in multiple security-related domains. Although these issues are largely discussed in the context of political disruption (e.g., Russian interference in the 2016 US Presidential election and beyond), disinformation has also been implicated in the inspiration and performance of extremist violence. This chapter will discuss how disinformation has been employed to promote radicalization and offer some solutions for identifying disinformation and stemming its influence.

Second, the reemergence of populist leaders coupled with the affordances offered by new communication technologies has resulted in a surge of right-wing terrorist violence. Investigations of these terrorist events often reveal that the perpetrators are inspired by public figures who have used inflammatory or aggressive language towards those victimized by the attacks. This represents a new form of political violence in which public figures do not overtly call for bloodshed, but their comments are suggestive enough that attackers interpret their words as implicit support for attacks against perceived enemies. This phenomenon has been called "stochastic terrorism," and it poses a unique challenge given that it requires counter-radicalization specialists to refute messages that are not overtly stated.

Finally, few technologies have advanced as quickly or as obviously as those intended to replicate images or sounds. One form of digital replication that has exploded since its emergence on the Internet in 2017 is the Deepfake – an audiovisual file that allows for the imitation of another person in any context that the producer wishes. Though Deepfake technology may have some positive applications, it has frightening implications for use by violent extremists. This chapter discusses these implications, as well as countermeasures that could be used to overcome the persuasive potential of Deepfakes.

Let's begin with one of the most pervasive problems of the early twenty-first century: online disinformation.

Online Disinformation by Extremist Groups and State-Sponsored Illicit Actors

In the weeks and months leading up to the 2016 US Presidential election, the Russian government engaged in a concerted effort to mislead American voters. Speaking to Congress, Facebook general counsel admitted that up to 126 million Facebook users were exposed to content that originated from a Russian disinformation campaign and 10 million users were exposed to advertisements purchased by Russian government operatives. Twitter did not fare much better; the company found over 2,700 accounts connected to the Russian government, as well as 36,000 bots that automatically tweeted statements meant to disinform those exposed to them.[1] The goals of this disinformation are multifaceted, but are generally intended to sow confusion, mistrust, and discord among countries in the European Union and the United States.

Unfortunately for these countries, Russia's disinformation efforts have been extremely effective and are likely to continue. Speaking about the Kremlin's use of disinformation, Danish Member of the European Parliament Jeppe Kofod described the magnitude of Russia's efforts, as well as the problems those efforts caused:

Let's not kid ourselves, Russian meddling in democratic elections is no longer the exception, it is becoming the norm. From the US presidential election to Brexit [the UK's vote to leave the European Union], the hands of the Kremlin have been busy dancing along keyboards, spreading disinformation – the full extent of which is yet to be understood by all of us.[2]

It's difficult to imagine how so many individuals were able to be misled by a foreign power, particularly given that Russian information operations are generally unsophisticated and require little technical complexity to perform.[3] But psychological research on how people engage with and assimilate information sheds some light on why disinformation campaigns can be so effective. Through an analysis of existing psychological research, RAND researchers Christopher Paul and Miriam Matthews found several reasons as to why disinformation might be accepted as truth by message recipients.[4]

First, people are generally not very skilled at distinguishing true information from false information. And even if an individual successfully identifies false information, he/she may not necessarily remember that the information was false when recalling it. Second, when faced with too much information, people tend to use cognitive shortcuts to determine whether that information is true or not. For example, someone attempting to process too much information may resort to deciding that information is true if it is endorsed by "experts" rather than systematically evaluating the content of messages.[5] Individuals also often accept information as true if that information comes from a source perceived to be objective – even if the source has no expertise on the topic. Third, messages that convey ideas that are familiar to message recipients are likely to be appealing to those recipients, even if the message contains information that is untrue. Finally, people tend to accept arguments if they are supported by evidence, even if the evidence itself is false.

Paul and Matthews's findings show why the Russian disinformation campaign was so effective – each of these outcomes are relatively easy to elicit. Flood message targets with disinformation so they can't systematically process the content of your messages. Trick them with the illusion of expertise and objectivity. Reinforce your arguments with evidence, even if that evidence is completely made up. If you can successfully employ these practices and tailor your messages so they align with your desired goals, congratulations; you have effectively weaponized false information. The ease with which this process was successfully used by Russian intelligence operatives is sobering.

The potential for disinformation to affect disorder in other contexts may be even more problematic.

∴

Russian intrusion into several countries' democratic processes has prompted a veritable flood of research on the topic. As such, a comprehensive review of disinformation and its effects is beyond the scope of this book.[6] But in the context of addressing communicative issues that have implications for radicalization and violent extremism, it is important to note what motivates the use of disinformation by state- and non-state actors to promote the assimilation of beliefs and attitudes consistent with extremist ideologies.

First, it is important to realize that entities that use disinformation strategies are incredibly varied in their motivations. Although you are presumably interested in disinformation's effects on processes related to radicalization and terrorism, researchers have identified several other reasons why disinformation might be deliberately spread online.

Most concern surrounding disinformation relates to its potential for undermining political beliefs and attitudes, but some individuals spread false information for much more superficial reasons. For instance, some individuals strategically use disinformation for financial gain.[7] These individuals typically seek to generate page clicks through fantastic claims that appeal to specific audiences. During the 2016 election, for example, teenagers in the Balkans commodified disinformation by posting false content about Hillary Clinton on websites they founded with conservative-sounding domain names.[8]

Other distributors of disinformation are motivated not by money, but status within the online communities they frequent. In some of these communities, individuals who manipulate large-scale institutions (like the media) are admired. As such, some users are motivated to be disruptive simply for the fun of it and to witness the confusion that results from their actions.[9] These individuals – colloquially referred to as "trolls" – tend to operate of their own accord. However, recent research has shown that governments have also used trolls to spread disinformation to achieve strategic objectives.[10]

More to the point of this chapter, disinformation can be employed by state- and non-state actors for the purpose of radicalization as well. Disaffected individuals who are steeped in Internet culture often come together in online forums and through social media platforms. There, they can find other individuals who share their frustrations within closed communicative systems. When disinformation is shared within these systems, it can reverberate within the ideological echo chamber, eventually becoming normalized among the individuals within it.

Marwick and Lewis described this phenomenon in the context of the far right and its various sub-movements. They explain how individuals within the "manosphere" (i.e., communities within the Internet dedicated to men's rights) seek to "red pill" others so they come to believe that men are oppressed.[11] The alt-right spreads disinformation about multiculturalism and globalism in an effort to promote ethnonationalism among whites. And white supremacists seek to "wake people up" with disinformation about shadowy Jewish leaders and the endangered future of the white race.

The use of disinformation for the purpose of ideological radicalization is not limited to the far right. Throughout the history of information warfare, political actors have spread false information related to other ideologies to foment extremism as part of a larger geopolitical strategy. Following the 1967 Six-Day War in which Israel routed two of the Soviet Union's most important allies in the Middle East, Egypt and Syria, KGB chairman Yuri Andropov sought to "repair the Kremlin's prestige by humiliating Israel."[12] Specifically, Andropov spread information depicting Zionism as a form of Nazi-style racism and training Palestinian terrorists to hijack El Al airplanes. To mask the KGB's involvement in the terrorist hijackings of the Israeli aircraft, Andropov allowed the Popular Front for the Liberation of Palestine to take credit.[13] In this way, the Soviet Union used disinformation in two ways against Israel – to justify Palestinian attacks through disinformation about Zionism and to provide cover for multiple attacks for which the KGB was responsible. By the early 1970s, Andropov's disinformation efforts were designed to persuade Muslims that with the help of the United States, Israel wanted to "transform the rest of the world into a Zionist fiefdom."[14]

This disinformation campaign had clear effects on the Islamic world's impressions of the United States and Israel. By Andropov's own admission, the KGB's intention was to arouse rage in the Muslim world to the point that they would engage in terrorism against the Soviet Union's enemies, Israel and the United States.[15]

The above example shows how a state actor can effectively leverage disinformation to stoke extremist beliefs and attitudes to advocate violence against its enemies. But in an age where anyone with an Internet connection can be instantaneously linked to anyone else, non-state actors can trigger violence with false information as well.

For instance, during the 2016 US Presidential election, the e-mails of Hillary Clinton's campaign manager John Podesta were hacked and subsequently released by Wikileaks. Following the release of the e-mails, a white supremacist Twitter account claimed that the New York Police Department was investigating the possibility that the e-mails contained evidence of Hillary Clinton's involvement in an international pedophilia ring. Clinton's supposed involvement in the ring was through James Alefantis, owner of the Comet Ping Pong pizza restaurant in Washington, DC. The fake story claims that Alefantis – who was mentioned in Podesta's e-mails – allowed Hillary and Bill Clinton to use the back room of Comet Ping Pong for pedophilic activities and child trafficking.[16]

The tweet from the white supremacist account was picked up by an online message board for conspiracy theories called Godlike Productions.[17] From there, Sean Adl-Tabatabai created a post for his website (previously called YourNewsWire.com, now called NewsPunch) claiming that FBI and NYPD sources found evidence on Bill and Hillary Clinton's involvement in the supposed child sex ring.[18] Adl-Tabatabai's only source for these claims was a thread on 4chan, a largely anonymous series of message boards.

The flimsiness of Adl-Tabatabai's source didn't matter. Alefantis and the staff of Comet Ping Pong received hundreds of death threats, including one message saying that his restaurant should be burned to the ground.[19] And on December 4, 2016, Edgar Maddison Welch walked into Comet with an AR-15 rifle and a .38 caliber handgun.[20] He fired several shots in the restaurant, but the employees escaped without injury. When questioned after the incident, Welch claimed he went there to investigate the reports of a child trafficking operation. Before leaving his home to head to Washington, Welch texted his friend to say he was "raiding a pedo ring" and that he would possibly "[sacrifice] the lives of a few for the lives of many."[21]

In a matter of days, a baseless rumor had mutated from tweet to viral story to manifest violence.

Both Andropov's disinformation campaign and the "Pizzagate" incident illustrate one of the central persuasive challenges associated with disinformation. When individuals encounter false information in echo chambers that reinforce their beliefs (whether political or conspiratorial in kind), it is incredibly difficult to break the cycle of belief reinforcement. Luckily, the proliferation of research on disinformation in the last few years has identified potential avenues for interrupting radicalization processes resulting from exposure to false content.

∴

Solutions geared towards addressing the problems caused by online disinformation typically fall into one of three categories – identification of false information, containment of false information, and promoting resilience among message targets to resist false information. Let's consider each of these solution types in turn.

The defining feature of effective disinformation is its capacity for fooling its audience into believing that the content of the disinformation message is real. Given this, the first (and most difficult) step for limiting disinformation's ability to promote the adoption of extremist beliefs and attitudes involves identifying that disinformation. To this end, it may be useful to use advanced automated technologies based on artificial intelligence and machine learning to quickly and accurately identify fake news when it emerges online. McGeehan contends that these advanced technologies could warn human analysts of the presence of disinformation in online spheres where it might arouse negative psychological responses among those exposed to it.[22] These technologies could further determine where the disinformation came from and direct users to information that debunks the false claims. Fried and Polyakova made a similar suggestion, arguing for a "24/7 warning system to track online disinformation."[23]

Although artificial intelligence and machine learning may be useful for identifying metadata and linguistic patterns that characterize disinformation, it is inevitable that disinformation will persuade some individuals. In these cases, McGeehan argues, it may be useful to adopt a public health/epidemiology approach whereby analysts identify a population at risk for "infection" by disinformation and preemptively provide them with true information to counter the falsehoods they may encounter online.[24] By using this kind of "information vaccination," analysts can create "herd immunity" within the targeted population such that enough people will have adequate defenses against disinformation that it will not spread within that population.

Some have argued that Internet companies that have been exploited for the purpose of spreading disinformation should also be more active in their efforts to contain false content. Fried and Polyakova admitted that companies like Facebook, Twitter, and Google can and should not be "arbiters of truth."[25] However, they can take practical steps to stop disinformation on their platforms, including identifying content from blatant propaganda organizations (e.g., RT, Sputnik), redesigning algorithms that better identify whether content is from a credible source or not, and revising advertising policies that ban ads that come from known propaganda outlets. Susan Morgan made similar recommendations, arguing that online companies should do more to remove bots capable of spreading disinformation from their platforms.[26]

Although identification and containment of false information are viable strategies for addressing problems associated with disinformation, they are only part of an overall solution. It is just as important to prepare potential targets of disinformation to resist it. By becoming knowledgeable about the online public sphere, Morgan argues, citizens will grow more resilient to disinformation that seeks to disrupt it.[27] In this vein, several researchers have advocated for educating online citizens so they are more informed about how and why disinformation is constructed and disseminated. Even more fundamental, citizens should be trained to engage in critical thinking in a new media environment where extremist groups can produce content and watch it propagate within online social networks not based on its authority, but on its popularity.[28] The inability of online citizens to objectively analyze the content they engage with[29] has been exploited by geopolitical enemies of the United States.[30] It is not a stretch to assume that terrorist groups – both foreign and domestic – will exploit the same analytical weaknesses.

One strategy that may be useful for informing the public sphere about potential disinformation is attitudinal inoculation. There is some evidence to show that when individuals are exposed to information refuting disinformation before they encounter it, they are less likely to develop beliefs, attitudes, or intentions consistent with the disinformation than those who are never pre-warned about it.[31] This would suggest that one of the most important strategies in dealing with disinformation that might promote extremist beliefs, attitudes, or intentions is "getting there first," meaning analysts must identify disinformation with the potential for spreading and refute it before it reaches the eyes of those vulnerable to assimilating it.

Deepfakes

In May of 2018, a Belgian political party called Socialistische Partij Anders (sp.a; translated to Socialist Party Differently) posted a video to the party's Twitter feed and Facebook page of US President Donald Trump expressing his feelings about the Paris Climate Accords.[32] Trump pulled no punches, telling them that he "had the balls to withdraw from the Paris climate agreement." Then, he offered some advice to the people of Belgium directly, telling them that they should follow suit and pressure their government to leave the Paris Climate Accords as well.

The video prompted an intense response from the sp.a's social media followers.[33] One commenter on the Facebook video was incredulous at Trump's arrogance:

Really? This ridiculous toddler video [is to] take over one of the most basic programs from Groen [a green political party in Belgium]? Does SP.a really have no idea[s] of its own anymore?

Said another commenter:

Americans themselves are as stupid as the back of a pig. Trump [should] return to [his] own door instead of blaming the Belgians for the climate because you are no better than the rest.

By and large, Belgian supporters of sp.a were unimpressed with the American president's attempt to influence the party's policies. There was only one problem; Donald Trump never made any comments about his "balls" to abandon the Paris Climate Accords or expressed any opinions about sp.a's leaving the agreement.

The video was a fake.[34] It was created by a production studio commissioned by the sp.a to capture its constituents' attention and direct them to a petition demanding that the Belgian government take steps to avert climate change. Socialist Party Differently members assumed that the poor quality of the video – Trump's lip movements in the video are particularly strange – would alert audience members to its being a forgery. But the party misjudged the degree to which those who saw the video would assume it to be authentic. Through its experiment in motivating its constituents, the sp.a accidentally showed how computer-generated imitations, even poorly constructed ones, can fire up audiences in politically charged environments. These kinds of media are commonly referred to as "Deepfakes."

Although "Deepfakes" typically refer to doctored video and imagery, the term refers to a range of different kinds of audiovisual material that has been manipulated to give the impression that an individual has done something that they have not. These kinds of manipulations can include imposing one person's face on another's body (face swaps), mimicking audio such that a sound clip seems to have originated from a specific speaker (voice swaps), mapping one face onto another to reenact facial gestures (deepfake puppetry), or creating synthetic video whereby footage of an individual's facial movements matches a specific audio file (deepfake lip-synching).[35]

Deepfakes originated in 2017 on Reddit, a media platform comprised of more than a million online communities dedicated to discussing specific topics and sharing content specific to those topics.[36] A user known as *u/deepfakes* created a subreddit (i.e., Reddit community) specifically associated with the creation and sharing of Deepfake files, the first of which were face swaps. It was in this subreddit where the first algorithm associated with the development of Deepfakes was made public. Some Redditors used the algorithm to impose faces of celebrities and other individuals onto pornographic material, giving the impression that the faces' owners had engaged in pornographic activity. Reddit eventually updated its rules, banning "involuntary pornography." As a result of this update, Reddit similarly banned the Deepfakes subreddit.[37] At this point, though, the horse was already out of the barn.

Since 2017, several techniques for developing increasingly convincing Deepfakes have been developed. Though an in-depth consideration of the technical specifications associated with these algorithms is beyond the scope of this book (and my understanding), these techniques are generally based on the use of artificial intelligence and "deep learning." Programmers use both tools to analyze and mimic large datasets comprising speech, audio, and imagery. These efforts have produced several easy-to-use platforms for the purpose of facial and body reenactment (e.g., Face2Face,[38] HeadOn,[39] and Deep Video Portraits[40]), facial replacement (e.g., DeepFaceLab[41]), or speech synthesis (e.g., Adobe VoCo,[42] Lyrebird[43]).

The rapid proliferation of these technologies has facilitated the development of misleading online audiovisual content of all types. In his Master's thesis on the topic, Tormod Fikse created a taxonomy of the different kinds of Deepfakes that have emerged in the online space.[44] The different categories of Deepfakes identified by Fikse are defined and illustrated via example in Table 7.1.[45]

Of these five categories, deceptive Deepfakes pose the greatest challenge for issues related to public trust and democracy. Senate Intelligence Committee Vice Chairman Mark Warner has said that deceptive Deepfakes represent the next phase of disinformation campaigns, and senior advisor with the Transatlantic Committee on Election Integrity has characterized them as "the next weapon in the [sic] disinformation warfare."[46]

In addition to the threats posed by deceptive Deepfakes to public trust and democracy, they can also have implications for the distribution of extremist propaganda and how violent extremist groups seek to influence their message targets. This is a disconcerting possibility, given the common understanding that as of early 2019, our capacity for countering disinformation resulting from Deepfakes is grossly underdeveloped.[47]

To understand how Deepfake technology could be exploited by violent extremists to achieve strategic objectives, it is useful to revisit why extremist groups communicate online at all. The communicative affordances provided by the Internet allow them to engage in all manner of interaction, but these actions are typically directed at a few broad

Table 7.1 *Fikse's taxonomy of Deepfake types*

Category	Description	Example
Technological demonstration	Intended to demonstrate how Deepfake technology operates. Typically include side-by-side comparisons of the original content and the manipulated content to show how Deepfake technology has altered the video	Comedian Jordan Peele demonstrates how former US President Barack Obama's likeness could be used to say things he has never said
Satirical	Content that is manipulated to offer political or social commentary. Not intended to be deceptive – the content is clearly doctored to ensure the audience recognizes its inauthenticity	Superimposition of Donald Trump and administration officials on characters being arrested by federal agents in the Netflix show, *Daredevil*
Meme-based	Deepfaked content that contributes to the larger online zeitgeist via shared ideas or symbols. Often intended to be funny, but may also be a form of political commentary	The regular imposition of actor Nicolas Cage's face on different individuals
Pornographic	Content taken from pornographic video or imagery in which the face of a non-pornographic actor/actress is imposed onto the body of the actor/actress of an individual in the video/picture	*Wonder Woman* actress Gal Gadot's face imposed on a pornography actress's body
Deceptive	Audiovisual material deliberately manipulated to give audiences the impression that an authority figure (e.g., politician, extremist leader, celebrity) is saying or doing something that they have not said or done	Face swaps of political leaders, including Vladimir Putin and Donald Trump, potentially allowing for disinformation dissemination from "viable" sources

categories of goals, including the radicalization of sympathetic audiences, the justification of violent activity, and the spread of fear to target populations. Deepfakes can strengthen their ability to achieve these goals, as well as others.

First, face swaps, voice synthesis, and lip-synching can allow extremist groups to produce messages from valuable "sources" that are, for one reason or another, unable to deliver those messages themselves. For example, Yemeni-American preacher and imam Anwar al-Awlaki was a notorious mouthpiece for al-Qaeda, producing several online lectures and propaganda in support of the group. Many of his online videos were found to have motivated Islamic terrorist incidents, including Roshonara Choudhry's stabbing attack of Labour MP Stephen Timms[48] and Faisal Shahzad's attempted bombing of Times Square in New York.[49] Al-Awlaki was also found to have been connected to Nidal Hasan, the perpetrator of the Fort Hood attack that killed thirteen US servicemen in 2009.[50]

The appeal of al-Awlaki's teachings was not lost on US intelligence or military personnel. As early as 2008, US Under-Secretary of Homeland Security for Intelligence and Analysis warned of al-Awlaki's sway with US Muslims and his propensity for inspiring them to engage in violence.[51] By 2011, President Barack Obama had grown to consider al-Awlaki's propaganda to be a central driver of Islamic terrorism aimed at the United States, and authorized a CIA-directed drone strike that killed the radical preacher.[52]

Obama hailed the death of al-Awlaki as a "major blow to al-Qaeda's most active operational affiliate" and a significant milestone in the fight against the group.[53] Indeed, few propagandists have been as productive or impactful as al-Awlaki was in the late 2000s and early 2010s.

Still, there is ample content available for al-Qaeda supporters to utilize Deepfake technology to develop and distribute a new message from "Anwar al-Awlaki." Such a video may show a computer-generated speaker who looks and sounds exactly like al-Awlaki, down to his verbal mannerisms and body language. Although viewers would likely know that the original al-Awlaki is dead, this kind of message could nonetheless be a powerful inspiration to those vulnerable to the messages that al-Awlaki was spreading while he was alive.

Perhaps more troublesome would be the ability of extremists to produce Deepfakes of individuals whose status is unknown by the US intelligence community. Recall, for example, the period between 2001 and 2011 when the status of Osama bin Laden was almost a complete mystery to the United States. Although al-Qaeda released a few videos of bin Laden following the September 11 attacks, he effectively disappeared following his escape from Tora Bora[54] until he was discovered and killed in Abbottabad, Pakistan almost a decade later.

Though bin Laden's successful retreat and concealment was a source of frustration for US officials, it had the benefit of precluding him making speeches or otherwise seeking to motivate new fighters to join al-Qaeda. If al-Qaeda had possessed Deepfake technology throughout the 2000s, they presumably could have produced propaganda videos featuring "bin Laden" to continue delivering his message in his absence.

In addition to replicating members of extremist groups, Deepfake technology could also be used to produce videos that appear to show enemies of the group engaged in activities that promote extremist beliefs, attitudes, or behaviors centered on those enemies. These activities could be as simple as making inflammatory statements against the extremist group's constituents or as provocative as the performance of war crimes against those the extremist group claims to defend.

Professors of Law Bobby Chesney and Danielle Citron described some of the ways that Deepfakes could threaten national security in this manner.[55] They proposed some sobering possibilities, including fake videos that show soldiers murdering innocent civilians in a war zone, falsified audio depicting US officials admitting to various kinds of war crimes and outrages, and individuals disparaging groups so intensely as to dehumanize or demonize them.

Real content like this has prompted extremist violence in the past. Following the release of photos showing the abuse and torture of prisoners at Abu Ghraib prison by US military personnel, al-Qaeda in Iraq engaged in a wave of violence, including video-recorded executions of their prisoners.[56] If this kind of content could be produced on demand, it could cause audiences to accept terrorist violence against supposed perpetrators as legitimate or motivate those audiences to engage in violence themselves.

At the very least, the production and distribution of material depicting crimes against an extremist group's constituents can put the depicted entities on the defensive. Said Michael Gross, Professor of International Relations and expert on military ethics, "information operations that exploit an adversary's killing of civilians may force an enemy to do what shells and rockets cannot: desist and stand down at little or no cost to guerrillas."[57] Deepfake technologies assist extremist groups in developing these kinds of videos – whether the subjects of the videos actually engaged in the activities or not.

Finally, Deepfake technology can assist extremist groups in their ability to make sophisticated threats and spread fear among target audiences.[58] Face-swapping can allow terrorist groups to impose the faces of its fighters on movie characters engaged in a violent attack against civilians. Deepfake lip-synching, voice swapping, or voice synthesis tools can be used to produce real-sounding audio clips of politicians and security experts warning of impending attacks and announcing natural or man-made catastrophes. Any of these practices could induce panic in a large audience, providing extremist groups with the chaos they need to influence their enemies to bend to their will.

Given these possibilities, the persuasion-specific challenges associated with Deepfakes are twofold. First, when extremist groups can effectively mimic individuals they mean to champion or demonize, the persuasive effects of their depictions are available on demand. Need a seasoned (but unavailable) veteran of your group to give a rousing speech to potential recruits? Produce a video in which your words come from his mouth. Need public outrage against an enemy group? Turn them into computer-generated puppets committing war crimes. Deepfake technology makes these processes a relatively simple endeavor.

Second, when messages can be produced to appear as if they come from any source, then the credibility of a message's source can be manufactured (or diminished) with a few mouse clicks.

Taken together, these implications demonstrate that extremist propaganda does not need to be genuine to be effective. The emergence of Deepfakes means that it can be manufactured and delivered as if it was produced by any source at any time.

∴

Just as artificial intelligence and deep learning can inform the development of Deepfakes to suit extremist groups' purposes, these tools can also be used to identify deceptive Deepfakes. To illustrate, some researchers have developed algorithms and programs to identify the use of fake video and voice synthesis techniques.[59] Others use neural networks to recognize Deepfakes,[60] an approach that can effectively identify over 97 percent of faked videos.[61] Still other programs are specifically tailored to spot irregularities in the characteristics of Deepfaked subjects. For example, Li and Lyu used predesigned Convolutional Neural Network models to identify the telltale warping of facial features in Deepfake videos.[62] Li, Chang, and Lyu similarly used neural networks to identify Deepfake videos by detecting the lack of eye-blinking among the videos' subjects.[63]

These kinds of solutions are promising for the detection of Deepfaked videos produced by extremist groups, but organizations in a position to implement them must first recognize the potential for Deepfakes to contribute to outcomes related to ideological radicalization. Once the scope of the threat is realized, these organizations can then partner with researchers like those referenced above to facilitate the use of their tools for the purpose of counter-radicalization.[64] The United Nations' Tech Against Terrorism initiative[65] and the Global Internet Forum for

Counter-Terrorism,[66] both of which have connections to salient Internet-industry organizations (e.g., Google, Facebook, YouTube) could be useful contexts for this kind of work.

Stochastic Terrorism

As long as terrorism has been a subject of empirical investigation, experts have argued over what constitutes terrorism and what doesn't. Researchers, analysts, and government officials have sparred over the nature of target types, motivations, perpetrator features, and a bevy of other factors that might characterize an act as terrorism. Despite perpetual debate surrounding terrorism's definition, for most of the history of terrorism studies, it has largely been considered to be an organizational enterprise.

At first, terrorism researchers focused on centrally structured organizations like the Provisional Irish Republican Army, the German Red Army Faction, and the Italian Red Brigades. These kinds of organizations were characterized by hierarchical structures in which ideological leaders would dictate operations. Although there may have been some flexibility in what small groups of fighters could do, orders largely filtered down from organizational leadership.

The emergence and widespread proliferation of the Internet in the 1990s had a significant influence on how terrorist organizations could communicate with audiences and coordinate activities. As a result, cell-based terrorist networks began to emerge in which small groups of fighters would self-organize and act on the basis of a terrorist ideology.[67] Although these cells sometimes take orders from a centralized authority structure (e.g., some cells from post-9/11 al-Qaeda), they can also operate without guidance from organizational leadership (e.g., Animal Liberation Front).

The Internet has even facilitated the emergence of individuals who engage in terrorist violence on their own – a phenomenon that the media and some researchers often (unfortunately) refer to as "lone wolf terrorism."[68] This term is largely a misnomer, suggesting that "lone wolves" operate completely of their own accord and without interpersonal links to larger movements. Work by Zoe Marchment, Paul Gill, Bart Schuurman, and others has suggested that it is more appropriate to refer to these individuals as "lone actors" because although they perpetrate violence alone, they are often inspired by extremist ideologies that they assimilated from social linkages to larger terrorist movements.[69] Regardless, this form of terrorism is distinct from the aforementioned types, given that it involves a solitary individual carrying out an attack.

Each of these phenomena have posed (and continue to pose) unique challenges to researchers, analysts, and counterterror practitioners. Unfortunately, another kind of ideologically driven violence has emerged in the age of online misinformation and disinformation – a form of terrorism inspired by persuasive rhetoric in which the speaker can deny his role in the performance of violence.

This form of terrorism – called stochastic terrorism[70] – has its origins in probability theory and mathematics.[71] A stochastic process is one that is based on a mathematical distribution of events such that an event will randomly occur at a given time and place. That is, stochastic events reliably occur, but are individually difficult to predict. Although stochastic functions are often used to model random natural occurrences (e.g., the development of bacteria in a Petri dish[72]), they have also been used to explain social phenomena, like fluctuations in financial markets.[73] Following from how stochastic processes have been studied in the natural and social sciences, some have begun to evaluate incitement of terrorism in a similar manner.

Stochastic terrorism refers to the "use of mass communications to incite random actors to carry out violent or terrorist acts that are statistically predictable but individually unpredictable."[74]

Psychologist Valerie Tarico argued that incidents of stochastic terrorism typically unfold over a series of steps that inevitably lead to a terrorist attack.[75] First, a public figure with access to a mass communication channel and a wide audience publicly demonizes a person or a group. Second, the targeted person or group is repeatedly verbally attacked until he/she/it is dehumanized and thought to be dangerous to the speaker's audience. At this point, message targets have likely developed a fear of those that have been dehumanized, as well as a moral disgust at the offenses the public figure accuses them of. Third, the public figure uses violent imagery, metaphors, jokes about violence, references to past "purges" of hated groups, and other aggressive rhetoric to refer to the targeted person or group – stopping just short of explicit calls to arms.

The casual use of violent rhetoric aimed at the dehumanized target group often leads to a member of the public figure's audience carrying out an act of terrorism. After the violent incident, the inciting party – the stochastic terrorist – condemns the act, claiming that it was impossible to foresee. By hiding behind a wall of plausible deniability, the public figure is absolved of any wrongdoing.

Because the stochastic terrorist disseminated the inciting message(s) over a wide audience, it is nearly impossible to predict when, where, and by whom a terrorist attack will be performed. However, *that* an attack will occur is a near certainty – the breadth of the audience that received the inciting message is sufficiently large that at least one individual will extrapolate from the speaker's words that he condones and supports the use of violence against those he rails at.

The issue of stochastic terrorism has come to the fore in recent years with the mainstreaming of the radical right since the ascension of populist politicians in the United States and Europe. Most notable of these politicians is US President Donald Trump, who has made several statements that have casually suggested or condoned the use of violence, some of which have been explicitly referenced by right-wing terrorists.

In response to a 2015 incident in which two Black Lives Matter activists came on stage at a rally for Presidential candidate Bernie Sanders and were given the microphone by a deferent Sanders, Trump suggested that he would never show such "weakness" and if such an incident happened to him, the activists would be subject to violence. Said Trump:

I thought that was disgusting. That showed such weakness, the way Sanders was taken away by two young women – the microphone – they just took the whole place over. That will never happen with me. I don't know I'll do the fighting myself or if other people will, but that was a disgrace.[76]

On the campaign trail a year later, Trump commented on the possibility of Hillary Clinton winning the election and choosing Supreme Court justices. In front of a Wilmington, North Carolina crowd, Trump alluded to the possibility that guns-rights advocates could do something about Clinton to keep her from appointing judges that do not align with their political preferences.

If she gets to pick her judges, nothing you can do, folks. Although the Second Amendment people, maybe there is. I don't know.[77]

The Trump campaign quickly walked back Trump's statement, saying that he meant to advocate for political unification to defeat Clinton at the ballot box. But as correctly argued by columnist David Cohen, it doesn't matter what Trump meant – with such a wide audience, "enough people will hear Trump's comments and think he's calling for people to take up arms against Clinton, her judges or both."[78]

Accidentally or not, some of Trump's statements have inspired terrorism. Following years of Trump's aggressive rhetoric against press organizations and Democratic politicians, in October of 2018, Cesar Sayoc mailed more than a dozen pipe bombs to targets that had been specifically named by Trump, including Hillary Clinton and CNN.[79] In February of 2019, Coast Guard Lieutenant Christopher Hasson was arrested with fifteen guns and more than 1,000 rounds of ammunition.

Like Sayoc, Hasson had compiled a hitlist of several prominent Democratic legislators, including Alexandria Ocasio-Cortez and Ilhan Omar. Also on the hitlist was Elizabeth Warren, whom Hasson listed as "poca warren" – a reference to Trump's derogatory nickname for the Massachusetts senator.[80] In addition to the hitlist, investigators also found that Hasson had performed online searches for "civil war if trump impeached" and "what if trump illegally impeached." In March of 2019, Brenton Tarrant killed forty-nine Muslim worshippers at a mosque in Christchurch, New Zealand. In a manifesto released in conjunction with the terrorist attack, Tarrant praised Trump "as a symbol of renewed white identity and common purpose," but not as a policymaker.[81]

Although Donald Trump is the most oft-cited source of language that has indirectly inspired terrorist attacks, he is hardly alone in this regard. Iowa Republican Representative Steve King has said things that could arguably be considered more inflammatory than what Trump has said. King has posted memes on social media suggesting that the South is better prepared for a new US civil war because southern states have "8 trillion bullets,"[82] dehumanized Mexican immigrants by referring to them as "dirt,"[83] and publicly questioned when the terms "white nationalist" and "white supremacist" became offensive.[84] Although Representative King may not mean to incite violence with these statements, they nonetheless normalize white supremacism and white nationalism, dehumanize non-white individuals, and support groups that would wage war against citizens that do not share his views.

Of course, stochastic terrorism is not unique to the United States. Some European officials have also made statements that could be interpreted as supportive of right-wing extremism and the violence that comes with it. In November of 2017, tens of thousands of demonstrators flooded the streets of Warsaw for Poland's Independence Day celebration. Among them were fascists and far-right nationalists advocating for a racially uniform culture. They wore masks, displayed white-power emblems, and chanted things like "Pure Poland, white Poland!" and "Refugees get out!" During a televised interview, one demonstrator said that the march was to "remove Jewry from power."[85] Across Europe, political commentators likened the rally to fascist movements that had been embraced by extremist politicians in the years prior to World War II. Following the celebration, Polish Interior Minister Mariusz Blaszczak called it a "beautiful sight," inherently condoning racist and xenophobic language that has justified violence against perceived "invaders" for decades.[86]

Stochastic terrorism is typically thought to occur via mass-mediated speeches that allow a public figure to vocalize their implicit support for extremism. However, the Internet's capacity for disseminating imagery and shorthand messages facilitates the performance of stochastic terror by other means as well.

For instance, Donald Trump has celebrated the notion of violence against those he sees as enemies using online memes. In July of 2017, he tweeted a meme video that depicts him attacking a figure with the CNN logo superimposed on his head.[87] As a caption to the video posted to Twitter, Trump added the hashtags #FraudNewsCNN and #FNN (presumably meant to mean "fake news network"). The video was tweeted in the weeks after a Republican candidate for the House of Representatives, Greg Gianforte, physically attacked a news reporter.[88] While discussing Gianforte's assault of the reporter at a rally, Trump called him "my guy" and stood watch over an applauding audience after he recounted how he heard about the incident. It's been reported that it was the first time that a president had openly and unabashedly praised the assault of a journalist on American soil.[89]

Stochastic terrorism poses two unique challenges to those who would develop messages intended for counter-radicalization. First, analysts can reasonably identify the themes that comprise traditional extremist propaganda, develop counter-messages that challenge those themes, and distribute those counter-messages to specifically targeted populations. However, when a public figure makes statements that *implicitly* support the use of terrorism – accidentally or not – it can be difficult to (1) determine how the figure's statement might be interpreted by those who would use it to justify violence, and (2) ensure that counter-messages that challenge those interpretations reach the potentially violent contingent of the audience.

Second, recall from Chapter 5 that reasoned action theory says that an individual's behaviors can be predicted, in part, by how that individual thinks those they care about (i.e., valued others) would judge their performance of those behaviors. This presents a daunting challenge for the prevention of violent radicalization via stochastic terrorism; the public figure that inspires the violent act is often also considered a valued other.

Consider Cesar Sayoc. His attempted attacks against critics of Donald Trump were inspired not only by Trump's identification of those critics as enemies, but also because Sayoc perceived Trump as a de facto father figure after being estranged from his own family.[90] Sayoc's perceived norms, which themselves were derived from what he thought Donald Trump would think of his behavior, grew to be consistent with the use of violence. Sayoc's case illustrates that intervening in the violent radicalization of someone inspired by a public figure's implicit promotion of violence requires not only overcoming the persuasiveness of the public figure's message, but also the message target's perceived norms derived from their beliefs about that figure.

∴

As you've learned from the previous chapters, targeting audiences is a critical element of persuasive messaging. Stochastic terrorism makes this very difficult since we are unable to know who will interpret inflammatory or aggressive messages as calls for violence. Here, it may be instructive to adopt a public health approach to communicative counter-radicalization. This approach involves delineating the different kinds of ways that we might respond to the threat of terrorism into primary, secondary, and tertiary prevention types. Primary prevention refers to efforts intended to avert politically motivated violence before it happens through large-scale education programs and campaigns. Secondary prevention efforts represent those activities that specifically target populations that are at risk for engaging in violence as a function of certain risk factors they possess. In the realm of violent extremism, tertiary prevention involves providing customized attention and/or care to individuals who are expressing signs of violent radicalization or have already performed an act of terrorism.[91]

In reviewing the different kinds of prevention afforded by a public health model, it immediately becomes clear that stochastic terrorism cannot be addressed with secondary or tertiary prevention. Stochastic-terrorism-inspired actors are too random and isolated to be targeted per secondary or tertiary prevention. Instead, it might be more effective to develop persuasive campaigns intended for wide distribution that challenge implicit calls for violence. These campaigns can be built on the foundation of the theories from the previous chapters, but would likely need to be disseminated via the Internet or more traditional mass media. By distributing the messages in this way, message designers and analysts could seek to engage with as wide an audience as possible in the hope that their messages reach those random individuals who might be at risk for engaging in violence.

Finally, message designers should be sure to administer surveys to supporters of the public figure that explicitly or implicitly advocates the use of violence. This will allow them to capture the beliefs and attitudes held by most of the audience, thereby informing the kinds of content that can be included in the counter-messages. Because the random individuals who would use violence will likely have established norms that align with their interpretations of the stochastic terrorist's words, it may be useful for designers to develop messages focusing on other factors that predict behavior per reasoned action theory. These factors include beliefs about the behavior and whether it will lead to positive outcomes and beliefs about whether the target of the message has control over his performance of a potential violent act.

Attitudinal inoculation may be useful in the latter case, as an inoculation message could suggest that the would-be terrorist would not be acting on his own accord but would essentially be a puppet of the stochastic terrorist. This threat to autonomy may trigger counter-arguing or anger towards the stochastic terrorist, both of which have been empirically shown to reduce support for violent extremism.[92]

∴

I'll admit it. This chapter has been bleak. Despite everything I promised you in the last few chapters regarding persuasion theory's potential for thwarting violent radicalization and its behavioral outcomes, this chapter shows you new ways that extremist groups can circumvent our efforts.

But take heart. I didn't bring you through seven chapters only to tell you it was all for naught. As I said at the beginning of this chapter, it's important that we keep our eyes on the horizon to see what's coming next. But what I didn't say earlier in this chapter is that threats are not the only things that come with a changing political, social, or technological landscape. Although this chapter focused on impending communicative challenges posed by violent extremist organizations, there are also *opportunities* that researchers, analysts, and practitioners can exploit to further improve our efforts geared towards counter-radicalization.

In the next and final chapter of the book, I will review the theories we covered earlier and offer brief discussions of three potential directions that we might take to use these theories and improve communicative counter-radicalization practices moving forward.

Notes

1 Miles Parks, "Russian Interference Campaign was Broader than First Known, Big Tech Tells Hill," *NPR* (October 31, 2017). Available at www.npr.org/ 2017/10/31/560481040/russian-interference-campaign-was-broader-than-first-known-big-tech-tells-hill; Philip Ewing, "Facebook Surrenders Russian-Linked Influence Ads to Congress," *NPR* (October 2, 2017). Available at www.npr .org/2017/10/02/555103005/facebook-surrenders-russian-linked-influence-ads-to-congress.
2 Jon Stone, "Russian Disinformation Campaign Has Been 'Extremely Successful' in Europe, Warns EU," *The Independent* (January 17, 2018). Available

at www.independent.co.uk/news/uk/politics/russian-fake-news-disinformation-europe-putin-trump-eu-european-parliament-commission-a8164526.html.

3 Rand Waltzmann, *The Weaponization of Information: The Need for Cognitive Security* (Santa Monica, CA: RAND Corporation, 2017), p. 4. Testimony presented before the Senate Armed Services Committee, Subcommittee on Cybersecurity on April 27, 2017 (CT-473).

4 Christopher Paul and Miriam Matthews, *The Russian "Firehose of Falsehood" Propaganda Model* (Santa Monica, CA: RAND Corporation, 2016).

5 Alice H. Eagley and Shelly Chaiken, "Process Theories of Attitude Formation and Change: The Elaboration Likelihood and Heuristic-Systematic Model," in *The Psychology of Attitudes*, ed. Alice H. Eagly and Shelly Chaiken, 303–350 (Orlando, FL: Harcourt Brace Jovanovich College Publishers, 1995).

6 For more comprehensive analyses of disinformation and its implications, see Ion Mihai Pacepa and Ronald J. Rychlak, *Disinformation: Former Spy Chief Reveals Secret Strategies for Undermining Freedom, Attacking Religion, and Promoting Terrorism* (Washington, DC: WND Books, 2013); Michael L. Gross and Tamar Meisels, eds., *Soft War: The Ethics of Unarmed Conflict* (Cambridge University Press, 2017).

7 Ibid.

8 Craig Silverman and Lawrence Alexander, "How Teens in the Balkans are Duping Trump Supporters with Fake News," *Buzzfeed News* (November 3, 2016). Available at www.buzzfeednews.com/article/craigsilverman/how-macedonia-became-a-global-hub-for-pro-trump-misinfo.

9 Whitney Phillips, *This is Why We Can't Have Nice Things: Mapping the Relationship between Online Trolling and Mainstream Culture* (Cambridge, MA: MIT Press, 2015).

10 Savvas Zannettou, Tristan Caulfield, William Setzer, Michael Sirivianos, Giancula Stringhini, and Jeremy Blackburn, "Who Let the Trolls Out? Towards Understanding State-Sponsored Trolls," *arXiv* (February 2019). Available at https://arxiv.org/abs/1811.03130; Savvas Zannettou, Tristan Caulfield, Emiliano De Cristofaro, Michael Sirivianos, Giancula Stringhini, and Jeremy Blackburn, "Disinformation Warfare: Understanding State-Sponsored Trolls on Twitter and Their Influence on the Web," *arXiv* (March 2019). Available at https://arxiv.org/abs/1801.09288.

11 Alice Marwick and Rebecca Lewis, "Media Manipulation and Disinformation Online," *Data & Society* (2017). Available at https://datasociety.net/pubs/oh/DataAndSociety_MediaManipulationAndDisinformationOnline.pdf.

12 Pacepa and Rychlak, *Disinformation*, p. 260.

13 Ibid.

14 Ibid., p. 261.

15 Ibid.

16 Kate Samuelson, "What to Know about Pizzagate, the Fake News Story with Real Consequences," *Time* (December 5, 2016). Available at http://time.com/4590255/pizzagate-fake-news-what-to-know/.

17 www.godlikeproductions.com.

18 Sean Adl-Tabatabai, "FBI Insider: Clinton Emails Linked to Political Pedophile Sex Ring," *NewsPunch* (October 31, 2016). Available at https://newspunch.com/fbi-clinton-email-pedophile-ring/.

19 Samuelson, "What to Know about Pizzagate."
20 Erik Ortiz, "'Pizzagate' Gunman Edgar Maddison Welch Sentenced to Four Years in Prison," *NBC News* (June 22, 2017). Available at www.nbcnews.com/news/us-news/pizzagate-gunman-edgar-maddison-welch-sentenced-four-years-prison-n775621.
21 Pete Williams, "'Pizzagate' Gunman Pleads Guilty to Carrying Firearm into D.C. Restaurant," *NBC News* (March 24, 2017). Available at www.nbcnews.com/news/us-news/pizzagate-gunman-pleads-guilty-carrying-firearm-d-c-res taurant-n738171.
22 Timothy P. McGeehan, "Countering Russian Disinformation," *Parameters* 48, no. 1 (2018): 49–57 (p. 53).
23 Daniel Fried and Alina Polyakova, *Democratic Defense against Disinformation* (Washington, DC: The Atlantic Council, 2018), p. 9.
24 McGeehan, "Countering Russian Disinformation," p. 54.
25 Fried and Polyakova, *Democratic Defense against Disinformation*, p. 11.
26 Susan Morgan, "Fake News, Disinformation, Manipulation and Online Tactics to Undermine Democracy," *Journal of Cyber Policy* 3, no. 1 (2018): 39–43 (pp. 42–43).
27 Ibid.
28 McGeehan, "Countering Russian Disinformation," p. 54.
29 See Nicholas G. Carr, *The Shallows: What the Internet is Doing to Our Brains* (New York: W. W. Norton, 2011), p. 6.
30 April Glaser, "Reddit is Finally Reckoning with How It Helped Spread Russian Propaganda in 2016," *Slate* (March 5, 2019). Available at https://slate.com/technology/2018/03/reddit-is-reckoning-with-how-it-helped-spread-russian-propaganda-in-2016.html.
31 Daniel Jolley and Karen M. Douglas, "The Effects of Anti-Vaccine Conspiracy Theories on Vaccination Intentions," *PLoS One* 9, no. 2 (2014): e89177.
32 sp.a, "Teken de Klimaatpetitie" [Facebook post]. Available at www.facebook.com/watch/?v=10155618434657151.
33 Both comments listed here were translated into English from their original Dutch.
34 Oscar Schwartz, "You Thought Fake News Was Bad? Deep Fakes Are Where Truth Goes to Die," *The Guardian* (November 12, 2018). Available at www.theguardian.com/technology/2018/nov/12/deep-fakes-fake-news-truth.
35 Yasmin Green, "Fake Video Will Soon Be Good Enough to Fool Entire Populations," *Wired* (January 12, 2019). Available at www.wired.co.uk/article/deepfake-videos-security.
36 Tormod Dag Fikse, "Imagining Deceptive Deepfakes," Master's thesis, University of Oslo, 2018.
37 Ibid., p. 17.
38 Justus Thies, Michael Zollhöfer, Marc Stamminger, Christian Theobalt, and Mattias Nießner, "Face2Face: Real-Time Face Capture and Reenactment of RGB Videos," *Communications of the ACM* 62, no. 1 (2019): 96–104.
39 Justus Thies, Michael Zollhöfer, and Mattias Nießner, "HeadOn: Real-Time Reenactment of Human Portrait Videos," *ACM Transactions on Graphics* 37, no. 4 (2018): article 164.

40 Hyeongwoo Kim, Pablo Garrido, Ayush Tewari, Weipeng Xu, Justus Thies, Mattias Nieβner, Patrick Perez, et al., "Deep Video Portraits," *ACM Transactions on Graphics* 37, no. 4 (2018): article 163.

41 See https://github.com/iperov/DeepFaceLab (accessed February 20, 2019).

42 Zeyu Jin, Gautham J. Mysore, Stephen Diverdi, Jingwan Lu, and Adam Finkelstein, "VoCo: Text-Based Insertion and Replacement in Audio Narration," *ACM Transactions on Graphics* 36, no. 4 (2017): article 96.

43 James Vincent, "Lyrebird Claims It Can Recreate Any Voice Using Just One Minute of Sample Audio," *The Verge* (April 24, 2017). Available at www.theverge.com/2017/4/24/15406882/ai-voice-synthesis-copy-human-speech-lyrebird.

44 Fikse, "Imagining Deceptive Deepfakes," pp. 20–25.

45 For the Deepfake examples referred to in Table 7.1, see: Amanda Kooser, "Jordan Peele Turns Obama into a Foul-Mouthed Fake-News PSA," *CNET* (April 17, 2018). Available at www.cnet.com/news/jordan-peele-buzzfeed-turn-obama-into-foul-mouthed-fake-news-psa/; 1oneclone, "It's Mueller Time! Trump Administration Season Ending" (August 18, 2017). Available at www.youtube.com/watch?v=d7Uy0Uznw4E; Limor Shifman, *Memes in Digital Culture* (Cambridge, MA: MIT Press, 2014); Stephen LaConte, "Ow Wow. Apparently If You Photoshop Nicolas Cage's Face Onto Ross Geller's Body, Your Brain Will Explode," *Buzzfeed* (February 4, 2019). Available at www.buzzfeed.com/stephenlaconte/nicolas-cage-ross-friends; Samantha Cole, "AI-Assisted Fake Porn is Here and We're All Fucked," *Vice Motherboard* (December 11, 2017). Available at https://motherboard.vice.com/en_us/article/gydydm/gal-gadot-fake-ai-porn. Gunn Enli refers to a situation in which audiences are deceived, thereby causing problems for those audiences and societal norms around truth and falsehood as an *authenticity scandal*. See Gunn Enli, *Mediated Authenticity: How the Media Constructs Reality* (New York: Peter Lang, 2015), p. 18. For face swaps, see Quartz, "Nothing is Real: How German Scientists Control Putin's Face" (April 6, 2016). Available at www.youtube.com/watch?v=ttGUiwfTYvg.

46 Olivia Beavers, "Washington Fears New Threat from 'Deepfake' Videos," *The Hill* (January 20, 2019). Available at https://thehill.com/policy/national-security/426148-washington-fears-new-threat-from-deepfake-videos.

47 See Chris Meserole and Alina Polyakova, "The West is Ill-Prepared for the Wave of 'Deep Fakes' that Artificial Intelligence Could Unleash," *Brookings* (May 25, 2018). Available at www.brookings.edu/blog/order-from-chaos/2018/05/25/the-west-is-ill-prepared-for-the-wave-of-deep-fakes-that-artificial-intelligence-could-unleash/.

48 Gordon Rayner and John Bingham, "Stephen Timms Stabbing: How Internet Sermons Turned Quiet Student into Fanatic," *The Telegraph* (November 2, 2010). Available at www.telegraph.co.uk/news/uknews/crime/8105516/Stephen-Timms-stabbing-how-internet-sermons-turned-quiet-student-into-fanatic.html.

49 Scott Shane and Mark Mazzetti, "Times Sq. Bomb Suspect is Linked to Militant Cleric," *New York Times* (May 6, 2010). Available at www.nytimes.com/2010/05/07/world/middleeast/07awlaki-.html.

50 Julian E. Barnes, "Gates Makes Recommendations in Ft. Hood Shooting Case," *LA Times* (January 15, 2010). Available at www.latimes.com/archives/la-xpm-2010-jan-15-la-na-fort-hood-pentagon16-2010jan16-story.html.
51 Gordon Rayner, "Muslim Groups Linked to September 11 Hijackers Spark Fury Over Conference," *The Telegraph* (December 27, 2008). Available at www.telegraph.co.uk/news/uknews/3966501/Muslim-groups-linked-to-September-11-hijackers-spark-fury-over-conference.html.
52 "Islamist Cleric Anwar al-Awlaki Killed in Yemen," *BBC* (September 30, 2011). Available at www.bbc.com/news/world-middle-east-15121879.
53 "Obama: Anwar al-Awlaki Death is Major Blow for al-Qaeda," *BBC* (September 30, 2011). Available at www.bbc.com/news/world-middle-east-15132308.
54 Mary Anne Weaver, "Lost at Tora Bora," *New York Times Magazine* (September 11, 2005). Available at www.nytimes.com/2005/09/11/magazine/lost-at-tora-bora.html.
55 Robert Chesney and Danielle Citron, "Deep Fakes: A Looming Crisis for National Security, Democracy, and Privacy?" *Lawfare* (February 21, 2018). Available at www.lawfareblog.com/deep-fakes-looming-crisis-national-security-democracy-and-privacy.
56 Steven H. Miles, *Oath Betrayed: Torture, Medical Complicity, and the War on Terror* (New York: Random House, 2006).
57 Michael L. Gross, *The Ethics of Insurgency: A Critical Guide to Just Guerrilla Warfare* (Cambridge University Press, 2015), p. 223.
58 Elliot Friedland, "Terrorists Will Soon be Able to Fake Any Video," *The Clarion Project* (March 14, 2018). Available at https://clarionproject.org/deep-fakes/.
59 Green, "Fake Video Will Soon Be Good Enough to Fool Entire Populations."
60 Pavel Korshunov and Sebastien Marcel, "DeepFakes: A New Threat to Face Recognition? Assessment and Detection," *arXiv* (December 2018). Available at https://arxiv.org/abs/1812.08685.
61 See David Güera and Edward J. Delp, "Deepfake Video Detection Using Recurrent Neural Networks," in *Proceedings of the 2018 IEEE International Conference on Advanced Video and Signal-Based Surveillance*, 127–132.
62 Yuezun Li and Siwei Lyu, "Exposing DeepFake Videos by Detecting Face Warping Artifacts," *arXiv* (March 2019). Available at https://arxiv.org/abs/1811.00656.
63 Yuezun Li, Ming-Ching Chang, and Siwei Lyu, "In Ictu Oculi: Exposing AI Generated Fake Face Videos by Detecting Eye Blinking," *arXiv* (June 2018). Available at https://arxiv.org/abs/1806.02877.
64 Meserole and Polyakova, "The West is Ill-Prepared for the Wave of 'Deep Fakes.'"
65 www.techagainstterrorism.org/.
66 www.gifct.org/about/.
67 See John Arquilla and David Ronfeldt, eds., *Networks and Netwars* (Santa Monica, CA: RAND Corporation, 2001).
68 See Mark S. Hamm and Ramon Spaaij, *The Age of Lone Wolf Terrorism* (New York: Columbia University Press, 2017), pp. 35–37.

69 Bart Schuurman, Lasse Lindekilde, Stefan Malthaner, Francis O'Connor, Paul Gill, and Noémie Bouhana, "End of the Lone Wolf: The Typology that Should Not Have Been," *Studies in Conflict & Terrorism* (in press); see also Zoe Marchment, Noémie Bouhana, and Paul Gill, "Lone Actor Terrorists: A Residence-to-Crime Approach," *Terrorism and Political Violence* (in press); plus, as Bart Schuurman, champion of the lupine community once joked, the term "lone wolf" is unfair to wolves.

70 https://stochasticterrorism.blogspot.com/.

71 See for example, Emanual Parzen, *Stochastic Processes* (San Francisco, CA: Holden-Day, 1962).

72 Miriam R. García, José A. Vázquez, Isabel G. Teixeira, and Antonio A. Alonso, "Stochastic Individual-Based Modeling of Bacterial Growth and Division using Flow Cytometry," *Frontiers in Microbiology* 8 (2018): article 2626.

73 See for example, J. Michael Steele, *Stochastic Calculus and Financial Applications* (New York: Springer-Verlag, 2001).

74 https://stochasticterrorism.blogspot.com/.

75 Valerie Tarico, "Christianist Republicans Systematically Incited Colorado Clinic Assault," personal website (November 28, 2015). Available at https://valerietarico.com/2015/11/28/christianist-republicans-systematically-incited-colorado-clinic-assault/.

76 "Trump, on Protest: I Don't Know if I'll Do the Fighting Myself Or if Other People Will," *C-SPAN* (August 11, 2015). Available at www.c-span.org/video/?c4762932/trump-protest-dont-ill-fighting-people; Meredith McGraw, "Trump: No Regrets for Praising Greg Gianforte for Body-Slamming Reporter," *ABC News* (October 19, 2018). Available at https://abcnews.go.com/Politics/montana-rally-president-trump-praises-greg-gianforte-body/story?id=58596529.

77 David S. Cohen, "Trump's Assassination Dog Whistle Was Even Scarier than You Think," *Rolling Stone* (August 9, 2016). Available at www.rollingstone.com/politics/politics-features/trumps-assassination-dog-whistle-was-even-scarier-than-you-think-112138/; Emily Crockett, "Trump's 2nd Amendment Comment Wasn't a Joke. It Was 'Stochastic Terrorism,'" *Vox* (August 11, 2016). Available at www.vox.com/2016/8/10/12422476/trump-second-amendment-hillary-stochastic-terrorism-anti-abortion-violence.

78 Cohen, "Trump's Assassination Dog Whistle Was Even Scarier than You Think."

79 Phil Helsel, Elisha Fieldstadt, and John Chandler, "Mail Bomber Cesar Sayoc Pleads Guilty; Devices Were Sent to Critics of Trump," *NBC News* (March 21, 2019). Available at www.nbcnews.com/news/us-news/alleged-mail-bomber-cesar-sayoc-pleads-guilty-devices-were-sent-n985786; Tarpley Hitt, "Mail Bomb Suspect Cesar Sayoc's Rage Against Mom Drove Him to Trump, Lawyer Claims," *The Daily Beast* (October 28, 2018). Available at www.thedailybeast.com/mail-bomb-suspect-cesar-sayocs-rage-against-mom-drove-him-to-trump-lawyer-claims.

80 Jon Swaine, "Neo-Nazi in Coast Guard Plotted Attack on Democrats and Journalists, Say Prosecutors," *The Guardian* (February 20, 2019). Available at

www.theguardian.com/us-news/2019/feb/20/neo-nazi-plotted-attack-on-democrats-journalists.

81 Colby Itkowitz and John Wagner, "Trump Says White Nationalism is Not a Rising Threat After New Zealand Attacks: 'It's a Small Group of People,'" *Washington Post* (March 15, 2019). Available at www.washingtonpost.com/politics/trump-offers-us-assistance-after-horrible-massacre-in-new-zealand/2019/03/15/931833d2-4712-11e9-aaf8-4512a6fe3439_story.html; Reuters, "White House Dismisses Trump Mention in Christchurch Shooter Manifesto," *The Guardian* (March 17, 2019). Available at www.theguardian.com/world/2019/mar/17/trump-christchurch-shooter-manifesto.

82 Reis Thebault, "Steve King Posts Meme Saying Red States Have '8 Trillion Bullets' in Event of Civil War," *LA Times* (March 19, 2019). Available at www.latimes.com/politics/la-na-pol-steve-king-civil-war-20190319-story.html.

83 Adam Rubenstein, "Did Steve King Just Refer to Immigrants as 'Dirt'?" *The Weekly Standard* (November 6, 2018). Available at www.weeklystandard.com/adam-rubenstein/did-steve-just-refer-to-immigrants-as-dirt.

84 Associated Press, "Republicans Slam Rep. Steve King for White Supremacist Remarks," *LA Times* (January 10, 2019). Available at www.latimes.com/ct-steve-king-republicans-20190110-story.html.

85 Matthew Taylor, "'White Europe': 60,000 Nationalists March on Poland's Independence Day," *The Guardian* (November 12, 2017). Available at www.theguardian.com/world/2017/nov/12/white-europe-60000-nationalists-march-on-polands-independence-day.

86 Paul Hockenos, "Poland and the Uncontrollable Fury of Europe's Far Right," *The Atlantic* (November 15, 2017). Available at www.theatlantic.com/international/archive/2017/11/europe-far-right-populist-nazi-poland/524559/.

87 Michael Edison Hayden, "Critics Pounce on Trump After CNN Wrestling Tweet," *ABC News* (July 2, 2017). Available at https://abcnews.go.com/Politics/critics-pounce-trump-cnn-wrestling-tweet/story?id=48405044.

88 Jonathan Martin, "Montana Republican Greg Gianforte, Charged with Assault, Awaits Fate in Vote," *New York Times* (May 24, 2017). Available at www.nytimes.com/2017/05/24/us/politics/greg-gianforte-montana-republican-body-slams-reporter.html.

89 Ed Pilkington, "'He's My Guy': Donald Trump Praises Gianforte for Assault on Guardian Reporter," *The Guardian* (October 19, 2018). Available at www.theguardian.com/us-news/2018/oct/18/trump-greg-gianforte-assault-guardian-ben-jacobs.

90 Hitt, "Mail Bomb Suspect Cesar Sayoc's Rage Against Mom Drove Him to Trump."

91 Michael Garcia, "A Public-Health Approach to Countering Violent Extremism," *Just Security* (April 3, 2019). Available at www.justsecurity.org/63455/a-public-health-approach-to-countering-violent-extremism/.

92 Kurt Braddock, "Vaccinating against Hate: Using Attitudinal Inoculation to Confer Resistance to Persuasion by Extremist Propaganda" (under review).

8 Fighting Back: Three Future Directions for Persuasion-Based Approaches to Counter-Radicalization

Following the last chapter, I wouldn't blame you for thinking that counter-radicalization efforts will perpetually lag behind the techniques that extremist groups use to reach audiences. The development and implementation of counter-radicalization programs requires ample support from large organizations. Unfortunately, government agencies, NGOs, universities, and other institutional entities involved in shaping viable counter-radicalization strategies are often characterized by organizational inertia, making them slow to react to changing communicative strategies employed by violent extremists. In contrast, the extremists are not constrained by the ethical or legal considerations that apply to counter-radicalization efforts. Moreover, extremists are often allowed to act of their own accord, limiting organizational interference in their interactions with audiences. This communicative agility makes violent extremists' persuasive messages adaptable to new communication technologies and shifting audience bases, making them all the more effective.

That said, throughout this book, I have tried to convey the notion that we can take advantage of the same cognitive outcomes of persuasive communication as the extremists. In this chapter, I want to reiterate this fact ... and go a step further. Here, I argue that we can apply our understanding of the persuasion theories described in the earlier chapters to develop *new* counter-radicalization practices that pull message targets away from extremist ideologies.

Though we want to be innovative in our development of communicative counter-radicalization techniques, it is important to realize that the theories and perspectives from Part II of this book describe psychological responses to persuasive communication in a general sense. Therefore, if we want to be successful as we look ahead, we must remember to look back. Regardless of how we develop and implement new counter-radicalization approaches, they must be grounded in proven theory. Times and tools change, but the psychological dynamics of persuasive communication remain constant.

In the spirit of looking forward while remaining cognizant of past empirical evidence on persuasive communication, this brief final chapter offers some cursory recommendations for future approaches to counter-radicalization designed on the basis of long-standing persuasion theory.

Specifically, the chapter will review three theories from Part II of this book – narrative theory, inoculation theory, and reasoned action theory – and offer possible routes that security researchers and practitioners might take to develop new counter-radicalization approaches. I do not cover discrete emotions in this chapter because the elicitation of emotional responses can be achieved in conjunction with any of the other theoretical approaches. As such, any counter-radicalization effort based on persuasive communication can be designed to elicit specific emotions and their corresponding behavioral responses.

However, narratives, attitudinal inoculation, and reasoned action each have specific characteristics that make them amenable to certain approaches to counter-radicalization. Technological advances in the realm of simulated reality hold significant promise in how we construct and distribute counter-narratives intended to reduce support for extremist groups. Entertainment-education programs – which have a long history in communication science but have not been applied to violent extremism – are uniquely suitable for inoculation messages. The capacity for Web 2.0 technologies to allow users to personalize their online experiences has significant implications for how those users develop beliefs and perceived norms about certain behaviors. A consideration of reasoned action theory in the development of counter-radicalization content to be distributed via Web 2.0 platforms allows us to better design that content.

This final chapter will not be a long one. The ideas I promote here are nascent to say the least, meaning that there has been little (if any) empirical analysis of their effectiveness in stemming violent radicalization. But as decades of social scientific research have shown us, the development of new solutions to existing problems begins by extending our established knowledge base. I hope this chapter prompts such an extension.

In a series of notes to himself containing ideas that he wished to keep in mind, Roman emperor and philosopher Marcus Aurelius wrote, "Never let the future disturb you. You will meet it, if you have to, with the same weapons of reason which today arm you against the present."[1]

Let us use our present weapons of reason to inform how we challenge extremist communication in the future.

Counter-Narratives and Immersive Technologies

Chapter 3 discussed narrative theory and how it can inform our development of counter-narratives intended to challenge extremist ideologies and prevent violent radicalization. In that chapter, I focused extensively on the *analysis* of extremist narratives to grasp the kinds of themes that comprise those narratives and promote psychological processes that facilitate persuasion via counter-narratives. A narrative's capacity for triggering these processes – psychological transportation, identification, and parasocial interaction – is based on the degree to which it provides audiences with an engaging, immersive, and relatable story. To this point, however, developers of counter-narratives have assumed that stories need to be told with standard text, video, or in some cases, in-person interventions. This is not without reason. The vast majority of research on narratives has investigated the persuasive efficacy of text- and video-based stimuli.[2]

However, recent technological advancements have made possible the development of narratives in media that, by their very nature, offer audiences more engaging narrative experiences. These media, called immersive virtual environments (IVEs), provide "synthetic representations of a natural or imagined environment."[3] They position audiences in two- or three-dimensional virtual spaces in which they can interact with their environment using input devices. While present in IVEs, users are often represented by avatars who mimic their actions or adopt a first-person perspective in which it seems that they are directly interacting with the virtual world.[4]

Research on social influence in IVEs has revealed a positive relationship between the realism of an immersive environment and the degree to which users are influenced by actors within the virtual world.[5] These studies have shown that virtual worlds can be useful for persuasion, provided the environments (and the actors within them) seem realistic. These results are consistent with more traditional research on narrative persuasion that has shown the realism of narratives to be connected to their capacity for promoting salient persuasive outcomes (e.g., transportation).

The most common forms of IVE are (1) immersive games in which users perceive themselves as being inside the game world and (2) virtual reality simulations in which users not only perceive themselves as being within the simulation, but are also aware of having arrived in and leaving that simulation, thereby giving them a heightened awareness of the virtual space within the virtual environment.[6]

Despite the technology's relative novelty, IVEs have been shown to be persuasive in multiple contexts. Much of the research on IVEs and their propensity for promoting persuasion has been done in the context of marketing,[7] but work in other areas has similarly shown IVEs to be effective for persuading users to adopt beliefs and attitudes consistent with message designers' goals. More specifically, immersive environments have affected users by reducing their intentions to drive drunk,[8] affecting their attitudes about fire safety,[9] diminishing their proclivity for engaging in risky sexual behaviors,[10] promoting their support of social causes,[11] facilitating their learning,[12] and influencing their perceptions of travel destinations.[13] Despite a relative lack of research on immersive virtual environments, it is clear that the technology can be used for persuasive purposes.

This begs a question – if immersive virtual environments have proven persuasive in such a variety of contexts, can they be used for the purpose of counter-radicalization? There is no research on virtual reality and counter-radicalization to date, but the wealth of support for the persuasive efficacy of virtual reality in these other domains suggests that it could be an extremely valuable resource for designers of messages intended to dissuade the adoption of extremist ideologies.

Some studies on user responses to virtual environments even suggest that they may be particularly suited to the sensitive context of violent extremism and counter-radicalization. For example, Jin Hammock and Moon Lee found that reticent individuals – those who hesitate to engage in social interaction – are more likely to engage in virtual worlds than in the real world (though the virtual world must be sufficiently realistic to prompt interaction).[14] This finding suggests that IVEs could be used to disseminate counter-narratives to populations who would otherwise be hesitant to engage with those who would be delivering the counter-narratives in a more traditional context.

Guadagno and colleagues also found that as long as a virtual avatar behaves "normally," individuals tend to be persuaded by them, *even if they know that they are computer generated*.[15] This has significant implications for the development and delivery of counter-narratives; no longer would message designers need to rely on the cooperation of trusted others to deliver counter-narrative content to those vulnerable to violent radicalization. Guadagno et al.'s findings suggest that even if an individual knows that a representation of a person is only a virtual avatar, the counter-narrative(s) told by that avatar are likely to be persuasive.

Related to this, Slater et al. found that virtual reality experiments can be useful for evaluating how individuals will react in real-world situations.[16] This means that the virtual presentation of a counter-narrative to individuals at risk for violent radicalization may help to predict how those individuals would react to similar counter-narratives encountered in more organic environments (e.g., as told to them by former extremists).

The question remains, what kinds of counter-narratives could be implemented with the use of IVEs? Interviews with former violent extremists can be instructive here. For example, many former terrorists have explained the disillusionment they felt upon becoming actively involved with their former organizations. Though they expected lives of adventure and political purpose, many found their involvement in terrorism to be bland and unsatisfying.[17] It may seem counterintuitive, but priming individuals to feel excitement at the prospect of joining a political extremist group, and then immersing them in a boring virtual narrative where their expectations fall flat may be an effective strategy for communicating the futility of engagement in terrorism. At the time of this writing, I am currently working on developing an experiment that will test the effectiveness of this kind of intervention.

Another kind of IVE-based counter-narrative approach might involve the use of video games. Burrows and Blanton showed that immersive video games can have positive persuasive effects on players' health outcomes.[18] It therefore follows that an effectively constructed video game that demonstrates the failures of violent extremism might represent an effective counter-narrative strategy.

Research on the persuasive efficacy of narratives presented via virtual reality is in its early stages, but the data are promising. As more work is performed, researchers and practitioners may want to consider implementing immersive virtual environments in their counter-radicalization efforts, as they can amplify the persuasive effects that result from the psychological processes outlined in Chapter 3.

Attitudinal Inoculation and Entertainment-Education Programming

Throughout the 1980s and 1990s, I was inundated with "very special episodes" of my favorite TV shows. Anyone who watched television during their adolescent and teenage years knows a very special episode when they see one. Viewers who would tune in for an entertaining, if vapid half-hour of hijinks was instead presented with a moral lesson related to some message that the show wanted its audience to assimilate. On *Saved by the Bell*, Zack Morris and the gang told us that "there's no hope with dope" as one of their favorite movie stars turns out to be a marijuana smoker. On *The Fresh Prince of Bel-Air*, Will and Carlton showed us the dangers of amphetamines when Carlton accidentally overdoses on speed that Will was using to stay awake and study. On *Family Matters*, Laura Winslow and Steve Urkel were victimized by anonymous racists in their school, showing us the ongoing struggle of African-Americans. Shawn Hunter of *Step by Step* was promised friendship and love at "The Center," which turned out to be a front for a cult led by a creepy, but charismatic leader. On *Diff'rent Strokes*, we were shown the dangers of sex predators, as Arnold and his friend Dudley are groomed by a seemingly friendly bicycle salesman, who gets the boys back to his home, shows them pornography, and takes pictures of them in various states of undress. Heavy-handed though these episodes might have been, they were instructive for young viewers about the kinds of threats they might face not only from their peers, but from other people as well.

Within communication and media studies, these kinds of programs are called entertainment-education. Entertainment-education refers to persuasive messages (typically prosocial) that are embedded in media that are typically meant for entertainment purposes.[19] Whereas narratives (and counter-narratives) as we discussed them in Chapter 3 are treated as independent segments, entertainment-education is often presented in the context of an established narrative structure (e.g., a television show). Moreover, entertainment-education differs from singular narratives because entertainment-education can be extended over a series of individual episodes. For example, on the popular medical drama *ER*, producers regularly embed multiple-episode storylines concerning health issues (e.g., HIV) that have been shown to have persuasive effects on those who have seen the storyline.[20]

The persuasive mechanisms of entertainment-education are largely similar to those discussed in Chapter 3, but Moyer-Gusé produced a model of persuasion via entertainment-education that includes mechanisms that are not as prominent in the narrative literature. This model, predicated on the Extended Elaboration Likelihood Model[21] and Social Cognitive Theory,[22] predicts the following processes result from consumption of entertainment-education programming:

- Narrative structure, parasocial interaction, and liking of a character reduces the tendency for audience members to experience psychological reactance.
- Transportation, identification, and parasocial interaction reduce the degree to which audiences counter argue against the messages in the program.

- Enjoyment of the program and identification with characters reduces audience tendency to selectively avoid messages embedded in the program that make them uncomfortable.
- Perceived similarity with characters and identification with those characters increases audience perceptions of vulnerability to the issues described in the entertainment-education programming and changes their expectations of outcomes related to the issue described.
- Parasocial interaction with characters changes audience perceptions of norms related to the behaviors highlighted in the entertainment-education programming.
- Perceived similarity with a character who effectively deals with the problems presented in the program increases audience perceptions of self-efficacy.

Moyer-Gusé contends that each of these processes predict the adoption of beliefs, attitudes, and behaviors consistent with those advocated (or warned against) in the story presented by the entertainment-education program. Based on what was covered in Chapter 3, her claim seems like it would hold water. However, entertainment-education is presented in a different manner than traditional narratives, suggesting its effectiveness may be different as well.

Luckily, there have been several meta-analyses on the topic of persuasion via entertainment-education. And although these studies have focused most heavily on health-related outcomes, they consistently show that entertainment-education has positive effects on message-consistent outcomes. That is, entertainment-education programming effectively shapes the beliefs, attitudes, intentions, and behaviors of those who are exposed to it.[23]

This begs the question: can entertainment-education be used in the context of violent extremism? The evidence suggests that the answer to this question is an unadulterated "yes." Although counter-messaging specialists have expended significant effort at developing and disseminating individual counter-narratives within vulnerable populations,[24] it seems to be a missed opportunity that messages intended to counter violent extremism have not been widely embedded in popular media. Clearly, popular media is not a new technology – but it represents a new opportunity.

Specifically, it offers an outlet through which analysts and practitioners can develop storylines that warn viewers about the dangers of adopting extremist ideologies, the presence of hate groups or extremist organizations in certain contexts (e.g., schools), or any other issue that message designers may want to raise.

To effectively use entertainment-education as an outlet through which counter-messages are distributed, government officials, researchers, and analysts will need to partner with producers of popular media in the same way that health communication researchers have. This will involve reaching out to television production studios and other producers of original content (e.g., Netflix) to inquire about the possibility of incorporating counter-ideological content into their programing.

One benefit of entertainment-education is its versatility. Message developers can produce any number of persuasive appeals to be embedded in entertainment-education programming. I would recommend that entertainment-education programs intended to dissuade the adoption of extremist ideologies (or violent behavior) would be best served by the inclusion of inoculation messages (like those described in Chapter 4).

My basis for recommending inoculation as a strategy to be employed in conjunction with entertainment-education is the regularity with which it has been tested as a vehicle for persuasion and its demonstrated effectiveness. Research in this area – which has also skewed heavily towards affecting health-related outcomes – has shown that inoculation messages intended to empower message recipients to avoid dangerous behaviors have been effective when embedded in entertainment-education programming.[25] This seems to be qualitatively consistent with the potential for using entertainment-education to inoculate audience attitudes against the dangers of violent extremism.

Of course, investigators must perform preliminary research on the efficacy of entertainment-education in the realm of radicalization before we can say how useful it might be or determine the kinds of programs that would be ideal for including content that would promote counter-radicalization. Still, the consistency with which entertainment-education has been shown to promote positive health outcomes suggests its promise for preventing the assimilation of extremist ideologies through a new kind of "very special episode."

Reasoned Action and Online Personalization and Customization: Self as Source

Within the literature on communication in the realm of violent extremism, there is an inherent assumption that the respective sources for extremist propaganda and counter-propaganda are extremist groups and those tasked with preventing radicalization (e.g., security personnel, researchers, analysts). This assumption is understandable, given that the foundation of most persuasion research is the notion that communication requires a message sender and a message receiver. One person speaks (or writes) and the other person listens (or reads). Simple.

However, the emergence of new communication technologies that allow message recipients to affect how they consume information blurs the line between message senders and receivers. Communication technology expert Shyam Sundar describes how some communication technologies allow users to influence the nature and process of a communicative interaction, making them feel as though they are an influential agent in the context of that interaction.[26] Sundar argues that when users perceive they have influence over the interactions they engage in, they are more amenable to different kinds of persuasive outcomes.

This agency-based model of customization[27] contends that the mechanism by which psychological benefits (like persuasion) can be derived from online content is an audience member's perception of "self-as-source." Sundar explains:

> According to this model, technological affordances imbue a higher sense of agency by allowing the user to serve as a source of his or her information, and thereby become the center of his or her interaction universe. This translates to positive cognitive, affective, and behavioral responses toward both the interface and the content of customizable media.[28]

To afford users the capacity to become the centers of their own interaction universe, platform designers must provide them with the tools needed to customize the information they encounter.[29] If these tools are relatively easy to use and users can successfully customize content to their liking, it should provide them with a sense of autonomy and self-efficacy, both of which can contribute to the persuasiveness of the customized content.[30]

Past research has shown that other factors influence the degree to which an individual will be persuaded by content that he or she has customized. First, a user's sense of identity may motivate them to customize content in such a way that it will be more persuasive.[31] By personalizing messages or the interface in which those messages are sent or received, users can feel unique relative to others, which promotes positive attitudes about the platform on which they engage with different messages.[32] And as I argued in my work with John Morrison, feelings of positivity towards a communicative interface can improve the persuasiveness of content intended for counter-radicalization.[33]

Second, the relevance of content that users engage with is an important predictor of whether that content will be persuasive.[34] In some cases, an online system will choose content to be presented to users based on their past online activity (i.e., personalization). In other cases, individuals will be afforded the opportunity to tailor content and the interface on which it appears of their own accord (customization). In either case, content is likely to match user interest, and is therefore likely to be deemed more credible.[35] There is a substantial amount of empirical research showing that messages that have been personalized or customized have had positive effects on different kinds of persuasive outcomes.[36]

In short, the recent history of research on how content is presented to users has shown that allowing users to customize their online communicative experiences can promote persuasion consistent with that which is advocated in the message they are exposed to. Given what we learned in Chapter 5, this makes sense. If personalization and customization enhance perceptions of source credibility and content credibility on the part of the user, it follows that this increased credibility will alter beliefs about the topics of the messages. In reasoned action theory terms, customized or personalized content can influence beliefs about a behavior, perceived norms, and perceived efficacy, all of which ultimately affect intentions and manifest behaviors.

How, then, can we leverage positive persuasive outcomes afforded by customization and personalization of online interfaces and content to affect counter-radicalization processes?

Answering this question effectively can be a tricky endeavor, given that content geared towards counter-radicalization is often tailored in a way to challenge specific elements of extremist propaganda. It would seem that this leaves us little room to allow our target audiences to customize that content. However, note that the positive outcomes associated with personalization and customization are not limited to content. Sundar and others have argued that allowing the user to influence *how* content is presented to them can offer similar persuasive benefits.

In this vein, it may benefit message developers to produce multifaceted counter-radicalization content (i.e., inoculation messages, counter-narratives, etc.) that can be presented to users in multiple ways. For instance, counter-narrative developers could build a "choose your own adventure" online platform that allows audiences to influence the direction of their story while maintaining control over the sorts of content that would reach those audiences, regardless of the choices they make. This may give users the impression of customizing their counter-narrative experience, despite the fact that the messages they will be exposed to will have the same counter-thematic content.

Another option involves allowing users to choose the trajectory they take through various counter-radicalization content. At present, some independent organizations are attempting to make use of online personalization to get vulnerable individuals to engage with counter-radicalization content. For instance, Moonshot CVE, an independent firm that develops CVE interventions, has developed a process whereby individuals who search for radicalizing content online are instead directed to thematically similar content that *counters* extremist propaganda. By giving users the impression that they are viewing material they found as a result of their own online search choices, Moonshot can increase users' perceptions of personalization, which can increase the degree to which they find the material they encounter persuasive.

∴

The suggestions I offer here do not represent a comprehensive list of the different ways that counter-radicalization researchers and practitioners can leverage new knowledge and technologies to fight extremist propaganda. I present them as jumping-off points – ideas that I hope prompt discussion and future research on new and creative ways to challenge the persuasive appeal of extremist communication.

I also hope that this book has provided you with ideas of your own on how we might develop empirically rigorous methods for beating extremists at their own communicative game. As I said in the introductory chapter, we have the tools to prevent vulnerable individuals from being seduced by ideologies built on violence and false promises. We have *always* had those tools in the form of long-validated social scientific theories; we need only look back in our respective disciplines to see how they have been applied to past social issues.

In doing so, we can bring them into the realm of violent extremism and protect those we hold most dear – not only those innocent bystanders who would be victimized by terrorist attacks, but also those lost souls who are at risk for being persuaded to perform them.

Notes

1 Marcus Aurelius, *Meditations* (Mineola, NY: Dover Publications, 1997), Book VII, 6.
2 See Kurt Braddock and James Price Dillard, "Meta-Analytic Evidence for the Persuasive Effect of Narratives on Beliefs, Attitudes, Intentions, and Behaviors," *Communication Monographs* 83, no. 4 (2016): 446–467.
3 Rosanna E. Guadagno, Jim Blascovich, Jeremy N. Bailenson, and Cade McCall, "Virtual Humans and Persuasion: The Effects of Agency and Behavioral Realism," *Media Psychology* 10, no. 1 (2007): 1–22; Jim Blascovich, Jack Loomis, Andrew C. Beall, Kimberly R. Swinth, Crystal L. Hoyt, and Jeremy N. Bailenson, "Immersive Virtual Environment Technology as a

Methodological Tool for Social Psychology," *Psychological Inquiry* 13, no. 2 (2002): 103–124; Jaron Lanier, "Tele-Immersion: Like Being There," *Scientific American* 284 (2001): 68–75.

4 Guadagno et al., "Virtual Humans and Persuasion."

5 Blascovich et al., "Immersive Virtual Environment Technology as a Methodological Tool for Social Psychology"; Maia Garau, "The Impact of Avatar Fidelity on Social Interaction in Virtual Environments," dissertation, University of London, 2003; Jeremy N. Bailenson, Kim Swinth, Crystal Hoyt, Susan Persky, Alex Dimov, and Jim Blascovich, "The Independent and Interactive Effects of Embodied-Agent Appearance and Behavior on Self-Report, Cognitive, and Behavioral Markers of Copresence in Immersive Virtual Environments," *PRESENCE: Teleoperators and Virtual Environment* 14 (2005): 379–396.

6 Iis Tussyadiah, Dan Wang, and Chenge (Helen) Jia, "Exploring the Persuasive Power of Virtual Reality Imagery for Destination Marketing," paper presented at the International Conference for Travel and Tourism Research Association, Vail, Colorado, June 14–16, 2016.

7 Dan Grigorovici, "Persuasive Effects of Presence in Immersive Virtual Environments," in *Being There: Concepts, Effects, and Measurements of User Presence in Synthetic Environments*, ed. G. Riva, F. Davide, and W. A. Ijsselsteijn, 191–207 (Amsterdam: Ios Press, 2003).

8 Christopher N. Burrows and Hart Blanton, "Real-World Persuasion from Virtual-World Campaigns: How Transportation into Virtual Worlds Moderates In-Game Influence," *Communication Research* 43, no. 4 (2016): 542–570.

9 Luca Chittaro and Nicola Zandgrando, "The Persuasive Power of Virtual Reality: Effects of Simulated Human Distress on Attitudes towards Fire Safety," in *Persuasive Technology: 5th International Conference, PERSUASIVE 2010*, ed. Thomas Ploug, Per Hasle, and Harri Oinas-Kukkonen, 58–69.

10 Stephen J. Read, Lynn C. Miller, Paul Robert Appleby, Mary E. Nwosu, Sadina Reynaldo, Ada Lauren, and Anila Putcha, "Socially Optimized Learning in a Virtual Environment: Reducing Risky Sexual Behavior among Men Who Have Sex with Men," *Human Communication Research* 32, no. 1 (2006): 1–33.

11 Kenneth C. C. Yang and Yowei Kang, "Augmented, Mixed, and Virtual Reality Applications in Cause-Related Marketing," in *Cases on Immersive Virtual Reality Techniques*, ed. Kenneth C. C. Yang, 217–240 (Hershey, PA: IGI Global, 2019).

12 Jeremy N. Bailenson, Nick Yee, Jim Blascovich, Andrew C. Beall, Nicole Lundblad, and Michael Jin, "The Use of Immersive Virtual Reality in the Learning Sciences: Digital Transformations of Teachers, Students, and Social Context," *The Journal of the Learning Sciences* 17 (2008): 102–141.

13 Iis P. Tussyadiah, Dan Wang, Timothy H. Jung, and M. Claudia tom Dieck, "Virtual Reality, Presence, and Attitude Change: Empirical Evidence from Tourism," *Tourism Management* 66 (2018): 140–154.

14 Jin K. Hammick and Moon J. Lee, "Do Shy People Feel Less Communication Apprehension Online? The Effects of Virtual Reality on the Relationship between Personality Characteristics and Communication Outcomes," *Computers in Human Behavior* 33 (2014): 302–310.

15 Guadagno et al., "Virtual Humans and Persuasion."
16 Mel Slater, Angus Antley, Adam Davison, David Swapp, Christopher Guger, Chris Barker, Nancy Pistrang, and Maria V. Sanchez-Vives, "A Virtual Reprise of the Stanley Milgram Obedience Experiments," *PLoS One* 1, no. 1 (2006): e39.
17 John Horgan, *Walking Away from Terrorism: Accounts of Disengagement from Radical and Extremist Movements* (Abingdon: Routledge, 2009).
18 Burrows and Blanton, "Real-World Persuasion from Virtual-World Campaigns."
19 Emily Moyer-Gusé, "Toward a Theory of Entertainment Persuasion: Explaining the Persuasive Effects of Entertainment-Education Messages," *Communication Theory* 18 (2008): 407–425 (p. 415).
20 Mollyann Brodie, Ursula Foehr, Vicky Rideout, Neal Baer, Carolyn Miller, Rebecca Flournoy, and Drew Altman, "Communicating Health Information through the Entertainment Media," *Health Affairs* 20, no. 1 (2001): 192–199.
21 Michael D. Slater, "Involvement as Goal-Directed Strategic Processing: Extending the Elaboration Likelihood Model," in *The Persuasion Handbook: Developments in Theory and Practice*, ed. James P. Dillard and Michael Pfau, 175–194 (Thousand Oaks, CA: Sage, 2002); Michael D. Slater and Donna Rouner, "Entertainment-Education and Elaboration Likelihood: Understanding the Processing of Narrative Persuasion," *Communication Theory* 12 (2002): 173–191.
22 Albert Bandura, *Social Foundations of Thought and Action: A Social Cognitive Theory* (Englewood Cliffs, NJ: Prentice Hall, 1986).
23 See, for example, Victor Orozco-Olvera, Fuyuan Shen, and Lucie Cluver, "The Effectiveness of Using Entertainment Education Narratives to Promote Safer Sexual Behaviors of Youth: A Meta-Analysis, 1985–2017," *PLoS One* 14, no. 2 (2019): e0209969; Fuyuan Shen and Jiangxue (Ashley) Han, "Effectiveness of Entertainment Education in Communicating Health Information: A Systematic Review," *Asian Journal of Communication* 24, no. 6 (2014): 605–616.
24 See Chapter 2 in this volume, as well as Kurt Braddock and John Horgan, "Towards a Guide for Constructing and Disseminating Counternarratives to Reduce Support for Terrorism," *Studies in Conflict & Terrorism* 39, no. 5 (2016): 381–404.
25 Youngju Shin, Michelle Miller-Day, Michael L. Hecht, and Janice L. Krieger, "Entertainment-Education Videos as a Persuasive Tool in the Substance Use Prevention Intervention 'Keepin' it REAL,'" *Health Communication* 33, no. 7 (2018): 896–906.
26 S. Shyam Sundar, Jeeyun Oh, Hyunjin Kang, and Akshaya Sreenivasan, "How Does Technology Persuade? Theoretical Mechanisms for Persuasive Technologies," in *The SAGE Handbook of Persuasion: Developments in Theory and Practice*, ed. James Price Dillard and Lijiang Shen, eds., 388–404 (Thousand Oaks, CA: Sage, 2013), p. 391.
27 S. Shyam Sundar, "Self as Source: Agency and Customization in Interactive Media," in *Mediated Interpersonal Communication*, ed. Elly A. Konjin, Sonja Utz, Martin Tanis, and Susan B. Barnes, 58–74 (New York: Routledge, 2008).

28 Sundar et al., "How Does Technology Persuade?," p. 392.
29 Per self-determination theory. See Richard M. Ryan and Edward L. Deci, "Self-Determination Theory and the Facilitation of Intrinsic Motivation, Social Development, and Well-Being," *American Psychologist* 55 (2000): 68–78.
30 Albert Bandura, *Self-Efficacy: The Exercise of Control* (New York: W. H. Freeman, 1997); Michael I. Norton, Daniel Mochon, and Dan Ariely, "The 'IKEA Effect': When Labor Leads to Love," Harvard Business School Marketing Unit Working Paper No. 11-091 (2011). Available at https://papers.ssrn.com/sol3/papers.cfm?abstract_id=1777100.
31 Sampada Marathe and S. Shyam Sundar, "What Drives Customization? Control or Identity?," in *Proceedings of the SIGCHI Conference on Human Factors in Computing Systems*, 781–790.
32 Richard E. Petty, S. Christian Wheeler, and George Y. Bizer, "Attitude Functions and Persuasion: An Elaboration Likelihood Approach to Matched Versus Mismatched Messages," in *Why We Evaluate: Functions of Attitudes*, ed. Gregory R. Maio and James M. Olson, 133–162 (Mahwah, NJ: Lawrence Erlbaum, 2000).
33 Kurt Braddock and John Morrison, "Cultivating Trust and Perceptions of Source Credibility in Online Counternarratives Intended to Reduce Support for Terrorism," *Studies in Conflict & Terrorism* (in press).
34 Sriram Kalyanaraman and S. Shyam Sundar, "The Psychological Appeal of Personalized Content in Web Portals: Does Customization Affect Attitudes and Behavior?," *Journal of Communication* 56, no. 1 (2006): 110–132.
35 S. Shyam Sundar and Sampada S. Marathe, "Personalization Versus Customization: The Importance of Agency, Privacy, and Power Usage," *Human Communication Research* 36 (2010): 298–322,
36 See, for example, Anke Oenema, Johanes Brug, Arie Dijkstra, Inge de Weerdt, and Hein de Vries, "Efficacy and Use of an Internet-Delivered Computer-Tailored Lifestyle Intervention, Targeting Saturated Fat Intake, Physical Activity and Smoking Cessation: A Randomized Controlled Trial," *Annals of Behavioral Medicine* 35, no. 2 (2008): 125–135; Bess H. Marcus, Beth A. Lewis, David M. Williams, Shira S. Dunsinger, John M. Jakicic, Jessica A. Whiteley, Anna E. Albrecht, et al., "A Comparison of Internet and Print-Based Physical Activity Interventions," *Archives of Internal Medicine* 167 (2007): 944–949.

Bibliography

Introduction

Barnard, Anne, and Hwaida Saad. "Raqqa: ISIS 'Capital,' is Captured, U.S.-Backed Forces Say." *New York Times*, October 17, 2017. www.nytimes.com/2017/10/17/world/middleeast/isis-syria-raqqa.html.

Bruce, James. "Inside the West's Secret War against ISIS." *The Arab Weekly*, July 3, 2016. https://thearabweekly.com/sites/default/files/pdf/2016/07/03-07/p1000.pdf.

Callimachi, Rukmini. "ISIS and the Lonely Young American." *New York Times*, June 27, 2015. www.nytimes.com/2015/06/28/world/americas/isis-online-recruiting-american.html.

Farwell, James P. "The Media Strategy of ISIS." *Survival: Global Politics and Strategy* 56, no. 6 (2014): 49–55.

Fenstermacher, Laurie, and Todd Leventhal, eds. *Countering Violent Extremism: Scientific Methods & Strategies*. Wright-Patterson Air Force Base, OH: Air Force Research Laboratory, 2011.

Katz, Rita. "The State Department's Twitter War with ISIS is Embarrassing." *Time*, September 16, 2014. http://time.com/3387065/isis-twitter-war-state-department/.

Kirk, Ashley. "Iraq and Syria: How Many Foreign Fighters are Fighting for ISIL?" *The Telegraph*, March 29, 2016. www.telegraph.co.uk/news/2016/03/29/iraq-and-syria-how-many-foreign-fighters-are-fighting-for-isil/.

Miller, Greg, and Scott Higham. "In a Propaganda War against ISIS, the U.S. Tried to Play by the Enemy's Rules." *The Washington Post*, May 8, 2015. www.washingtonpost.com/world/national-security/in-a-propaganda-war-us-tried-to-play-by-the-enemys-rules/2015/05/08/6eb6b732-e52f-11e4-81ea-0649268f729e_story.html.

Teng, Poh Si, and Ben Laffin. "Flirting with the Islamic State." *New York Times*, June 27, 2015. www.nytimes.com/video/world/100000003749550/flirting-with-the-islamic-state.html.

Tzu, Sun. *The Art of War*. London: Everyman's Library, 2018.

Chapter 1: Radicalization and Persuasion

Akhtar, Salman. "The Psychodynamic Dimension of Terrorism." *Psychiatric Annals* 29, no. 6 (1999): 350–355.

Aronson, Elliot, Timothy D. Wilson, and Robin M. Akert. *Social Psychology: The Heart and the Mind*. New York: HarperCollins, 2002.

Bakker, Edwin. *Jihadi Terrorists in Europe: Their Characteristics and the Circumstances in Which They Joined the Jihad—An Exploratory Study*. The Hague: Clingendael Institute, 2006.

Bar-Tal, Daniel. *Shared Beliefs in a Society: Social Psychological Analysis*. Thousand Oaks, CA: Sage, 2000.

Beck, Aaron T. *Cognitive Therapy and the Emotional Disorders*. New York: Plume, 1979.

Berman, Mark. "Prosecutors Say Dylann Roof 'Self-Radicalized' Online, Wrote another Manifesto in Jail." *The Washington Post*, August 22, 2016. www.washingtonpost.com/news/post-nation/wp/2016/08/22/prosecutors-say-accused-charleston-church-gunman-self-radicalized-online.

Blackwell, Dick. "Tune In! Turn On! Sell Out! The Dissolution of Radicalism in Analytic Psychotherapy." *European Journal of Psychotherapy & Counselling* 6 (2003): 21–34.

Blinder, Alan, and Kevin Sack. "Dylann Roof, Addressing Court, Offers No Apology or Explanation for Massacre." *New York Times*, January 4, 2017. www.nytimes.com/2017/01/04/us/dylann-roof-sentencing.html.

Bowyer-Bell, J. *The Dynamics of Armed Struggle*. London: Frank Cass, 1998.

Braddock, Kurt. "Fighting Words: The Persuasive Effect of Online Extremist Narratives on the Radicalization Process." PhD dissertation, The Pennsylvania State University, 2012.

Brown, Rupert. "Social Identity Theory: Past Achievements, Current Problems, and Future Challenges." *European Journal of Social Psychology* 30 (2000): 745–778.

Cilluffo, Frank J., Sharon L. Cardash, and Andrew J. Whitehead. "Radicalization: Behind Bars and Beyond Borders." *The Brown Journal of World Affairs* 13, no. 2 (2007): 113–122.

CNN. "Controversial Cleric of UK Mosque." April 1, 2003. www.cnn.com/2003/WORLD/europe/01/20/uk.hamzaprofile/.

Cohen, Amit. "Hamas Dot Com." *Ma'ariv*, July 2, 2003. www.tomgrossmedia.com/mideastdispatches/archives/000294.html.

Combs, Cynthia C. "The Media as a Showcase for Terrorism." In *Teaching Terror*, ed. James J. F. Forest, 133–154. Oxford: Rowman & Littlefield, 2006.

Creed, W. E. Douglas. "Voice Lessons: Tempered Radicalism and the Use of Voice and Silence." *Journal of Management Studies* 40 (2003): 1502–1536.

de Rosa, Annamaria Silvana. "The Boomerang Effect of Radicalism in Discursive Psychology: A Critical Overview of the Controversy with the Social Representations Theory." *Journal for the Theory of Social Behavior* 36 (2006): 161–201.

Della Porta, Donatella. "Recruitment Processes in Clandestine Political Organizations: Italian Left-Wing Terrorism." In *From Structure to Action: Comparing Social Movement Research across Cultures*, ed. Bert Klandermans, Hanspeter Kriesi, and Sidney G. Tarrow, 155–171. Greenwich, CT: JAI Press, 1988.

Drash, Wayne. "Inside the Bible Study Massacre: A Mom 'Laid in Her Son's Blood.'" *CNN*, December 17, 2015. www.cnn.com/2015/06/19/us/inside-charleston-bible-study-massacre/index.html.

Ferree, Myra Marx. "Resonance and Radicalism: Feminist Framing in the Abortion Debates of the United States and Germany." *American Journal of Sociology* 109, no. 2 (2003): 302–344.

Fishbein, Martin, and Icek Ajzen. *Belief, Attitude, Intention, and Behavior: An Introduction to Theory and Research.* Reading, MA: Addison-Wesley, 1975.

   Predicting and Changing Behavior: The Reasoned Action Approach. New York: Routledge, 2010.

Flam, Helena. "Anger in Repressive Regimes: A Footnote to *Domination and the Arts of Resistance* by James Scott." *European Journal of Social Theory* 7 (2004): 171–188.

Forest, James J. F. "Training Camps and Other Centers of Learning." In *Teaching Terror*, ed. James J. F. Forest, 69–110. Oxford: Rowman & Littlefield, 2006.

Forsythe, Donelson R. *Group Dynamics.* Belmont, CA: Brooks/Cole, 1999.

Fuchs, Douglas, and Lynn. S. Fuchs. "Inclusive Schools Movement and the Radicalization of Special Education Reform." *Exceptional Children* 60, no. 4 (1994): 294–309.

Goodwin, Jeff, James F. Jasper, and Francesca Polletta, eds. *Passionate Politics: Emotions and Social Movements.* University of Chicago Press, 2001.

Gunaratna, Rohan. "Al Qaeda's Lose and Learn Doctrine: The Trajectory from Oplan Bojinka to 9/11." In *Teaching Terror*, ed. James J. F. Forest, 171–188. Oxford: Rowman & Littlefield, 2006.

Hegghammer, Thomas. "Terrorist Recruitment and Radicalization in Saudi Arabia." *Middle East Policy* 13, no. 4 (2006): 39–60.

Hoffman, Bruce. *Al Qaeda, Trends in Terrorism and Future Potentialities: An Assessment.* Santa Monica, CA: RAND Corporation, 2003.

   Inside Terrorism. New York: Columbia University Press, 1998.

Horgan, John. "From Profiles to Pathways and Roots to Routes: Perspectives from Psychology on Radicalization into Terrorism." *Annals of the American Academy of Political and Social Science* 618 (2008): 80–94.

   The Psychology of Terrorism. Abingdon: Routledge, 2014.

   Walking Away from Terrorism: Accounts of Disengagement from Radical and Extremist Movements. Abingdon: Routledge, 2009.

International Criminal Court. "Warrant of Arrest Unsealed against Five LRA Commanders." www.icc-cpi.int/Pages/item.aspx?name=warrant%20of%20arrest%20unsealed%20against%20five%20lra%20commanders.

Jackson, Brian A. "Training for Urban Resistance: The Case of the Provisional Irish Republican Army." In *The Making of a Terrorist: Recruitment, Training, and Root Causes, Vol. 2*, ed. James J. F. Forest, 119–135. Westport, CT: Praeger.

Jäger, Herbert. "The Individual Dimension of Terrorist Action" [in German]. In *Lebenslaufanalysen*, ed. Herbert Jäger, Gerhard Schmidtchen, and Lieselotte Sullwold, 141–174. Opladen: Westdeutscher, 1981.

Jünschke, Klaus. *Spätlese: Texte zu Raf und Knast.* Frankfurt: Verlag Neue Kritik.

Kemper, Theodore D. "Social Constructionist and Positivist Approaches to the Sociology of Emotions." *American Journal of Sociology* 87 (1981): 336–362.

Kilcullen, David. *The Accidental Guerrilla*. Oxford University Press, 2009.

McCauley, Clark. "Jujitsu Politics: Terrorism and Response to Terrorism." In *Collateral Damage: The Psychological Consequences of America's War on Terrorism*, ed. Paul Kimmel and Chris E. Stout, 45–65. Westport, CT: Praeger, 2006.

McCauley, Clark, and Sophia Moskalenko. *Friction: How Radicalization Happens to Them and Us*. Oxford University Press, 2011.

———. "Mechanisms of Political Radicalization: Pathways toward Terrorism." *Terrorism and Political Violence* 20, no. 3 (2008): 415–433.

———. "Understanding Political Radicalization: The Two-Pyramid Model." *American Psychologist* 72, no. 3 (2017): 205–216.

McClatchy. "Sen. Clementa Pinckney on Walter Scott Killing." *The State*, February 7, 2015. www.thestate.com/latest-news/article25339573.html.

Miller, Gerald R. "On Being Persuaded: Some Basic Distinctions." In *The SAGE Handbook of Persuasion: Developments in Theory and Practice*, ed. James Price Dillard and Lijiang Shen, 70–82. Thousand Oaks, CA: Sage, 2013.

Moghaddam, Fathali M. "The Staircase to Terrorism: A Psychological Exploration." *American Psychologist* 60, no. 2 (2005): 161–169.

Morgan, Stephen J. *The Mind of a Terrorist Fundamentalist: The Psychology of Terror Cults*. Brussels: Institute Spiritus Vitus, 2001.

Mullen, Brian. Atrocity as a Function of Lynch Mob Composition." *Personality and Social Psychology Bulletin* 12 (1986): 187–197.

National Commission on Terrorist Attacks Upon the United States. *9/11 Commission Report*. New York: W. W. Norton, 2004.

Neidhardt, Friedhelm. "Soziale Bedingungen Terroristischen Handelns: Das Beispiel der 'Baader-Meinhof-Gruppe' (RAF)." In *Gruppenprozesse*, ed. Wanda von Kaeyer-Katte, Dieter Claessens, Hubert Feger, and Friedhelm Neidhardt, 318–391. Opladen: Westdeutscher, 1982.

Newman, Edward. "Exploring the 'Root Causes' of Terrorism." *Studies in Conflict & Terrorism* 29, no. 8 (2006): 749–772.

O'Neill, Ann. "The 13th Juror: The Radicalization of Dzhokhar Tsarnaev." *CNN*, March 30, 2015. www.reuters.com/article/us-boston-bombings-trial/boston-bomb-suspect-influenced-by-al-qaeda-expert-witness-idUSKBN0MJ0Z620150323.

Ortiz, Erik, and Daniel Arkin. "Dylann Roof 'Almost Didn't Go Through' with Charleston Church Shooting." *NBC News*, June 19, 2015. www.nbcnews.com/storyline/charleston-church-shooting/dylann-roof-almost-didnt-go-through-charleston-church-shooting-n378341.

Palestinian Center for Policy and Survey Research. Palestinian Public Opinion Poll #27. www.pcpsr.org/survey/polls/2008/p27e1.html.

Pappas, Takis S. "Political Leadership and the Emergence of Radical Mass Movements in Democracy." *Comparative Political Studies* 41 (2008): 1117–1140.

Post, Jerrold M., and Gabriel Sheffer. "The Risk of Radicalization and Terrorism in U.S. Muslim Communities." *The Brown Journal of World Affairs* 13, no. 2 (2007): 101–112.

Pressman, Elaine. "Exploring the Sources of Radicalization and Violent Radical-ization: Some Transatlantic Perspectives." *Journal of Security Studies* 2 (2008): 1–20.

Reicher, Stephen, Russell Spears, and Tom Postmes. "A Social Identity Model of Deindividuation Phenomena." *European Review of Social Psychology* 6 (1995): 161–198.

Rubenstein, Richard E. *Alchemists of Revolution.* New York: Basic Books, 1987.

Sageman, Marc. *Leaderless Jihad.* Philadelphia, PA: University of Pennsylvania Press, 2008.

——— *Understanding Terror Networks.* Philadelphia, PA: University of Pennsylvania Press, 2004.

Schmidt, Michael S. "Charleston Suspect was in Contact with Supremacists, Officials Say." *New York Times,* July 3, 2015. www.nytimes.com/2015/07/04/us/dylann-roof-was-in-contact-with-supremacists-officials-say.html.

Seib, Philip, and Dana M. Janbek. *Global Terrorism and New Media: The Post al-Qaeda Generation.* New York: Routledge, 2010.

Shamir, Ronen. "The De-Radicalization of Corporate Social Responsibility." *Critical Sociology* 30 (2004): 669–689.

Shiffman, John. "From Abuse to a Chat Room, A Martyr is Made." Reuters. December 7, 2012. http://graphics.thomsonreuters.com/12/12/JihadJaneAll.pdf.

Silber, Mitchell D., and Arvin Bhatt. *Radicalization in the West: The Homegrown Threat.* New York: NYPD Intelligence Division, 2007. https://sethgodin.typepad.com/seths_blog/files/NYPD_Report-Radicalization_in_the_West.pdf.

Silke, Andrew. "Becoming a Terrorist." In *Victims, and Society: Psychological Perspectives on Terrorism and its Consequences,* ed. Andrew Silke, 29–53. London: John Wiley & Sons, 2003.

Singer, Margaret Thaler. *Cults in Our Midst: The Continuing Fight against their Hidden Menace.* San Francisco, CA: Jossey-Bass, 1995.

Stahelski, Anthony. "Terrorists Are Made, Not Born: Creating Terrorists Using Social Psychological Conditioning." *Cultic Studies Review* 4, no. 1 (2005): 30–40.

Taylor, Max, and John Horgan. "A Conceptual Framework for Addressing Psychological Process in the Development of the Terrorist." *Terrorism and Political Violence* 18, no. 4 (2006): 585–601.

Taylor, S. Levi, Edgar C. O'Neal, Travis Langley, and Ann Houston Butcher. "Anger Arousal, Deindividuation, and Aggression." *Aggressive Behavior* 17, no. 4 (1991): 193–206.

Thayer, Carlyle Alan. "Explaining 'Clean Skins': The Dynamics of Small Group Social Networks and the London Bombers." Paper presented at the Work-shop on Sacrificial Devotion in Comparative Perspective: Tamil Tigers and Beyond, Adelaide, Australia, December 5–7, 2005. www.scribd.com/document/18260792/Thayer-Terrorism-Radicalization-Through-Social-Networks.

US Department of Justice. "Abu Hamza Arrested in London on Terrorism Charges Filed in the United States." Press Release #371, May 27, 2004. www.justice.gov/archive/opa/pr/2004/May/04_crm_371.htm.

Valdmanis, Richard. "Boston Bomb Suspect Influenced by Al Qaeda: Expert Witness." Reuters, March 23, 2015. www.reuters.com/article/us-boston-bombings-trial/boston-bomb-suspect-influenced-by-al-qaeda-expert-witness-idUSKBN0MJ0Z620150323.

Waller, James. *Becoming Evil: How Ordinary People Commit Genocide and Mass Killing*. Oxford University Press, 2002.

Wangsness, Lisa, and Brian Ballou. "Islam Might Have Had Secondary Role in Boston Attacks." *Boston Globe*, April 20, 2013. www.bostonglobe.com/metro/2013/04/19/scholars-caution-against-drawing-easy-religious-conclusions-about-suspects-boston-marathon-bombings/a5Iucv4ntQHgSvXchQqKOM/story.html.

Wasmund, Klaus. "The Political Socialization of West German Terrorists." In *Political Violence and Terror: Motifs and Motivations*, ed. Peter H. Merkl, 191–228. Berkeley, CA: University of California Press, 1986.

Weimann, Gabriel. "New Terrorism and New Media." *Wilson Center Research Series Vol. 2*, 2014. www.wilsoncenter.org/sites/default/files/STIP_140501_new_terrorism_F_0.pdf.

Terrorism on the Internet: The New Arena, the New Challenges. Washington, DC: United States Institute of Peace Press, 2006.

Chapter 2: Lessons from Past and Current Counter-Radicalization Efforts

Active Change Foundation. "Preventing Extremism: One-Day Prevent Extremism Training." www.activechangefoundation.org/Event/preventing-extremism.

Agenfor International. "EuRad: Shari'ah Based Counterradicalization." www.agenformedia.com/international-projects/eurad.

"ISDEP: Improving Security by Democratic Participation." www.agenformedia.com/international-projects/isdep.

Beirich, Heidi. "The Year in Hate: Rage against Change." *Southern Poverty Law Center Intelligence Report* (February 20, 2019). www.splcenter.org/fighting-hate/intelligence-report/2019/year-hate-rage-against-change.

Benmelech, Efraim, and Esteban F. Klor. "What Explains the Flow of Foreign Fighters to ISIS?" NBER Working Paper 22190 (2016). National Bureau of Economic Research. www.nber.org/papers/w22190.pdf.

Bertelsen, Preven. "Danish Preventative Measures and De-radicalization Strategies: The Aarhus Model." *Panorama* 1 (2015): 241–253.

Boucek, Christopher. "Saudi Arabia's 'Soft' Counterterrorism Strategy: Prevention, Rehabilitation, and Aftercare." *Carnegie Papers* 97 (2008). https://carnegieendowment.org/files/cp97_boucek_saudi_final.pdf.

Braddock, Kurt, and John Horgan. "Towards a Guide for Constructing and Disseminating Counternarratives to Reduce Support for Terrorism." *Studies in Conflict & Terrorism* 39, no. 5 (2016): 381–404.

Braddock, Kurt, and John F. Morrison. "Cultivating Trust and Perceptions of Source Credibility in Online Counternarratives Intended to Reduce Support for Terrorism." *Studies in Conflict & Terrorism* (in press).

Bundesamt für Migration und Flüchtlinge, *Faith or Extremism? Help for Relatives: The Advice Centre on Radicalisation.* www.bamf.de/SharedDocs/Anlagen/EN/Publikationen/Broschueren/glaube-oder-extremismus.pdf.

Calgary Police Service. "ReDirect: About Us." www.redirectprogram.ca/.

Cartwright, Mark. "Sphinx." *Ancient History Encyclopedia*, September 8, 2012. www.ancient.eu/sphinx/.

Casebeer, William D., and James A. Russell. "Storytelling and Terrorism: Towards a Comprehensive 'Counter-Narrative' Strategy." *Strategic Insights* 4, no. 3 (2005). https://apps.dtic.mil/dtic/tr/fulltext/u2/a521449.pdf.

Centre for Sustainable Conflict Resolution. *BRAVE: Building Resilience against Violent Extremism.* http://braveprogram.org.

Counter Extremism Project. "Digital Disruption: Fighting Online Extremism." www.counterextremism.com/digital-disruption.

Davey, Melissa. "Victoria's Deradicalisation Plan: A 'Soviet-Style' Idea that Will Only Alienate—Expert." *The Guardian*, June 8, 2015. www.theguardian.com/australia-news/2015/jun/08/victorias-deradicalisation-plan-a-soviet-style-idea-that-will-only-alienate-expert.

Federal Bureau of Investigation. *Don't Be a Puppet.* https://cve.fbi.gov/home.html.

Frazer, Sir James George, ed. *Apollodorus Library.* www.perseus.tufts.edu/hopper/text?doc=Apollod.

Government of India Ministry of Communications. "Website Blocked Following Court Order." December 31, 2014. http://pib.nic.in/newsite/mbErel.aspx?relid=114259.

Harrigan, Jane. "The Rise of Religious-Based Radicalism and the Deradicalisation Programme in Bangladesh." In *Deradicalising Violent Extremists: Counter-Radicalisation and Deradicalisation Programmes and their Impact in Muslim Majority States*, ed. Hamed El-Said and Jane Harrigan, 50–73. London: Routledge, 2013.

HM Government. *Channel Duty Guidance: Protecting Vulnerable People from being Drawn into Terrorism.* London: Crown Copyright, 2015.

Horgan, John, and Mary Beth Altier. "The Future of Terrorist De-Radicalization Programs." *Georgetown Journal of International Affairs* 13, no. 2 (2012): 83–90.

Horgan, John, and Kurt Braddock. "Rehabilitating the Terrorists? Challenges in Assessing the Effectiveness of De-radicalization Programs." *Terrorism and Political Violence* 22, no. 2 (2010): 267–291.

Institute for Strategic Dialogue. *Case Study Report: Community Policing and the Prevention of Radicalisation, Belgium.* www.counterextremism.org/download_file/88/134/117/.

Case Study Report: Slotevaart Action Plan to Prevent Radicalisation. www.counterextremism.org/download_file/205/134/508/.

Extreme Dialogue. https://extremedialogue.org/sites/isd.hocext.co.uk/files/2018-03/ISD-Brochure-Web.pdf.

Katz, Rita. "The State Department's Twitter War with ISIS is Embarrassing." *Time*, September 16, 2014. http://time.com/3387065/isis-twitter-war-state-department/.

Köhler, Daniel. *Understanding Deradicalization: Methods, Tools and Programs for Countering Violent Extremism*. London: Routledge, 2017.

Langat, Anthony. "Muslim Leaders are Trying to Change the Way Kenya Fights Terrorism." *Agence France-Presse*, August 23, 2015. www.pri.org/stories/2015-08-23/muslim-leaders-are-trying-change-way-kenya-fights-terrorism.

Leuprecht, Christian, Todd Hataley, Sophia Moskalenko, and Clark McCauley. "Winning the Battle but Losing the War? Narrative and Counter-Narratives Strategy." *Perspectives on Terrorism* 3, no. 2 (2009): 25–35.

Life After Hate. "Our Programs." www.lifeafterhate.org/programs.

"Who We Are." www.lifeafterhate.org/about-us-1.

Miller, Greg, and Scott Higham. "In a Propaganda War against ISIS, the U.S. Tried to Play by the Enemy's Rules." *The Washington Post*, May 8, 2015. www.washingtonpost.com/world/national-security/in-a-propaganda-war-us-tried-to-play-by-the-enemys-rules/2015/05/08/6eb6b732-e52f-11e4-81ea-0649268f729e_story.html.

Morlin, Bill. "The 'Alt-Right' is Still Killing People." *Southern Poverty Law Center Intelligence Report* (February 20, 2019). www.splcenter.org/sites/default/files/intelligence_report_166.pdf.

Mothers for Life Network. "About the Mothers for Life Network." www.mothersforlife.org/en/about-us.

Noricks, Darcy M. E. "Disengagement and Deradicalization: Processes and Programs." In *Social Science for Counterterrorism*, ed. Paul K. Davis and Kim Cragin, 299–322. Santa Monica, CA: RAND Corporation, 2009.

Qadir, Zahra. "Preventing Extremism." Active Change Foundation. www.activechangefoundation.org/blog/blog-post-3.

Schmid, Alex, and Albert Jongman. *Political Terrorism: A New Guide to Actors, Authors, Concepts, Databases, Theories and Literature*. Amsterdam: North Holland Publishing, 1988.

Stampnitzky, Lisa. "Disciplining an Unruly Field: Terrorism Experts and Theories of Scientific/Intellectual Production." *Qualitative Sociology* 34, no. 1 (2011): 1–19.

Stop Djihadisme. "Fight against Jihadist Propaganda on the Internet" [in French]. www.stop-djihadisme.gouv.fr/que-faire/relayer-contre-discours/lutter-contre-propagande-djihadiste-internet.

"How to Prevent and Fight against the Radicalization of Minors?" [in French]. www.stop-djihadisme.gouv.fr/lutte-contre-terrorisme-radicalisation/prevention-radicalisation/comment-prevenir-lutter-contre.

The Local. "Extremism Hotline Swamped with Calls." *The Local – Austria*, January 21, 2015. www.thelocal.at/20150121/austrian-extremism-hotline-swamped-with-calls.

"Swedish Extremism Hotline Prepares to Open." *The Local – Sweden*, October 29, 2015. www.thelocal.se/20151029/swedish-extremism-hotline-prepares-to-open.

The Redirect Method: Results. https://redirectmethod.org/pilot/#results.

The Redirect Method: Targeting. https://redirectmethod.org/pilot/#targeting.

Thomas, Paul. "Failed and Friendless: The UK's 'Preventing Violent Extremism' Programme." *The British Journal of Politics and International Relations* 12 (2010). 442–458.

"Youth, Terrorism and Education: Britain's Prevent Programme." *International Journal of Lifelong Education* 35, no. 2 (2016): 171–187.

Tuck, Henry, and Tanya Silverman. *The Counter-Narrative Handbook*. Washington, DC: ISD Global, 2016. www.isdglobal.org/wp-content/uploads/2018/10/Counter-narrative-Handbook_1_web.pdf.

VINK. "Are You Worried about Someone You Know?" [in Danish]. City of Copenhagen. https://vink.kk.dk/indhold/er-du-bekymret-en-du-kender.

Chapter 3: Extremist Narratives and Counter-Narratives

"3 Men Charged in Bombings of Seven Abortion Facilities." *New York Times*, January 20, 1985. www.nytimes.com/1985/01/20/us/3-men-charged-in-bombings-of-seven-abortion-facilities.html.

Abbott, H. Porter. *The Cambridge Introduction to Narrative*, 2nd edition. New York: Cambridge University Press, 2008.

Alhabash, Saleem, and Anna R. McAlister. "Redefining Virality in Less Broad Strokes: Predicting Viral Behavioral Intentions from Motivations and Uses of Facebook and Twitter." *New Media & Society* 17, no. 8 (2015): 1317–1339.

Allen, Mike, and Raymond W. Preiss. "Comparing the Persuasiveness of Narrative and Statistical Evidence using Meta-Analysis." *Communication Research Reports* 14 (1997): 125–131.

Allocca, Kevin. "Why Videos Go Viral." *TED Talks*. November, 2011. www.ted.com/talks/kevin_allocca_why_videos_go_viral/up-next.

Ashour, Omar. "Online De-Radicalization? Countering Violent Extremist Narratives: Message, Messenger and Media Strategy." *Perspectives on Terrorism* 4, no. 6 (2010). www.terrorismanalysts.com/pt/index.php/pot/article/view/128/html.

Baesler, E. James, and Judee K. Burgoon. "The Temporal Effects of Story and Statistical Evidence on Belief Change." *Communication Research* 21, no. 5 (1994): 582–602.

Bandura, Albert. "Social Cognitive Theory in Cultural Context." *Applied Psychology* 51, no. 2 (2002): 269–290.

Barthes, Roland. "Introduction to the Structural Analysis of Narrative." In *A Barthes Reader*, ed. Susan Sontag, 251–295. New York: Hill & Wang, 1982.

Bass, Bernard M. "Leadership: Good, Better, Best." *Organizational Dynamics* 13, no. 3 (1985): 26–40.

Berelson, Bernard. *Content Analysis in Communication Research*. New York: Free Press, 1952.

Berger, Jonah, and Katherine L. Milkman. "Emotion and Virality: What Makes Online Content Go Viral?" *GfK Marketing Intelligence Review* 5, no. 1 (2013): 19–23.

Bernardi, Daniel Leonard, Pauline Hope Cheong, Chris Lundry, and Scott W. Ruston. *Narrative Landmines: Rumors, Islamist Extremism, and the Struggle for Strategic Influence*. New Brunswick, NJ: Rutgers University Press, 2012.

Bloom, Mia, Hicham Tiflati, and John Horgan. "Navigating ISIS's Preferred Platform: Telegram." *Terrorism and Political Violence* (in press). doi:10.1080/09546553.2017.1339695.

Bouncken, Ricarda B., Aim-Orn Imcharoen, and Wilma Klaasen-van-Husen. "What Does Collectivism Mean for Leadership and Teamwork Performance? An Empirical Study in Professional Service Firms." *Journal of International Business and Economics* 7, no. 2 (2007): 5–9.

Boyatzis, Richard E. *Transforming Qualitative Information: Thematic Analysis and Code Development.* Thousand Oaks, CA: Sage, 1998.

Braddock, Kurt. "Developing and Disseminating Narratives for Countering Violent Extremism: The Utility of Former Offenders." Presentation at the Understanding Terrorism and Political Violence Conference, Cork, Ireland, March 30, 2015.

——— "Fighting Words: The Persuasive Effect of Online Extremist Narratives on the Radicalization Process." PhD dissertation, The Pennsylvania State University, 2012.

——— "The Talking Cure? Communication and Psychological Impact in Prison De-Radicalisation Programmes." In *Prisons, Terrorism, and Extremism: Critical Issues in Management, Radicalisation and Reform*, ed. Andrew Silke, 60–74. London: Routledge, 2014.

——— "The Utility of Narratives for Promoting Radicalization: The Case of the Animal Liberation Front." *Dynamics of Asymmetric Conflict* 8, no. 1 (2011): 38–59.

Braddock, Kurt, and James Price Dillard. "Meta-Analytic Evidence for the Persuasive Effect of Narratives on Beliefs, Attitudes, Intentions, and Behaviors." *Communication Monographs* 83, no. 4 (2016): 446–467.

Braddock, Kurt and John Horgan. "Towards a Guide for Constructing and Disseminating Counternarratives to Reduce Support for Terrorism." *Studies in Conflict & Terrorism* 39, no. 5 (2016): 381–404.

Braddock, Kurt, and John F. Morrison. "Cultivating Trust and Perceptions of Source Credibility in Online Counternarratives Intended to Reduce Support for Terrorism." *Studies in Conflict & Terrorism.* Under review.

Brehm, Jack W. *A Theory of Psychological Reactance.* New York: Academic Press, 1966.

Brown, Jane D., Kim Walsh Childers, and Cynthia S. Waszak. "Television and Adolescent Sexuality." *Journal of Adolescent Health Care* 11 (1990): 62–70.

Burgoon, Michael, Eusebio Alvaro, Joseph Grandpre, and Michael Voloudakis. "Revisiting the Theory of Psychological Reactance." In *The Persuasion Handbook: Theory and Practice*, ed. James Price Dillard and Michael Pfau, 213–232. Thousand Oaks, CA: Sage, 2002.

Busselle, Rick, and Helena Bilandzic. "Fictionality and Perceived Realism in Experiencing Stories: A Model of Narrative Comprehension and Engagement." *Communication Theory* 18 (2008): 255–280.

Carter, Owen, Robert Donovan, and Geoffrey Jalleh. "Using Viral E-mails to Distribute Tobacco Control Advertisements: An Experimental Investigation." *Journal of Health Communication* 16 (2011): 698–707.

CBS News Staff. "McVeigh Vents on '60 Minutes.'" *CBS News*, March 13, 2000. www.cbsnews.com/news/mcveigh-vents-on-60-minutes/.

Cohen, Jacob. "A Coefficient of Agreement for Nominal Scales." *Educational and Psychological Measurement* 20, no. 1 (1960): 37–46.

Cohen, Jonathan. "Defining Identification: A Theoretical Look at the Identification of Audiences with Media Characters." *Mass Communication and Society* 4, no. 3 (2001): 245–264.

Conway, Maura. "Terrorism and the Internet: New Media – New Threat?" *Parliamentary Affairs* 59, no. 2 (2006): 283–298.

Corman, Steven R. "Understanding the Role of Narrative as Extremist Strategic Communication." In *Countering Violent Extremism: Scientific Methods and Strategies*, ed. Laurie Fenstermacher and Todd Levanthal, 36–43. Washington, DC: Air Force Research Laboratory, 2011. https://apps.dtic.mil/dtic/tr/fulltext/u2/a552480.pdf.

Corman, Steven R., and Jill S. Schiefelbein. "Communication and Media Strategy in the Islamist War of Ideas." Consortium for Strategic Communication Report #0601, Arizona State University, April 20, 2006. http://csc.asu.edu/wp-content/uploads/2012/06/119.pdf.

Couch, Christina. "Life After Hate: Recovering from Racism." Master's thesis, Massachusetts Institute of Technology, 2015.

Dahlstrom, Michael F. "The Role of Causality in Information Acceptance in Narratives: An Example from Science Communication." *Communication Research* 37, no. 6 (2010): 857–875.

Eckler, Petya, and Paul Bolls. "Spreading the Virus: Emotional Tone of Viral Advertising and its Effect on Forwarding Intentions and Attitudes." *Journal of Interactive Advertising* 11, no. 2 (2011): 1–11.

Fisher, Walter R. *Human Communication as Narration: Toward a Philosophy of Reason, Value, and Action*. Columbia, SC: University of South Carolina Press, 1987.

Furlow, R. Bennett, and H. L. Goodall. "The War of Ideas and the Battle of Narratives." *Cultural Studies ←→ Critical Methodologies* 11, no. 3 (2011): 215–223.

Genette, Gérard. *Figures of Literary Discourse*. New York: Columbia University Press, 1982.

Gesser-Edelsburg, Anat, and Ronit Endevelt. "An Entertainment-Education Study of Stereotypes and Prejudice against Women: An Evaluation of *Fat Pig*." *Health Education Journal* 70, no. 4 (2011): 374–382.

Gill, Paul, Emily Corner, Maura Conway, Amy Thornton, Mia Bloom, and John Horgan. "Terrorist Use of the Internet by the Numbers." *Criminology and Public Policy* 16, no. 1 (2017): 99–117.

Goodall Jr., H. L. *Counter-Narrative: How Progressive Academics Can Challenge Extremists and Promote Social Justice*. Walnut Creek, CA: Left Coast Press, 2010.

Goodstein, Laurie. "U.S. Muslims Take on ISIS' Recruiting Machine." *New York Times*, February 19, 2015. www.nytimes.com/2015/02/20/us/muslim-leaders-in-us-seek-to-counteract-extremist-recruiters.html.

Goossens, Luc, Wim Beyers, Mieke Emmen, and Marcel A. G. Van Aken. "The Imaginary Audience and Personal Fable: Factor Analyses and Concurrent

Validity of the 'New Look' Measures." *Journal of Research on Adolescence* 12, no. 2 (2002): 193–215.

Gray, Jennifer B., and Nancy G. Harrington. "Narrative and Framing: A Test of an Integrated Message Strategy in the Exercise Context." *Journal of Health Communication* 16, no. 3 (2011): 264–281.

Green, Melanie C. "Narratives and Cancer Communication." *Journal of Communication* 56 (2006): S163–S183.

Green, Melanie C., and Timothy C. Brock. "In the Mind's Eye: Transportation-Imagery Model of Narrative Persuasion." In *Narrative Impact: Social and Cognitive Foundations*, ed. Melanie C. Green, Jeffrey J. Strange, and Timothy C. Brock, 315–341. Mahwah, NJ: Lawrence Erlbaum Associates, 2002.

Green, Melanie C., and Timothy C. Brock. "The Role of Transportation in the Persuasiveness of Public Narratives." *Journal of Personality and Social Psychology* 79, no. 5 (2000): 701–721.

Greene, Kathryn, and Laura S. Brinn. "Messages Influencing College Women's Tanning Bed Use: Statistical versus Narrative Evidence Format and a Self-Assessment to Increase Perceived Susceptibility." *Journal of Health Communication* 8, no. 5 (2003): 443–461.

Gruen, Lori, and Peter Singer. *Animal Liberation: A Graphic Guide*. London: Camden Press, 1987.

Gumbel, Andrew, and Roger G. Charles. *Oklahoma City: What the Investigation Missed – and Why it Still Matters*. New York: William Morrow, 2012.

Halverson, Jeffry R., H. L. Goodall Jr., and Steven R. Corman. *Master Narratives of Islamic Extremism*. New York: Palgrave Macmillan, 2011.

Heath, Chip, and Dan Heath. *Made to Stick: Why Some Ideas Survive and Others Die*. New York: Doubleday, 2007.

Heimbach, Irina, Benjamin Schiller, Thorsten Strufe, and Oliver Hinz. "Content Virality on Online Social Networks: Empirical Evidence from Twitter, Facebook, and Google+ on German News Websites." *Proceedings of the 26th ACM Conference on Hypertext & Social Media* (2015): 39–47. http://dynamic-networks.org/publications/papers/papers/content-virality.pdf.

Hinyard, Leslie J., and Matthew W. Kreuter. "Using Narrative Communication as a Tool for Behavior Change: A Conceptual, Theoretical, and Empirical Overview." *Health Education & Behavior* 34, no. 5 (2007): 777–792.

Hogan, Patrick Colm. *The Mind and its Stories: Narrative Universals and Human Emotion*. New York: Cambridge University Press, 2003.

Homeland Security Committee Task Force on Combating Terrorist and Foreign Fighters Travel. *Final Report*. Washington, DC: Homeland Security Committee, 2015.

Horgan, John. *The Psychology of Terrorism*, 2nd edition. London: Routledge, 2014.

Hovland, Carl I., and Walter Weiss. "The Influence of Source Credibility on Communication Effectiveness." *Public Opinion Quarterly* 15, no. 4 (1951): 635–650.

Kazoleas, Dean. "A Comparison of the Persuasive Effectiveness of Qualitative versus Quantitative Evidence: A Test of Explanatory Hypotheses." *Communication Quarterly* 41, no. 1 (1993): 40–50.

Khader, Majeed, Neo Loo Seng, Gabriel Ong, Eunice Tan Mingyi, and Jeffry Chin, eds. *Combating Violent Extremism and Radicalization in the Digital Era.* Hershey, PA: IGI Global, 2016.

Kim, Hyun Suk, Sungkyoung Lee, Joseph N. Capella, Lisa Vera, and Sherry Emery. "Content Characteristics Driving the Diffusion of Antismoking Messages: Implications for Cancer Prevention in the Emerging Public Communication Environment." *Journal of the National Cancer Institute Monographs* 47 (2013): 182–187.

Kopfman, Jenifer E., Sandi W. Smith, James K. Ah Yun, and Annemarie Hodges. "Affective and Cognitive Reactions to Narrative versus Statistical Evidence Organ Donation Messages." *Journal of Applied Communication Research* 26, no. 3 (1998): 279–300.

Lemal, Marijke, and Jan Van den Bulck. "Testing the Effectiveness of a Skin Cancer Narrative in Promoting Positive Health Behavior: A Pilot Study" *Preventative Medicine* 51, no. 2 (2010): 178–181.

Leuprecht, Christian, Todd Hataley, Sophia Moskalenko, and Clark McCauley. "Winning the Battle but Losing the War? Narrative and Counter-Narratives Strategy." *Perspectives on Terrorism* 3, no. 2 (2009): 25–35.

Levanthal, Howard. "Findings and Theory in the Study of Fear Communications." In *Advances in Experimental Social Psychology*, Volume 5, ed. Leonard Berkowitz, 119–186. New York: Academic Press, 1970.

McGrane, Wendy L., Eric B. Allely, and Frank J. Toth. "The Use of Interactive Media for HIV/AIDS Prevention in the Military Community." *Military Medicine* 155, no. 6 (1990): 235–240.

McVeigh, Tracy. ""The McVeigh Letters: Why I Bombed Oklahoma." *The Guardian*, May 6, 2001. www.theguardian.com/world/2001/may/06/mcveigh.usa.

Mills, Adam J. "Virality in Social Media: The SPIN Framework." *Journal of Public Affairs* 12, no. 2 (2012): 162–169.

Moyer-Gusé, Emily. "Toward a Theory of Entertainment Persuasion: Explaining the Persuasive Effects of Entertainment-Education Messages." *Communication Theory* 18 (2008): 407–425.

Onega, Susana, and José Ángel Garcia Landa, eds. *Narratology.* New York: Routledge, 2014.

Patton, Michael Quinn. *Qualitative Research & Evaluation Methods.* Thousand Oaks, CA: Sage, 2002.

Pennebaker, James W., and Janet D. Seagal. "Forming a Story: The Health Benefits of Narrative." *Journal of Clinical Psychology* 55 (1999): 1243–1254.

Prati, Gabriele, Luca Pietrantoni, and Bruna Zani. "Influenza Vaccination: The Persuasiveness of Messages Among People Aged 65 Years and Older." *Health Communication* 27, no. 5 (2012): 413–420.

Prentice, Deborah A., Richard J. Gerrig, and Daniel S. Bailis. "What Readers Bring to the Processing of Fictional Texts." *Psychonomic Bulletin & Review* 4, no. 3 (1997): 416–420.

Quiggin, Tom. "Understanding al-Qaeda's Ideology for Counter-Narrative Work." *Perspectives on Terrorism* 3, no. 2 (2009). www.terrorismanalysts.com/pt/index.php/pot/article/view/67/html.

Richardson, Brian. *Narrative Dynamics: Essays on Time, Plot, Closure, and Frames.* Columbus, OH: Ohio State University Press, 2002.

Rimmon-Kenan, Shlomith. *Narrative Fiction: Contemporary Poetics*. London: Routledge, 1996.

Ryan, Marie-Laure. "Toward a Definition of Narrative." In *The Cambridge Companion to Narrative*, ed. David Herman, 22–36. New York: Cambridge University Press, 2007.

Sageman, Marc. *Understanding Terror Networks*. Philadelphia, PA: University of Pennsylvania Press, 2004.

Schiappa, Edward, Peter B. Gregg, and Dean E. Hewes. "Can a Television Series Change Attitudes about Death? A Study of College Students and *Six Feet Under*." *Death Studies* 28, no. 5 (2004): 459–474.

Screier, Margrit. *Qualitative Content Analysis in Practice*. London: Sage, 2012.

Shelley, Cameron. "Analogical Counterarguments: A Taxonomy for Critical Thinking." *Argumentation* 18 (2004): 223–238.

Slater, Michael D. "Choosing Audience Segmentation Strategies and Methods for Health Communication." In *Designing Health Messages: Approaches from Communication Theory and Public Health Practice*, ed. Edward Maibach and Roxanne Louiselle Parrott, 186–198. Thousand Oaks, CA: Sage, 1995.

Slater, Michael D., and Donna Rouner. "Entertainment-Education and Elaboration Likelihood: Understanding the Processing of Narrative Persuasion." *Communication Theory* 12, no. 2 (2002): 173–191.

Thomas, Pierre. "Army of God Letters Claim Responsibility for Clinic Bombing." *CNN*, February 2, 1998. www.cnn.com/US/9802/02/clinic .bombing.530pm/index.html?_s=PM:US.

Waldman, Peter, and Hugh Pope. "Crusade Reference Reinforces Fears War on Terrorism is Against Muslims." *The Wall Street Journal*, September 21, 2001. www.wsj.com/articles/SB1001020294332922160.

Walsh, Nick Paton, Salma Abdelaziz, Mark Phillips, and Mehamed Hasan. "ISIS Brides Flee Caliphate as Noose Tightens on Terror Group." *CNN*, July 17, 2017. www.cnn.com/2017/07/17/middleeast/raqqa-isis-brides/index.html

Weng, Lilian, Filippo Menczer, and Yong-Yeol Ahn. "Virality Prediction and Community Structure in Social Networks" *Scientific Reports* 3, no. 2522 (2013). www.nature.com/articles/srep02522.pdf.

Wilkin, Holley A., Thomas W. Valente, Sheila Murphy, Michael J. Cody, Grace Huang, and Vicki Beck. "Does Entertainment-Education Work with Latinos in the United States? Identification and the Effects of a Telenovela Breast Cancer Storyline." *Journal of Health Communication* 12, no. 5 (2007): 455–469.

Wood, Graeme. "What ISIS Really Wants." *The Atlantic*, March, 2015. www .theatlantic.com/magazine/archive/2015/03/what-isis-really-wants/384980/.

Yalch, Richard F., and Rebecca Elmore-Yalch. The Effect of Numbers on the Route to Persuasion." *Journal of Consumer Research* 11 (1984): 522–527.

Chapter 4: Attitudinal Inoculation, Radicalization, and Counter-Radicalization

Abramson, Joseph. "Comparing Advertising, Inoculation Theory, and the Prevention of Attitude Change among Brand Loyal Consumers: A Laboratory Experiment." Dissertation, Louisiana State University, 1977.

An, Chasu. "Efficacy of Inoculation Strategies in Promoting Resistance to Political Attack Messages: Source Credibility Perspective." Dissertation, University of Oklahoma, 2003.

An, Chasu, and Michael Pfau. "The Efficacy of Inoculation in Televised Political Debates." *Journal of Communication* 54, no. 3 (2004): 421–436.

Banas, John A., and Stephen A. Rains. "A Meta-Analysis of Research on Inoculation Theory." *Communication Monographs* 77, no. 3 (2010): 281–311.

Bernard, Mark M., Gregory B. Maio, and James M. Olson. "The Vulnerability of Values to Attack: Inoculation of Values and Value-Relevant Attitudes." *Personality and Social Psychology Bulletin* 29, no. 1 (2003): 63–75.

Bither, Stewart, Ira J. Dolich, and Elaine B. Nell. "The Application of Attitude Immunization Techniques in Marketing." *Journal of Marketing Research* 8 (1971): 56–61.

Borchgrevink, Aage. *A Norwegian Tragedy: Anders Behring Breivik and the Massacre on Utøya.* Cambridge: Polity Press, 2013.

Braddock, Kurt. "Developing and Disseminating Narratives for Countering Violent Extremism: The Utility of Former Offenders." Paper presented at the Understanding Terrorism and Political Violence Conference, Cork, Ireland, March 2015.

"Vaccinating against Hate: Using Inoculation to Confer to Resistance to Persuasion by Extremist Propaganda." *Journal of Communication* (in press).

Braddock, Kurt, and John Horgan. "Towards a Guide for Constructing and Disseminating Counternarratives to Reduce Support for Terrorism." *Studies in Conflict & Terrorism* 39, no. 5 (2016): 381–404.

Braddock, Kurt, and John Morrison. "Cultivating Trust and Source Credibility in Online Counternarratives Intended to Reduce Support for Terrorism." *Studies in Conflict & Terrorism* (in press).

Brehm, Jack Williams. *A Theory of Psychological Reactance.* New York: Academic Press, 1966.

Brehm, Sharon S., and Jack W. Brehm. *Psychological Reactance: A Theory of Freedom and Control.* New York: Academic Press, 1981.

Compton, Josh. "Inoculation Theory." In *The SAGE Handbook of Persuasion: Developments in Theory and Practice*, ed. James Price Dillard and Lijiang Shen, 220–236. Thousand Oaks, CA: Sage, 2013.

Compton, Josh, Ben Jackson, and James A. Dimmock. "Persuading Others to Avoid Persuasion: Inoculation Theory and Resistant Health Attitudes." *Frontiers in Psychology* 7 (2016): article 122.

Compton, Josh, and Michael Pfau. "Inoculating against Pro-Plagiarism Justifications: Rational and Affective Strategies." *Journal of Applied Communication Research* 36, no. 1 (2008): 98–119.

"Inoculation Theory of Resistance to Influence at Maturity: Recent Progress in Theory Development and Application and Suggestions for Future Research." In *Communication Yearbook 29*, ed. Pamela J. Kalbfleisch, 97–145. New York: Routledge, 2005.

"Use of Inoculation to Foster Resistance to Credit Card Marketing Targeting College Students." *Journal of Applied Communication Research* 32 (2004): 343–364.

Dillard, James Price, and Lijiang Shen. "On the Nature of Reactance and its Role in Persuasive Health Communication." *Communication Monographs* 72 (2005): 144–168.

El-Khoury, Christine. "Anti-Muslim Extremists: How Far Will They Go?" *Australian Broadcasting Corporation*, November 22, 2015. www.abc.net.au/radionational/programs/backgroundbriefing/anti-muslim-extremists-how-far-will-they-go/6954442.

Esposito, John L. *The Oxford Dictionary of Islam*. Oxford University Press, 2003.

Godbold, Linda C., and Michael Pfau. "Conferring Resistance to Peer Pressure among Adolescents: Using Inoculation Theory to Discourage Alcohol Use." *Communication Research* 27, no. 4 (2000): 411–437.

Horgan, John. *Walking Away from Terrorism: Accounts of Disengagement from Radical and Extremist Movements*. Abingdon: Routledge, 2009.

Interfaith Voices. "Losing a Child to Extremism, Stopping Others" [podcast]. http://interfaithradio.org/Archive/2016-June/Losing_a_Child_to_Extremism__Stopping_Others.

Ivanov, Bobi. "Designing Inoculation Messages for Health Communication Campaigns." In *Health Communication Message Design: Theory and Practice*, ed. Hyunyi Cho, 73–93. Thousand Oaks, CA: Sage, 2012.

Ivanov, Bobi, William J. Burns, Timothy L. Sellnow, Elizabeth L. Petrun Sayers, Shari R. Veil, and Marcus W. Mayorga. "Using an Inoculation Message Approach to Promote Public Confidence in Protective Agencies." *Journal of Applied Communication Research* 44, no. 4 (2016): 381–398.

Ivanov, Bobi, Michael Pfau, and Kimberly A. Parker. "The Attitude Base as a Moderator of the Effectiveness of Inoculation Strategy." *Communication Monographs* 76, no. 1 (2009): 47–72.

Kamins, Michael A., and Henry Assael. "Two-Sided Versus One-Sided Appeals: A Cognitive Perspective on Argumentation, Source Derogation, and the Effect of Disconfirming Trial on Belief Change." *Journal of Marketing Research* 24 (1987): 29–39.

Lim, Joon Soo, and Eyun-Jung Ki. "Resistance to Ethically Suspicious Parody Video on YouTube: A Test of Inoculation Theory." *Journalism and Mass Communication Quarterly* 84, no. 4 (2007): 713–728.

Mason, Alicia M., and Claude H. Miller. "Inoculation Message Treatments for Curbing Noncommunicable Disease Development." *Pan American Journal of Public Health* 34, no. 1 (2013): 29–35.

McGuire, William J. "Inducing Resistance to Persuasion: Some Contemporary Approaches." In *Advances in Experimental Social Psychology 1*, ed. Leonard Berkowitz, 191–229. New York: Academic Press, 1964.

"The Effectiveness of Supportive and Refutational Defenses in Immunizing and Restoring Beliefs against Persuasion." *Sociometry* 24, no. 2 (1961): 184–197.

McGuire, William J., and Demetrios Papageorgis. "Effectiveness of Forewarning in Developing Resistance to Persuasion." *The Public Opinion Quarterly* 26, no. 1 (1962): 24–34.

"The Relative Efficacy of Various Types of Prior Belief-Defense in Producing Immunity against Persuasion." *Journal of Abnormal and Social Psychology* 62 (1961): 327–337.

Miller, Claude H., Bobi Ivanov, Jeanetta Sims, Josh Compton, Kylie J. Harrison, Kimberly A. Parker, James L. Parker, and Joshua M. Averbeck. "Boosting the Potency of Resistance: Combining the Motivational Forces of Inoculation and Psychological Reactance." *Human Communication Research* 39 (2013): 127–155.

News Corp Australia. "Australian Man Brenton Tarrant Named as Christchurch Gunman as Four Taken into Custody." *The West Australian*, March 15, 2019. https://thewest.com.au/news/terrorism/australian-man-brenton-tarrant-named-as-christchurch-gunman-as-four-taken-into-custody-ng-b881137083z.

Parker, Kimberly A., Bobi Ivanov, and Josh Compton. "Inoculation's Efficacy with Young Adults' Risky Behaviors: Can Inoculation Confer Cross-Protection over Related but Untreated Issues?" *Health Communication* 27, no. 3 (2012): 223–233.

Parker, Kimberly A., Stephen A. Rains, and Bobi Ivanov. "Examining the 'Blanket of Protection' Conferred by Inoculation: The Effects of Inoculation Messages on the Cross-Protection of Related Attitudes." *Communication Monographs* 83, no. 1 (2016): 49–68.

Pfau, Michael. "Designing Messages for Behavioral Inoculation." In *Designing Health Messages: Approaches from Communication Theory and Public Health Practice*, ed. Edward Maibach and Roxanne Louiselle Parrott, 99–113. Thousand Oaks, CA: Sage, 1995.

"The Inoculation Model of Resistance to Influence." In *Progress in Communication Sciences: Advances in Persuasion, Vol. 13*, ed. George Barnett and Franklin J. Bostner, 133–171. Greenwich, CT: Ablex, 1997.

"The Potential of Inoculation in Promoting Resistance to the Effectiveness of Comparative Advertising Messages." *Communication Quarterly* 40, no. 1 (1992): 26–44.

Pfau, Michael, Joshua Compton, Kimberly A. Parker, Elaine M. Witenberg, Chasu An, Monica Ferguson, Heather Horton, and Yuri Malyshev. "The Traditional Explanation for Resistance Versus Attitude Accessibility: Do They Trigger Distinct or Overlapping Processes of Resistance?" *Human Communication Research* 30, no. 3 (2004): 329–360.

Pfau, Michael, Michael Haigh, Andeelynn Fifrick, Douglas Holl, Allison Tedesco, Jay Cope, David Nunnally, Amy Schiess, Donald Preston, Paul Roszkowski, and Marlon Martin. "The Effects of Print News Photographs of the Casualties of War." *Journalism & Mass Communication Quarterly* 83, no. 1 (2006): 150–168.

Pfau, Michael, Michael Haigh, Jeanetta Sims, and Shelley Wigley. "The Influence of Corporate Front-Group Stealth Campaigns." *Communication Research* 34, no. 1 (2007): 73–99.

Pfau, Michael, R. Lance Holbert, Stephen J. Zubric, Nilofer H. Pasha, and Wei-Kuo Lin. "Role and Influence of Communication Modality in the Process of Resistance to Persuasion." *Media Psychology* 2, no. 1 (2000): 1–33.

Pfau, Michael, Bobi Ivanov, Brian Houston, Michel Haigh, Jeanetta Sims, Eileen Gilchrist, Jason Russell, Shelley Wigley, Jackie Eckstein, and Natalie Richert. "Inoculation and Mental Processing: The Instrumental Role of Associative Networks in the Process of Resistance to Counterattitudinal Influence." *Communication Monographs* 72, no. 4 (2005): 414–441.

Pfau, Michael, and Henry C. Kenski. *Attack Politics: Strategy and Defense.* Santa Barbara, CA: Praeger, 1990.

Pfau, Michael, Henry C. Kenski, Michael Nitz, and John Sorenson. "Efficacy of Inoculation Strategies in Promoting Resistance to Political Attack Messages: Application to Direct Mail." *Communication Monographs* 57, no. 1 (1990): 25–43.

Pfau, Michael, Shane M. Semmler, Leslie Deatrick, Alicia Mason, Gwen Nisbett, Lindsay Lane, Elizabeth Craig, Jill Underhill, and John Banas. "Nuances about the Role and Impact of Affect in Inoculation." *Communication Monographs* 76, no. 1 (2009): 73–98.

Pfau, Michael, Kyle James Tusing, Ascan F. Koerner, Waipeng Lee, Linda C. Godbold, Linda J. Penaloza, Violet Shu-huei Yang, and Yah-Huei Hong. "Enriching the Inoculation Construct: The Role of Critical Components in the Process of Resistance." *Human Communication Research* 24, no. 2 (1997): 187–215.

Pfau, Michael, and Steve Van Bockern. "The Persistence of Inoculation in Conferring Resistance to Smoking Initiation among Adolescents: The Second Year." *Human Communication Research* 20, no. 3 (1994): 413–430.

Pfau, Michael, Steve Van Bockern, and Jong Geun Kang. "Use of Inoculation to Promote Resistance to Smoking Initiation among Adolescents." *Communication Monographs* 59, no. 3 (1992): 213–230.

Picciolini, Christian. *Romantic Violence: Memoirs of an American Skinhead.* Chicago: Goldmill Group, 2015.

Quick, Brian L., and Michael T. Stephenson. "Further Evidence that Psychological Reactance Can Be Modeled as a Combination of Anger and Negative Cognitions." *Communication Research* 34, no. 3 (2007): 255–276.

Rains, Stephen A., and Monique Mitchell Turner. "Psychological Reactance and Persuasive Health Communication: A Test and Extension of the Intertwined Model." *Human Communication Research* 33 (2007): 241–269.

Reuters. "'Islamophobic Terrorism Must Stop': World Reacts in Horror to New Zealand Mosque Attacks." *News18*, March 15, 2019. www.news18.com/news/world/islamophobic-terrorism-must-stop-world-reacts-in-horror-to-new-zealand-mosque-attacks-2067551.html.

Richards, Adam, and John A. Banas. "Inoculation against Resistance to Persuasive Health Messages." *Health Communication* 30 (2015): 451–460.

Safi, Michael. "Sydney Siege: Anonymous Warning about Man Haron Monis Followed Up, Says PM." *The Guardian*, December 21, 2014. www.theguardian.com/australia-news/2014/dec/21/sydney-siege-anonymous-warning-about-man-haron-monis-followed-up-says-pm.

Sageman, Marc. *Leaderless Jihad.* Philadelphia, PA: University of Pennsylvania Press, 2008.

Understanding Terror Networks. Philadelphia, PA: University of Pennsylvania Press, 2004.

Schmid, Alex P. "Challenging the Narrative of the 'Islamic State.'" ICCT Research Paper (2015). https://icct.nl/wp-content/uploads/2015/06/ICCT-Schmid-Challenging-the-Narrative-of-the-Islamic-State-June2015.pdf.

Seierstad, Åsne. *One of Us: The Story of a Massacre in Norway and its Aftermath*. New York: Farrar, Straus & Giroux, 2016.

Simmonds, Kylie. "Sydney Siege: Police Respond to Anti-Muslim Sentiment in Wake of Lindt Café Shootout." *Australian Broadcasting Corporation*, December 16, 2014. www.abc.net.au/news/2014-12-17/anti-muslim-senti ment-sydney-siege-auburn-mosque-threat/5972784.

Stiff, James B., and Paul A. Mongeau. *Persuasive Communication*. New York: Guilford Press, 2002.

Wong, Norman C. H., and Kylie J. Harrison. "Nuances in Inoculation: Protecting Positive Attitudes toward the HPV Vaccine & the Practice of Vaccinating Children." *Journal of Women's Health, Issues and Care* 3, no. 6 (2014).

Chapter 5: The Reasoned Action of Radicalization and Counter-Radicalization

Ajzen, Icek. "From Intentions to Actions: A Theory of Planned Behavior." In *Action Control: From Cognition to Behavior*, ed. Julius Kuhl and Jürgen Beckman, 11–39. Heidelberg: Springer, 1985.

"The Theory of Planned Behavior." *Organizational Behavior and Human Decision Processes* 50 (1991): 179–211.

"The Theory of Planned Behaviour: Reactions and Reflections." *Psychology & Health* 26, no. 9 (2011): 1113–1127.

Ajzen, Icek, and Martin Fishbein. "Attitudinal and Normative Variables as Predictors of Specific Behavior." *Journal of Personality and Social Psychology* 27 (1973): 41–57.

Albarracín, Dolores, Blair T. Johnson, Martin Fishbein, and Paige A. Muellerleile. "Theories of Reasoned Action and Planned Behavior as Models of Condom Use." *Psychological Bulletin* 127, no. 1 (2011): 142–161.

Bronstein, Scott, and Drew Griffin. "Young ISIS Recruit: I was Blinded By Love." *CNN*, December 6, 2016. www.cnn.com/2016/12/02/us/mississippi-isis-muhammad-dakhlalla-interview/index.html.

Cooke, Richard, and David P. French. "How Well Do the Theory of Reasoned Action and Theory of Planned Behaviour Predict Intentions and Attendance at Screening Programmes? A Meta-Analysis." *Psychology & Health* 43 (2008): 745–765.

Fishbein, Martin. "Attitude and the Prediction of Behavior." In *Readings in Attitude Theory and Measurement*, ed. Martin Fishbein, 477–492. New York: Wiley, 1967.

"Developing Effective Behavior Change Interventions: Some Lessons Learned from Behavioral Research." In *Reviewing the Behavioral Sciences Knowledge Base on Technology Transfer*, ed. Thomas E. Backer, Susan L. David, and Gerald Saucy, 246–261. Rockville, MD: National Institute on Drug Abuse, 1995. https://archives.drugabuse.gov/sites/default/files/mono graph155.pdf.

"The Role of Theory in HIV Prevention." *AIDS Care* 12 (2000): 273–278.

Fishbein, Martin, and Icek Ajzen. *Belief, Attitude, Intention, and Behavior: An Introduction to Theory and Research*. Reading, MA: Addison-Wesley, 1975. *Predicting and Changing Behavior: The Reasoned Action Approach*. New York: Routledge, 2010.

Fishbein, Martin, and Mark Stasson. "The Role of Desires, Self-Predictions, and Perceived Control in the Prediction of Training Session Attendance." *Journal of Applied Social Psychology* 20 (1990): 173–198.

Fishbein, Martin, and Marco C. Yzer. "Using Theory to Design Effective Health Behavior Interventions." *Communication Theory* 13, no. 2 (2003): 164–183.

Gibbons, Frederick X., Meg Gerrard, Hart Blanton, and Daniel W. Russell. "Reasoned Action and Social Reaction: Willingness and Intention as Independent Predictors of Health Risk." *Journal of Personality and Social Psychology* 74 (1998): 1164–1180.

Giles, M., C. Liddell, and M. Bydawell. "Condom Use in African Adolescents: The Role of Individual and Group Factors." *AIDS Care* 17, no. 6 (2005): 729–739.

Green, Emma. "How Two Mississippi College Students Fell in Love and Decided to Join a Terrorist Group." *The Atlantic*, May 1, 2017. www.theatlantic.com/politics/archive/2017/05/mississippi-young-dakhlalla/524751/.

Hornik, R., Allyson C. Volinsky, Shane Mannis, Laura A. Gibson, Emily Brennan, Stella J. Lee, and Andy S. L. Tan. "Validating the Hornik & Woolf Approach to Choosing Media Campaign Themes: Do Promising Beliefs Predict Behavior Change in a Longitudinal Study?" *Communication Methods and Measures* 13, no. 1 (2019): 60–68.

Hornik, R., and Kimberly Duyck Woolf. "Using Cross-Sectional Surveys to Plan Message Strategies." *Social Marketing Quarterly* 5 (1999): 34–41.

"Mississippi ISIS Recruit: 'The FBI, They Really Saved My Life.'" *CBS News*, August 25, 2016. www.cbsnews.com/news/mississippi-isis-recruit-muhammad-dakhlalla-fbi-saved-my-life/.

Pertl, M. M., David Hevey, Kent Steven Thomas, Agnella Craig, Siobhan Ní Chuinneagáin, and Laura Maher. "Differential Effects of Self-Efficacy and Perceived Control on Intention to Perform Skin Cancer-Related Health Behaviours." *Health Education Research* 25 (2010): 769–779.

Terry, Deborah J., and Joanne E. O'Leary. "The Theory of Planned Behaviour: The Effects of Perceived Behavioural Control and Self-Efficacy." *British Journal of Social Psychology* 34, no. 2 (1995): 199–220.

Van den Putte, Bas. "On the Theory of Reasoned Action." Dissertation, University of Amsterdam, 1993.

Warshaw, Paul R., and Fred D. Davis. "Disentangling Behavioral Intention and Behavioral Expectation," *Journal of Experimental Social Psychology* 21, no. 3 (1985): 213–228.

Yzer, Marco. "Reasoned Action Theory: Persuasion as Belief-Based Behavior Change." In *The SAGE Handbook of Persuasion: Developments in Theory and Practice*, ed. James Price Dillard and Lijiang Shen, 120–136. Thousand Oaks, CA. Sage, 2013.

Chapter 6: Emotion in Extremist Propaganda and Counter-Propaganda

Abdullah X. "Abdullah X." www.youtube.com/user/abdullahx.

Aly, Anne, Dana Weimann-Saks, and Gabriel Weimann. "Making 'Noise' Online: An Analysis of the Say No to Terror Online Campaign." *Perspectives on Terrorism* 8, no. 5 (2014): 33–47.

Antonetti, Paolo, Paul Baines, and Shailendra Jain. "The Persuasiveness of Guilt Appeals Over Time: Pathways to Delayed Compliance." *Journal of Business Research* 90 (2018): 14–25.

Associated Press (Baghdad). "Muslim Clerics Denounce 'Savage' ISIS Murder of Jordanian Pilot." *The Guardian*, February 6, 2015. www.theguardian.com/world/2015/feb/06/muslim-clerics-denounce-jordanian-pilot-execution-kasasbeh.

Averill, James R. "Studies on Anger and Aggression: Implications for Theories of Emotion." *American Psychologist* 38, no. 11 (1983): 1145–1160.

Bandura, Albert. *Social Foundations of Thought and Action*. Englewood Cliffs, NJ: Prentice Hall, 1986.

BBC News. "1987: Bomb Kills 11 at Enniskillen." November 8, 1987. http://news.bbc.co.uk/onthisday/hi/dates/stories/november/8/newsid_2515000/2515113.stm.

"Jordan Pilot Hostage Moaz al-Kasasbeh 'Burned Alive'." February 3, 2015. www.bbc.com/news/world-middle-east-31121160.

Boudewyns, Vanessa, Monique M. Turner, and Ryan S. Paquin. "Shame-Free Guilt Appeals: Testing the Emotional and Cognitive Effects of Shame and Guilt Appeals." *Psychology & Marketing* 30, no. 9 (2013): 811–825.

Bowlby, John. *Attachment and Loss*, 3 vols. New York: Basic Books, 1980.

Braddock, Kurt. "Fighting Words: The Persuasive Effect of Online Extremist Narratives on the Radicalization Process." PhD dissertation, The Pennsylvania State University, 2012.

Brader, Ted. "Striking a Responsive Chord: How Political Ads Motivate and Persuade Voters by Appealing to Emotions." *American Journal of Political Science* 49, no. 2 (2005): 388–405.

Campbell, Lisa J. "The Use of Beheadings by Fundamentalist Islam." *Global Crime* 7, no. 3–4 (2006): 583–614.

Cardona, Claire Z. "Turn in 'Illegal Aliens': Posters Call on UT-Arlington Campus to Do So as 'Civic Duty.'" www.dallasnews.com/news/higher-education/2017/04/24/turn-illegal-aliens-ut-arlington-students-urged-fliers-found-campus.

Center for Strategic Studies, University of Jordan. "Public Opinion Survey: Some Current National Issues – February 2015 Main Findings." http://jcss.org/Photos/635608078830183108.pdf.

Chadwick, Amy E. "Toward a Theory of Persuasive Hope: Effects of Cognitive Appraisals, Hope Appeals, and Hope in the Context of Climate Change." *Health Communication* 30 (2015): 598–611.

Chang, Chun-Tuan. "Guilt Appeals in Cause-Related Marketing." *International Journal of Advertising: The Review of Marketing Communications* 30, no. 4 (2011): 587–616.

Chulov, Martin, and Shiv Malik. "ISIS Video Shows Jordanian Hostage Being Burned to Death." *The Guardian*, February 3, 2015. www.theguardian.com/world/2015/feb/03/isis-video-jordanian-hostage-burdning-death-muadh-al-kasabeh.

Cialdini, Robert B., Richard J. Borden, Avril Thorne, Marcus Randall Walker, Stephen Freeman, and Lloyd Reynolds Sloan. "Basking in Reflected Glory: Three (Football) Field Studies." *Journal of Personality and Social Psychology* 34, no. 3 (1976): 366–375.

Cialdini, Robert B., Stephanie L. Brown, Brian P. Lewis, Carol Luce, and Steven L. Neuberg. "Reinterpreting the Empathy–Altruism Relationship: When One into One Equals Oneness." *Journal of Personality and Social Psychology* 73, no. 3 (1997): 481–494.

Cohen-Charash, Yochi. "Episodic Envy." *Journal of Applied Social Psychology* 39, no. 9 (2009): 2128–2173.

Coulter, Robin Higie, and Mary Beth Pinto. "Guilt Appeals in Advertising: What Are Their Effects?" *Journal of Applied Psychology* 80, no. 6 (1995): 697–705.

Crossley-Holland, Dominic. Age of Terror (Episode 2): 10 Days of Terror *[television program]*. BBC.

Crusius, Jan, and Jens Lange. "What Catches the Envious Eye? Attentional Biases within Malicious and Benign Envy." *Journal of Experimental Social Psychology* 55 (2014): 1–11.

de Hoog, Natascha, Wolfgang Stroebe, and John B. F. de Wit. "The Impact of Fear Appeals on Processing and Acceptance of Action Recommendations." *Personality and Social Psychology Bulletin* 31, no. 1 (2005): 24–33.

Dillard, James Price, and Robin L. Nabi. "The Persuasive Influence of Emotion in Cancer Prevention and Detection Messages." *Journal of Communication* 56, no. S1 (2006): S123–S139.

Dillard, James Price, and Eugenia Peck. "Persuasion and the Structure of Affect: Dual Systems and Discrete Emotions as Complementary Models." *Human Communication Research* 27, no. 1 (2001): 38–68.

Dillard, James Price, Courtney A. Plotnick, Linda C. Godbold, Vicki S. Freimuth, and Timothy Edgar. "The Multiple Affective Outcomes of AIDS PSAs: Fear Appeals Do More than Scare People." *Communication Research* 23, no. 1 (1996): 44–72.

Dillard, James Price, and Kiwon Seo. "Affect and Persuasion." In *The SAGE Handbook of Persuasion: Developments in Theory and Practice*, ed. James Price Dillard and Lijiang Shen, 150–166. Thousand Oaks, CA: Sage, 2013.

Duffy, Michelle K., Kristin L. Scott, Jason D. Shaw, Bennett J. Tepper, and Karl Aquino. "A Social Context Model of Envy and Social Undermining." *Academy of Management Journal* 55, no. 3 (2012): 643–666.

Ekman, Paul, Robert W. Levenson, and Wallace V. Friesen. "Automatic Nervous System Activity Distinguishes among Emotions." *Science* 221, no. 46416 (1983): 1208–1210.

Estés, Clarissa Pinkola. *Women Who Run with the Wolves: Myths and Stories of the Wild Woman Archetype.* New York: Ballantine Books, 1992.

Fein, Melvyn. *I.A.M.: A Common Sense Guide to Coping with Anger.* Westport, CT: Praeger.

Fiske, Susan T. "Envy Up, Scorn Down: How Comparison Divides Us." *American Psychologist* 65, no. 8 (2010): 698–706.

Fox News. "ISIS Burns Hostage Alive." February 3, 2015. https://video.foxnews.com/v/4030583977001/#sp=show-clips.

Franz, Barbara. "Europe's Muslim Youth: An Inquiry into the Politics of Discrimination, Relative Deprivation, and Identity Formation." *Mediterranean Quarterly* 18, no. 1 (2007): 89–112.

Frijda, Nico H. *The Emotions*. Cambridge University Press, 1986.

Frijda, Nico H., Peter Kuipers, and Elisabeth ter Schure. "Relations among Emotion, Appraisal, and Emotional Action Readiness." *Journal of Personality and Social Psychology* 57, no. 2 (1989): 212–228.

Gardham, Duncan, and John Hall. "Was Jordanian Pilot Burned Alive after Sick Twitter Campaign among ISIS Supporters to Name His Method of Death?" *Daily Mail*, February 4, 2015. www.dailymail.co.uk/news/article-2939196/Was-Jordanian-pilot-burned-alive-sick-Twitter-campaign-ISIS-supporters-method-death.html.

Griffin, Andrew. "ISIS Militants Using Twitter to Ask for Suggestions on How to Kill Jordanian Pilot." *The Independent*, December 30, 2014. www.independent.co.uk/life-style/gadgets-and-tech/news/isis-polls-twitter-for-gruesome-suggestions-of-how-to-kill-jordanian-pilot-9949550.html.

Griffin-Nolan, Ed. "Keeping Perspective and Overreactions." *The Syracuse New Times*, September 17, 2014. www.syracusenewtimes.com/keeping-perspective-and-overreactions/.

Hearst, David. "Ulster Terrorist Bomb Kills 11." *The Guardian*, November 9, 1987. www.theguardian.com/uk/1987/nov/09/northernireland.davidhearst.

Hendriks, Hanneke, Bas van den Putte, and Gert-Jan de Bruijn. "Changing the Conversation: The Influence of Emotions on Conversational Valence and Alcohol Consumption." *Prevention Science* 15, no. 5 (2013): 684–693.

Higbee, Kenneth L. "Fifteen Years of Fear Arousal: Research on Threat Appeals 1953–1968." *Psychological Bulletin* 72, no. 6 (1969): 426–444.

Hovland, Carl I., Irving L. Janis, and Harold H. Kelley. *Communication and Persuasion: Psychological Studies of Opinion Change*. New Haven, CT: Yale University Press, 1953.

Insko, Chester A., Abe Arkoff, and Verla M. Insko. "Effects of High and Low Fear-Arousing Communications upon Opinions toward Smoking." *Journal of Experimental Social Psychology* 1 (1965): 256–266.

Isen, Alice M. "Positive Affect and Decision Making." In *Handbook of Emotions*, ed. Michael Lewis and Jeanette M. Haviland, 261–277. New York: Guilford Press, 1993.

"ISIS Video Purports to Show Jordanian Pilot Burned Alive." *CBS News*, February 3, 2015. www.cbsnews.com/news/isis-hostage-jordanian-pilot-muath-al-kaseasbeh-purportedly-burned-alive-in-video/.

Izard, Carroll E. *Differential Emotions Theory*. New York: Springer Science + Business Media, 1977.

———. "Emotion Theory and Research: Highlights, Unanswered Questions, and Emerging Issues." *Annual Review of Psychology* 60 (2009): 1–25.

———. *Human Emotions*. New York: Plenum Press, 1977.

———. *The Psychology of Emotions*. New York: Plenum Press, 1991.

Janis, Irving L., and Seymour Feshbach. "Effects of Fear-Arousing Communications." *Journal of Abnormal and Social Psychology* 48, no. 1 (1953): 78–92.

Janis, Irving L., and Robert F. Terwilliger. "An Experimental Study of Psychological Resistance to Fear Arousing Communications." *Journal of Abnormal and Social Psychology* 65 (1962): 403-410.

Kang, Yahui, and Joseph N. Capella. "Emotional Reactions to and Perceived Effectiveness of Media Messages: Appraisal and Message Sensation Value." *Western Journal of Communication* 72, no. 1 (2008): 40–61.

Kemp, Elyria, My Bui, Anjala Krishen, Pamela Miles Homer, and Michael S. LaTour. "Understanding the Power of Hope and Empathy in Healthcare Marketing." *Journal of Consumer Marketing* 34, no. 2 (2017): 85–95.

Kemp, Elyria, Pamela A. Kennett-Hensel, and Jeremy Kees. "Pulling on the Heartstrings: Examining the Effects of Emotions and Gender in Persuasion Appeals." *Journal of Advertising* 42, no. 1 (2013): 69–79.

Kim, Hyo J., and Glen T. Cameron. "Emotions Matter in Crisis: The Role in Anger and Sadness in the Publics' Response to Crisis news Framing and Corporate Crisis Response." *Communication Research* 38, no. 6 (2011): 826–855.

King, Tom. *House of Commons Official Report.* November 9, 1987.

Krusemark, Elizabeth A., and Wen Li. "Do All Threats Work the Same Way? Divergent Effects of Fear and Disgust on Sensory Perception and Attention." *Journal of Neuroscience* 31, no. 9 (2011): 3429–3434.

Lazarus, Richard S. *Emotion and Adaptation.* New York: Oxford University Press, 1991.

"From Psychological Stress to the Emotions: A History of Changing Outlooks." *Annual Review of Psychology* 44 (1993): 1–21.

Lazarus, Richard S., and Bernice N. Lazarus. *Passion and Reason: Making Sense of Our Emotions.* Oxford University Press, 1994.

Leach, Colin Wayne, Nastia Snider, and Aarti Iyer. "'Poisoning the Consciences of the Fortunate': The Experience of Relative Advantage and Support for Social Equality." In *Relative Deprivation: Specification, Development, and Integration*, ed. Iain Walker and Heather J. Smith, 136–163. Cambridge University Press, 2002.

Leventhal, Howard, and Robert P. Singer. "Affect Arousal and Positioning of Recommendations in Persuasive Communications." *Journal of Personality and Social Psychology* 4, no. 2 (1966): 137–146.

Leventhal, Howard, and Jean C. Watts. "Sources of Resistance to Fear-Arousing Communications on Smoking and Lung Cancer." *Journal of Personality* 34 (1966): 155–175.

Life After Hate, Inc. *Exit USA.* www.lifeafterhate.org/exitusa.

Louro, Maria J., Rik Pieters, and Marcel Zeelenberg. "Negative Returns on Positive Emotions: The Influence of Pride and Self-Regulatory Goals on Repurchase Decisions." *Journal of Communication Research* 31, no. 4 (2005): 833–840.

Lu, Hang. "The Effects of Emotional Appeals and Gain Versus Loss Framing in Communicating Sea Star Wasting Disease." *Science Communication* 38, no. 2 (2016): 143–169.

MacInnis, Deborah J., and Gustavo E. de Mello. "The Concept of Hope and its Relevance to Product Evaluation and Choice." *Journal of Marketing* 69, no. 1 (2005): 1–14.

Mackie, Diane M., and Leila T. Worth. "Feeling Good, but Not Thinking Straight: The Impact of Positive Mood on Persuasion." In *Emotion & Social Judgments*, ed. Joseph P. Forgas, 201–220. New York: Pergamon Press, 1991.

Manning, Maurice. *Senead Eireann*, Volume 17 Column 1346. November 11, 1987.

Markiewicz, Dorothy. "Effects of Humor on Persuasion." *Sociometry* 37, no. 3 (1974): 407–422.

McCarthy, John, Marvin Minsky, Claude E. Shannon, and Phyllis Fox. "*Artificial Intelligence.*" Computation Center, Massachusetts Institute of Technology. https://dspace.mit.edu/bitstream/handle/1721.1/53496/RLE_QPR_060_XVI.pdf.

Meczkowski, Eric J., and James Price Dillard. "Fear Appeals in Strategic Communication." In *The International Encyclopedia of Media Effects*, ed. Patrick Rössler. Hoboken, NJ: John Wiley & Sons, 2017.

Montada, Leo, and Angela Schneider. "Justice and Emotional Reactions to the Disadvantaged." *Social Justice Research* 3, no. 4 (1989): 313–344.

Nabi, Robin L. "A Cognitive Functional Model for the Effects of Discrete Negative Emotions on Information Processing, Attitude Change, and Recall." *Communication Theory* 9, no. 3 (1999): 292–320.

"Discrete Emotions and Persuasion." In *The Persuasion Handbook: Developments in Theory and Practice*, ed. James Price Dillard and Michael Pfau, 289–308. Thousand Oaks, CA: Sage, 2002.

Nabi, Robin L., and Lauren Keblusek. "Inspired by Hope, Motivated by Envy: Comparing the Effects of Discrete Emotions in the Process of Social Comparison to Media Figures." *Media Psychology* 17, no. 2 (2014): 208–234.

Nerb, Josef, and Hans Spada. "Evaluation of Environmental Problems: A Coherence Model of Cognition and Emotion." *Cognition and Emotion* 15, no. 4 (2011): 521–551.

Nordland, Rod, and Anne Barnard. "Militants' Killing of Jordanian Pilot Unites the Arab World in Anger." *New York Times*, February 4, 2015. www.nytimes.com/2015/02/05/world/middleeast/arab-world-unites-in-anger-after-burning-of-jordanian-pilot.html.

O'Keefe, Daniel J. "Guilt as a Mechanism of Persuasion." In *The Persuasion Handbook: Developments in Theory and Practice*, ed. James Price Dillard and Michael Pfau, 329–344. Thousand Oaks, CA: Sage, 2002.

O'Keefe, Daniel. "Guilt and Social Influence." *Annals of the International Communication Association* 23, no. 1 (2000): 67–101.

Parrott, W. Gerrod, and Richard H. Smith. "Distinguishing the Experiences of Envy and Jealousy." *Journal of Personality and Social Psychology* 64, no. 6 (1993): 906–920.

Peters, Gyalt-Jorn Ygram, Robert A. C. Ruiter, and Gerjo Kok. "Threatening Communication: A Critical Re-Analysis and a Revised Meta-Analytic Test of Fear Appeal Theory." *Health Psychology Review* 7, no. S1 (2013): S8–S31.

Pfau, Michael, Erin Alison Szabo, Jason Anderson, Joshua Morrill, Jessica Zubric, and Hua-Hsin Wan. "The Role and Impact of Affect in the Process of Resistance to Persuasion." *Human Communication Research* 27, no. 2 (2001): 216–252.

Phan, K. Luan, Tor Wager, Stephan F. Taylor, and Israel Liberson. "Functional Neuroanatomy of Emotion: A Meta-Analysis of Emotion Activation Studies in PET and fMRI." *NeuroImage* 16, no. 2 (2002): 331–348.

Raihani, N. J., and Katherine McAuliffe. "Human Punishment is Motivated by Inequity Aversion, Not a Desire for Reciprocity." *Biology Letters* 8, no. 5 (2012): 802–804.

Rains, Howell. "With Latest Bomb, I.R.A. Injures its Own Cause." *New York Times*, November 15, 1987. www.nytimes.com/1987/11/15/weekinreview/the-world-terrorism-with-latest-bomb-ira-injures-its-own-cause.html.

Reiser, Christa. *Reflections on Anger: Women and Men in a Changing Society*. Westport, CT: Praeger, 1999.

"Revulsion in Government at Enniskillen Bomb Outrage Revealed." *Irish Independent*, December 29, 2017. www.independent.ie/irish-news/revulsion-in-government-at-enniskillen-bomb-outrage-revealed-36443145.html.

Rogers, Ronald W. "A Protection Motivation Theory of Fear Appeals and Attitude Change." *Journal of Psychology* 91, no. 1 (1975): 93–114.

Russell, James A., and Lisa Feldman Barrett. "Core Affect, Prototypical Emotional Episodes, and other Things Called Emotion: Dissecting the Elephant." *Journal of Personality and Social Psychology* 76, no. 5 (1999): 805–819.

Say No to Terror. "Know Your Enemy" [in Arabic]. www.youtube.com/watch?v=2NpEXoCjsKE.

Say No to Terror. "Who We Are" [in Arabic]. www.sntt.me/our-message/.

Silke, Andrew. "Becoming a Terrorist." In *Terrorists, Victims, and Society: Psychological Perspectives on Terrorism and its Consequences*, ed. Andrew Silke, 29–54. Chichester: Wiley & Sons, 2003.

Smith, Richard H., and Sung Hee Kim. "Comprehending Envy." *Psychological Bulletin* 133, no. 1 (2007): 46–64.

Sones, Matthew C. "Fear vs. Hope: Do Discrete Emotions Mediate Message Frame Effectiveness in Genetic Cancer Screening Appeals?" Doctoral dissertation, Georgia State University, 2017.

Stahelski, Anthony. "Terrorists Are Made, Not Born: Creating Terrorists Using Social Psychological Conditioning." *Cultic Studies Review* 4, no. 1 (2004): 30–40.

Sternthal, Brian, and C. Samuel Craig. "Humor in Advertising." *Journal of Marketing* 37, no. 4 (1973): 12–18.

Straumsheim, Carl. "Stop the Presses." *Inside Higher Ed*, March 29, 2016. www.insidehighered.com/news/2016/03/29/simple-potentially-serious-vulnerability-behind-anti-semitic-fliers.

Su, Alice. "It Wasn't Their War." *The Atlantic*, February 5, 2015. www.theatlantic.com/international/archive/2015/02/jordan-isis-pilot-response/385199/.

Tai, Kenneth, Jayanth Narayanan, and Daniel J. McAllister. "Envy as Pain: Rethinking the Nature of Envy and its Implications for Employees and Organizations." *Academy of Management Review* 37, no. 1 (2012): 107–129.

Tajfel, Henri, and John Turner. "An Integrative Theory of Intergroup Conflict." In *Intergroup Relations*, ed. Michael A. Hogg and Dominic Abrams, 71–90. Philadelphia, PA: Psychology Press, 2001.

Tangney, June Price, Rowland S. Miller, Laura Flicker, and Deborah Hill Barlow. "Are Shame, Guilt, and Embarrassment Distinct Emotions?" *Journal of Personality and Social Psychology* 70, no. 6 (1996): 1256–1269.

Tannenbaum, Melanie B., Justin Hepler, Rick S. Zimmerman, Lindsey Saul, Samantha Jacobs, Kristina Wilson, and Dolores Albarracín. "Appealing to Fear: A Meta-Analysis of Fear Appeal Effectiveness and Theories." *Psychological Bulletin* 161, no. 6 (2015): 1178–1204.

Thomas, Sandra P. "Anger and its Manifestation in Women." In *Women and Anger*, ed. Sandra P. Thomas, 40–67. New York: Springer, 1993.

Thompson, Geir, Lars Glasø, and Øyvind Martinson. "Antecedents and Consequences of Envy." *Journal of Social Psychology* 156, no. 2 (2016): 139–153.

Tomkins, Silvan S. *Affect, Imagery, Consciousness: The Complete Edition*. New York: Springer, 1962.

Turner, Monique Mitchell. "Using Emotion in Risk Communication: The Anger Activism Model." *Public Relations Review* 33 (2007): 114–119.

Turner, Monique, Elena Bessarabova, Kathryn Hambleton, Maribeth Weiss, Sanja Sipek, and Kristen Long. "Does Anger Facilitate or Debilitate Persuasion? A Test of the Anger Activism Model." *Paper presented at the annual meeting of the International Communication Association*, Dresden, Germany, 2006.

Ubayasiri, Kasun. "Virtual Hostage Dramas and Real Politics." *ejournalist* 4, no. 2 (2004): 1–25.

van de Ven, Niels. "Envy and Admiration: Emotion and Motivation Following Upward Social Comparison." *Cognition and Emotion* 31, no. 1 (2017): 193–200.

van de Ven, Niels, Marcel Zeelenberg, and Rik Pieters. "Leveling Up and Down: The Experience of Benign and Malicious Envy." *Emotion* 9, no. 3 (2009): 419–429.

van Doorn, Janne, Marcel Zeelenberg, and Seger M. Breugelmans. "The Impact of Anger on Donations to Victims." *International Review of Victimology* 23, no. 3 (2017): 303–312.

Waller, James. *Becoming Evil: How Ordinary People Commit Genocide and Mass Killing*. Oxford University Press, 2007.

Watson, David, and Lee Anna Clark. *The PANAS-X: Manual for the Positive and Negative Affect Schedule*. https://ir.uiowa.edu/cgi/viewcontent.cgi?referer=https://www.google.com/&httpsredir=1&article=1011&context=psychology_pubs/.

Weinberger, Marc G., and Charles S. Gulas. "The Impact of Humor in Advertising: A Review." *Journal of Advertising* 21, no. 4 (1992): 35–59.

Weiner, Norbert. "Cybernetics." *Scientific American* 179, no. 5 (1948): 14–19.

Witte, Kim. "Fear Control and Danger Control: A Test of the Extended Parallel Process Model (EPPM)." *Communication Monographs* 61, no. 2 (1994): 113–134.

"Fear as Motivator, Fear as Inhibitor: Using the EPPM to Explain Fear Appeal Successes and Failures." In *The Handbook of Communication and Emotion*, ed. Peter Andersen and Laura Guerrero, 423–450. New York: Academic Press, 1998.

Witte, Kim, and Mike Allen. "A Meta-Analysis of Fear Appeals: Implications for Effective Public Health Campaigns." *Health Education & Behavior* 27, no. 5 (2000): 591–615.

Woody, Sheila R., and Bethany A. Teachman. "Intersection of Disgust and Fear: Normative and Pathological Views." *Clinical Psychology: Science and Practice* 7, no. 3 (2000): 291–311.

Xu, Zhan, and Hao Guo. "A Meta-Analysis of the Effectiveness of Guilt on Health-Related Attitudes." *Health Communication* 33, no. 5 (2018): 519–525.

Zelin, Aaron. "New Video Nashind from The Islamic State: 'Blood for Blood.'" *Jihadology*, April 29, 2016. https://jihadology.net/2016/04/29/new-video-nashid-from-the-islamic-state-blood-forblood/.

Chapter 7: Three Future Challenges in Radicalization and Counter-Radicalization

1oneclone. "It's Mueller Time! Trump Administration Season Ending." YouTube Video, August 18, 2017. www.youtube.com/watch?v=d7Uy0Uznw4E.

Adl-Tabatabai, Sean. "FBI Insider: Clinton Emails Linked to Political Pedophile Sex Ring." *NewsPunch*, October 31, 2016. https://newspunch.com/fbi-clinton-email-pedophile-ring/.

Arquilla, John, and David Ronfeldt, eds. *Networks and Netwars*. Santa Monica, CA: RAND Corporation, 2001.

Associated Press. "Republicans Slam Rep. Steve King for White Supremacist Remarks." *LA Times*, January 10, 2019. www.latimes.com/ct-steve-king-republicans-20190110-story.html.

Barnes, Julian E. "Gates Makes Recommendations in Ft. Hood Shooting Case." *LA Times*, January 15, 2010. www.latimes.com/archives/la-xpm-2010-jan-15-la-na-fort-hood-pentagon16-2010jan16-story.html.

Beavers, Olivia. "Washington Fears New Threat from 'Deepfake' Videos." *The Hill*, January 20, 2019. https://thehill.com/policy/national-security/426148-washington-fears-new-threat-from-deepfake-videos.

BBC News. "Islamist Cleric Anwar al-Awlaki Killed in Yemen." September 30, 2011. www.bbc.com/news/world-middle-east-15121879.

"Obama: Anwar al-Awlaki Death is Major Blow for al-Qaeda." September 30, 2011. www.bbc.com/news/world-middle-east-15132308.

Braddock, Kurt. "Vaccinating against Hate: Using Attitudinal Inoculation to Confer Resistance to Persuasion by Extremist Propaganda" (under review).

Carr, Nicholas G. *The Shallows: What the Internet is Doing to Our Brains*. New York: W. W. Norton, 2011.

Chesney, Robert, and Danielle Citron. "Deep Fakes: A Looming Crisis for National Security, Democracy, and Privacy?" *Lawfare*, February 21, 2018. www.lawfareblog.com/deep-fakes-looming-crisis-national-security-democracy-and-privacy.

Cohen, David S. "Trump's Assassination Dog Whistle Was Even Scarier than You Think." *Rolling Stone*, August 9, 2016. www.rollingstone.com/politics/ politics-features/trumps-assassination-dog-whistle-was-even-scarier-than-you-think-112138/.

Cole, Samantha. "AI-Assisted Fake Porn is Here and We're All Fucked." *Vice Motherboard*, December 11, 2017. https://motherboard.vice.com/en_us/art icle/gydydm/gal-gadot-fake-ai-porn.

Crockett, Emily. "Trump's 2nd Amendment Comment Wasn't a Joke. It Was 'Stochastic Terrorism.'" *Vox*, August 11, 2016. www.vox.com/2016/8/10/ 12422476/trump-second-amendment-hillary-stochastic-terrorism-anti-abor tion-violence.

Eagley, Alice H., and Shelly Chaiken. "Process Theories of Attitude Formation and Change: The Elaboration Likelihood and Heuristic-Systematic Model." In *The Psychology of Attitudes*, ed. Alice H. Eagly and Shelly Chaiken, 303–350. Orlando, FL: Harcourt Brace Jovanovich College Publishers, 1995.

Enli, Gunn. *Mediated Authenticity: How the Media Constructs Reality*. New York: Peter Lang, 2015.

Ewing, Philip. "Facebook Surrenders Russian-Linked Influence Ads to Congress." NPR, October 2, 2017. www.npr.org/2017/10/02/555103005/face book-surrenders-russian-linked-influence-ads-to-congress.

Fikse, Tormod Dag. "Imagining Deceptive Deepfakes." Master's thesis, University of Oslo, 2018.

Fried, Daniel, and Alina Polyakova. *Democratic Defense against Disinformation*. Washington, DC: The Atlantic Council, 2018.

Friedland, Elliot. "Terrorists Will Soon be Able to Fake Any Video." *The Clarion Project*, March 14, 2018. https://clarionproject.org/deep-fakes/.

Garcia, Michael. "A Public-Health Approach to Countering Violent Extremism." *Just Security*, April 3, 2019. www.justsecurity.org/63455/a-public-health-approach-to-countering-violent-extremism/.

García, Miriam R., José A. Vázquez, Isabel G. Teixeira, and Antonio A. Alonso. "Stochastic Individual-Based Modeling of Bacterial Growth and Division using Flow Cytometry." *Frontiers in Microbiology* 8 (2018): article 2626.

Glaser, April. "Reddit is Finally Reckoning with How It Helped Spread Russian Propaganda in 2016." *Slate*, March 5, 2019. https://slate.com/technology/ 2018/03/reddit-is-reckoning-with-how-it-helped-spread-russian-propa ganda-in-2016.html.

Green, Yasmin. "Fake Video Will Soon Be Good Enough to Fool Entire Populations." *Wired*, January 12, 2019. www.wired.co.uk/article/deepfake-videos-security.

Gross, Michael L. *The Ethics of Insurgency: A Critical Guide to Just Guerrilla Warfare*. Cambridge University Press, 2015.

Gross, Michael L., and Tamar Meisels, eds. *Soft War: The Ethics of Unarmed Conflict*. Cambridge University Press, 2017.

Güera, David, and Edward J. Delp. "Deepfake Video Detection Using Recurrent Neural Networks." In *Proceedings of the 2018 IEEE International Conference on Advanced Video and Signal-Based Surveillance*, 127–132.

Hamm, Mark S., and Ramon Spaaij. *The Age of Lone Wolf Terrorism*. New York: Columbia University Press, 2017.

Hayden, Michael Edison. "Critics Pounce on Trump After CNN Wrestling Tweet." *ABC News*, July 2, 2017. https://abcnews.go.com/Politics/critics-pounce-trump-cnn-wrestling-tweet/story?id=48405044.

Helsel, Phil, Elisha Fieldstadt, and John Chandler. "Mail Bomber Cesar Sayoc Pleads Guilty; Devices Were Sent to Critics of Trump." *NBC News*, March 21, 2019. www.nbcnews.com/news/us-news/alleged-mail-bomber-cesar-sayoc-pleads-guilty-devices-were-sent-n985786.

Hitt, Tarpley. "Mail Bomb Suspect Cesar Sayoc's Rage Against Mom Drove Him to Trump, Lawyer Claims." *The Daily Beast*, October 28, 2018. www.thedailybeast.com/mail-bomb-suspect-cesar-sayocs-rage-against-mom-drove-him-to-trump-lawyer-claims.

Hockenos, Paul. "Poland and the Uncontrollable Fury of Europe's Far Right." *The Atlantic*, November 15, 2017. www.theatlantic.com/international/archive/2017/11/europe-far-right-populist-nazi-poland/524559/.

Itkowitz, Colby, and John Wagner. "Trump Says White Nationalism is Not a Rising Threat After New Zealand Attacks: 'It's a Small Group of People.'" *Washington Post*, March 15, 2019. www.washingtonpost.com/politics/trump-offers-us-assistance-after-horrible-massacre-in-new-zealand/2019/03/15/931833d2-4712-11e9-aaf8-4512a6fe3439_story.html.

Jin, Zeyu, Gautham J. Mysore, Stephen Diverdi, Jingwan Lu, and Adam Finkelstein. "VoCo: Text-Based Insertion and Replacement in Audio Narration." *ACM Transactions on Graphics* 36, no. 4 (2017): article 96.

Jolley, Daniel, and Karen M. Douglas. "The Effects of Anti-Vaccine Conspiracy Theories on Vaccination Intentions." *PLoS One* 9, no. 2 (2014): e89177.

Kim, Hyeongwoo, Pablo Garrido, Ayush Tewari, Weipeng Xu, Justus Thies, Mattias Nießner, Patrick Perez, et al. "Deep Video Portraits." *ACM Transactions on Graphics* 37, no. 4 (2018): article 163.

Kooser, Amanda. "Jordan Peele Turns Obama into a Foul-Mouthed Fake-News PSA." *CNET*, April 17, 2018. www.cnet.com/news/jordan-peele-buzzfeed-turn-obama-into-foul-mouthed-fake-news-psa/.

Korshunov, Pavel, and Sebastien Marcel. "DeepFakes: A New Threat to Face Recognition? Assessment and Detection." *arXiv*, December 2018.

LaConte, Stephen. "Ow Wow. Apparently If You Photoshop Nicolas Cage's Face Onto Ross Geller's Body, Your Brain Will Explode." *Buzzfeed*, February 4, 2019. www.buzzfeed.com/stephenlaconte/nicolas-cage-ross-friends.

Li, Yuezun, Ming-Ching Chang, and Siwei Lyu. "In Ictu Oculi: Exposing AI Generated Fake Face Videos by Detecting Eye Blinking." *arXiv*, June 2018.

Li, Yuezun, and Siwei Lyu. "Exposing DeepFake Videos by Detecting Face Warping Artifacts." *arXiv*, March 2019.

Marchment, Zoe, Noémie Bouhana, and Paul Gill. "Lone Actor Terrorists: A Residence-to-Crime Approach." *Terrorism and Political Violence* (in press).

Martin, Jonathan. "Montana Republican Greg Gianforte, Charged with Assault, Awaits Fate in Vote." *New York Times*, May 24, 2017. www.nytimes.com/2017/05/24/us/politics/greg-gianforte-montana-republican-body-slams-reporter.html.

Marwick, Alice, and Rebecca Lewis. "Media Manipulation and Disinformation Online." *Data & Society* (2017). https://datasociety.net/pubs/oh/DataAndSociety_MediaManipulationAndDisinformationOnline.pdf.

McGeehan, Timothy P. "Countering Russian Disinformation." *Parameters* 48, no. 1 (2018): 49–57.

McGraw, Meredith. "Trump: No Regrets for Praising Greg Gianforte for Body-Slamming Reporter." *ABC News*, October 19, 2018. https://abcnews.go.com/Politics/montana-rally-president-trump-praises-greg-gianforte-body/story?id=58596529.

Meserole, Chris, and Alina Polyakova. "The West is Ill-Prepared for the Wave of 'Deep Fakes' that Artificial Intelligence Could Unleash." *Brookings*, May 25, 2018. www.brookings.edu/blog/order-from-chaos/2018/05/25/the-west-is-ill-prepared-for-the-wave-of-deep-fakes-that-artificial-intelligence-could-unleash/.

Miles, Steven H. *Oath Betrayed: Torture, Medical Complicity, and the War on Terror*. New York: Random House, 2006.

Morgan, Susan. "Fake News, Disinformation, Manipulation and Online Tactics to Undermine Democracy." *Journal of Cyber Policy* 3, no. 1 (2018): 39–43.

Ortiz, Erik. "'Pizzagate' Gunman Edgar Maddison Welch Sentenced to Four Years in Prison." *NBC News*, June 22, 2017..nbcnews.com/news/us-news/pizzagate-gunman-edgar-maddison-welch-sentenced-four-years-prison-n775621.

Pacepa, Ion Mihai, and Ronald J. Rychlak. *Disinformation: Former Spy Chief Reveals Secret Strategies for Undermining Freedom, Attacking Religion, and Promoting Terrorism*. Washington, DC: WND Books, 2013.

Parks, Miles. "Russian Interference Campaign was Broader than First Known, Big Tech Tells Hill." *NPR*, October 31, 2017. www.npr.org/2017/10/31/560481040/russian-interference-campaign-was-broader-than-first-known-big-tech-tells-hill.

Parzen, Emanual. *Stochastic Processes*. San Francisco, CA: Holden-Day, 1962.

Paul, Christopher, and Miriam Matthews. *The Russian "Firehose of Falsehood" Propaganda Model*. Santa Monica, CA: RAND Corporation, 2016.

Phillips, Whitney. *This is Why We Can't Have Nice Things: Mapping the Relationship between Online Trolling and Mainstream Culture*. Cambridge, MA: MIT Press, 2015.

Pilkington, Ed. "'He's My Guy': Donald Trump Praises Gianforte for Assault on Guardian Reporter." *The Guardian*, October 19, 2018. www.theguardian.com/us-news/2018/oct/18/trump-greg-gianforte-assault-guardian-ben-jacobs.

Quartz. "Nothing is Real: How German Scientists Control Putin's Face." YouTube Video. April 6, 2016. www.youtube.com/watch?v=ttGUiwfTYvg.

Rayner, Gordon. "Muslim Groups Linked to September 11 Hijackers Spark Fury Over Conference." *The Telegraph*, December 27, 2008. www.telegraph.co.uk/news/uknews/3966501/Muslim-groups-linked-to-September-11-hijackers-spark-fury-over-conference.html.

Rayner, Gordon, and John Bingham. "Stephen Timms Stabbing: How Internet Sermons Turned Quiet Student into Fanatic." *The Telegraph*, November 2, 2010. www.telegraph.co.uk/news/uknews/crime/8105516/Stephen-Timms-stabbing-how-internet-sermons-turned-quiet-student-into-fanatic.html.

Reuters. "White House Dismisses Trump Mention in Christchurch Shooter Manifesto." *The Guardian*, March 17, 2019. www.theguardian.com/world/2019/mar/17/trump-christchurch-shooter-manifesto.

Rubenstein, Adam. "Did Steve King Just Refer to Immigrants as 'Dirt'?" *The Weekly Standard*, November 6, 2018. www.weeklystandard.com/adam-rubenstein/did-steve-just-refer-to-immigrants-as-dirt.

Samuelson, Kate. "What to Know about Pizzagate, the Fake News Story with Real Consequences." *Time*, December 5, 2016. http://time.com/4590255/pizzagate-fake-news-what-to-know/.

Schuurman, Bart, Lasse Lindekilde, Stefan Malthaner, Francis O'Connor, Paul Gill, and Noémie Bouhana. "End of the Lone Wolf: The Typology that Should Not Have Been." *Studies in Conflict & Terrorism* (in press).

Schwartz, Oscar. "You Thought Fake News was Bad? Deep Fakes are Where Truth Goes to Die." *The Guardian*, November 12, 2018. www.theguardian.com/technology/2018/nov/12/deep-fakes-fake-news-truth.

Shane, Scott, and Mark Mazzetti. "Times Sq. Bomb Suspect is Linked to Militant Cleric." *New York Times*, May 6, 2010. www.nytimes.com/2010/05/07/world/middleeast/07awlaki-.html.

Shifman, Limor. *Memes in Digital Culture*. Cambridge, MA: MIT Press, 2014.

Silverman, Craig, and Lawrence Alexander. "How Teens in the Balkans are Duping Trump Supporters with Fake News." *Buzzfeed News*, November 3, 2016. www.buzzfeednews.com/article/craigsilverman/how-macedonia-became-a-global-hub-for-pro-trump-misinfo.

sp.a. "Teken de Klimaatpetitie." www.facebook.com/watch/?v=10155618434657151.

Steele, J. Michael. *Stochastic Calculus and Financial Applications*. New York: Springer-Verlag, 2001.

Stone, Jon. "Russian Disinformation Campaign Has Been 'Extremely Successful' in Europe, Warns EU." *The Independent*, January 17, 2018. www.independent.co.uk/news/uk/politics/russian-fake-news-disinformation-europe-putin-trump-eu-european-parliament-commission-a8164526.html.

Swaine, Jon. "Neo-Nazi in Coast Guard Plotted Attack on Democrats and Journalists, Say Prosecutors." *The Guardian*, February 20, 2019. www.theguardian.com/us-news/2019/feb/20/neo-nazi-plotted-attack-on-democrats-journalists.

Tarico, Valerie. "Christianist Republicans Systematically Incited Colorado Clinic Assault." November 28, 2015. https://valerietarico.com/2015/11/28/christianist-republicans-systematically-incited-colorado-clinic-assault/.

Taylor, Matthew. "'White Europe': 60,000 Nationalists March on Poland's Independence Day." *The Guardian*, November 12, 2017. www.theguardian.com/world/2017/nov/12/white-europe-60000-nationalists-march-on-polands-independence-day.

Thebault, Reis. "Steve King Posts Meme Saying Red States Have '8 Trillion Bullets' in Event of Civil War." *LA Times*, March 19, 2019. www.latimes.com/politics/la-na-pol-steve-king-civil-war-20190319-story.html.

Thies, Justus, Michael Zollhöfer, and Mattias Nießner. "HeadOn: Real-Time Reenactment of Human Portrait Videos." *ACM Transactions on Graphics 37*, no. 4 (2018): article 164.

Thies, Justus, Michael Zollhöfer, Marc Stamminger, Christian Theobalt, and Mattias Nießner. "Face2Face: Real-Time Face Capture and Reenactment of RGB Videos." *Communications of the ACM* 62, no. 1 (2019): 96–104.

"Trump, on Protest: I Don't Know if I'll Do the Fighting Myself Or if Other People Will." *C-SPAN*, August 11, 2015. www.c-span.org/video/?c4762932/trump-protest-dont-ill-fighting-people.

Vincent, James. "Lyrebird Claims It Can Recreate Any Voice Using Just One Minute of Sample Audio." *The Verge*, April 24, 2017. www.theverge.com/2017/4/24/15406882/ai-voice-synthesis-copy-human-speech-lyrebird.

Waltzman, Rand. *The Weaponization of Information: The Need for Cognitive Security*. Santa Monica, CA: RAND Corporation, 2017.

Weaver, Mary Anne. "Lost at Tora Bora." *New York Times Magazine*, September 11, 2005. www.nytimes.com/2005/09/11/magazine/lost-at-tora-bora.html.

Williams, Pete. "'Pizzagate' Gunman Pleads Guilty to Carrying Firearm into D.C. Restaurant." *NBC News*, March 24, 2017. www.nbcnews.com/news/us-news/pizzagate-gunman-pleads-guilty-carrying-firearm-d-c-restaurant-n738171.

Zannattou, Savvas, Tristan Caulfield, Emiliano De Cristofaro, Michael Sirivianos, Giancula Stringhini, and Jeremy Blackburn. "Disinformation Warfare: Understanding State-Sponsored Trolls on Twitter and Their Influence on the Web." *arXiv*, March 2019. https://arxiv.org/abs/1801.09288.

Zannattou, Savvas, Tristan Caulfield, William Setzer, Michael Sirivianos, Giancula Stringhini, and Jeremy Blackburn. "Who Let the Trolls Out? Towards Understanding State-Sponsored Trolls." *arXiv*, February 2019. https://arxiv.org/abs/1811.03130.

Chapter 8: Three Future Directions for Persuasion-Based Approaches to Counter-Radicalization

Aurelius, Marcus. *Meditations*. Mineola, NY: Dover Publications, 1997.

Bailenson, Jeremy N., Kim Swinth, Crystal Hoyt, Susan Persky, Alex Dimov, and Jim Blascovich. "The Independent and Interactive Effects of Embodied-Agent Appearance and Behavior on Self-Report, Cognitive, and Behavioral Markers of Copresence in Immersive Virtual Environments." *PRESENCE: Teleoperators and Virtual Environment* 14 (2005): 379–396.

Bailenson, Jeremy N., Nick Yee, Jim Blascovich, Andrew C. Beall, Nicole Lundblad, and Michael Jin. "The Use of Immersive Virtual Reality in the Learning Sciences: Digital Transformations of Teachers, Students, and Social Context." *The Journal of the Learning Sciences* 17 (2008): 102–141.

Bandura, Albert. *Self-Efficacy: The Exercise of Control*. New York: W. H. Freeman, 1997.

———. *Social Foundations of Thought and Action: A Social Cognitive Theory*. Englewood Cliffs, NJ: Prentice Hall, 1986.

Blascovich, Jim, Jack Loomis, Andrew C. Beall, Kimberly R. Swinth, Crystal L. Hoyt, and Jeremy N. Bailenson. "Immersive Virtual Environment Technology as a Methodological Tool for Social Psychology." *Psychological Inquiry* 13, no. 2 (2002): 103–124.

Braddock, Kurt, and James Price Dillard. "Meta-Analytic Evidence for the Persuasive Effect of Narratives on Beliefs, Attitudes, Intentions, and Behaviors." *Communication Monographs* 83, no. 4 (2016): 446–467.

Braddock, Kurt, and John Horgan. "Towards a Guide for Constructing and Disseminating Counternarratives to Reduce Support for Terrorism." *Studies in Conflict & Terrorism* 39, no. 5 (2016): 381–404.

Braddock, Kurt, and John Morrison. "Cultivating Trust and Perceptions of Source Credibility in Online Counternarratives Intended to Reduce Support for Terrorism." *Studies in Conflict & Terrorism* (in press).

Brodie, Mollyann, Ursula Foehr, Vicky Rideout, Neal Baer, Carolyn Miller, Rebecca Flournoy, and Drew Altman. "Communicating Health Information through the Entertainment Media." *Health Affairs* 20, no. 1 (2001): 192–199.

Burrows, Christopher N., and Hart Blanton. "Real-World Persuasion from Virtual-World Campaigns: How Transportation into Virtual Worlds Moderates In-Game Influence." *Communication Research* 43, no. 4 (2016): 542–570.

Chittaro, Luca, and Nicola Zandgrando. "The Persuasive Power of Virtual Reality: Effects of Simulated Human Distress on Attitudes towards Fire Safety." In *Persuasive Technology: 5th International Conference, PERSUASIVE 2010*, ed. Thomas Ploug, Per Hasle, and Harri Oinas-Kukkonen, 58–69.

Garau, Maia. "The Impact of Avatar Fidelity on Social Interaction in Virtual Environments." Dissertation, University of London, 2003.

Grigorovici, Dan. "Persuasive Effects of Presence in Immersive Virtual Environments." In *Being There: Concepts, Effects, and Measurements of User Presence in Synthetic Environments*, ed. G. Riva, F. Davide, and W. A. Ijsselsteij, 191–207. Amsterdam: Ios Press, 2003.

Guadagno, Rosanna E., Jim Blascovich, Jeremy N. Bailenson, and Cade McCall. "Virtual Humans and Persuasion: The Effects of Agency and Behavioral Realism." *Media Psychology* 10, no. 1 (2007): 1–22.

Hammick, Jin K., and Moon J. Lee. "Do Shy People Feel Less Communication Apprehension Online? The Effects of Virtual Reality on the Relationship between Personality Characteristics and Communication Outcomes." *Computers in Human Behavior* 33 (2014): 302–310.

Horgan, John. *Walking Away from Terrorism: Accounts of Disengagement from Radical and Extremist Movements.* Abingdon: Routledge, 2009.

Kalyanaraman, Sriram, and S. Shyam Sundar. "The Psychological Appeal of Personalized Content in Web Portals: Does Customization Affect Attitudes and Behavior?" *Journal of Communication* 56, no. 1 (2006): 110–132.

Lanier, Jaron. "Tele-Immersion: Like Being There." *Scientific American* 284 (2001): 68–75.

Marathe, Sampada, and S. Shyam Sundar. "What Drives Customization? Control or Identity?" In *Proceedings of the SIGCHI Conference on Human Factors in Computing Systems*, 781–790.

Marcus, Bess H., Beth A. Lewis, David M. Williams, Shira S. Dunsinger, John M. Jakicic, Jessica A. Whiteley, Anna E. Albrecht, et al. "A Comparison of Internet and Print-Based Physical Activity Interventions." *Archives of Internal Medicine* 167 (2007): 944–949.

Moyer, Gusé, Emily. "Toward a Theory of Entertainment Persuasion: Explaining the Persuasive Effects of Entertainment-Education Messages." *Communication Theory* 18 (2008): 407–425.

Norton, Michael I., Daniel Mochon, and Dan Ariely. "The 'IKEA Effect': When Labor Leads to Love." Harvard Business School Marketing Unit Working Paper No. 11-091 (2011). https://papers.ssrn.com/sol3/papers.cfm?abstract_id=1777100.

Oenema, Anke, Johanes Brug, Arie Dijkstra, Inge de Weerdt, and Hein de Vries. "Efficacy and Use of an Internet-Delivered Computer-Tailored Lifestyle Intervention, Targeting Saturated Fat Intake, Physical Activity and Smoking Cessation: A Randomized Controlled Trial." *Annals of Behavioral Medicine* 35, no. 2 (2008): 125–135.

Orozco-Olvera, Victor, Fuyuan Shen, and Lucie Cluver. "The Effectiveness of Using Entertainment Education Narratives to Promote Safer Sexual Behaviors of Youth: A Meta-Analysis, 1985–2017." *PLoS One* 14, no. 2 (2019): e0209969.

Petty, Richard E., S. Christian Wheeler, and George Y. Bizer. "Attitude Functions and Persuasion: An Elaboration Likelihood Approach to Matched Versus Mismatched Messages." In *Why We Evaluate: Functions of Attitudes*, ed. Gregory R. Maio and James M. Olson, 133–162. Mahwah, NJ: Lawrence Erlbaum.

Read, Stephen J., Lynn C. Miller, Paul Robert Appleby, Mary E. Nwosu, Sadina Reynaldo, Ada Lauren, and Anila Putcha. "Socially Optimized Learning in a Virtual Environment: Reducing Risky Sexual Behavior among Men Who Have Sex with Men." *Human Communication Research* 32, no. 1 (2006): 1–33.

Ryan, Richard M., and Edward L. Deci. "Self-Determination Theory and the Facilitation of Intrinsic Motivation, Social Development, and Well-Being." *American Psychologist* 55 (2000): 68–78.

Shen, Fuyuan, and Jiangxue (Ashley) Han. "Effectiveness of Entertainment Education in Communicating Health Information: A Systematic Review." *Asian Journal of Communication* 24, no. 6 (2014): 605–616.

Shin, Youngju, Michelle Miller-Day, Michael L. Hecht, and Janice L. Krieger. "Entertainment-Education Videos as a Persuasive Tool in the Substance Use Prevention Intervention 'Keepin' it REAL.'" *Health Communication* 33, no. 7 (2018): 896–906.

Slater, Mel, Angus Antley, Adam Davison, David Swapp, Christopher Guger, Chris Barker, Nancy Pistrang, and Maria V. Sanchez-Vives. "A Virtual Reprise of the Stanley Milgram Obedience Experiments." *PLoS One* 1, no. 1 (2006): e39.

Slater, Michael D. "Involvement as Goal-Directed Strategic Processing: Extending the Elaboration Likelihood Model." In *The Persuasion Handbook: Developments in Theory and Practice*, ed. James Price Dillard and Michael Pfau, 175–194. Thousand Oaks, CA: Sage, 2002.

Slater, Michael D., and Donna Rouner. "Entertainment-Education and Elaboration Likelihood: Understanding the Process of Narrative Persuasion." *Communication Theory* 12 (2002): 173–191.

Sundar, S. Shyam. "Self as Source: Agency and Customization in Interactive Media." In *Mediated Interpersonal Communication*, ed. Elly A. Konjin, Sonja Utz, Martin Tanis, and Susan B. Barnes, 58–74. New York: Routledge, 2008.

Sundar, S. Shyam, and Sampada S. Marathe. "Personalization Versus Customization: The Importance of Agency, Privacy, and Power Usage." *Human Communication Research* 36 (2010): 298–322.

Sundar, S. Shyam, Jeeyun Oh, Hyunjin Kang, and Akshaya Sreenivasan. "How Does Technology Persuade? Theoretical Mechanisms for Persuasive Technologies." In *The SAGE Handbook of Persuasion: Developments in Theory and Practice*, ed. James Price Dillard and Lijiang Shen, 388–404. Thousand Oaks, CA: Sage, 2013.

Tussyadiah, Iis, Dan Wang, and Chenge (Helen) Jia. "Exploring the Persuasive Power of Virtual Reality Imagery for Destination Marketing." Paper presented at the International Conference for Travel and Tourism Research Association, Vail, Colorado, June 14–16, 2016.

Tussyadiah, Iis P., Dan Wang, Timothy H. Jung, and M. Claudia tom Dieck. "Virtual Reality, Presence, and Attitude Change: Empirical Evidence from Tourism." *Tourism Management* 66 (2018): 140–154.

Yang, Kenneth C. C., and Yowei Kang. "Augmented, Mixed, and Virtual Reality Applications in Cause-Related Marketing." In *Cases on Immersive Virtual Reality Techniques*, ed. Kenneth C. C. Yang, 217–240. Hershey, PA: IGI Global, 2019.

Index

Printed in Great Britain
by Amazon

64107854R00173